Money Talks

Money Talks

*Speech, Economic Power, and the
Values of Democracy*

Martin H. Redish

NEW YORK UNIVERSITY PRESS

New York and London

NEW YORK UNIVERSITY PRESS
New York and London

Library of Congress Cataloging-in-Publication Data
Redish, Martin H.
Money talks : speech, economic power, and the values of democracy /
Martin H. Redish.
p.   cm.
Includes bibliographical references and index.
ISBN 0-8147-7538-1 (cloth : alk. paper)
1. Campaign funds—United States. 2. Freedom of speech—United
States.   I. Title.
JK1991 .R423 2001
323.44'3'0973—dc21   2001001102

New York University Press books are printed on acid-free paper,
and their binding materials are chosen for strength and durability.

Manufactured in the United States of America
10 9 8 7 6 5 4 3 2 1

To Jessica and Elisa, who have put their powers of free expression to wondrous use

Contents

Preface

In many ways, this book is the culmination of thirty years of First Amendment scholarship. During my third year of law school and my Second Circuit clerkship the following year, I authored my first two scholarly articles: *The First Amendment in the Marketplace: Commercial Speech and the Values of Free Expression*, 39 George Washington Law Review 429 (1971), and *Campaign Spending Laws and the First Amendment*, 46 N.Y.U. Law Review 900 (1971). In those articles, I provided a somewhat primitive foundation for much of the analysis that appears in this book. I argued in both articles that civil libertarians' traditional disdain for economic rights had misled them into summarily rejecting First Amendment protection for expression designed to promote commercial and economic interests. I argued that once one got past constitutional liberals' almost reflexive bias against powerful economic interests, one would recognize that speech promoting commercial sale and campaign contributions or expenditures substantially furthered long-recognized free speech values.

At the time, few scholars or jurists even acknowledged the possibility that substantial First Amendment interests were implicated by the regulation of economic power for expressive purposes. Since then, however, many courts and commentators have come to acknowledge this fact, though theoretical controversy and doctrinal confusion continue to prevail. In this book, I seek to develop a coherent theoretical rationale to support the view that restrictions on the expression of the economically powerful or the use of money for expression threaten fundamental First Amendment values.

A number of the chapters derive from articles that I have authored or coauthored since 1990. These include: Martin H. Redish, *Product Health Claims and the First Amendment: Scientific Expression and the Twilight Zone of Commercial Speech*, 43 Vanderbilt Law Review 1433 (1990); Martin H. Redish and Gary Lippman, *Freedom of Expression and the Civic Republican*

Revival in Constitutional Theory: The Ominous Implications, 79 California Law Review 267 (1991); Martin H. Redish and Daryl Kessler, *Government Subsidies and Free Expression*, 80 Minnesota Law Review 543 (1996); Martin H. Redish, *First Amendment Theory and the Demise of the Commercial Speech Distinction: The Case of the Smoking Controversy*, 24 Northern Kentucky Law Review 553 (1997); Martin H. Redish and Howard M. Wasserman, *What's Good for General Motors: Corporate Speech and the Theory of Free Expression*, 66 George Washington Law Review 235 (1998); and Martin H. Redish and Kirk J. Kaludis, *The Right of Expressive Access in First Amendment Theory: Redistributive Values and the Democratic Dilemma*, 93 Northwestern University Law Review 1085 (1999).

To the extent the chapters herein reproduce material from those articles, they do so with the permission of the reviews in which the articles were published. Several of the chapters draw on articles coauthored with one or another of my former students, including Kirk Kaludis, Daryl Kessler, Gary Lippman, and Howard Wasserman. Each deserves significant credit for his contribution. However, to the extent that the chapters depart from or modify those articles, the views expressed should not necessarily be attributed to them.

I should note, for purposes of full disclosure, that on a number of occasions over the last fifteen years I have either consulted with or represented a variety of corporations on matters involving regulation of their free speech rights. However, all of the views expressed here are solely my own and should not be attributed to any of my past or future clients. More importantly, I should emphasize that my fundamental views on these subjects were formed long before I began such representation, as my 1971 articles quite clearly demonstrate.

Numerous individuals and institutions deserve thanks for providing me invaluable assistance in preparing this book. In particular, I owe a great deal to the Northwestern University School of Law and its dean, David Van Zandt, who have provided significant financial and moral support to this effort, including resources to support both my individual research and a symposium on free speech and economic power held at Northwestern in October 1998 and later reproduced in a symposium issue of the Northwestern Law Review. I also acknowledge the valuable input I received on portions of the book at symposiums or workshops held at the University of Kentucky, Northern Kentucky University, Rutgers University–Camden, and the University of San Diego Law Schools. I owe special thanks also to my secretary, Melaney Petty, who has done everything possible to ease the burden on one as technologically challenged as I am. My research assistants, Tracy LeRoy and Aimee Mackay, provided valuable research help.

Finally, my wife, Caren, and my daughters, Jessica and Elisa, are and always will be most important to me.

Money Talks

1

Introduction

The Intersection between Free Speech and Economic Power

Everyone, at some point, has heard the phrase "money talks." To most people, it probably implies that those with economic power enjoy a level of influence unjustified by any rational theory of dessert, and that more appropriate criteria for the allocation of entitlements and authority—for example, intelligence, moral worth, or talent—are often pushed aside in favor of money and power.

The phrase has an ironically special significance in the expressive marketplace. In recent years respected scholars and jurists have argued that the private accumulation of money and economic power has a deleterious, almost pathological impact on the viability of both free expression and the democratic system of which it is a central part.[1] They have therefore proposed significant restrictions on the use of economic power for expressive purposes. Moreover, these commentators have argued that the nation's primary sources of communication are largely controlled by economically powerful private forces, and have therefore urged that government create rights of access to these communication centers on behalf of those who lack such resources.[2] Some have contended that speech motivated by profit maximization fails to further the purposes served by the constitutional protection of free expression, and therefore it may appropriately be regulated by government without violating the First Amendment's guarantee of free speech.[3]

Those concerned about the expressive influence of economic power have advocated the control of such influence by means of two fundamental strategies: (1) limiting the use of economic power for purposes of expression; and (2) controlling the expression of the economically powerful. While these strategies are in no sense mutually exclusive, neither are they identical. The strategy of limiting the use of economic power seeks

1

to remove any advantage the economically powerful might have in the expressive marketplace, by imposing an artificial and confining form of equality of expressive expenditures among would-be speakers. In so doing, this strategy will inevitably diminish the sum total of available expressive activity on the part of those who could afford to engage in expression beyond the limits imposed by government.

The second strategy, in contrast, seeks to restrain the expression of the economically powerful directly but selectively, by excluding from the scope of free speech protection expressive categories that are a priori most likely to be employed by the economically powerful: commercial speech and speech by corporations. While these two categories of expression may appear similar, in important ways they are quite distinct. Commercial speech may be defined either in terms of the commercial motivation of the speaker or the commercial subject of the expression.[4] Corporate speech, on the other hand, may concern any subject matter, even the purely political, and need not be directly intended to promote sale. The only defining characteristic of corporate speech is that it has been issued by a corporate entity.[5]

The goal of this book is to refute both the conclusions and the underlying theoretical rationales of those who believe that money and economic power cause significant harm to the systems of free expression and democracy, and therefore that regulation of corporate and commercial speech is consistent with the First Amendment's free expression guarantee. My underlying thesis is that neither the fact that expression has been paid for nor the presence of an underlying motivation of profit maximization detracts from the social, political, or constitutional values fostered by such expressive activity. To the contrary, governmentally imposed restrictions on expressive expenditures and profit-motivated expression cause serious harm both to the interests of free expression and to the values of democracy, on multiple levels. Hence, these expressive categories should be no more subject to regulation than any other type of fully protected speech.

This thesis derives from a synthesis of six foundational propositions, which are grounded in both modern economic reality and normative principles of democratic theory:

1. In light of modern economic realities and the structure of modern communications, expression often requires significant financial resources in order to be effective. Therefore, restricting the use of financial resources for expressive purposes will necessarily reduce the sum total of

available expression. In short, if "money talks," then restricting the use of money in the expressive marketplace silences.

2. A reduction in the sum total of available expression undermines the values fostered by the free expression guarantee, whether one employs an individual self-realization rationale or a democratic process-based communitarian rationale.

3. The fact that expression has been disseminated for purposes of financial gain or personal profit is never thought to dictate a reduced level of constitutional protection in most First Amendment contexts, and no basis in free speech theory exists to justify the disparate treatment of corporate or commercial speech on the basis of its profit motive.

4. The concern for equality often claimed to rationalize the modern assault on expressive economic power in actuality represents a perversion of the true form of equality that underlies the theory of free expression. Concern for *the equality of ideas and opinions* is the central element of First Amendment theory; for the most part, concern for other forms of equality are either in tension with or irrelevant to the values fostered by the constitutional protection of expression.

5. While the concern for equality is arguably more appropriately intertwined with expressive values when relied upon to rationalize the creation of a private right of expressive access to privately owned sources of communication, such forced access nevertheless violates fundamental values underlying the system of free expression.

6. To a significant extent, the modern scholarly assault on expressive economic power appears to be driven by considerations of normative political ideology, in contravention of the principle of "epistemological humility" on questions of normative value, which is central to the principles of both democratic theory and free speech protection.

Ideological considerations may explain the attack on expressive economic power in two ways. On one level, this attack may represent little more than the regulator's normative disagreement with the substance of the political and economic positions taken by the majority of economically powerful speakers. In more concrete terms, it may well be no coincidence that those who oppose the use of expressive power for the most part favor liberal or left-wing political positions, while those who exercise significant economic power for expressive purposes often advocate causes traditionally associated with conservative political ideology. On another level, such attacks on the expressive use of economic power may be rationalized on grounds of civic republican theory, a philosophy of government that opposes—on both moral and political grounds—personal or social choices motivated exclusively or predominantly by considerations of narrow personal gain. Expressive restrictions premised on this philosophy represent a perversion of the regulatory neutrality among competing normative viewpoints that is so necessary to maintaining an effective system of free expression.

Taken together, the six propositions listed above refute the arguments that have been made in support of the restriction of expressive economic power. The first proposition makes the deceptively simple observations that effective expression in modern society is often difficult or impossible without the use of economic resources, and that restriction on the use of economic resources for expressive purposes will therefore reduce the dissemination of information and opinion. This point is often selectively and inconsistently ignored by those who advocate restricting expressive economic power. On the one hand, commentators who advocate such limitations seek to provide a First Amendment justification for the restriction of the use of money on the grounds that such expenditures do not themselves constitute speech, but rather merely the exercise of non-speech property rights.[6] Through resort to such reasoning, they attempt to exclude such uses of economic power from the scope of the First Amendment. Yet the same commentators often seek to regulate the use of economic power for expressive purposes for the very reason that the exercise of such power provides an improper advantage in the expressive arena.[7]

The point of the first proposition is not to resolve all of the issues of free speech theory that are implicated by the use of expressive economic power. The goal, rather, is simply to establish that the restriction of economic power at the very least raises serious concerns for free speech theory. Because restrictions on the use of money for expressive purposes inevitably reduce the sum total of expressive activity in society, they require careful scrutiny under the First Amendment.

Several scholars have argued that even this seemingly uncontroversial assertion is inaccurate. They contend that there exists a "limited pie" of potential expressive activity, and that restricting the use of economic power for expressive purposes will have the salutary effect of opening up channels of communication for those who would otherwise lack such power.[8] They make such assertions, however, without the slightest empirical grounding or support. Indeed, in most situations it would be counterintuitive to believe that permitting expressive activity on the part of speaker A somehow denies speaker B an opportunity to convey her message, or, correspondingly, that reducing the ability of speaker A to communicate somehow expands the opportunity of speaker B to communicate. Indeed, where speaker B lacks sufficient resources to reach the populace, in most situations, the only inevitable effect of a reduction in the ability of speaker A to communicate will be increased ignorance among the populace about the views of speaker A. Speaker B's ability to communicate will in no sense have been improved, except in a purely relative sense. Such a governmentally orchestrated increase in public ignorance is surely inconsistent with the values served by the protection of free expression, however one chooses to characterize those values.

Advocates of restrictions on expressive economic power occasionally respond that the harmful impact of the exercise of such power derives from the confusion and dilution caused by the resulting tidal wave of expression on the minds of the populace. Given the populace's often limited attention span, the argument goes, widespread dissemination of the views of the economically powerful effectively "drowns out" the expression of the less economically powerful.[9] Yet once again, these commentators provide no empirical or psychological support for their assertion.

More importantly, this view contravenes two normative precepts that are central to any effective system of free expression: (1) that government may not restrict expression out of a paternalistic fear that the citizenry is not sufficiently intelligent to understand or process such expression; and (2) that absent compelling justification government may not determine, ex ante, that at some predetermined point there has been "enough" expression on a particular issue or viewpoint.[10]

The former precept derives from the essential premise of democratic theory that the citizens themselves must be allowed to decide what information or opinion is to be deemed valuable or persuasive. Therefore, any governmental regulation of expression motivated by a paternalistic concern over the citizens' ability to comprehend the expression constitutes an impermissible affront to the dignity of the individual citizen. Moreover, such regulation improperly skews the community's self-governing process.

The latter precept disposes of what could be called "the town meeting fallacy," namely, the fallacious assumption that society functions like a self-contained town meeting. In the town meeting, Alexander Meiklejohn has argued, there is no need to have different citizens repeat the same views, because once the position has been expressed it has been heard by all.[11] Those who argue that expenditures for expression should be restricted are implicitly assuming that society operates similarly, and that expression may be restricted where the positions to be communicated have already been disseminated. Of course, nothing could be further from the truth. No one can be certain when and by what means citizens are exposed to the expression of particular views or information. Thus, there can be no predetermined point at which government may decide that one particular view has been sufficiently disseminated.

The book's second proposition draws normative theoretical implications from acceptance of the factual assertions contained in the first proposition. Under the second proposition, the reduction in the sum total of available expressive activity is deemed to undermine the values served by the constitutional protection of free expression. This is true whether one adopts an individualized self-realization theory as the rationale for such protection[12] or instead views the purpose of free expression to be solely to facilitate the community's self-governing process.[13]

Some might respond that an increase in the sum total of available expression will not necessarily further the democratic value of maintaining an informed public, because not all expression contributes valuable information or argumentation. Such an argument is unacceptable, however, for two reasons. First, even if some official authority were deemed competent to make such a determination on behalf of the citizenry—a dubious proposition, to be sure—there is absolutely no basis, ex ante, on which to conclude that it is the expression of those who possess economic power, rather than the expression of those who do not, that is deserving of such a negative characterization.

More importantly, the essential premises of democracy and its logical corollary, what can appropriately be described as the "principle of epistemological humility," preclude government from regulating private expressive activity on the basis of the government's judgment of the value of that expression. The principle of epistemological humility dictates that in a democratic society, where the moral validity of the form of government is measured not by an external judgment as to the propriety of substantive outcomes but rather solely in terms of the process's consistency with representative norms, society may not properly presuppose substantive moral truth, untied ultimately to the direct or indirect choices of the electorate. Any other result would necessarily contradict the fundamental precept of democratic theory—namely, the requirement that governmental decisions be made with the consent of the governed.[14] Pursuant to this principle, then, governmental paternalism in the regulation of expression is inherently inconsistent with the fundamental democratic notions of individual dignity and societal self-rule.

The third proposition seeks to refute one of the primary rationales that has been widely relied upon to justify suppression of the expression of the economically powerful. It has often been argued, either explicitly or implicitly, that commercial or corporate expression is undeserving of constitutional protection because it is designed for narrow purposes of personal economic gain. But such an argument proves far too much, since much concededly protected expressive activity could be characterized in exactly the same manner.

In any event, it is by no means clear that the use of expression as a means of enabling the speaker to improve her personal situation is in any way inconsistent with the self-determination values underlying modern democratic theory. To the contrary, a motivation of personal gain may be extremely beneficial to the values a system of free expression seeks to foster, since it will often result in the dissemination of information and opinion that would otherwise have been unavailable to the citizenry.

The fact that expression is motivated by personal gain in no way automatically implies that the speech will be either fraudulent or harmful. In fact, our legal system has often recognized the beneficial effects that a motivation of personal gain may have. The requirement of personal injury to satisfy the standing requirements in an Article III federal court and the nation's conscious commitment to an adversary legal system demonstrate the point. In both instances, our legal system has made the a priori judgment that the existence of a motivation of personal gain will likely lead to greater enthusiasm and effort on the part of the actor, ultimately benefitting society as a whole.

It is important to note recognizing the potential value of profit-motivated speech does not necessarily imply accepting a political theory premised upon the narrow, self-interested atomistic pluralism often attacked by modern moral theorists. The version of democratic theory that serves as the normative framework for my defense of economically motivated speech is far different from the mechanistic, non-deliberative pluralistic model caricatured and criticized by modern civic republican and communitarian scholars. On the other hand, the version of democratic theory adopted here also differs dramatically from the civic republican and communitarian theories, which for the most part refuse to recognize the fundamental importance of individual growth and personal development within a democratic system.

The form of democratic theory on which my free speech arguments rely emphasizes the value of the personal and intellectual development that result when people participate in making life-affecting decisions, either collectively or individually. A portion of such decision making will take place solely for the purpose of bettering the lives of the individual or her family. Another portion will be made by and affect the democratic community as a whole, either directly or indirectly through the society's selection of governing representatives. But even those who refuse to acknowledge that any independent moral value derives from individual development need to recognize that any democratic community that fails to acknowledge the individual members of that community as developing entities worthy of respect is doomed to failure. The success of a democratic society ultimately depends on the wise choices of its individual citizens. If those citizens are viewed as nothing more than dependant cogs in a communitarian wheel, they will never be in a position to develop the decision-making ability required in a democratic society.[15]

Profit-motivated expression may further the values of democracy in several ways. Initially, to the extent individuals employ expressive activity as a means of achieving their predetermined physical, moral, or social ends, such expression may foster the personal development of the speakers by helping them attain their life goals. The fact that such expression may be designed primarily to facilitate personal gain does not necessarily detract from or undermine such development. In addition, such expression may simultaneously further the personal development of the individual listeners and facilitate societal decisions of the democratic community as a whole.[16]

The fourth proposition is designed to refute the argument against expressive economic power grounded in principles of equality. To be sure, the fact that the restriction of the expression of the economically powerful would tend to equalize the expressive power of both the powerful and the powerless does provide a superficially appealing basis for the belief that such restriction furthers the value of expressive equality. There are, however, significant flaws in such overly simplistic reasoning.

The form of equality brought about by the reduction in the expressive ability of the economically powerful is inconsistent with the values of free expression. This can be seen simply by hypothesizing a law that prohibits *anybody* from saying *anything*. From the narrow equality perspective, one presumably could find no problem with such a law; all speakers are being treated "equally." But surely, such a law must be deemed a violation of the right of free expression, if that right is to continue to retain independent and coherent meaning. To bring about an equality of public ignorance most assuredly fails to further the values fostered by the guarantee of free expression, however those values are described. Thus, the values fostered by free expression and those fostered by equality are in no sense identical.

Moreover, producing economic equality among speakers naturally leaves untouched numerous other inequalities, many of which have little or no relevance to the merits of the speaker's expression. Examples include inequalities in levels of public awareness caused by differences in the speakers' prior involvement in public life, as when one speaker has been an actor, astronaut, or athlete, and another has not. Indeed, differences in relative economic resources may have the effect of neutralizing such non-economic advantages. Thus, the economic equality sought by restricting the use of economic resources for expressive purposes may actually increase certain forms of inequality.

This analysis is not intended to suggest that concepts of equality are wholly irrelevant to the theory of free expression. To the contrary, one form of equality is central to any system of free speech. However, that concept focuses on the equality of ideas: No viewpoint may be deemed by government to be normatively superior to any other, for purposes of the regulation or suppression of the expression of private individuals or organizations. Rejection of the precept of an equality of ideas would violate the principle of epistemological humility that inheres in a society's commitment to the concept of democracy. A democratic system that completely insulates particular substantive moral positions from public debate or perusal is effectively no democracy at all. In such a society, elections would not differ from those held in the Communist nations of Eastern Europe during the Cold War. In both situations, the citizenry is allowed to make governing choices only so long as those choices are normatively consistent with a preexisting moral structure derived from sources external to the wishes of the populace. In such a society, the principle of free expression is reduced to nothing more than a political tool, employed selectively by those in power as a means of suppressing dissent and solidifying power.

As the sixth proposition indicates, the book will argue that restrictions on the expression of the economically powerful represent considerably more than merely a failure to promote precepts of First Amendment equality. Such restrictions affirmatively violate the dictate of equality of ideas on one of two ideological levels. On the most concrete level, restrictions on the expression of the economically powerful will value only one side of a current political or social debate. For example, if one were to accept the theory that so-called commercial speech is undeserving of free speech protection, the inevitable result—as a practical matter, if not a theoretical one—will be that consumer advocates who attack the safety or efficacy of a commercial product will receive full constitutional protection for those attacks. Yet the corporate entities who are responsible for the challenged product will be denied similar constitutional protection for their attempts to promote or defend their product through advertising.

When a commercial speech dichotomy is employed, then, significant expressive inequalities in public debates are created on such questions as corporate environmental responsibility, product safety, and tobacco use. In effect, if not in motivation, the exclusion of commercial expression from the scope of the First Amendment would give rise to a stark gradation in the level of constitutional protection for expression solely on the basis of which side of a controversy the expression takes. It would be difficult to imagine a more blatant violation of the principle of epistemological humility.[17]

The second level on which restrictions on the expression of the economically powerful can be seen to be an outgrowth of the regulator's normative ideological predisposition implicates somewhat broader issues of economic theory. In a number of ways, such restrictions appear to be motivated by a normative choice in favor of the substantive value of economic redistribution. From this perspective, restrictions on the speech of the economically powerful are properly viewed instrumentally, merely as a means of fostering attainment of the predetermined normative objective of economic redistribution. Relying on normative economic theory to rationalize the restriction of economically powerful speech undermines the process-based values favoring citizen choice that are inherent in the society's initial commitment to democracy.[18] Moreover, in no other segment of free speech theory or doctrine do we penalize expression on the basis of the speaker's underlying motivation of personal gain. Indeed, much fully protected expression is motivated by personal gain in one sense or another. To reduce the level of constitutional protection for commercial speech on the basis of the presence of a profit motive, then, would categorically discriminate against expression that fosters the capitalist system.

Chapter 2 explores these themes in the context of the debate over the level of First Amendment protection to be given to commercial speech.

There I argue that in light of the definitional models of the concept of commercial speech that most scholars and jurists have adopted (i.e., speech designed to promote a commercial transaction, as opposed solely to speech concerning commercial products and services), the widespread theoretical disdain for commercial speech is in reality nothing more than the outgrowth of a predetermined commitment to specific normative ideological precepts. As such, efforts to reduce the level of First Amendment protection given to commercial speech constitute unacceptable interferences with epistemological humility and value neutrality.

Chapter 3 examines the doctrinal and theoretical issues surrounding the level of constitutional protection to be given to what is concededly non-commercial speech when that speech is disseminated by profit-making corporations. I argue that such expression deserves full First Amendment protection, and I reject scholarly arguments that corporate speech fails to aid in the personal self-realization process. I also reject arguments premised on concerns about forced shareholder expression and the need to bring about speaker equality.

Chapter 4 examines the First Amendment implications of both proposed and existing forms of campaign finance regulation, particularly limitations on campaign expenditures and financial contributions. I also explore the theoretical, empirical, and conceptual flaws that plague the arguments traditionally made to support the constitutionality of such regulations.

Chapter 5 examines a complex issue of First Amendment equality: the governmental creation of a private right of forced access to privately owned communicative sources. Examples include right-of-reply statutes and the Federal Communications Commission's fairness doctrine. The equality issue is complicated in this context, because unlike the regulation of corporate speech and campaign finance reform, where the avowed goal is to bring about equality through silencing, in the case of the right of access equality is sought through the overall expansion of expressive activity.

Ultimately, however, the dangers to free speech values caused by the creation of forced access rights are far greater than the potential benefits. These dangers include public humiliation, personal demoralization, and cognitive dissonance on the part of the private individual or entity forced to provide access. All three results threaten the core free speech values of personal self-realization and communitarian self-governance.

In addition, there exists a serious danger that governmentally created rights of access will be become inextricably intertwined with the substantive normative values of economic redistribution. I seek to establish such a linkage by initially conceptualizing rights of expressive access as nothing more than a subset of broader governmentally imposed economic redistribution.

Chapter 6 considers a separate but nevertheless related issue of free speech theory and doctrine, namely, the First Amendment implications of the governmental subsidization of private expression. I begin by recognizing the constitutional dilemma inherent in governmental subsidization of expression. On the one hand, government quite obviously needs to be able to inform the citizenry of its programs and actions. Moreover, subsidizing private expression can further all of the traditionally accepted free speech values by enabling private speakers to express themselves or to communicate information and opinion to others. On the other hand, the power to selectively subsidize private speech enables the government to undermine First Amendment interests by distorting the expressive marketplace and penalizing those who wish to express views that the government deems unacceptable. I develop a categorically based model to be used to determine under what circumstances such subsidization in general or the particular restrictions that government imposes on that subsidization are constitutional.

No doubt many will find the positions taken in these pages quite controversial. One might argue, not unreasonably, that the unrestrained use of money for expressive purposes leads to invidious inequalities in the ability of citizens to communicate information or to express themselves. But it must be recalled that such expressive inequalities derive, not from direct governmental manipulation of the expressive marketplace, but rather from events and actions wholly untied to the communicative system or its regulation. To expect all participants to enter that system with completely identical resources and capabilities is at best quixotic and at worst counterproductive to the interest and values of free speech. It is quixotic because it is absurdly unrealistic to assume that such a result could ever be achieved. It is counterproductive because any attempt to bring it about would undoubtedly require a reduction of private expression to the lowest common denominator, at best leading only to an equality of ignorance.

Of course, commentators who advocate restrictions on the expression of the economically powerful may have alternative underlying agendas. Speakers who possess economic power will generally advocate positions that, if accepted, would enable them to maintain or increase their power. One can safely predict, then, that restriction of their expression will likely benefit the political interests of those who lack economic power. As brilliant as this approach may be as a form of left-wing political strategy, however, it is—for reasons to be explored in detail in the chapters that follow—disastrous as a theory of free expression.

2

Commercial Speech and Democratic Values

The Evolution of Modern Commercial Speech Protection

Though the First Amendment has been part of the Constitution for more than two hundred years, for most of that time the category of expression known as "commercial speech" remained completely unprotected.[1] In its 1943 decision in *Valentine v. Chrestensen*,[2] the Supreme Court summarily but unequivocally held that commercial advertising fell outside the First Amendment's scope.[3] For the next thirty years commercial speech protection lay completely dormant, receiving barely even a reference in the Court's decisions.[4] It was not until 1976 that the Supreme Court, in its watershed decision in *Virginia State Board of Pharmacy v. Virginia Citizens Consumer Council, Inc.*,[5] finally extended something approaching meaningful free speech protection to truthful commercial advertising.

In the years immediately following this case, which marked the first time the Supreme Court provided more than negligible First Amendment protection to commercial speech, the Court afforded commercial speech "a limited measure of protection, commensurate with its subordinate position in the scale of First Amendment values."[6] As a result, the Court on occasion upheld speech regulations that would quite probably have been deemed unconstitutional if imposed on non-commercial expression.[7] In *Central Hudson Gas & Electric Corp. v. Public Service Commission*,[8] four years after *Virginia Board*, the Court established a four-part test to determine the constitutionality of commercial speech regulation that has, for the most part, withstood the test of time. The first element of the test—which was, in at least one direction, outcome-determinative—asked whether the speech sought to be regulated was false or misleading, or advocated unlawful activity. If the answer to either question was yes, governmental restriction of that speech would automatically be deemed valid under the First Amendment. The second element of the test asked whether government regulation furthered a substantial interest. The third inquired whether the regulation directly advanced that interest. The fourth asked whether the governmental interest could be equally served "by a more limited restriction on commercial speech."[9]

Although the *Central Hudson* test is susceptible to a wide variety of interpretations, some more speech-protective than others, at some fundamental level the test inherently limits the extent to which it can insulate commercial speech from restriction. None of the test's factors authorizes a reviewing court to take into account the harm that the restriction causes to First Amendment values. For example, at no point does the test ask whether the "substantial" governmental interest may be outweighed by the harm to free speech interests caused by the restriction on expression—an inquiry that is universally undertaken in areas of traditional First Amendment analysis.[10] Evidence that, at least in its origins, the test established in *Central Hudson* was not intended to provide a level of protection equivalent to that provided by traditionally speech-protective First Amendment standards can be found in the Court's dictum in that very decision, accepting the theoretical propriety of an avowedly paternalistic explanation for government's attempt to regulate commercial expression.[11]

Commercial speech protection reached its post–*Virginia Board* low point in the Supreme Court's 1986 decision in *Posadas de P.R. Associates v. Tourism Co. of Puerto Rico.*[12] There the Court propounded the inherently fallacious—and now expressly repudiated[13]—theory that the supposedly greater power to regulate conduct logically included within it the assumed lesser power to regulate expression promoting that conduct.[14] Some doubt existed whether the *Posadas* Court ever really intended to adopt such an extreme position.[15] In upholding the challenged regulation of commercial speech, the Court in that case purported to apply the *Central Hudson* test.[16] Yet even in its least protective form, that test provides commercial speech with substantially greater constitutional protection than has been extended to commercial conduct in modern times under the substantive due process protection of the Fifth and Fourteenth Amendments.[17] Thus, if the Court had truly intended to adopt a "greater-includes-the-lesser" approach, there would have been no point in considering the applicability of the *Central Hudson* factors. Because government's constitutional power to regulate the underlying commercial conduct was clear, its power to regulate the "lesser" activity of commercial advertising should have been equally clear. The very fact that the Court considered it necessary to examine the *Central Hudson* factors tends to demonstrate that it did not intend to subsume commercial speech protection within the parameters of substantive due process.

Subsequent Supreme Court decisions appeared to take a considerably more protective approach to commercial speech than had been suggested in *Posadas*.[18] It was not until the Court's decision in *44 Liquormart v. Rhode Island*,[19] however, that a significant segment of the Court explicitly adopted the view that the protection given commercial speech, for the most part,[20] should approach the stringent level of protection afforded traditional categories of expression.

In *44 Liquormart*, the Supreme Court held unconstitutional Rhode Island statutes prohibiting the advertising of liquor prices other than at the location of sale. Four separate opinions were written. Justice Stevens, announcing the judgment of the Court, spoke for three Justices when he wrote:

> Advertising has been a part of our culture throughout our history. Even in colonial days, the public relied on "commercial speech" for vital information about the market. Indeed, commercial messages played such a central role in public life prior to the Founding that Benjamin Franklin authored his early defense of a free press in support of his decision to print, of all things, an advertisement for voyages to Barbados.[21]

Justice Stevens accepted that commercial speech may constitutionally be regulated in order to avoid deceptive advertising or to "restrict some forms of aggressive sales practices that have the potential to exert 'undue influence' over consumers."[22] He nevertheless concluded that "when a State entirely prohibits the dissemination of truthful, nonmisleading messages for reasons unrelated to the preservation of a fair bargaining process, there is far less reason to depart from the rigorous review that the First Amendment generally demands."[23] Justice Stevens also put an end to the Court's flirtation with the specious logic of *Posadas*:

> Contrary to the assumption made in *Posadas*, we think it quite clear that banning speech may sometimes prove far more intrusive than banning conduct.... [W]e reject the assumption that words are necessarily less vital to freedom than actions, or that logic somehow proves that the power to prohibit an activity is necessarily "greater" than the power to suppress speech about it.[24]

Justice Thomas, in a separate concurring opinion, expressed the view that "[i]n cases in which the government's asserted interest is to keep legal users of a product or service ignorant in order to manipulate their choices in the marketplace, the balancing test adopted in *Central Hudson* should not be applied. . . . Rather, such an 'interest' is per se illegitimate and can no more justify regulation of 'commercial' speech than it can justify regulation of 'noncommercial' speech."[25] In reaching this conclusion, he emphasized a number of distinct factors. These included the importance of free dissemination of information about commercial choices in a market economy; the antipaternalistic premises of the First Amendment; the impropriety of manipulating consumer choices or public opinion by suppressing accurate commercial information; the near impossibility of severing "commercial" speech from speech necessary to democratic decision making; and the dangers of permitting the government to do covertly what it might not have been able to muster the political support to do openly.[26]

Four members of the Court in *44 Liquormart* thus adopted the view that, at least under most circumstances, commercial speech is to be treated fungibly with traditionally protected categories of expression in terms of the standard of review.[27] Even Justice O'Connor, who—speaking for four members of the Court[28]—refused to accept Justice Stevens's equation of commercial and non-commercial speech,[29] both explicitly rejected the *Posadas* logic[30] and applied a highly speech-protective version of the *Central Hudson* test.[31]

There can be little question that the decision in *44 Liquormart* represented a dramatic breakthrough in commercial speech theory.[32] Though their reasoning differed in certain respects, all members of the Court adopted a much more protective approach to commercial speech than previous decisions generally had employed.

To the Court's credit, the opinions in *44 Liquormart* contain more thoughtful analysis of the role of commercial speech in First Amendment theory than either the pre–*Virginia Board* Court's summary and conclusory rejection of First Amendment protection or the post–*Virginia Board* Court's half-hearted extension of the First Amendment guarantee. At no point in the opinions, however, do any of the Justices engage in a thorough critical overview of the theoretical arguments for and against the continued second-class status of commercial speech. Perhaps that would be too much to expect of a judicial opinion in any event. But as close as the Court has now come to placing commercial speech on the same plane as more traditionally protected expression, such a theoretical reconsideration is most certainly in order.

As a doctrinal matter, the *44 Liquormart* decision represents the zenith of the Court's protection of commercial speech.[33] Yet even given its broadest reading, the decision fails definitively to equate commercial speech protection with that given more traditional forms of protected expression. Moreover, the overwhelming majority of post–*44 Liquormart* lower court decisions have viewed that decision as little more than a reaffirmation of the relatively reduced level of protection provided formally by the four-pronged *Central Hudson* test, albeit in its most protective form.[34] Thus, today it would probably be accurate to assert that commercial speech receives at least a slightly lower level of First Amendment protection than more traditionally protected categories of expression such as political or literary speech. A number of respected commentators have long argued, for a variety of reasons, that commercial speech deserves either significantly reduced protection or even no First Amendment protection at all.[35]

For reasons I have explored in detail elsewhere, it has long been my belief that this conclusion is incorrect.[36] More significant than the ultimate conclusion, however, are the constitutional and political implications of the theoretical rationales used to justify the conclusion. A careful analysis of these rationales reveals an ominous subtext: Much of the modern scholarly attack on commercial speech protection is implicitly but unequivocally premised on substantive ideological preferences—a practice that is both anathema to the fundamental assumptions of democratic theory and inconsistent with the essential framework of any meaningful system of free expression.

The Definition of Commercial Speech: Determining the Constitutional Stakes

The justification of the asserted distinction between commercial speech and more traditionally protected forms of expression, not surprisingly, varies on the basis of how one chooses to define commercial speech.[37] For example, if one were to distinguish commercial speech from protected expression solely or primarily in terms of the subject matter of the expression, one could conceivably justify a reduced level of constitutional protection for commercial speech on the grounds of the expression's relative lack of importance to the values fostered by the First Amendment guarantee.[38] By its nature, commercial speech concerns the qualities and characteristics of consumer products and services. If one believes that the defining characteristic of commercial speech is its subject matter, its exclusive focus on the relative merits of competing commercial products or services could arguably remove it from the scope of a free speech guarantee deemed exclusively to foster the political process.[39] The politically based free speech theories of renowned commentators Alexander Meiklejohn and Robert Bork could arguably support such a conclusion.[40]

Such reasoning is seriously flawed in a number of important respects. Initially, it is often impossible to distinguish speech concerning commercial products and services from speech concerning matters of public importance, for the simple reason that the two subjects of expression are in no sense mutually exclusive. Discussion of the relative values and risks of commercial products quite often implicates issues of public and political importance. Secondly, even in those instances in which the two categories of expression do not overlap, speech concerning commercial services and products should be deemed to foster exactly the same values fostered by political expression. Just as respected theorists have asserted that political speech facilitates the process of self-government by making the individual a more informed voter,[41] so, too, does commercial speech facilitate the process of private self-government, by making individuals better informed in making private life-affecting choices. Both types of expression, then, foster the same free speech value because both promote and inform the exercise of self-governing decision making. In this sense, both forms of expression facilitate the fundamental democratic values of self-determination and self-realization.

To be sure, this analysis is by no means immune from challenge. The theoretical debate on this issue was, as a practical matter, largely mooted, however, by the definition of commercial speech ultimately adopted by the Supreme Court. In extending a comparatively limited form of constitutional protection to commercial speech, the Court has uniformly confined this expressive category to speech that promotes a commercial transaction.[42] While the Court's attempts to define the concept of commercial speech have varied in several respects and have often suffered from ambiguities and inconsistencies, they have never varied in this one important respect: Speech that does not propose or promote a commercial transaction does not qualify as commercial speech.[43] Thus, under governing Supreme Court standards, to fall within the less-protected category of commercial speech, expression must, at the very least, advocate commercial purchase.

Omitted from the Court's definition of commercial speech is expression concerning commercial products or services that is either neutral about or negative toward the possibility of purchase. For example, under the Court's definition, Ralph Nader's description of the dangers or inadequacies of the Chevrolet Corvair—even when appearing in the form of an advertisement—would necessarily be deemed fully protected non-commercial speech. On the other hand, an advertisement by General Motors extolling the virtues of the Corvair, thereby promoting purchase, would presumably constitute less-protected commercial speech. Similarly, commentary in *Consumer Reports Magazine* concerning the relative merits of various commercial products quite clearly receives full constitutional protection,[44] though the very same information conveyed in the form of an advertisement advocating purchase would undoubtedly receive the reduced protection afforded commercial speech.

In distinguishing commercial speech primarily on the basis of advocacy of purchase, the Supreme Court has effectively conceded that the subject of the worth of commercial products or services is not inherently deserving of reduced constitutional protection. It is, rather, solely when the discussion of the subject appears in the context of promoting purchase that the less protective commercial speech standard is triggered.

One cannot explain this dichotomy on the basis of the relative unimportance of expression concerning commercial products or services, because to the extent one were to make this claim it would apply to speech opposed to purchase as much as it would to speech advocating purchase. While several conceivable rationales for the distinction have been suggested, none has proper grounding in generally accepted First Amendment theory. More troubling, however, is the fact that most of these conceivable rationales reflect—either directly or indirectly—substantive ideological biases that can have no legitimate relevance to the structure of First Amendment protection. If governmental institutions are able to vary the level of constitutional protection afforded to speech on the basis of their agreement with the ideological positions expressed in that speech, the First Amendment will have been reduced to little more than a result-oriented, manipulative political tool, to be employed by those in power strategically as a means of suppressing their enemies.

The current debate over the appropriate level of First Amendment protection to be extended to commercial speech contains a significant and ominous irony. On the one hand, reduced protection for commercial speech has often been justified on the grounds that because of the very nature of such expression there can be no real fear that improper or ulterior considerations influenced the regulatory decision or that government is abusing its power, as there could be when the subject of regulation involves matters of political concern.[45] On the other hand, careful exploration of the conceivable rationales for the advocacy-of-purchase distinction inescapably demonstrates a blatant underlying ideological bias, which virtually all modern free speech doctrine considers anathema both to the First Amendment and to the democratic system of which it is a part.[46] Far from innocuously avoiding the dangers of tyrannical abuse inherent in politically selective viewpoint-based suppression, then, the very existence of the commercial speech distinction itself threatens the ideological neutrality that is central to the viability of the free speech guarantee.

There are seven conceivable rationales for an advocacy-based definition of commercial speech: (1) the "substantive due process" rationale; (2) the "heartiness" rationale; (3) the speech–action dichotomy; (4) the corporate speaker rationale; (5) the "self-interest" rationale; (6) the ideological rationale; and (7) the "deliberation" rationale. The first rationale is far and away the least compelling, since it completely ignores the well-established constitutional dichotomy between speech and action. The second and third justifications represent unambiguous distortions of generally accepted free speech theory. They are, in short, improper extrapolations and applications of generally accepted principles of First Amendment exposition. While the remaining four rationales represent equally invalid or distorted applications of free speech theory, they additionally assume a troubling anti-democratic cast. All four are in some way premised on principles of First Amendment explication that, either directly or indirectly, favor speech advocating one particular political or ideological viewpoint over expression advocating competing viewpoints. In essence, these rationales derive from the strategic goal of protecting anti-capitalistic speech—or at least speech that will either have the effect of harming capitalistic interests or will have no impact one way or the other on such interests—at the expense of speech designed to promote capitalism or capitalistic interests. These rationales, then, support a constitutional doctrine that is structured largely as a means of burdening one particular side of a political struggle, solely because of distaste for the underlying ideological position fostered by the expression supporting that side of the debate.

Before we can fully understand the problematic nature of these rationales for an advocacy-based definition of commercial speech, we must first understand certain baseline principles of free speech theory. These principles, I believe, represent a widely shared consensus about the theoretical underpinnings of the free speech guarantee—a consensus that has shaped the core of modern First Amendment doctrine in cases that involve traditionally protected categories of expression.

These conceptual baselines underscore the inextricable intersection between free expression and democratic theory, and the centrality of viewpoint neutrality in shaping the structure of both. Hence the next section will provide the general theoretical background necessary to fully understand the broader analytical implications of the commercial speech distinction. After describing the elements of this constitutional baseline, I critique each of the seven conceivable rationales for an advocacy-based definition of commercial speech, pointing out how each either misapplies accepted First Amendment precepts or undermines the value neutrality that is essential to free and open debate in a democratic society. In so doing, I demonstrate how the true rationale underlying a reduced level of protection for commercial speech actually implicates invidious threats to the viability of both free speech and democracy. The section that follows considers the implications of the extension of full commercial speech protection for the regulation of false advertising. The final section examines the implications of the theoretical analysis for one of the most controversial issues of commercial speech regulation, tobacco advertising.

The Baseline of Free Speech Theory: Freedom of Expression as an Outgrowth of the Commitment to Self-Determination

As might be expected, theorists have differed dramatically over the values and scope of the constitutional protection of free expression.[47] Several scholars have focused exclusively on the role that free speech serves in checking government excess,[48] while others have highlighted the facilitative role that speech serves in the conduct of the political process.[49] Still others have seen development of the individual as the overarching principle.[50] Finally, some have seen in the First Amendment a conglomeration of developmental and societal benefits.[51]

Despite this mixture, it is possible to glean from respected scholarly and judicial writings a certain consensus baseline of free speech theory, without which the concept of free speech would be rendered either trivial or meaningless. Simply stated, that baseline is that the First Amendment both reflects and implements a belief in the ability of adult individuals to judge for themselves the wisdom or persuasiveness of expressed viewpoints advocating lawful conduct, free from paternalistic governmental intrusion or selective governmental interference. Censorship of private expression on the basis of a governmentally determined perception of the common good simultaneously hinders peaceful societal change through citizen choice and stunts the individual's personal and intellectual growth.

Certain modern theorists might respond to these claims by suggesting that to the extent the implications of the precepts underlying the reduced level of protection for commercial speech are inconsistent with basic notions of free speech theory, it is the latter that should be found to fail the normative challenge. However, such baseline free speech principles are so centrally intertwined with the values that underlie democratic structure—in particular, popular sovereignty and self-determination—that abandoning the former would be impossible without weakening or abandoning the latter. The First Amendment, much like the concept of democracy itself, is ultimately premised on a belief that individuals are capable of influencing decisions that directly affect their lives and morally deserve to do so. Moreover, denial of the power of societal self-determination undermines respect for society's members and would inevitably stunt the individual's personal, moral, and intellectual growth.[52]

Total individualized control over decisions affecting one's life is impossible within the broad framework of what is fundamentally a communal society. However, the next-best solution (from a moral perspective) is some type of majoritarian rule, combined with a right to free and open debate for individual members of society, allowing them to contribute to the self-governing process.

Of course, this is in no way to suggest that the constitutional protection given conduct is equivalent to the constitutional protection given expression. By its terms, the First Amendment extends its powerful reach only to the latter. In part, this is because expression involves uniquely human qualities of thought, deemed to be central to the operation of a democratic system. The speech–conduct distinction is also drawn in part because it is widely assumed that the harms of conduct are considerably more acute and direct than those of expression. Thus, our constitutional structure draws a clear distinction between the levels of protection given the two activities. This fact, however, has never altered the behavior-facilitating rationale for free speech protection, at least when the speech involves or advocates activities that society permits.

Such a theoretical construct views the individual both as an integrated whole worthy of respect and as a free and functioning citizen within a broader community. Thus, the often-perceived conflict between individualism and communitarianism as rationales for free speech protection—at least in this broad structural sense—is illusionary. A vibrant self-governing community cannot function successfully unless individual citizens are themselves intellectually active and respected members of that community.[53] Although theorists may differ over which is the ends and which is the means, it is clear that individual integrity and democratic community are intertwined in a symbiotic relationship.[54]

It is, then, fallacious to assume—as some modern theorists suggest—that recognition of the central role played by individual integrity as an element of both free speech theory and democratic government will necessarily degenerate into some form of the base, possessive individualism or atomization that characterizes much libertarian theory.[55] As political theorist Thomas Spragens has warned, it is incorrect to confuse the pluralistic libertarianism universally condemned by modern civic republicans with the liberalism of Locke and Mill. "The pluralist conception of democracy," Thomas Spragens writes, "is more in the tradition of Hume's utilitarian conservatism than of Mill."[56] That is,

> like Hume, [the modern libertarians] take stability and moderation—rather than like Mill, individual improvement—as the decisive tests of a good polity. Participation, therefore, loses its standing; for participation seems clearly less essential to system stability and moderation than it is to individual development. Indeed, participation can be seen as potentially unsettling if it is too extensive.[57]

Although liberal democratic theory places value on the individual and her role within the community, the goal, in the words of political theorist David Held, is simply to "attempt to define a private sphere independent of the state."[58] It is this form of individualism, not the mechanistic, non-deliberative "free market" model of the modern pluralists,[59] that both democratic theory and the First Amendment are designed to foster. According to Held, "liberalism became associated with the doctrine that freedom of choice should be applied to matters as diverse as marriage, religion, economic and political affairs—in fact, to everything that affected daily life. Liberalism upheld the values of reason and toleration in the face of tradition and absolutism."[60]

It does not follow, however, that an individual's use of her deliberative powers as a means of furthering her personal interests is somehow immoral or improper. Control of—or at least influence on—decisions that affect one's life is an essential element of one's human dignity, and thus lies at the heart of the moral rationale for democratic theory. Indeed, absent such concern, no moral basis would exist on which to prefer representative democracy to benevolent but despotic forms of government in the first place.

In contrast to the narrow, mechanistic implications of pluralistic forms of individualism, liberal democratic theory holds that assertion of one's personal interest can be tempered by altruistic or empathetic considerations.[61] Moreover, also unlike the possessive pluralist model, in liberal democratic theory individual decision making may rely exclusively or primarily on the processes of thought and deliberation.

Of course, if one were to reject an initial normative commitment to the values of popular sovereignty and self-determination, then the derivative free speech postulates would likely also fall. Since a belief in societal self-determination underlies our entire political system and constitutional structure, however, one cannot reject that belief without simultaneously rejecting the entire foundation of the American form of government. An initial rejection of the moral value of societal self-determination would necessarily constitute a rejection of the First Amendment, rather than an interpretation of it.

This is not to suggest that the theories of liberal democracy are completely free of moral question or difficulty. Certain political theorists have questioned "[t]he extent to which individuals are 'free' in contemporary liberal democracies."[62] For example, political scientist Carole Pateman has argued that "the 'free and equal' individual, is, in practice, a person found much more rarely than liberal theory suggests."[63] As David Held has articulated the position:

> Liberal theory—in its classical and contemporary guises—generally assumes what has, in fact, to be carefully examined: namely, whether the existing relationships among men and women, working, middle and upper classes, blacks and whites, and various ethnic groups allows [sic] formally recognized rights to be actually realized. The formal existence of certain rights in democratic theory and ideology is, while not unimportant, of little value if they cannot be exercised in everyday practice.[64]

Held further noted that "[i]f liberals or neo-liberals were to take these issues seriously, they would discover that massive numbers of individuals are restricted systematically—for want of a complex mix of resources and opportunities—from participating actively in political and civic life."[65]

From a purely moral or social perspective, the problems to which these scholars point may be deemed real ones. The problems were surely greater, however, prior to the enactment of modern legislation that has effectively, albeit not completely, increased the influence and equality of these previously subjugated groups.[66] Ironically, enactment of this legislation was achieved in large part by a process in which citizens exerted power in the political marketplace in order to protect and promote their self-interest, in the classic democratic fashion. The same is largely true of the economically disadvantaged classes: Our post–New Deal welfare state structure was implemented through traditional representative democratic processes.

It would be naive to dismiss completely the moral and political problems caused by the discrimination and poverty currently tolerated within our democratic system.[67] The question that the critics of classical democracy need to answer, however, is exactly what the preferable alternative system is. Should we impose a czar, empowered to right all moral wrongs perceived by scholars of the New Left, regardless of the will of the populace? Superimposition of a Marxist governmental structure without the consent of the governed would contravene the most basic notion of democratic theory. Thus, while no one rationally could claim that democracy is free from all moral problem or doubt, consideration of all the alternatives reaffirms the wisdom of Churchill's classic assertion that democracy is the worst governmental system—except for all the others.[68]

In any event, attacks on classical democracy based on considerations of distributive justice underscore the mutually exclusive relationship between democratic theory and governmental commitment to a precept of objective moral truth. A belief that one can ascertain and impose on society some form of absolute moral truth, derived by a means external to an assessment of public will, is fundamentally at odds with a belief in either societal or individual self-determination. If one believes in the imposition of externally derived moral truth, the concept of democracy is rendered at best a nuisance and at worst a serious social harm. By definition, a democratic system places ultimate moral and social decision-making power in the electorate. Either because of practical necessity or purposeful design, day-to-day political decision making may be one or more steps removed from the direct expression of popular will. But unless those who are making those decisions are somehow representative of and accountable to the electorate, the fundamental premise of democracy will be absent, on definitional, pragmatic, and moral grounds.

If one were to assert both knowledge of objective moral truth and the desire to impose that moral truth on society, then that operation of the principle of direct or indirect self-determination would make no sense. Under these circumstances, the possibility would surely exist that whatever majorities are necessary to make moral choices will choose a course opposite to, or at least different from, the externally derived moral truth.

One could, perhaps, seek to synthesize objective moral truth and societal self-determination, by viewing the collectivist deliberative process as a means of implementing that moral truth. The "freedom" of society to select only the moral choices some external source has already made, however, is no freedom at all. It would be a "democratic" system only in the same hollow and Orwellian sense that any totalitarian government that holds "elections" with only the government's candidates running can be considered democratic. Hence, if one chooses to adopt a fundamentally democratic system of self-determination, one must logically first reject a belief in the power and ability of government to discern and impose binding substantive moral truth untied to the expression, at some level, of popular will.[69] Moreover, even when the popular will has spoken, that decision must in some sense always be open for future public reflection and reconsideration.

Some who believe firmly in the superior moral truth of their substantive value structure could, quite reasonably, oppose committing their values to the test of the democratic process altogether, despite the obvious interference with self-determination that would result. The problem, however, is that others may feel equally justified in attempting to foist their own moral choices on society. Without some form of plebiscite, it is difficult to deny to others the same right to resist the imposition of our substantive value structure absent resort to the democratic process. Of course, we might argue that the difference between the two substantive moral structures is that ours is right and theirs is wrong, but they will, quite naturally, say the same. If some form of popular sovereignty is not deemed a prerequisite to the exercise of societal political choice on a moral level, then any political decision could be legitimated solely by reference to an external moral framework chosen by those in power.

Following this reasoning, democracy could be defended as a strategic device by reference to the Rawlsian construct of the veil of ignorance. When those of us in the mythical state of nature establish our governmental structure, none of us knows who in society will be a part of which moral faction, or which moral faction will be more powerful.[70] The members of society are, then, sufficiently risk-averse to leave the ultimate moral choice to some form of the expression of popular will, rather than decreeing, ex ante, that the faction with greater physical power will prevail. We further agree that once those choices have been made, those in power may not suppress the expression of those who disagree with those choices.

This "bet-hedging" rationale does not represent a firmly held theory of moral epistemology so much as an instrumental construct designed to avoid totalitarianism. Thus, the Rawlsian model does not presume a societal commitment to some form of ethical relativism. One may simply believe that the government, ex ante, must be guided by such a principle in order to prevent ideologically based takeovers that undermine the process-based values fostered by self-determination.

Presumably, this exact reasoning rationalizes a governmental stance favoring the societal commitment to freedom of religion. Surely, one need not personally reject a belief in the objective superiority of a particular religion in order to advocate a governmental stance of "epistemological humility" toward religion in general, for the simple reason that such a stance is essential to the prevention of government interference with the exercise of religious freedom. Application of the principle of epistemological humility to government's moral choices implies that private citizens themselves possess the ability to determine the "correct" moral choice. But as long as the principle of popular choice is restricted at the outset by super-majoritarian constitutional protections of foundational ethical principles (for example, the prohibitions of slavery and racial discrimination and the guarantee of free expression), the popular-choice solution is far preferable to reliance on a test grounded in physical or political power.

Of course, the system our nation selected is not based purely on popular sovereignty. Rather, our society has developed a complex mixture of popular sovereignty, republican-like procedural hurdles to collective action, and counter-majoritarian constitutional limitations. However, existing constitutional limitations on popular sovereignty are not identical to externally imposed substantive moral restraints on societal self-determination. Unlike such external restraints, constitutionally imposed limitations were initially considered and ratified by society itself. Also, unlike external moral restraints, constitutional limitations are subject to super-majoritarian repeal or modification.[71] Finally, it is important to note that in no instance do constitutional prohibitions on private or governmental behavior in any way prohibit debate or discussion about the merits of those prohibitions—a commitment that those who adopt a belief in the implementation of ab-solute moral truth at the societal level are not likely to make.[72]

It is this last point that most underscores the link between democratic processes and free speech. Core principles of free speech are widely thought to derive from our society's initial commitment to some form of popular sovereignty.[73] On one level, free speech may be seen as a neces-sary catalyst for the operation of self-government: Effective performance of the self-governing function requires a free flow of information and opinion about all issues potentially open to collective decision. On an-other level, the same normative principles that lead to the commitment to popular sovereignty in the first place also logically lead to a conclusion in favor of the protection of free speech.

The Baseline of Free Speech Doctrine: The Unbending Prohibition on Viewpoint Regulation

If one could point to a single principle to which virtually all modern free speech decisions of the Supreme Court adhere, it would be the principle of epistemological humility. "[T]here is," the Court has said, "no such thing as a false idea."[74] The statement represents the Court's means of assuring that government is prohibited from regulating or suppressing speech because it dislikes or disagrees with the viewpoint being expressed.[75]

The prohibition of normative viewpoint regulation represents the ini-tial societal commitment to self-determination and to the instrumental construct of epistemological humility. Justice Holmes put it well:

> Persecution for the expression of opinions seems to me perfectly logical. If you have no doubt of your premises or your power and want a certain re-sult with all your heart you naturally express your wishes in law and sweep away all opposition. To allow opposition by speech seems to indicate you think the speech impotent . . . or that you doubt either your power or your premises.[76]

Though Holmes's "marketplace" theory has often been subjected to mod-ern scholarly attack,[77] it would be difficult to deny the relevance of his reasoning to the basic epistemological premises of democratic theory.

Ultimately, the rationale for a total rejection of government's power to regulate viewpoints it finds offensive or disagrees with is that any such power would be inherently boundless. In other words, one could not

authorize a reviewing court to distinguish acceptable viewpoint regulations from impermissible ones. How could a court rationally confine the
government's power within the bounds of such a structure? By reference
to widespread popular opinion? Such a "limitation" would effectively
lock in existing societal preferences, a result completely inconsistent with
fundamental notions of democracy. Nor could a court confine the power
by reference to the judges' agreement or disagreement with the views expressed, because such an unprincipled point of demarcation would effectively allow the court to shape debate in any manner it wanted. In short,
abandonment of the absolute prohibition of viewpoint regulation would
effectively gut any meaningful concept of free speech protection.

To be sure, the viewpoint bar arguably possesses several doctrinal
qualifications. If, in a particular context, expression of a viewpoint is
likely to give rise immediately to criminal conduct, regulation might be
permissible.[78] Moreover, in certain restricted environments, such as
schools or the military, the government is given considerably broader lee-
way to control expression.[79] It is certainly conceivable that, in practice,
any of these limitations might be abused in such a manner as to threaten
the core principle. But at least in its theoretically pure state, the principle
disallowing viewpoint regulation stands as the cornerstone of the
Supreme Court's First Amendment jurisprudence, as well as the starting
point of most free speech scholarship.[80]

Another principle of free speech that plays an important role in the
Supreme Court's modern First Amendment jurisprudence is the precept
that a speaker's motivation is irrelevant to the level of constitutional protection given to his speech.[81] This postulate derives in part from recognition of the obvious difficulties in deciphering such a subjective factor.
Additionally, gradating the level of constitutional protection on the basis
of personal motivation might lead to an indirect form of viewpoint regulation. For example, a court's reduction of First Amendment protection
to speech made in order to promote one's own private economic interests
might be considered judicial disdain for a free enterprise system. Finally,
if one accepts the principle that an important element of the First
Amendment right is tied to the receipt of information and opinion,[82]
then exclusion of expression from First Amendment protection solely on
grounds of motivation makes little sense. The listener may benefit, regardless of the speaker's underlying motivation.

Supreme Court decisions also widely accept that the constitutional
protection of free speech extends to an individual's chosen manner of ex-

pression as well as to the content of that expression.[83] Under an "individualist" model of the First Amendment, such a conclusion makes perfect sense: An individual's choice of how to express her views is inherently intertwined with the creative and developmental processes that the First Amendment is designed to foster.

It must be conceded that some restrictions on the manner of expression do not violate the First Amendment. Presumably, one may be constitutionally prohibited from choosing to convey one's message by means of a marching band at midnight in a hospital zone. But the Supreme Court has drawn a sharp distinction between permissible and impermissible manner regulations: The latter are premised on popular ideological distaste for or substantive disagreement with the chosen means of expression.[84]

The postulates of free speech theory and doctrine described in the preceding discussion may be grouped together as core principles. The following section will explain the numerous ways in which the asserted or conceivable rationales for rejecting or reducing the level of First Amendment protection given to commercial speech violate those core principles.

Critiquing the Rationales for the Commercial Speech Distinction

Substantive Due Process

It could be argued that commercial speech is simply one form of commercial conduct, and that since the New Deal, it has been established that the substantive due process protection given to commercial conduct is at best minimal. Such an argument must be rejected, for the simple reason that commercial speech is no more commercial conduct than political speech is political conduct. The First Amendment protects the advocacy of violent overthrow of the government, at least to a certain extent; the Constitution provides absolutely no protection to an actual attempted overthrow. There is no reason, either conceptual or practical, to burden commercial speech protection with the constitutional standards relevant to commercial conduct.

"Heartiness" and Objective Verifiability

In *Virginia State Board of Pharmacy*, as noted previously, the Supreme Court extended a substantial but nevertheless reduced level of constitutional protection to commercial speech. The Court suggested two reasons to explain the "commonsense distinction" between commercial speech and traditionally protected forms of expression that it was drawing. First, "[t]he truth of commercial speech may be more easily verifiable by its disseminator than news reporting or political commentary."[85] Second, "[s]ince advertising is the sine qua non of commercial profits, there is little likelihood of it being chilled by proper regulation."[86] Justice Stevens in *44 Liquormart* expressed serious doubt about these rationales,[87] and with good reason.

Three problems plague both of these suggested distinctions. Initially, even if one were to assume their accuracy, at most they represent grounds to distinguish First Amendment protection for regulation of false advertising from First Amendment protection extended to false and defamatory statements concerning public figures pursuant to the doctrine of *New York Times Co. v. Sullivan*.[88] In *New York Times*, the Supreme Court protected false and defamatory statements about public officials, because of the fear that allowing such regulation might chill even truthful comments. In *Virginia Board*, the Court found this rationale applicable to commercial speech. We need not fear chilling truthful advertising by prohibiting false advertising, the argument asserts, because advertising claims involve factual assertions that are verifiable with relative ease. In any event, the argument proceeds, the existence of a profit incentive will preclude such a chill.

At most, such reasoning makes sense solely in the context of false advertising regulation. When the issue turns from the regulation of false advertising to the constitutionality of blanket prohibitions on what is concededly truthful commercial speech, the "heartiness" and "verifiability" rationales are rendered wholly irrelevant. What difference could it possibly make that a commercial enterprise may have an increased incentive to advertise due to its profit motive, if the government has completely prohibited it from advertising?

Second, it would be absurd to suggest that the existence of a financial incentive for expression is somehow uniquely confined to commercial advertising. The ultimate irony in such a position is that the speech sought to be penalized in the *New York Times* case itself—where the Court waxed eloquent about the dangers of a chilling effect on free expression that might be caused by defamation actions brought by public officials[89]—came in the form of a paid advertisement appearing in the newspaper.[90] Surely, much fully protected political speech is motivated by considerations of personal benefit. This is true whether the speaker is a candidate for political office or a person seeking to influence the outcome of the political process.[91] Somehow, that fact does not cause the Supreme Court less concern about the possible chill on personally motivated expression that defamation suits might create. It is difficult to understand why a different standard should be applied to commercial expression on the grounds that the existence of a profit motive assures expressive "heartiness."

Finally, it is by no means obvious that claims made in commercial advertisements are necessarily more objectively verifiable than many of those made in the political realm. Often, political speech is composed, not of assertions of normative political theory, but rather of simple statements of allegedly objective fact—for example, a candidate's assertion that her opponent failed to file his federal tax return. The same is true of speech in other non-commercial categories of expression. Surely, the assertions contained in *Consumer Reports Magazine* are no more or less objectively verifiable than are the claims of commercial advertisers. Yet under the definition of commercial speech traditionally employed by the Supreme Court, the former receive full First Amendment protection while the latter do not.

The Speech–Action Dichotomy

Perhaps the Court's focus on the proposal of a commercial transaction as the defining element of commercial speech can be grounded on the well-established speech–action dichotomy. Both textually and theoretically, the First Amendment protects speech, not actions.[92] To the extent expression promoting commercial transactions is "linked inextricably" to the commercial transactions themselves,[93] arguably the speech collapses into the non-expressive commercial transaction. As a result its status as protected speech is at least diluted if not completely revoked.[94]

At most, this reasoning could arguably have relevance to promotion at the point of sale.[95] It is only at the point of sale that commercial advocacy is even arguably so temporarily linked to the acts of purchase and sale that it can realistically be deemed an element of these acts. Moreover, to suggest that speech that advocates action is automatically rendered the equivalent of action would defy both conceptual reality and at least seventy years of the Supreme Court's First Amendment jurisprudence. The Court has long held that many forms of advocacy of conduct receive full First Amendment protection, even though the advocated conduct is itself unlawful.[96] Thus, speech that advocates action is for that reason no less classifiable as "speech," for purposes of First Amendment protection. Indeed, speech advocating some alteration in listener behavior is in many ways at the core of the constitutional protection, which recognizes the inherent intersection between expression and political choice. Thus, the speech–action dichotomy fails to justify a categorical distinction between commercial and noncommercial expression.

The Corporate Nature of the Speaker

Yet another conceivable rationale for the commercial speech distinction is the fact that the speaker in the context of commercial promotions will generally—though presumably not always—be a corporate entity.[97] A number of commentators believe that the values traditionally served by the protection of free speech are inapplicable in the context of corporate speech.[98]

Purely as a doctrinal matter, however, it would be awkward for the Supreme Court to rely on the corporate nature of the speaker to justify reduced protection for commercial speech. The Court has long held that in matters of general public interest, corporations have available to them the "full panoply" of free speech rights.[99] While the Court has on occasion wavered in its resolve on this issue,[100] its decisions recognizing the free speech rights of corporations remain good law.[101] The Court, then, could hardly ground its reduced protection of commercial speech on the corporate nature of the advertiser.

Moreover, as will be shown in detail in the next chapter, as a theoretical matter a speaker's corporate status should in no way diminish the level of First Amendment protection accorded its expression.[102] The primary argument against the protection of corporate speech is that such expression is not the product of free will, but rather nothing more than a slavish, robot-like response to market forces.[103] Even if one were to accept these assertions, however, it would not follow that corporate speech is necessarily beneath First Amendment concerns. According to respected precepts of free speech theory, at least a significant portion of the value served by free expression is the benefit received by the reader, viewer, or listener.[104] But if one important rationale for free speech protection is the speech's value to the listener or reader, then logically neither the motivation for the speech nor its effect on the speaker should be dispositive of its First Amendment status.

In any event, the view of corporate expression as something other than the exercise of free will is unduly myopic, for it completely ignores the exercise of free will that enters into the formation of the corporate entity in the first place. The entire history of the American corporation is tied to the democratic goals of personal self-development and advancement.[105] It is, then, appropriate to view the corporation's speech as a means of facilitating the voluntary self-governing choices and self-development of those who formed and operated the corporation. Thus, corporate expression deserves full First Amendment protection. The corporate nature of the speaker therefore fails to rationalize the commercial speech distinction.

Speaker Self-Interest

The most obvious rationale available to support the Supreme Court's distinction, for purposes of First Amendment protection, between commercial advertising and such expressive forms as *Consumer Reports Magazine* commentary is the latter's presumed objectivity. A commercial advertiser, quite naturally, possesses an inherent economic interest in persuading the listener or reader to buy its product. In contrast, the editors of *Consumer Reports* can reasonably be presumed to have no special interest in whether or not its readers purchase the products rated in their magazine.

One might reason that speech uttered for purposes of personal financial gain is undeserving of constitutional protection for two reasons. First, scholars have argued that the First Amendment was not designed to protect "a seller hawking his wares."[106] In the words of two voluble critics of commercial speech protection, there exists a "dissonance between today's commercial expression and the noble purposes of the First Amendment. . . . [T]he real reason for constitutional protection of modern mass advertising is less ennobling: It is speech in the service of selling."[107] In short, the argument is that the First Amendment was designed to foster higher values than the base pursuit of personal profit. Secondly, it could be argued that speech uttered for purposes of financial gain is inherently untrustworthy, because, the speaker's self interest will necessarily cause her to distort reality.

A distinction based on the personal interest of the speaker cannot withstand close analytical scrutiny. In no other area of First Amendment construction does a speaker's lack of objectivity or the presence of a speaker's personal or financial interest in gaining acceptance of the viewpoint expressed in her expression in any way reduce the constitutional protection afforded to that expression. A candidate for political office, for example, obviously lacks objectivity of expression; anything the candidate says will, in at least some sense, be uttered with the purpose of furthering her chances of electoral success. Yet her speech—quite correctly—is afforded full First Amendment protection. The same could be said of the speech of countless private interest groups that seek to shape public opinion. In fact, it is likely that most contributions to public debate today are motivated by the desire to further one personal interest or another. This fact hardly leads to a reduction in their First Amendment protection. It is unclear, then, why the very same factor should reduce the protection given to commercial advertising.

If one were starting from first principles, one could perhaps fashion a normative free speech theory that consciously excluded from protection personally motivated or non-objective expression. However, such a theory of free expression would be totally inconsistent with the historical and philosophical traditions of the democratic system, premised on a fundamental belief in respect for the dignity of the individual, as well as a belief in the individual's ability to influence decisions that directly impact her. It is not surprising, then, that in contexts outside the narrow scope of commercial speech the Supreme Court has unhesitatingly extended full constitutional protection to self-interested and economically motivated speech.[108]

Moreover, purely as a practical matter, any free speech theory that excludes protection for self-interested speech would effectively turn our existing political structure on its head. It is an undisputed fact of modern political life that individuals often speak in order to promote their own interests through the governing process, by seeking either to convince those in power to take or not to take certain actions or to convince the electorate to replace those in power with individuals who will further the speakers' personal interests. Exclusion of such speech from the scope of the First Amendment would leave precious little expression remaining in the protected category.

One could attempt to rationalize a theory that rejects constitutional protection for self-interested speech on the basis of the theories of modern civic republican scholars.[109] In the words of David Held, modern republicanism posits that "freedom is marked by the ability to participate in the public sphere by the subordination of egoistic concerns to the public good, and by the subsequent opportunity this creates for the expansion of welfare."[110] In certain respects modern civic republican theory can be linked to the theories of Rousseau,[111] who believed that "[t]he role of the citizen is the highest to which an individual can aspire."[112]

The essential link among the modern variants of republican theory is a belief that one should eschew the pursuit of purely private interests in favor of the pursuit of a common good and civic virtue, distinct from the narrow interests of the individual.[113] In modern republican theory, the individual fulfills his morally valid role not within the private sphere of his existence but rather in his capacity as a citizen within the public sphere. Beyond this common link, however, there are theoretical variants that have different normative implications for free speech theory.

For purposes of testing its implications for free speech protection, civic republican theory may initially be divided into two categories: the "communitarian-determinative" and "external-objective" models. The latter model, which I associate primarily with the works of Cass Sunstein, posits the possibility of arriving at universal moral agreement on substantively correct answers through the use of "practical reason."[114] The former model, in contrast, assumes no externally derived moral absolutes, but instead places total reliance on subjective communitarian choices as a measure of the common good. In short, both submodels of civic republican theory place supreme value on ascertaining the common good at the expense of the pursuit of purely private, individual interests, but it is there that the similarity ends. While the "external-objective" model posits the existence of an objectively derivable common good, divorced from the collective perception of what that common good is, the "communitarian-determinative" model equates the common good with the collective's own view of that concept.

Although both models suffer from fundamental flaws, it is easy to gradate the two models in terms of the threat each poses to the baseline principles of free speech theory. Since its origins in the Greek city-state, civic republican theory has been grounded in a fundamental belief in the value of collective self-determination.[115] Pursuant to this theory, the polity is to decide for itself how it will be governed. Any theoretical structure that relies on the communitarian deliberative process simply as a means of achieving a set of predetermined or externally derived ideological ends, disguised under the heading of "practical reason,"[116] therefore conflicts with the key assumption of the traditional republican model. The "external-objective" model, then, threatens the very premise of self-determination underlying the theory of representative democracy.[117] Once one assumes that society may employ the deliberative process as a means of attaining universal agreement on some form of objective moral truth through the use of "practical reason,"[118] one has laid the logical groundwork for the rationalization of governmentally imposed viewpoint regulation.[119] Yet once one discards the core premise that viewpoint-based regulation is unacceptable, little remains of the free speech guarantee. Because governmental regulation of viewpoint could be limited only by a wholly unprincipled and subjective judicial judgment as to the substantive moral correctness or wisdom of the viewpoint being regulated, the barrier between citizen choice and governmental usurpation would, as a practical matter, have fallen.

The "communitarian-determinative" branch of civic republican theory, on the other hand, at least retains the comparative advantage of preserving a basic belief in societal self-determination. The impact of the "communitarian-determinative" model on the core free speech principles, however, also remains problematic.

All branches of civic republicanism threaten key principles underlying free speech theory, because of their near-universal dismissal of the individual's value, other than as a political spoke in the communitarian wheel.[120] While the "communitarian-determinative" model is free of externally imposed moral judgments, it ignores the essential symbiotic intersection between individual development and integrity and performance of the communitarian function of self-government. Civic republican theories that fall within the "external-objective" model, on the other hand, suffer from deeper problems. Modern theorists who advocate this view, such as Cass Sunstein, generally posit a simultaneous belief in pursuit of the common good and a rejection of the pursuit of purely private interests.[121] The logical implication of this political theory is that the expression of one found to be speaking in pursuit of his own personal interests will receive less protection than the expression of one who seeks to contribute to the pursuit of the common good. If accepted, for reasons already discussed such logic would profoundly alter the accepted First Amendment doctrine that the motivation for expression is irrelevant to the level of constitutional protection.

Such logic would also have a dramatic impact on the conduct of the modern political process. As an example, consider how this approach would treat expression by American autoworkers urging an increase in tariffs on Japanese cars. It would, of course, be naive to believe that such expression was not heavily tainted with personal economic motivation. Yet to deny or reduce protection to such speech would profoundly reduce the amount of debate conducted in this country, where those with the most to gain or lose often contribute most heavily.

More importantly, acceptance of civic republican philosophy would threaten meaningful individuality or creativity, because the theory filters the constitutional protection of expression through the potentially stifling concepts of "civic virtue" and "common good." One can imagine authoritarian societies in which individuals are forced—either directly or through communitarian pressure—to dress, act, and think alike, and in which any assertion of individuality is viewed as a selfish and dangerous aberration from pursuit of the greater common good. It is all but impossible to envision meaningful individual discourse, thought, or creativity under such conditions. It is also impossible to imagine that such a society could foster the "human flourishing" that civic republicans proclaim to be their goal.[122]

For these reasons, modern conceptions of American democracy and freedom are incommensurable with the Athenian view of the individual as nothing more than a citizen.[123] As modern political theorists have asserted, "[c]ontemporary thinking about democratic governance builds primarily on premises of individualism and self-interest. Ideas of governors pursuing an autonomous public virtue and collective purpose have been subordinated to ideas of negotiation, political coalition, and competition."[124] In the modern democratic world, as Professor Sartori has told us, an individual is more than a citizen of a state. "In our conception," he asserts, "a human being cannot be reduced to his or her citizenness. For purposes of modern democratic society, a man is not merely a member of a collective. Modern democracy is meant to protect the freedom of the individual as a person—a freedom that cannot be entrusted to . . . the 'subjection of the individual to the power of the whole.'"[125] Once one acknowledges that at least in part the constitutional protection of free expression is designed to foster a normative commitment to the value of individual development, the extension of such protection to self-interested speech follows logically.

Recognizing self-interest as a legitimate motivating force for expression does not necessarily mean embracing the caricaturist pluralism both described and attacked by modern public choice theorists.[126] The concept of self-interest does not automatically imply mechanistic, non-deliberative pursuit of selfish interests. By accepting the legitimacy of self-interest, rather, one merely recognizes that by means of his rational processes the individual can determine what actions or results will serve his personal interests most effectively, and, by means of communication, seek to persuade others to allow or affirmatively bring about such results. In this sense, self-interested communication serves as both a symbol of individual integrity and as an essential facilitator in the process of personal self-realization.

There are, moreover, strong practical and strategic reasons to protect self-interested speech. As political scientist Jane Mansbridge has shown, to be truly effective a wholly communitarian form of government must be employed within a society that is relatively confined and homogeneous, where individuals possess a shared substantive goal.[127] In contrast, in a large and heterogeneous society such as ours, it is grossly unrealistic to assume a cohesive and cooperative society working toward a common end. Under these circumstances, then, the primary benefit of a democratic system is to enable individuals to protect their own interests from threats posed by the government or by other private interests—a system that Mansbridge calls "adversary democracy." This form of democracy, she notes, is "built on self-interest." "In current adversary theory," she writes, "there is no common good or public interest. Voters pursue their individual interests by making demands on the political system in proportion to the intensity of their feelings. . . . From the interchange between self-interested voters and self-interested brokers emerge decisions that come as close as possible to a balanced aggregation of individual interests."[128]

Our society's choice to adopt the adversary system in its legal structure implicitly signals a recognition of the potential benefits brought about by the individual's pursuit of her own self-interest. Rather than relying on objective and disinterested government officials to conduct the factual investigation in a case, the adversary system employs individuals whose primary responsibility is to protect and further the interest of the client.[129] When an attorney makes an argument to a court, presumably the judge is (or should be) fully aware that the argument is being made, not necessarily because the attorney believes it to be morally, factually, or legally correct, but rather because it would help the attorney win the case. No doubt, the judge will, with appropriate skepticism, discount the persuasiveness of the argument in light of the attorney's obvious self-interest in gaining its acceptance. It surely does not follow, however, that the judge will or should automatically ignore the merits of the argument, or that because of the attorney's self-interest the argument will be less than compelling. The system provides the attorney with the incentive to develop the argument, because of the very self-interest that inheres in the structure of the adversary system. Implicit in the establishment of the adversary system, then, is the recognition that the clash between competing self-interested individuals or entities will likely maximize the welfare of the society.

Similarly, the law of standing in federal court, derived from the case-or-controversy requirement contained in Article III of the Constitution, is premised on a societal preference for including a self-interest prerequisite as an assurance of that litigants are serious in both purpose and motivation.[130] The Supreme Court has made clear that pure ideological interest provides an insufficient basis on which to establish constitutional standing.[131] To be sure, in part this "private rights" model of adjudication is premised on notions of separation of powers and the nature of the judicial function.[132] But it derives as well from the assumption that self-interest will provide the necessary incentive to assure full preparation of a case.[133]

Far from the antisocial negative force described by modern civic republican and communitarian scholars, then, an individual's pursuit of her self-interest is widely thought to better society as a whole—a fact recognized in all aspects of free speech theory other than commercial speech. One can only wonder, then, why an exception for self-interested speech is recognized in the area of commercial advertising.

The Ideological Rationale

As the preceding sections have shown, the conceivable rationales for an advocacy-based commercial speech distinction that purport to be premised on the traditional analytical tools of free speech theory are inadequate on both conceptual and practical grounds. Once one chooses to define the concept of commercial speech by reference to a factor other than its subject matter[134]—an approach that the Supreme Court has quite clearly adopted— the remaining conceivable rationales suffer from a blatant inconsistency with either established precepts of First Amendment doctrine, widely held notions of American political theory, or both.[135]

The primary alternative explanation for the reduced level of First Amendment protection afforded commercial advertising is some sort of ideologically or policy-based distaste for, or rejection of, the normative values served by the commercial promotion of a product or service. This ideological rationale can take one of two forms. First, it may represent a generic ideological rejection of the very economic system out of which commercial advertising grows. Second, it may constitute a narrower form of policy preference that condemns the particular product or service being promoted by the commercial advertising in question. The thinking behind this narrower rationale is presumably that, as a practical matter, the only individuals who possess sufficient incentive to promote the product or activity to the public are those seeking to sell it. Thus, to stop the commercial advertising is tantamount to halting all promotion of the use of the product or service. Under such a regulatory approach, it would make perfect sense to extend full protection to the speech of those attacking the product or service, but either no protection or only limited protection to speech promoting its purchase or use, simply because the former category of expression furthers the predetermined policy goal while the latter undermines it.

The problem with either of the conceivable forms of an ideological or policy-based rationale is that both of them are fundamentally inconsistent with the core premises of a system of meaningful free speech protection and the democratic structure of which free expression is a central element. Surely, the Supreme Court today would not countenance a law restricting pro-socialist expression on the grounds that those in power believe that socialism is unwise or immoral and fear that such expression might lead to society's adoption of socialist precepts. Nor would it uphold a law restricting anti-socialist expression because those in power have deemed socialism to be the preferred social economic theory. Under such a blatantly viewpoint-based form of selective protection, the control of expression would be reduced to nothing more than a struggle for political power. Whichever side attains political power would presumably be able constitutionally to shut off all expression that it found to be ideologically distasteful or in disagreement with the currently predominating ideology.

The so-called "neutral principles" theory of constitutional interpretation advocated by Herbert Wechsler many years ago[136] has come under strong attack in recent years.[137] Yet if there exists any area of constitutional analysis where it is essential that constitutional rules are established and followed without concern for the identity of the particular views or parties involved in the litigation, it is the enforcement of the free expression guarantee. As already established, the ideological neutrality of the system of free expression is essential to that system's very existence; without it, the system will inevitably implode.

It could be deemed presumptuous to question the underlying ideological motivations behind the scholarly attack on commercial speech protection. Yet on occasion, critics of commercial speech have openly acknowledged the relevance to their analysis of either ideologically oriented concerns or subjective social or political values. For example, R. George Wright, a strong and articulate opponent of commercial speech protection, recently argued: "[C]ommercial getting and spending is, except in the case of the poor, at best weakly correlated with happiness or well-being."[138] He further expressed concern over "the ways in which commercialism and commercial values affect how we experience the otherwise noncommercial elements of our lives."[139] Wright thus overtly demonstrated his subjective ideological distaste for commercial speech as a predicate for his attack on its constitutional protection.

Many of those who today attack commercial speech protection have long been associated with the Critical Legal Studies movement within legal academia, a group whose members share an epistemological perspective that rejects the viability of legal analysis divorced from purely political considerations and a political ideology that is extremely antagonistic to the capitalistic interests associated with and promoted by commercial advertising.[140] It is thus certainly not far-fetched to suggest that the rejection or reduction of First Amendment protection for commercial advertising advocated by such scholars ultimately amounts to little more than an ideologically grounded (and thus wholly unacceptable) rationale.

Reliance on such ideological motivations effectively reduces free speech doctrine to a Hobbesian state of nature, in which there exists a political "war of all against all." In such circumstances, whichever ideological camp attains political power may, quite legitimately, suppress the speech of its opposition on no grounds other than naked distaste for the political viewpoints expressed in that speech. However, life in such a constitutional state of nature is, as Hobbes warned, likely to be nasty, brutish, and short.[141] As a theoretical matter, then, preference for a particular ideology should never play any part in justifying governmental restriction of expression.

The Deliberation Rationale

The final rationale that has been urged to support the advocacy-based commercial speech distinction shares many of the invidious characteristics of the ideological rationale, but is potentially more dangerous because of its superficially and misleadingly innocuous appearance. Under what can be called the "deliberation" rationale, commercial advertising is deemed worthy of reduced or no First Amendment protection because it does nothing more than artificially create irrational wants among consumers. Moreover, the argument proceeds, commercial advertising induces purchase, not through appeal to rational or carefully reasoned considerations but rather by resort to non-rational or persuasional methods that seek to tap reflexive and unthinking consumer response. In the words of two leading critics of modern commercial advertising: "In the regime of pecuniary truth, successful advertising techniques use words and images to push expectations beyond their reasonable orbit so that the consumer may yield uncritically to an ad's persuasive force."[142] "[I]n much of our culture," they further argue, "image is all, truth is irrelevant, there is no right to know, and we are as we consume."[143]

Underlying the deliberation rationale is the idea that, from the perspective of the values traditionally deemed to be fostered by the free speech guarantee, protection of commercial advertising would actually prove to be counterproductive. The free speech guarantee is widely assumed either to develop the individual's abilities and capacities or to facilitate both the governing process and the search for the common good by encouraging careful deliberation. On the basis of this assumption, some have argued that commercial advertising not only fails to foster deliberative values, it actually gives rise to the antithesis of deliberation—that is, reflexive, irrational, and non-deliberative behavior. Advertising therefore appropriately falls outside the scope of the free speech guarantee.

For a variety of reasons, the deliberation rationale provides an improper basis on which to ground the commercial speech dichotomy. Those reasons fall into two basic categories: (1) even assuming the rationale's premises, it cannot justify the commercial speech distinction; and (2) it is inherently inconsistent with fundamental free speech values.

The first basis on which to reject the deliberation rationale is the less controversial of the two. Put simply, the deliberation rationale is simultaneously over- and under-inclusive as an explanation for a rigid dichotomy between commercial and non-commercial speech. Most obviously, whether or not it is accurate to assert that expression that induces non-deliberative or irrational actions on the part of readers or listeners is undeserving of First Amendment protection, there can be little question that a considerable amount of non-commercial speech does exactly the same thing. Certainly, a reviewing court could, without controversy, take judicial notice of a similar effect caused by much political advertising, as well as by numerous communicative elements in today's pop culture. Thus, even were one to assume its validity, the deliberation rationale proves too much. It is unable rationally to explain the drawing of a rigid line of demarcation between commercial and non-commercial speech.

On the other hand, to assume that all commercial advertising appeals to non-rational and reflexive impulses in the consuming public is to engage in a wholly unsupported and often inaccurate generalization. It is true, of course, that advertising, by its nature, constitutes advocacy. Thus, one can reasonably expect that it will not be objective or complete in its description of a product or service. But one should not assume that only objective expression induces deliberation. Rational appeals can be fashioned and rational arguments made, even though they are developed in support of only one side of an issue that is subject to debate. Any other conclusion, at least when tied to the determination of the scope of First Amendment protection, could have profoundly disastrous consequences on current First Amendment standards. The simple reality is that much of the core modern political expression is advocacy, which is likely to be neither objective nor complete. For example, the expression of the National Rifle Association is no more likely to include references to the number of accidental deaths caused by handguns than that of anti-gun activists is likely to make reference to the studies suggesting that the widespread availability of handguns actually reduces the risks of gun violence. Moreover, no one could reasonably expect any other result. To deny protection to expression on the grounds that it is neither objective nor complete would deprive much modern political debate of its fundamental character.

Even if one were to adopt the deliberative model of free speech theory, then, one could not automatically exclude all commercial advertising from the protected category. Rather, one would have to engage in a case-by-case inquiry to determine whether the speech in question promoted or undermined true deliberation. The dangers in such a narrow, content-based approach, however, should be obvious. Imposition of a deliberation prerequisite on particular expression before First Amendment protection is triggered would be devastating to the values of both democracy and free expression.

This is not to suggest that the theory of "deliberative democracy," to which democratic theorists have devoted substantial attention in recent years, is necessarily harmful to the attainment of many of the values fostered by free speech protection. The theory of deliberative democracy, in the words of its leading advocates, "address[es] the challenge of moral disagreement by developing a conception of democracy that secures a central place for moral discussion in political life."[144] The core idea is that "when citizens or their representatives disagree morally, they should continue to reason together to reach mutually acceptable decisions."[145] One may contrast this theory with the mechanistic, robot-like pursuit of self-interest traditionally associated with pluralist theories of democracy. Contrary to the pluralist view, the theory of deliberative democracy asserts that "politics involves a public activity that cannot be reduced to the private choices of consensus in the 'market.'"[146]

Purely as a theory of normative behavior and decision making, one may reasonably prefer a theoretical model grounded in the value of careful review about the moral implications of conceivable self-governing choices over one that inexorably and mechanistically pursues self-interest at the expense of all other potentially relevant moral considerations. From the perspective of First Amendment theory, however, the issue is not that simple. As demonstrated earlier, in its essence democracy is largely a theory of process. Its success or failure cannot be judged systemically by how some external force chooses normatively to characterize either the wisdom or moral value of the substantive choices made by the democratic process. Otherwise, the central element of democracy—societal self-determination—would be contravened. The essential premise of free speech theory has always been a prohibition on viewpoint-based governmental regulation of expression. Because by definition a democratic society may, through majoritarian processes, ultimately choose *any* substantive result, even one thought by some to be irrational (if only through the super-majoritarian process of constitutional amendment), and because the populace needs a free flow of competing information and opinion to facilitate the self-governing process, it is improper for government to suppress expression for no reason other than the supposed incorrectness or irrationality of the viewpoint being expressed.

Were one to superimpose the precepts of deliberative democracy as limitations on the protections of the First Amendment, this fundamental principle of value neutrality would inescapably be violated. Such a prerequisite would effectively operate as a type of a priori and externally imposed value restriction on the exercise of free expression.

One could fashion a number of responses to this attack on the relevance of deliberative precepts to First Amendment theory. Initially, one might contend that deliberative democracy is inherently a procedural mechanism: It concerns only how someone is to go about making substantive moral choices, rather than what those substantive choices should be. Thus, to have First Amendment protection turn on the extent to which expression is deliberative in no way preempts the electorate or its representatives from making their own substantive value choices.

Second, one could argue that deliberative democracy actually furthers the widely accepted First Amendment values of personal and intellectual self-development, because it emphasizes the importance—and induces the increased use—of self-reflection and the meaningful exercise of individual reasoning processes. Purely mechanistic and privatist pluralism, the argument proceeds, cannot be deemed consistent with the values of free expression, because it places no importance on the Millian value of personal moral and intellectual development through the exercise of free will in the making of self-governing decisions.[147]

Finally, one might argue that the restrictions imposed by the requirement of value neutrality invidiously shut off normative debate on both the process and substance of important value choices. By focusing on the normative importance of the exercise of moral reason, the argument proceeds, deliberative democratic theory serves a valuable function, through which individuals better themselves by means of the use of their uniquely human intellectual abilities to employ the rational process.

Despite their superficial appeal, all of these arguments ultimately fail. None of them justifies the use of deliberative democratic theory as a type of litmus test for First Amendment protection. Initially, one may question the extent to which deliberative democracy is, in fact, a uniquely procedural concept. One could persuasively argue that the procedural and substantive inquiries effectively collapse into a single inquiry, because of the assumption that unless the individual's reasoning process reaches a particular substantive result, she could not have been deliberating properly.

There appears to be some level of confusion among modern deliberative theorists over the extent to which one may properly divorce the theory of deliberative democracy from a perception of substantive moral rightness. On the one hand, certain theorists seek to show how a proceduralist account of legitimacy is compatible with epistemic criteria of rightness.[148] They have argued that deliberative democracy is not merely based on a procedural conception of politics, but rather a means to achieve predetermined normative goals.[149] Yet many of the same theorists simultaneously seek to "avoid the overly epistemic view associated with correctness theories, which identify legitimacy with correctness of outcome."[150]

The inextricable intersection between deliberative democracy and substantive theories of moral correctness is underscored by the close association the theory has with the modern revival of communitarian-oriented theories of civic republicanism. For example, the leading advocate of the civic republican revival in modern constitutional theory, Cass Sunstein, has connected the seemingly procedural precept of deliberation with externally derived principles of practical reason and moral universalism.[151] He grounds the connection in the assumption that use of a truly deliberative process will necessarily produce substantive moral decisions that are dictated by a predetermined conception of the public interest. Pursuant to Sunstein's analysis, if one were to reach contrary substantive conclusions, one could not possibly have deliberated adequately.[152]

To the extent that deliberative democratic theory does, in fact, intersect with substantive republican values, there can be little doubt that use of a deliberative filter for purposes of determining First Amendment protection effectively destroys the principle of epistemological humility that underlies the entire concept of free speech protection.[153] In short, free speech protection cannot be made to turn on either the regulator's or the judicial reviewer's agreement with the normative positions being expressed, lest free speech protection degenerate into an ideological tool to be used by those in power to suppress those who are not. Thus, if a preference for deliberative democracy does indirectly represent a substantive preference for a type of civic republican communitarianism over a pluralistic form of privatism, its use in First Amendment analysis as a type of censorial filter constitutes a violation of the most fundamental premise of free speech theory.

Even were deliberation to be viewed as an entirely process-based mechanism, its use as a First Amendment filter raises troubling questions under the core free speech premise of epistemological humility. For even when viewed this narrowly, a preference for deliberation still represents a normative choice in favor of one particular methodology of decision making. This is a choice that neither the electorate nor its representatives in a democratic society are bound to accept, regardless of how favorably we as individuals may choose to view that methodology.

The arguments supporting the deliberative rationale, however, are not exclusively tied to civic republican theory. Though the modern theoretical association between deliberation and civic republicanism cannot be denied, one could fashion an argument that the systemic value to which deliberation gives rise is equally consistent with the more individualistic developmental theories of free expression. From this perspective, one might defend deliberation on the grounds that the values of personal and intellectual growth—which, according to these theoretical models, underlie the protection of free expression—can be fostered only through use of a truly deliberative process. The assumption behind this argument is that a reflexive preference for and pursuit of narrow private interests is actually counterproductive to the pursuit of the values that the free speech guarantee seeks to foster. Such an unthinking and narrow approach, the argument proceeds, can result in no form of meaningful human growth. In this sense, the deliberative value can be grounded in John Stuart Mill's unique form of democratic individualism and self-realization—a value that has long been associated with many of the modern rationales for free speech protection.[154]

Such an argument has a superficially seductive appeal, especially to those scholars who find a purely communitarian-based free speech theory both conceptually contradictory and pragmatically ominous. If one begins with the premise that a successful democratic community ultimately requires free-thinking and intellectually active individuals, perhaps one should logically be receptive to a theory of free expression that seeks to protect only expression that actually fosters personal and intellectual growth. A system in which irrational or non-rational appeals are permitted to influence individual decision making could reasonably be characterized as harmful to the interest in developing the intellectual capacities of the members of the polity.

One should not be deluded by false hopes for attaining a system of free expression that will protect only speech that positively promotes intellectual growth, however. It is at this point that the values of intellectual and personal growth that properly underlie free speech protection arguably clash head-on with the foundational principle of epistemological humility, producing a Hegelian-like synthesis that could be described as "the self-realization paradox." The self-realization paradox posits that any governmentally imposed censorial structure designed to foster an individual's moral and intellectual development will, by its very existence, undermine and stunt that development. In other words, such a censorial structure would bring about the very result sought to be avoided in the first place, namely, stunting an individual's intellectual growth.

The obvious problem with such a censorial system is that any externally objective measurement of intellectual or moral worth—with the possible exception of limited restricted environments, such as schools or the military—inherently undermines the values of individual worth and growth by denying the individual the power to make her own choices as to which arguments and appeals to find persuasive. Thus, such a system necessarily reflects a paternalistic disdain for and mistrust of the individual's ability to determine for herself what expression is persuasive—a result that hardly could be deemed consistent with a model of either democracy or free expression premised on a normative foundation of respect for the intellectual autonomy and abilities of the individual.

One can readily discern the inherent defects that plague such an epistemologically arrogant censorial system simply by applying it to an expressive context other than commercial speech —for example, to the governmental regulation of literature or political advocacy. The thought that government could censor literary or political expression because it judged the mode of argumentation employed in that expression to be irrational is so inconsistent with the premises of a system of free expression that it must be summarily rejected. This is so even if, in a particular case, the consensus—indeed, even universal—perception is that the substance of that expression is illogical, unworthy, or immoral. For similar reasons, commercial speech regulation cannot be justified on the grounds that its appeal is, on the basis of some externally derived objective standard, judged to be irrational.

One might seek to distinguish a free speech attack, grounded in disdain for epistemological arrogance, against externally imposed censorship in the political or literary contexts from a similar attack in the commercial speech context on the basis of what can be called a "censorial innocence" rationale. The argument would be that such substantively based censorship is unacceptable in areas of traditionally protected expression, because in those contexts history teaches that an inherent mistrust of government's regulatory motivations is fully justified. Government, according to this argument, is usually motivated by a desire to perpetuate itself in power, and it can best accomplish this goal by suppressing the speech of its political opposition. If government is successful in this endeavor, tyranny becomes a dangerously real possibility.[155] From this perspective, the role of the free speech guarantee is exclusively to stand as a protection against the growth of political tyranny.

Under this "garrison state" approach to First Amendment protection, the free speech guarantee naturally prevents those in power from censoring political expression because they disagree with the substance of that expression.[156] Nor would the government's characterization of the political expression as "irrational" in some objective sense insulate the censorship from First Amendment scrutiny, because to allow government to exercise such a power would be to invite the growth of tyranny through the back door. Were government able to defuse First Amendment scrutiny so easily, government could simply label much or all of its opposition's expression as "irrational." Further, though scholarly unanimity would not exist on the point, most commentators would extend such constitutional skepticism to governmental regulation of the substance of literary expression, as well.

Some no doubt believe that, because commercial speech in no way threatens the accretion of governmental power, government has no self-protective incentive to censor it. Therefore, its suppression does not give rise to the fear of governmental abuse that is normally associated with the censorship of traditionally protected categories of expression.

This "censorial innocence" theory, however, fails completely to distinguish commercial speech from the other fully protected expressive categories. At best, this asserted basis for distinction could work only if one defined "commercial speech" in terms of the subject matter of the expression. Speech concerning commercial products or services, the argument would proceed, is necessarily divorced from issues that might induce the abuse of governmental power or the growth of tyranny. For reasons that will be discussed, even this argument is woefully naive and unrealistic. But, more importantly, such an argument completely ignores the indisputable doctrinal fact that the Supreme Court has not defined commercial speech exclusively by reference to the subject matter of the expression. Presumably, the same lack of concern about governmental regulation should logically affect any speech exclusively concerning the merits and qualities of commercial products and services. Yet the Court has confined the definition of the lesser-protected commercial speech category solely in terms of the commercially motivated advocacy of the purchase of such products or services.

It would, in any event, be incorrect to assume that there is no danger of governmental abuse in the regulation of expression concerning the qualities of commercial products and services, because the assertion of governmental regulatory power and the sale of commercial products and services often overlap. It therefore would ignore reality to suggest that the two activities somehow follow purely non-intersecting paths. Moreover, as the preceding section has already demonstrated, an advocacy-based definition of commercial speech necessarily implicates serious ideological concerns, because it selectively protects speech solely by reference to the side of the argument that speech supports. Thus, those in power could choose to regulate speech promoting commercial transactions as a means of suppressing expression that either seeks to advance, or has the effect of advancing, capitalistic interests.

In any event, modern public choice theorists point out the dangers of political abuse inherent in the government regulation of commercial promotion. According to the insights of public choice theory, legislative decisions are motivated not by concerns of finding the best means of promoting the public interest but rather by an almost mechanistic desire to "sell" legislative goods to the highest bidding private interest.[157]

Ironically, many of the leading constitutional scholars who have accepted these public choice insights are also the staunchest opponents of the constitutional protection of commercial speech.[158] Yet the insights of public choice theory warn us that government may often regulate commercial speech, not out of any overarching judgment about the public interest, but rather as a means of providing a legislative or administrative benefit to the regulated party's competitors. Surely, such regulation of expression would constitute blatant and impermissible abuse of governmental power, under any of the modern theories of free speech protection.

Most importantly, the "censorial innocence" rationale for distinguishing between commercial and non-commercial speech misses the fundamental point. The "garrison state" logic that provides this basis for the asserted distinction ignores the key fact that the avoidance of tyranny is not an end in itself. It is, rather, a means of assuring that citizens—either as individuals or as members of a broader political community—have the opportunity to develop their faculties through the exercise of the powers of free will and self-government. Such development is inconceivable under totalitarian rule. To the extent governmental regulation or suppression of expression unduly stifles the attainment of these values, it matters not at all whether that regulation represents intentional governmental abuse of its power or merely well-intentioned governmental overzealousness. In both cases, the negative impact on the positive values the free speech guarantee seeks to foster is identical.

It should be evident that such overzealousness is a danger inherent in governmental regulation of speech. Governmental regulators exist to regulate. They cannot realistically be deemed objective observers in the conflict between the interest in regulation on the one hand and free speech concerns on the other. Thus, the need for judicial intervention in order to assure a balanced and fair constitutional judgment is as great in the area of commercial expression as it is in the context of political expression. This is so even in the unlikely event that one were properly to conclude that the dangers of improper motivation or intentional abuse do not exist in the context of commercial regulation.

Rationalizing the Commercial Speech Distinction: A Summary

Once one rejects subject matter as a rationale for reducing or excluding First Amendment protection for commercial speech, the remaining rationales fall as quickly and easily as a stack of dominoes. More importantly, exclusion of subject matter as the sole defining factor of commercial speech all but certainly reveals an underlying ideological rationale inherent in the commercial speech distinction. It is not that the debate over the merits of commercial products or services falls beyond the scope of the First Amendment, but rather that the expression of those most likely to advocate one side of that debate is deemed unworthy of such protection.

This point effectively underscores the inherent difficulty in drawing a distinction between commercial and political expression in the first place. Speech does not come in neat, severable units. Both the operation of commercial enterprises and the quality of their products and services give rise to inescapable social and political implications. The very fact that those who seek to reduce free speech protection for commercial speech are today so anxious to exclude from that less-protected category expression concerning commercial products or services that does not promote purchase tends to confirm the political implications inherent in all commercial speech.

The Problem of False Advertising

If one concludes that commercial speech deserves full First Amendment protection, a natural question arises concerning the extent to which false advertising is also to be protected. Under the currently controlling *Central Hudson* test, false or misleading advertising is automatically excluded from protection.[159] However, the *Central Hudson* Court developed its test while recognizing the "commonsense distinction" between commercial and non-commercial speech.[160] If, as advocated here, the Court were to extend full First Amendment protection to commercial speech, one might reasonably assume that false commercial speech would also receive full protection.

This conclusion need not automatically follow, however. In *44 Liquor-mart*,[161] for example, Justice Stevens, announcing the judgment of the Court, rejected the commercial speech distinction for purposes of truthful expression but continued the exclusion of false and misleading advertising from the scope of First Amendment protection.[162] Indeed, as previously noted, all of the reasons the Supreme Court originally gave to justify the reduced level of protection for commercial speech at most justified reduced protection for false advertising.[163] It is at least conceivable, then, that one could extend full First Amendment protection to truthful commercial advertising, yet still deny any protection to false or misleading advertising.

It is by no means clear, however, that false or misleading advertising should be totally excluded from First Amendment protection. Under certain circumstances, false non-commercial speech receives full protection under the First Amendment, and to distinguish commercial speech under identical conditions may well be irrational. To illustrate the point, it is appropriate to consider a hypothetical situation. Imagine that Congress has enacted the "False and Misleading Medical and Scientific Reporting Act of 2001." The law is premised on a fear that scientific quackery may cause significant societal harm by confusing the public and inducing its members to seek out costly, worthless, and possibly harmful medical cures or supposed scientific advances. The Act establishes a special commission of scientific and medical experts to rule on the accuracy of any proposed scientific or medical theory that conceivably could cause public harm or confusion. Such scientific or medical assertions must be substantiated to the commission's satisfaction, or the speaker risks issuance of a cease and desist order, imposition of criminal penalties, or both.

Only the narrowest of free speech theorists would find this statute to meet the requirements of the First Amendment.[164] Indeed, most observers would recoil at the creation of such a governmentally imposed "Big Brother" of scientific inquiry. In part, this is because imposing a governmental pall of intellectual orthodoxy is inconsistent with the assumptions traditionally deemed to underlie a free society. The ability to engage in uninhibited intellectual inquiry and communication is essential to the mental and personal development of the individual. This development is indispensable if individuals are to participate actively in the governing of their lives, an activity inherent in a democratic system.

Despite the protection given by traditional First Amendment theory to scientific assertions, when the very same assertions are included as part of a commercial promotion of a product, attitudes change dramatically. Governmental regulation of product health claims demonstrates the clearest application of this dichotomy today. Because of the public's strong desire for information about how the use or consumption of a product may affect one's health, as well as the often uncertain, controversial, and changing nature of medical science, the government has often regulated health claims made on behalf of various commercial products. Both the Federal Trade Commission (FTC)[165] and the Food and Drug Administration (FDA)[166] exercise regulatory authority over health claims for various products. Regulation also has been sought at the state level, primarily through attempted judicial enforcement against allegedly deceptive product health claims.[167]

Of course, one might seek to distinguish scientific expression from commercial advertising making the exact same claims on the grounds that commercial advertising is disseminated because of a profit motivation. Arguably, this fact renders the claims made in the advertisements "hardier" than claims made directly by scientists. As the Supreme Court has reasoned, "[s]ince advertising is the sine qua non of commercial profits, there is little likelihood of its being chilled by proper regulation."[168] For two reasons, however, this reasoning is flawed. First, it would defy reality to suggest that a scientist does not have an equally strong motivation to promote the validity of her own scientific theories; the success of her entire career will often depend on public acceptance. Second, to focus on the supposed absence of chilling misses the point. The absence of a chill is relevant only when government seeks to suppress unprotected speech but a concern exists that the speaker will be deterred from expressing protected expression for fear that it will be confused with the suppressed speech. Here, however, the concern is that government, by regulating so-called "false" advertising, will be suppressing the dissemination of legitimate scientific debate. The fact that commercial advertising may be hardier is irrelevant if the advertiser is directly prohibited from disseminating valuable expression.

To extend First Amendment protection to commercial speech, it should be emphasized, does not necessarily imply that government should be deprived of any opportunity to regulate any form of false advertising. At least under certain circumstances, government has power to regulate false non-commercial speech. For example, even in the area of political speech concerning public officials or public figures, defamation disseminated with knowledge of falsity or reckless disregard of truth or falsity falls outside the scope of First Amendment protection.[169] It would be perfectly appropriate to incorporate the reckless disregard–knowledge of falsity standard as a qualification on the free speech protection afforded to commercial speech. Thus, where government could establish that the false commercial speech was uttered with knowledge of falsity or reckless disregard of truth falsity, constitutional protection would be lost.

It does not necessarily follow that use of this qualification would afford commercial speech the same level of protection traditionally received by all forms of non-commercial expression. It is not entirely clear whether, in the area of political speech, the exclusion from First Amendment protection applies solely to consciously false defamatory expression, as opposed to consciously false non-defamatory expression.

While the Court has to this point applied this exception solely in defamation cases, one can certainly hypothesize other forms of purely political expression where conscious falsehoods would undoubtedly fall outside the scope of constitutional protection. For example, imagine a situation in which a candidate for political office speaks at a meeting of the Veterans of Foreign Wars. In his speech, he informs the veterans that he understands their problems, because he, too, is a veteran, having seen combat in Vietnam. On the basis of this representation, he asks the veterans to make financial contributions to his campaign. Based on this assertion, veterans contribute substantial sums to the candidate's campaign fund. In reality, however, the candidate is not a veteran and never experienced combat; the statement was simply a lie. This is a non-defamatory political statement. Yet no one could reasonably believe that the First Amendment would protect such a misrepresentation. Regardless of its political context, the statement constitutes unprotected fraud. Similarly, consciously or recklessly false factual assertions concerning the qualities of a commercial product or service are also fraudulent, and there should therefore be little question that such statements fall outside the scope of First Amendment protection. This is true even if truthful commercial speech receives full constitutional protection.[170]

The Smoking Controversy: The Commercial Speech Distinction in Microcosm

Much as the Spanish Civil War served as a testing ground for many of the weapons that were later employed in considerably broader theaters of combat, the issue of First Amendment protection for tobacco advertising can serve as a measuring stick for the overall theoretical grounding of the commercial speech distinction. Though the restrictions on advertising accepted by the tobacco industry as part of the national tobacco settlement now render the issue largely one of more limited reach, the arguments against First Amendment protection for tobacco advertising nevertheless underscore every one of the theoretical flaws underlying the commercial speech distinction.

No one could seriously dispute that smoking is a social and political issue of enormous intensity and import. The smoking controversy involves a variety of heavily contested issues, implicating questions of scientific theory, individual free choice, social responsibility, and the scope of governmental power—issues that constitute the very meat of the expression traditionally receiving full First Amendment protection.

In order to demonstrate the point, one need only inquire whether full First Amendment protection would extend to the commentary of anti-tobacco activists either asserting the scientific case for the link between smoking and illness or directly urging individuals not to smoke. The answer, quite obviously, is that such expression would and should receive full First Amendment protection. Presumably, even the most ardent advocate of a narrow, politically based First Amendment would have to concede that such expression lies at the core of free speech protection, because it implicates issues at the very center of the political process. But if this is true for the expression of those advocating that individuals refrain from smoking, it logically must be equally true of speech on the other side of the issue. The label of "political speech" cannot properly be attributed only to one side of a political debate.

As noted throughout this chapter, if there is one unbending principle of First Amendment theory and doctrine it is that government may not shut off one side of a political debate because of disagreement with the position that side seeks to express.[171] To uphold such a restriction would allow government to skew the democratic process in order to achieve an externally preordained result. It would, moreover, reflect government's paternalistic mistrust of its citizens' ability to make lawful choices on the basis of free and open debate.[172] Additionally, selective governmental suppression of speech on the basis of government's perception of the speech's wisdom or persuasiveness undermines the basic premises of governmental epistemological humility, without which the First Amendment cannot survive. Yet the consequence of—indeed, the motivating force behind—the regulation of tobacco advertising is that one side of this important public controversy is to be stifled, so that only the expression of the other side can be heard.

The reduced level of protection for tobacco advertising cannot be justified on the basis of the subject matter of the advertisements, because the expression urging individuals not to smoke, of course, deals with the same subject matter. Nor can it be justified on the basis of the self-interest of the tobacco companies, because, as explained previously, self-interest has never been thought to justify reduced protection of expression that is part of a public debate (nor could it, without significantly disrupting the existing system of free expression).[173]

Advocates of a ban on tobacco advertising might respond, however, that tobacco advertising is qualitatively different from traditionally protected political advocacy, simply because of the enormity of the physical harm claimed to be caused by smoking. But even if assumed to be true, this fact does not distinguish tobacco advertising from the manner in which government might reasonably view much political expression. For example, in the 1950s government might have believed, not unreasonably, that unilateral disarmament would have led either to a Soviet nuclear attack or to Communist enslavement, obviously causing disaster and ruin well beyond anything that smoking could conceivably cause. If the government were permitted to proceed under a paternalistic assumption of the public's inability to process competing information and opinion, it could reasonably have concluded that the citizenry at that time could not be trusted to make proper judgments after hearing arguments made by advocates of unilateral disarmament.

Similarly, in the 1960s the government firmly believed that, pursuant to the so-called "domino theory," losses to the Communists in Southeast Asia would eventually lead to the destruction of all free nations until the United States was forced to stand alone against the forces of world Communist domination. Government officials could therefore have reasoned that allowing people to oppose the war effort in Vietnam might effectively "dupe" the public into seriously compromising the nation's security. Finally, speech advocating either racial inferiority or racial violence, if effective, most assuredly could lead to political and social results deemed by many to be truly disastrous. In all of these hypotheticals, the judiciary naturally would construe the First Amendment to deny government the power to suppress political expression on the basis of the fear that citizens might be improperly influenced to make what the government deems to be unwise political choices.

The point, in short, is that if our constitutional system permits government to control expression out of a fear that the public cannot be trusted to make proper judgments on the basis of that expression, the only remaining question concerns which potential public choices the government deems to be both unwise and harmful. No system of free expression could flourish if government possessed such a power. At least since the famed concurring opinion of Justice Brandeis in *Whitney v. California*,[174] it has been widely accepted that the answer to supposedly harmful speech is not governmental expression, but rather counterspeech. Under current free speech doctrine, government may not, consistent with the First Amendment, censor political communication on the basis of fears that the citizenry will be influenced to make unwise judgments. Yet, a tobacco advertising ban would reflect just such governmental mistrust of individual decision-making ability. If the Supreme Court were to accept the premise that the public cannot be trusted to make choices on the basis of advocacy on behalf of a lawful activity, it is difficult to see how government could be denied the exact same power when political choices are involved.

It could be argued that even were one to concede—as one reasonably must—that the smoking controversy implicates a matter of legitimate public debate, it does not logically follow that tobacco advertising constitutes a real contribution to the debate. The advertisements provide no concrete information. Rather, they convey nothing more than the frivolous and misleading idea that smoking is a pleasurable activity that increases the individual's personal attractiveness and social acceptability.[175] The flaw in this reasoning, however, is evident on the argument's face. Ironically, this attack on tobacco advertising itself constitutes proof that such advertising represents a contribution to the smoking debate. Far from failing to contribute to a public debate, the advertisements assume the validity of one very clear choice in the smoking controversy. Especially once the required warnings are included, the advertisements can be read to urge individuals to risk the possibility of future health injury in order to obtain certain largely intangible social or personal benefits, as is true of an individual's choice to participate in numerous other risk- producing activities.

Even if there were not such an intense controversy over the ills of smoking, it would be difficult to distinguish appeals made in tobacco advertisements from debate concerning social and political issues traditionally subjected to full First Amendment protection. Such appeals promote lawful lifestyle choices available to the individual. When one recognizes the existence of the intense public controversy over smoking, regulation of such advocacy takes on the ominous character of governmentally orchestrated suppression, manipulation, and mind control—the epitome of the type of expressive regulation the First Amendment precludes.

The fact that the government finds the arguments made in advocating a lawful activity to be unpersuasive or unwise, of course, makes such advocacy no less part of the public debate. There can be little question, then, that tobacco advertising is today the subject of potential regulation for the very reason that it conveys an unpopular (albeit perfectly lawful) social message that challenges the views of those who presently hold political power.[176] Far from being justified as merely regulations of the expression of "a seller hawking his wares,"[177] then, the restriction of tobacco advertising in reality represents the most ominous form of thought suppression.

Once one acknowledges that the regulation of tobacco advertising constitutes governmental suppression of an unpopular social message, the arguments traditionally relied upon to reduce protection for commercial speech disintegrate. The facts that tobacco advertising may not provide a complete picture concerning the dangers of tobacco use, or that the tobacco industry's promotions are motivated out of concern for profits, in no way distinguish the tobacco industry's message from the overwhelming majority of fully protected contributions to public debate. The argument that tobacco advertising misleadingly fails to provide a complete picture no more justifies reduced protection here than it does in any other area of speech regulation. Virtually no contribution to public debate is free of personal motivation or bias. Nor do virtually any such contributions even purport to convey a complete or objective portrayal of the issues.

The system of free expression seeks to deal with the negative consequences that may flow from these factors in a number of ways. First, recipients of such contributions to public debate are generally expected to discount the arguments in light of the speaker's self-interest. Second, the concept of a free marketplace in ideas and information presumes that the arguments and facts unstated by one group of speakers will at some point be provided by competing groups of speakers. As in the legal and economic spheres, the implicit assumption is that the self-interest of those harmed by the expression will induce counterspeech. Thus, the very factor that is widely relied upon to justify reduced constitutional protection for commercial speech actually serves as the theoretical linchpin for the successful operation of the marketplace of ideas.

To be sure, reliance on the marketplace to assure that all aspects of an issue are adequately explored in the course of public debate will prove unreliable in certain instances. But for this reason government may choose to contribute to public debate by warning the public of what it deems the erroneous or unwise positions taken by private speakers.[178] It does not follow, however, that government may skew the debate by means of outright suppression of private expression. Such a cure would be considerably more harmful than the disease.

At least in the specific context of the smoking controversy, concern about the absence of counterspeech is, of course, moot. The fear of an expressive imbalance could hardly justify suppression of the tobacco industry's position, since no one could reasonably dispute the empirical reality of the widespread—indeed, pervasive—presence of the anti-smoking position.

Conclusion

The puzzling (and frustrating) element in the analysis of the constitutionality of tobacco advertising regulation is that virtually no free speech scholar (at least those lacking an overriding, ideologically based result orientation) would suggest that either the personal interest of the speaker or the biased and incomplete nature of expression somehow reduces the level of First Amendment protection given to traditional contributions to public debate. Nor would the expressive market's possible failure to portray all viewpoints ever be allowed to justify suppression of popularly held partisan positions. Fundamental precepts of free speech theory obviously preclude such governmental tinkering with the expressive marketplace. Yet when commercial advertising is involved, for some reason, factors that are routinely ignored in traditional First Amendment analysis appear—inconsistently—to assume overriding theoretical importance.

Recognition of the important role that commercial advertising plays in shaping social attitudes and values, manifested by the Supreme Court in its decision in *44 Liquormart*, logically dictates the need to accord such expression full First Amendment protection. Neither distaste for the message nor the existence of the advertiser's self-interest nor the non-objective nature of the expression can justify its suppression any more than it does in the case of traditionally protected advocacy.

Under well-established First Amendment precepts, protected speech may be self-interested, incomplete, and even irrational. Even at their worst, then, contributions to public debate that come in the form of commercial advertising differ in no meaningful way from many traditionally protected contributions to the expressive marketplace. There is therefore no principled theoretical basis on which to distinguish commercial advertising from any other category of fully protected expression.

3

Corporate Speech and the Theory of Free Expression

When Charles Wilson, president of General Motors and President Eisenhower's nominee to be Secretary of Defense, in 1953 boldly asserted that what is good for our country is good for General Motors, and vice versa,[1] he was subjected to intense ridicule and criticism in certain political and intellectual circles for simplistically and greedily equating his company's own private economic concerns with those of the national interest. To be sure, Wilson was espousing a controversial—albeit venerable—political and economic theory that draws no distinction between the interests of the private and public spheres.[2] On at least one level, however, Wilson was recognizing an indisputable fact of modern political life: Whatever the government does will inescapably have an immeasurable impact on the health and welfare of the private corporate world and vice versa.

Some will no doubt reject Wilson's suggestion that the intersection will always be one of positive correlation; they may well believe, instead, that what benefits large corporate interests often will harm the public interest.[3] But no one realistically could deny the inevitable existence of the intersection, for good or ill. As Charles Lindblom has correctly noted, government and business share "the major leadership roles in the politic[o]-economic order."[4]

The indisputability of the intersection between governmental and corporate interests renders puzzling the views of numerous scholars that the expression of profit-making corporations is either completely undeserving of First Amendment protection[5] or entitled to only a limited or reduced level of free speech protection,[6] even on subjects of central concern to the governing process.[7] Who, one reasonably could ask, has a greater interest in what actions the government takes with regard to the economy than corporations, whose very survival may well turn on the success or failure of those actions? Who possesses more firsthand knowledge and expertise on issues relevant to potential governmental regulation of private economic activity? To exclude corporate expression from the scope of the free speech clause, then, would be unwisely to shut out from public debate a substantial amount of relevant, provocative, and potentially vital information and opinion on issues of fundamental importance to the polity.

Purporting to recognize the existence of the political-economic intersection, the Supreme Court in *First National Bank v. Bellotti*[8] held that otherwise protected expression did not lose its protected status because its source was a corporation.[9] Although the Court subsequently reaffirmed[10] and applied[11] this holding and has never actually overruled *Bellotti*, in later decisions the Court has implicitly but clearly pulled back from this stance.[12] In so doing, the Court appears to have either ignored or at least partially abandoned the principles it had wisely recognized in *Bellotti*.

Those scholars who oppose protection of corporate speech have suggested superficially persuasive rationales for their position. They have asserted that, unlike individuals, corporations are incapable of truly exercising liberty or obtaining the benefits of personal self-realization, factors that they deem to be the *sine qua non* of free expression. Instead, they argue, corporations are nothing more than mindless, faceless entities, robotically driven by the need for profit maximization. Their expression is therefore undeserving of First Amendment protection.[13] Moreover, they argue, protecting corporate speech improperly and artificially alters the proper balance of expressive power in society and would threaten to "drown out" all possibly competing expression.[14] Finally, scholars have noted that protecting corporate speech could effectively force dissenting shareholders to associate themselves with the corporation's expression, a harm to the shareholders' own free speech interests that should be avoided.[15]

None of these assertions justifies such an exclusion or even a reduction in the reach of constitutional protection.[16] Moreover, commentators who oppose constitutional protection for corporate speech have incorrectly ignored the numerous ways in which such expression actually fulfills the values served by the constitutional guarantee of free speech.[17] Viewing corporations as nothing more than faceless, robotic profit maximizers unduly truncates the proper perspective on the nature and status of corporations because it ignores both the beneficial social purposes that legal recognition of the corporate form was initially designed to serve and the reasons that individuals choose to take advantage of the corporate form in the first place.[18] Viewed from this more complete social and economic perspective, the corporate form performs an important democratic function in facilitating the self-realization of individuals who have chosen to make use of it.[19] One should view corporate speech, then, as a form of indirect or catalytic self-realization, no less valuable than the more obvious and direct modes of self-development, and thus fully consistent with the purposes served by the constitutional protection of speech.[20]

Even if the concept of catalytic self-realization were rejected, however, it would not follow that corporate speech should be excluded from the scope of the First Amendment. Regardless of the expression's source, such speech undoubtedly has the effect of aiding the self-realization of the recipients of that expression, an obvious fact often mystifyingly ignored by commentators who wrongly reject constitutional protection for corporate speech.[21]

In addition to furthering these positive values of free expression, protection of corporate speech precludes the serious negative results that traditionally flow from a failure to guarantee the freedom of speech. Regardless of the speaker's motive for the expression, corporate speech may serve a vital role in checking potential governmental excesses.[22] Although this role traditionally is thought to be performed by the institutional press, it is widely recognized today that the press, at least on occasion, has failed to perform that function effectively.[23] Thus, it is important to recognize that alternative institutions in the private sector may have sufficient built-in incentives to perform the governmental checking function in ways that the institutional press will not or cannot perform.[24]

Finally, it is important to recognize the ideological biases that almost inevitably underlie the exclusion of corporate speech from the First Amendment's reach. It is not difficult to predict that the speech of profit-making corporations will widely espouse views consistent with a capitalistic economic and political philosophy. The decision to exclude corporate speech from the First Amendment's scope, then, can hardly be made behind a viewpoint-neutral "veil of ignorance,"[25] generally deemed a prerequisite for the government's regulation of expression.[26] It therefore requires only minimal extrapolation to view such exclusion as an indirect but nonetheless invidious form of viewpoint regulation—a result widely considered an egregious violation of fundamental First Amendment principles.[27]

The first part of this chapter briefly describes the doctrinal development of the current Supreme Court position on corporate speech. I demonstrate that, although the doctrinal messages sent by the Court have been mixed, the modern trend is moving away from extending full-fledged constitutional protection to corporate speech. In the second part, I make the theoretical case for the constitutional protection of corporate speech from both the positive and negative perspectives of First Amendment theory. In the final part, I respond to the theories that support the total exclusion of corporate speech from the scope of the constitutional guarantee, concluding that none of these theories in any way justifies such exclusion.

Corporate Speech in the Supreme Court

Over the years, the Court implicitly recognized corporate speech rights in numerous decisions that struck down generally applicable free speech restrictions when applied to an incorporated entity.[28] No law had singled out corporate speech for special burdens or restrictions, so the Court had not been required to determine expressly whether the free speech rights of corporations differed in any way from those of the individual. The fact that the Court was willing to extend First Amendment protection even though corporate entities were asserting the right, however, would seem to indicate the Court's implicit assumption that corporations fell within the scope of the free speech clause.

In 1978, the Court faced this issue directly, concluding unequivocally that the First Amendment speech right protected corporations.[29] However, later decisions have left the current doctrinal status of that protection largely in a state of confusion.

Speech-Protective Decisions

FIRST NATIONAL BANK V. BELLOTTI

In *First National Bank v. Bellotti*,[30] the first case considering a statute that directly targeted corporate speech for restriction, the Court struck down a state law that prohibited corporations from making expenditures to influence issue elections other than those "materially affecting any of the property, business or assets of the corporation."[31] The Court expressly rejected the idea that speech otherwise protected by the First Amendment lost that protection because of the speaker's corporate identity.[32]

Three corporations and two banks had challenged the law, seeking to speak in opposition to a referendum on a state constitutional amendment that would have created a graduated individual income tax.[33] The Court, in a 5–4 decision authored by Justice Powell, noted the uncontested point that the material in question would be immune from state regulation if issued by a non-corporate source and held that "[t]he inherent worth of the speech in terms of its capacity for informing the public d[id] not depend upon the identity of its source, whether corporation, association, union, or individual."[34] This was especially true of the political speech at issue that was deemed "indispensable to decisionmaking in a democracy."[35]

The Court focused on the role of speech in "affording the public access to discussion, debate, and the dissemination of information and ideas," as well as the First Amendment's role in "prohibit[ing] government from limiting the stock of information from which members of the public may draw."[36] The Court was especially wary in a case, such as the one before it, in which the law "suggest[ed] an attempt to give one side of a debatable public question an advantage in expressing its views to the people."[37]

The decision rejected several asserted justifications for the law. First, the state did not persuade the Court that powerful corporate speech "may drown out other points of view," at least in the absence of some showing that corporate voices had been overwhelming or even significant in influencing state referenda or in causing a loss of citizen confidence in the electoral process.[38] Second, the Court reaffirmed that "the concept that government may restrict the speech of some elements of our society in order to enhance the relative voice of others is wholly foreign to the First Amendment."[39] Third, the Court rejected the state's asserted interest in protecting dissenting shareholders from having their investments used to fund speech with which they did not agree.[40] The Court found that the statute did not truly serve that interest because it left the corporation free to speak using shareholder funds in other, non-referendum contexts.[41]

PACIFIC GAS & ELECTRIC CO. V. PUBLIC UTILITIES COMMISSION

In *Pacific Gas & Electric Co. v. Public Utilities Commission*,[42] the Court reversed an order of the state Public Utilities Commission that required a utility company to permit Toward Utility Rate Normalization (TURN), a citizen's advocacy organization opposing the company on rate issues, to use the "extra space" in the company's billing envelopes to solicit funds and distribute a newsletter advocating its position on rate issues.[43] TURN would have been able to use the envelope space four times a year, and the utility company could respond to TURN's position in its own newsletter.[44]

Justice Powell, writing for the plurality, adhered to the principles established in *Bellotti*, noting the public interest in receiving information and the irrelevance of the speaker to the question of constitutional protection.[45] The "critical considerations," wrote Justice Powell, "were that the State sought to abridge speech that the First Amendment is designed to protect, and that such prohibitions limited the range of information and ideas to which the public is exposed."[46] The Court focused on two problems it found in the law. First, the law discriminated on the basis of the selected speaker's viewpoint;[47] access to the envelope space was available only to a group such as TURN, which held positions in opposition to the utility company and disagreed with the company's views.[48] Second, the commission's order gave rise to a problem of forced speech because the company was required to associate with and disseminate a message with which it likely disagreed by having to include the message in envelopes with its return address.[49]

Non-Protective Decisions

FEC V. MASSACHUSETTS CITIZENS FOR LIFE, INC.

In *FEC v. Massachusetts Citizens for Life*,[50] the Court, in an opinion written by Justice Brennan (who dissented in *Bellotti*), held a federal law prohibiting expressive corporate expenditures "in connection with" any federal election unconstitutional as applied to a not-for-profit corporation.[51] The law prohibited corporations from using treasury funds in connection with a federal election, requiring instead that such expenditures be made from a segregated fund.[52] The case revolved around the activities of Massachusetts Citizens for Life (MCFL), which published an occasional newsletter and it's one-time "Special Edition," which was a voting guide showing the voting records of all primary election candidates on abortion issues.[53]

Justice Brennan noted that although the law "is not an absolute restriction on speech, it is a substantial one,"[54] placing a more stringent restriction on MCFL because it is incorporated,[55] and that its "practical effect may be to discourage protected speech."[56] Such a restriction might have been permissible to control the "corrosive influence of concentrated corporate wealth" that gives corporations advantages and interferes with the marketplace of political ideas, he reasoned.[57] Because MCFL was not a traditional profit-making enterprise organized for economic gain, however, it did not pose the same danger of corruption.[58] The resources it had amassed were the product of its popularity in the political marketplace, not its success in the economic marketplace.[59] Thus, the speech prohibition was unconstitutional as applied to MCFL.[60] The First Amendment, the Court concluded, fully protected the expression of corporations, such as MCFL, that were "more akin to voluntary political organizations than business firms."[61]

The Court pointed to three features of MCFL that brought its expression within the First Amendment's scope. First, MCFL was formed for the express purpose of promoting political ideas. Second, no shareholders were affected. Third, MCFL was not established by a business corporation and was not otherwise connected with business corporations.[62]

AUSTIN V. MICHIGAN CHAMBER OF COMMERCE

The Court appeared to pull back on the protection of profit-making corporate speech in *Austin v. Michigan Chamber of Commerce*.[63] The Chamber was a nonprofit corporation of eight thousand members, many of them for-profit corporations, whose purpose was to (1) promote economic conditions favorable to private enterprises, (2) disseminate information and educate its members about laws of interest to the business community, and (3) publicize to the government the views of the business community on public policy matters.[64] The Chamber had sought to place an advertisement supporting one candidate in a local newspaper, reading in part: "Michigan Needs Richard Bandstra to Help Us be Job Competitive Again."[65]

In *Austin*, unlike *MCFL*, the Supreme Court upheld a state law, modeled on the federal law challenged in *MCFL*, prohibiting corporate expenditures "in support of, or in opposition to, any candidate in elections for state office" except when the expenditure was made through a segregated fund.[66] Justice Marshall, writing for a 6–3 majority, acknowledged that use of funds to place advertisements urging support of a political candidate is protected speech.[67] Further, according to Justice Marshall, the fact that the Chamber is a corporation did not remove the speech "from the ambit of the First Amendment."[68] The Court adhered to its prior decision in *MCFL*, recognizing that the law burdened expressive activity, thus requiring a compelling interest to support it.[69]

The Court then held that the restriction on corporate speech was aimed at "a different type of corruption in the political arena: The corrosive and distorting effects of immense aggregations of wealth that are accumulated with the help of the corporate form and that have little or no correlation to the public's support for the corporation's political ideas."[70] Corporations were found to possess certain state-awarded advantages, such as limited liability, perpetual life, and favorable treatment of the accumulation and distribution of assets to enable them to maximize shareholders' returns.[71] Speech by a business corporation, given its perceived power and persuasiveness, thus was to be deemed per se a form of corruption that the state could regulate constitutionally.[72]

Justice Marshall rejected the suggestion that the law impermissibly equalized voices by restricting corporate speech; rather, the law's purpose and effect were to ensure that corporate expenditures "reflect actual public support for the political ideas espoused by corporations."[73] Moreover, the state did not need to show a problem of corporate dominance; the "potential" for distorting the political process was enough to justify restricting the speech of one powerful voice.[74]

The Court proceeded to hold that, although the Chamber was a non-profit ideological corporation, the law was constitutionally applicable because it did not share the three key characteristics that had exempted MCFL.[75] The distinction primarily revolved around the Chamber's links to business—many of its members were either business corporations or involved in business, and its activities related not only to political issues but also to economic, civic, and business conditions and practices.[76] Additionally, there would be an economic disincentive for members to disassociate from the Chamber if they disagreed with any of its political positions.[77]

Summary

Although the Supreme Court's speech-protective decisions remain good law, subsequent trends clearly reflect the Court's hesitancy to protect profit-making corporate speech, at least in certain contexts. As subsequent analysis will demonstrate, however, the Court's speech protective decisions more accurately reflect appropriate precepts of First Amendment theory.

The Case for Corporate Speech

The Positive–Negative Dichotomy

Although the theoretical arguments supporting full First Amendment protection for corporate speech are many, they may be grouped under two broad conceptual headings: those that appeal to positive free speech theories, and those that appeal to negative free speech theories. Positive theories focus upon the affirmative benefits to which free speech gives rise, both to the individual and to society. Negative theories derive from the skeptical, mistrustful strain underlying American democratic theory, manifested more generally in the theory of separation of powers.[78] They recognize the inherently vulnerable nature of a democratic system in general and of the commitment to free expression in particular.[79] Negative theories focus upon both the hostile forces in society that constantly threaten free speech protection and the harms that would ensue from undermining such protection.[80]

The two categories, it should be emphasized, are by no means mutually exclusive. Indeed, contrary to the implicit assumptions of certain commentators,[81] the two concepts actually function in a symbiotic relationship: Negative theories act as a bodyguard for the positive theories. In other words, the purpose of the negative theories is to assure that the positive benefits fostered by the commitment to free expression can be attained, free from undermining by hostile external forces.[82]

Corporate Speech and Positive Free Speech Theory

Any discussion of the scope of First Amendment protection should focus, at least in part, "on the positive role of the free speech guarantee as a catalyst in tapping and developing the uniquely human creative and intellectual capacities of the individual."[83] Although the free speech guarantee is phrased as a negative,[84] it has long been recognized that the societal commitment to a system of free expression serves a variety of positive purposes.[85] Positive theories are premised on the notion that speech enriches and enhances the lives and abilities of individuals—both speakers and listeners—as well as the democratic society as a whole.

THE FIRST AMENDMENT AS A VEHICLE OF INDIVIDUAL SELF-REALIZATION

The fundamental, positive value of the constitutional free speech guarantee is furtherance of individual self-realization, a broad value that includes (1) the individual's development of her personal powers and abilities, and (2) the individual's ability and opportunity to make all levels of life-affecting decisions, thereby controlling and determining her life's course.[86] The value of free speech is simultaneously intrinsic and instrumental. It is intrinsic, as I have previously argued, in the sense that "the very exercise of one's freedom to speak, write, create, appreciate, or learn represents a use, and therefore a development, of an individual's uniquely human faculties."[87] It is instrumental in that the receipt of a broad range of information and opinion facilitates the making of life-affecting decisions.[88] This dual nature of self-realization means speech or advocacy functions both as an end in itself and as a means to an end.

The theory of individual self-realization is not universally accepted as the definitive rationale for free speech protection.[89] Several theorists instead have focused primarily or exclusively upon more communitarian-based notions, such as society's performance of the democratic governing function.[90] For purposes of the present analysis, however, accepting such a communitarian theory actually would strengthen the case for corporate speech protection.[91] But more important, the mistake of these theorists is their failure to ask the fundamental question: Why a democratic system in the first place? Our society chooses to function as a democracy for the very reason that we value individual autonomy and self-realization.[92] Otherwise, democracy could not be morally justified. Society, after all, is made up of individuals, and if one places no value on a single individual's exercise of autonomy, it is impossible to justify placing a value on the collective exercise of autonomy.[93] Thus, in this sense a communitarian approach is not necessarily inconsistent with the more individualized self-realization model because the government itself is ultimately premised on a belief in the individual's worth.[94] Both concepts dictate a commitment to a democratic form of government because—as the classical democratic theorists argued—democracy enables individuals to develop their human faculties and control their own destinies.[95]

Whatever value one derives from a democratic system, there can be little question that a commitment to democracy logically dictates a commitment to free expression. The concept of free speech, then, flows from the same overarching value that underlies the commitment to democracy in the first place, and if society chooses the latter political structure, it also must protect the former.

The positive rationales for protecting free expression focus on the benefits that the speech brings to individuals, both personal and political, and to society as a whole. In the next section I consider the manner in which extending full protection to corporate speech fosters these values and benefits.

CORPORATIONS, SOCIAL WELFARE, AND THE
DEMOCRATIC PROCESS

Whatever normative conclusion one reaches about the role that corporations should play in modern society,[96] it would be difficult to deny corporate activity's enormous impact on both the nation's welfare and the government's success. Issues such as the best means to avoid inflation and unemployment—both of which may well be as attributable to business performance as they are to government decision making—are only two of the many socio-economic issues facing the polity.[97] Moreover, even governmental decisions that do not deal directly with economic issues can have a significant impact on the economy and therefore on corporate well-being.

David Millon has described this intersection as the "public law" conception of corporate law,[98] which acknowledges the substantial societal significance of corporate activity.[99] This conception represents a theoretical recognition that, at some level, Charles Wilson was correct in asserting that General Motors' welfare is intertwined with the country's welfare.[100]

Recognition of the public–corporate intersection acknowledges that corporate use of economic power will inevitably have a social and political impact beyond the narrow interests of the corporation itself.[101] In the words of political scientist Peter Bachrach, corporate leaders "significantly influence societal values directly and in the short run. And once a national issue has come to public attention, they frequently exercise their influence whether they want to or not. Their sheer existence, owing to their size, power, ubiquity, and public acceptance, leaves them no alternative."[102] Economist Adolf Berle long ago recognized that "[t]he corporation [had become], essentially, a nonstatist political institution."[103]

A number of scholars do not find this a positive development. One commentator, for example, has argued that because the economy's health generally is dependent upon the magnitude of corporate expenditures on capital goods, "public policy necessarily tends to be oriented, especially over the long run, in a direction which is fundamentally in line with the interests of the great corporate enterprises. And this will be true even if the interests of the giants are in conflict with other social goals."[104]

In a similar vein, Lindblom has pointed to what he describes as the danger of "circularity": the fear that, because of corporate power's distorting effect, political choices are effectively made by the very economic interests that the system was intended to regulate.[105] In the words of

Owen Fiss, under the circularity principle, "[v]oters were not actually considering the continued viability of capitalism, the justness of market distributions, or the structure within which organized labor was allowed to act because . . . of the control exercised by corporate interests over the political agenda."[106]

Even a casual examination of modern history tends to show, however, that Lindblom substantially overstates the level of political power that "dominant" corporate interests exercise. It would be absurd, of course, to suggest that large corporate interests have exercised little or no influence over modern economic and regulatory policies. But the very creation of the New Deal, as well as the enactment of the social welfare legislation of the "Great Society" programs in the 1960s, the heavy federal regulation of the tobacco and drug industries, and the modern congressional failure to enact federal tort reform legislation that would substantially benefit corporate defendants, all tend to demonstrate that large corporate interests have not always had their way in the political process.[107] Indeed, one probably could make an empirical case that over the last two-thirds of the twentieth century, the political power exercised by organized labor has been at least as great as that of the corporate giants. It likely would be more accurate to state that the corporate interest is merely one of several powerful voices that are widely heard in the political process.

More important for present purposes, Lindblom's analysis cannot be deemed relevant to the issue of First Amendment protection for corporate speech because the analysis is inherently and substantively viewpoint-based. In other words, Lindblom's entire theory is premised on the normative assumption that governmental regulation of economic interests is itself a good. The theory thus adopts a normative position on a fundamental substantive political issue—an approach that is, of course, perfectly appropriate. Yet in shaping the structure of First Amendment protection, it is entirely inappropriate to proceed on the basis of one particular set of substantive political value choices.[108] The whole point of the First Amendment, rather, is to allow free and open debate on the merits of competing approaches to those very issues. Thus, freed—as it constitutionally must be—from its moorings in normative economic and political philosophy, Lindblom's theory merely underscores the empirical accuracy of the asserted intersection between issues affecting corporate interests and those affecting the polity as a whole.

The public law understanding of the corporation's role, then, rests upon a view of the profit-making corporation as a participant in the policy deliberations of the government and as a performer of a leadership role in the political-economic order.[109] This view has significant and obvious implications for extending the scope of the First Amendment to corporate expression. Because of their expertise, resources, and incentives, corporations are uniquely suited to inform the electorate about many of the socio-economic issues facing the nation. Moreover, the very fact that a major profit-making corporation is of the opinion that a particular candidate or a particular policy is important to the community's prosperity may reasonably influence individual judgments on the matter.[110] The corporate viewpoint, of course, need not be accepted, but it should be made available as one option for the polity to assess.

Recognizing both the role that corporations play in a democratic society and their potential influence over government policies logically dictates extending full First Amendment protection to corporate speech. Any other conclusion would deprive the polity of potentially valuable input into the exercise of their self-governing power.[111]

Lindblom has argued that profit-making corporations have "become a kind of public official and exercise what, on a broad view of their role, are public functions."[112] This insight helps to explain the modern treatment of plaintiff corporations in defamation actions. The Court has recognized a strong state interest in protecting corporations from statements that are "clearly damaging" to their reputations.[113] This recognition is consistent with a view that a corporation's interests are intertwined with the broader interests of society as a whole.[114] The Court also has recognized that corporate plaintiffs are public figures for purposes of First Amendment defamation standards,[115] and thus, in order to recover damages, must demonstrate that a false statement was made with "'actual malice'—that is, with knowledge that it was false or with reckless disregard of whether it was false or not."[116] The standard's original premise was the need to insulate speakers from libel damages to insure that "debate on public issues should be uninhibited, robust, and wide-open."[117] The public law conception of the corporation is fully consistent with that underlying premise.[118]

At the same time, viewing corporations as public figures for purposes of the First Amendment privilege in libel suits underscores the important socio-political role that corporations play in society. In *Gertz v. Robert Welch, Inc.*,[119] the Court held that private-person plaintiffs were not subject to the actual malice standard, relying in part on the fact that public plaintiffs "usually enjoy significantly greater access to the channels of effective communication and hence have a more realistic opportunity to counteract false statements."[120] In other words, public persons have the ability to use mass media to speak in their own defense and contradict or correct the false statements.

In extending the status of public figure to a large corporation, the Court recognized that a business corporation enjoys "increased and more meaningful access to channels of communication for rebutting defamatory falsehood."[121] In so doing, the Court necessarily assumed that the corporation possesses the constitutional right to use those channels and to speak in its own defense. If the state were allowed to burden or otherwise interfere with corporate speech, the logic of *Gertz* would not permit the actual malice standard to apply to corporations.

One could argue, of course, that the corporate response to a defamatory statement serves an important role in furthering and protecting the corporation's business, because a corporate rebuttal to that false statement is necessary to maintain the corporation's reputation and thus maintain a profitable business. Such expression might be distinguishable from speech surrounding an election campaign, which arguably is not necessary to maintain the corporate reputation.[122] The two categories, however, share many similarities. The economic and regulatory choices made by elected officials can significantly affect corporations' profitability and success.[123] Thus, corporate interests may be promoted as much by expression endorsing candidates or commenting on public issues as by speech responding to defamatory statements.

CORPORATIONS, DEMOCRATIC THEORY, AND THE CONCEPT OF "CATALYTIC SELF-REALIZATION"

Respected scholars—in particular, C. Edwin Baker and Randall P. Bezanson—have argued that corporate speech does not deserve First Amendment protection because it fails to foster the values of personal liberty and self-expression that exclusively underlie the free speech right.[124] Far from being the product of a voluntarily chosen expression of the inner self, they contend, corporate speech amounts to nothing more than a mechanistic, involuntary attempt to maximize profits, ineluctably dictated by the corporate entity's inherent nature.[125]

Their rejection of First Amendment protection for corporate speech derives from both the absence of a human source of the expression and the presence of an inexorable profit motivation. The corporate ideas do not originate with any single individual or other intentional communicative act, these scholars argue, and the speech does not reflect any individual's voluntarily adopted political views.[126] Bezanson has asserted that speech by a business entity is "a machine programmed in a general direction which, when fed by the owners, channels its energy to particular ends that cannot be predicted at the time of feeding."[127]

Such a theory totally ignores whatever self-developmental benefit corporate expression might have on its recipients. Whether one should accept so truncated a version of the value of free expression in the first place is itself questionable.[128] But even were we to assume, solely for purposes of argument, that to fall within the First Amendment's protective umbrella expression must be the voluntarily chosen product of a self-realizing individual or association of individuals, it still would not follow that corporate speech is undeserving of constitutional protection. Such a conclusion improperly ignores the important elements of voluntary human choice that enter into individuals' resort to the corporate form in the first place, as well as the means by which the corporate form helps those individuals attain their goals. The profit-making corporation should be seen as an important catalyst in the process of individual self-realization, as has long been recognized in the case of unincorporated associations and nonprofit corporations.[129]

Alexis de Tocqueville recognized that the right and ability of individuals to form voluntary associations constituted an integral part of the fabric of American democratic society, in which the people had "carried to the highest perfection the art of pursuing in common the object of their common desires" and applied it to the "greatest number of purposes."[130] Americans associated not only for exclusively political purposes, he noted, but also for "commercial and manufacturing companies" and for all purposes "serious, futile, general or restrictive, enormous or diminutive."[131] As with political activity, such associations were deemed necessary to enhance the influence of individually powerless citizens by allowing them to unite in order to amass power.[132]

As previously noted, democracy is most appropriately characterized as a system both logically dependent upon and designed to further self-realization.[133] Associations may serve effectively as important vehicles through which individuals attain their personal and economic goals. This process could be described as "catalytic self-realization" because these associations serve as catalysts in enabling people to use and develop their human faculties and control their own destinies by pursuing their chosen purposes in society.

The business corporation arose from many of the same associational goals grounded in democratic theory as did other forms of association.[134] Indeed, the most common purpose of civil associations in the 1830s, other than political parties, was to further commerce and manufacturing.[135] Such organizations were examples of the many associations of individuals deemed by Tocqueville to be necessary elements of a democratic society. Indeed, during the Jacksonian period, the corporation was seen as a means to equalize otherwise unbalanced competing economic forces.[136] Absent the special economic and legal advantages of the corporate form, individual entrepreneurs who lacked personal fortunes were unable to compete effectively with those who possessed such wealth. Thus, the corporation's growth represented "the economic aspect of the political and social forces that democratized the United States during the Age of Jackson."[137] Corporations were recognized as "useful instrument[s] of regular business."[138]

Although corporations historically were subjected to some degree of attack on equality grounds, according to a leading authority, "[t]he compatibility of corporate status with individual equality under law raised issues of procedure rather than of substance. . . . The valid egalitarian point was simply that [the corporate form] should be available by a simple procedure on equal terms to all who saw use for them in ordinary business associations."[139] To enhance the success of such organizations, states legislatively authorized general incorporation, which made the formation of business corporations and individual investment in them easier and more commonplace.[140] Thus, during and after the presidency of Andrew Jackson, corporations not only were deemed to be consistent with the individual equality precept, but were viewed as a response to the "demand that all should have reasonably equal access to the benefits of incorporation."[141]

Although it would be naive to suggest that the role played by the modern corporation is identical to that of its Jacksonian ancestor, many striking similarities persist. One should not forget that ultimately the "corporation is its people and they are not detached from society."[142] Hence, for purposes of self-realization theory, one should view the corporation as merely one form of voluntary association, an aggregation of talent and resources, consciously entered into by individuals. In so doing, these individuals are seeking to self-realize by engaging and investing in business and by participating in and personally benefiting from the political-economic system through the power of collective action.[143] The corporate form enables individuals to pool their resources and, like other associations, pursue their chosen goals in a more efficient and effective manner.

It also enables individuals to engage in business and investment activity that they otherwise would be unable to perform as effectively on their own.[144] Further, it enables these individuals to speak in support of attaining those economic goals in a stronger, more effective voice.[145] In short, the business corporation may serve as a catalyst for the process of individual self-realization.

This analysis applies as much to the use of the corporate form in the economic arena as it does to the use of association in the political arena. Much as a common trust fund, composed of a grouping of smaller individual trusts, is designed and intended to geometrically increase investment benefits on the basis of the aggregated capital,[146] an individual shareholder's or corporate manager's ability to realize his economic goals can be magnified many times in both breadth and force.

The corporation's use of expression may significantly further fulfillment of the corporation's purpose. Just as the corporation serves as a catalyst for individual self-realization, so, too, does its speech play an important role in the attainment of the goals that its managers and investors have set for it. The activity of associating provides not only for collective and powerful action but also for a collective and powerful voice. The speaker whose individual message might not be as effective standing alone gains audibility and effectiveness by advocating her positions through group association.[147] A group can explain, advance, defend, and seek support for its purposes or positions in a manner that most individuals could not hope to achieve acting alone. This is especially true of the corporation, with its emphasis on centralized and efficient decision making and action.

The fact that a corporation's speech is directed toward economic gain should not distinguish it from other associational forms for First Amendment purposes. It is not uncommon for means of expression or communication to further one's own economic interests. One may advance such interests by persuading or influencing government or private individuals or entities either to take action or to refrain from taking action. Just as the individual's ability to maximize economic gain increases geometrically by resort to the streamlined methods of the corporate form, so, too, does the individual's ability to communicate in an effort to increase profits expand dramatically when filtered through the corporation's structure. It is therefore appropriate to recognize how use of the corporate form may magnify dramatically the communication's power and reach.

The fact that the corporation's primary purpose and function do not themselves constitute expression or communication also should not in any way reduce the level of First Amendment protection given to corporate speech. In its instrumental form, speech is not an end in itself but rather a means of facilitating personal or collective goals.[148] Thus, expression that fosters attainment of non-expressive goals fits well within the First Amendment's theoretical framework.

CORPORATE SPEECH AND THE LISTENER'S FIRST AMENDMENT RIGHT

Even if one ultimately rejected the catalytic self-realization concept, either in the abstract or in its specific application to corporations,[149] it does not necessarily follow that corporate speech falls outside the bounds of the First Amendment. Such expression can serve an important function both by fostering the democratic process on a collective level and by helping its recipients with self-realization on an individual level. Free expression facilitates the democratic process[150] because a free flow of information and opinion is essential for an individual to make life-affecting choices. Likewise, individuals develop their personal and intellectual faculties by receiving and processing information. The value of self-realization may be fostered as much by the receipt of expression as by the act of expressing.[151] Because the listener and the speaker receive the identical benefit from the speech, the listener's rights should be recognized as an independent basis on which to protect expression.[152]

A focus on the interests of recipients has played a venerable role in the development of modern free speech theory. Most significant is Alexander Meiklejohn's politically based theory of free speech, which viewed as the primary concern "not that everyone shall speak, but that everything worth saying shall be said."[153] This approach protects "those activities of thought and communication by which we govern."[154] To Meiklejohn, speech's value lay entirely in enabling voters to "acquire the intelligence, integrity, sensitivity, and generous devotion to the general welfare" necessary to act in a democratic government.[155] This ability derives from the receipt of "information or opinion or doubt or disbelief or criticism which is relevant to that issue."[156]

According to Meiklejohn, the First Amendment prohibits government from preventing individuals from learning any opinions or ideas relevant to the governing process.[157] An individual thus is exercising her First Amendment rights when she receives and intellectually processes information and opinion. The Court has recognized this independently grounded listener's right to receive information and ideas as a "necessary predicate to the recipient's meaningful exercise of his own rights of speech, press, and political freedom."[158]

This analysis provides an independent basis for protecting corporate speech in order to protect the First Amendment rights of those potential listeners who will hear, process, learn from, and make decisions based partially upon this information.[159] This logic in large part provided the basis for the Court's initial decision to protect corporate speech in *Bellotti*, in which the Court emphasized the First Amendment's "role in affording the public access to discussion, debate, and the dissemination of information and ideas" and in prohibiting the "government from limiting the stock of information from which members of the public may draw."[160]

The conceivable response that the listener's right does not justify protection of corporate speech because others will convey the same opinion or information is unpersuasive for several reasons. Initially, the identity of the source of speech may matter in providing context to the message as "an important component of many attempts to persuade."[161] The message's overall nature may change when the messenger changes; similarly, the degree of effectiveness and credibility may change depending on the source.[162] The same statement from different speakers may constitute a different message. As the Court has noted, an "espousal of socialism may carry different implications when displayed on the grounds of a stately mansion than when pasted on a factory wall or on an ambulatory sandwich board."[163] Thus, recognition of the listener's right logically dictates that all possible different versions of a statement may be made available for the listeners to see and react to in their own ways.[164] To a listener who dislikes or mistrusts corporations or big businesses, explicit support for a candidate or issue by a powerful corporation might dictate that listener's opposition to that candidate. Conversely, a person who approves of the role and influence of corporations might be predisposed to agree with the message for the very same reason. In either case, that message, with the corporation as its source, is relevant to the individual's decision.[165]

More important, it is by no means clear that the same information or opinion will be disseminated—at least anywhere near as effectively—absent corporate contributions to public debate. Corporations invariably will possess both the economic incentive and resources to express their views effectively and persuasively. We cannot be certain that any other entities or individuals will possess either quality to the same extent or degree. Ironically, although corporations' wealth and power are often what cause opponents of corporate speech to call for its restriction,[166] that very power is what makes corporate speech most valuable to both the democratic process and the listener's self-realization. The result of restricting the corporate voice, then, is that debate on a political issue is considerably less "uninhibited, robust, and wide-open"[167] than the First Amendment commands.

Baker and Bezanson have argued, however, that the exclusive basis of First Amendment protection is the volitional speaker's liberty. To them, the key is the act of speaking, not the speech itself.[168] Because a corporation's speech is "speakerless," under their view, it is not entitled to protection.[169] This is one of several conceivable rationales to support the view that the listener's rights are irrelevant if the speaker has no independently grounded right to speak.[170] The problem with such an argument is that it begs the very question that is the subject of the debate, because it simply assumes that the listener has no rights absent a voluntary speaker. The argument thus fails to respond to the contention that the speaker should have a right to speak for the very reason that the listener's receipt of the expression would foster First Amendment values.

It is true, of course, that recognition of a listener's right could not reasonably force either an unwilling private speaker to speak[171] or the government to disclose information it does not wish to divulge. Regardless of how one ultimately resolves the debate about the "voluntariness" of corporate expression,[172] surely no external force is "compelling" the expression. Hence, accepting an independently grounded listener's right does, in fact, resolve the issue of corporate speech protection.

A second argument against recognition of this independently grounded listener's right, made by Baker, focuses on the supposed lack of a logical stopping point for that right. He fears that this broad conception of respect for listener autonomy would prevent the government from denying the listener information even if on balance it concludes that the speech does not contribute to the good and even if it is acting either as a speaker or as a regulator of entities that have no autonomy rights.[173]

By his own words, however, Baker demonstrates his analysis's failure, for his words prove far too much. The government surely has no power to control what a speaker can say based on what the government concludes does not contribute to the public good.[174] Such a view necessarily violates the premise of epistemological humility so fundamental to First Amendment theory and doctrine.[175] Indeed, Baker's own liberty theory inherently recognizes this fact because he insists that "the collective must respect the equality and autonomy of individuals," thus "limiting the collective's decisionmaking authority" and permitting speech that the majority may deem unwise or objectionable.[176]

Once society grants to the government the power to prevent listeners from receiving expression based on the government's determination of the public good, there is no logical stopping point and therefore no reason not to grant the government the same power to prevent speakers from creating and disseminating expression that the government deems unwise. Baker attempts to tie everything back to speaker—as opposed to listener—autonomy as the key element in determining which communications the government can or cannot restrict in the name of the public good.[177] Yet, once it is recognized that both the speaker and listener derive similar benefits from the autonomy involved in the process of free expression, any rational basis for that distinction disappears.

Corporate Speech and the "Negative" Theory of the First Amendment

Although the free speech guarantee fosters the positive values associated with collective democracy and individual self-realization, the democratic system's inherent vulnerability requires constant vigilance in order to ensure that hostile forces do not undermine it. Thus, several theories concerning the First Amendment's scope have focused wisely on speech's role in preventing the government from acting in ways that may threaten the onset of tyranny.

This negative conception is apparent in two approaches to First Amendment interpretation, both of which may be understood as subvalues that serve the broader, more positive self-realization value.[178] First, and best known, is Vincent Blasi's theory of the "checking" function, which focuses on the value the First Amendment serves in checking governmental misconduct and public officials' abuse of power.[179] A second form of the negative theory seeks to prohibit the government from artificially enhancing its own position and power by controlling or manipulating lawful individual choices. The government may not seek to achieve its desired results by selectively censoring information and opinion that might be relevant to those choices.[180]

The First Amendment as a Check on Government

The best known of the negative theories is Blasi's checking function, which posits that the uppermost value of the First Amendment is "checking the abuse of power by public officials."[181] The central premise of Blasi's theory is that the First Amendment's fundamental role is to counter governmental misconduct by "facilitating a process by which countervailing forces check the misuse of official power."[182]

The checking function employs an "essentially pessimistic view of human nature and human institutions,"[183] similar in many ways to the view that underlies the separation of powers concept. Both are based on recognition of the need for "countervailing power in a democratic state"[184] necessary to "control the abuses of government."[185] As James Madison wrote in *The Federalist*, "[i]f angels were to govern men, neither external nor internal controls on government would be necessary."[186] Because that option obviously was not available, controls over the government had to be institutionalized.[187] Separation of powers and the First Amendment's checking function both require formal, organized, and prophylactic structures to continually police potential abuses before the government is allowed to subvert liberty.[188]

As fashioned by Blasi, the theory underlying the checking function is plagued with ambiguities.[189] For example, although Blasi describes the especially serious evil to which free speech protection is directed as "misconduct by government officials,"[190] it is not clear whether he intends to confine this concept to breaches of ethical or criminal prohibitions by government officials, or to include as well any substantive governmental decisions or choices deemed—by whom, it is also unclear—to be improper. If he intends the latter, he fails to define adequately such a concept. Nevertheless, Blasi's recognition of the pessimistic underside of the First Amendment represents an important contribution to First Amendment thought, for surely checking governmental abuse is an important role played by that constitutional protection. Corporate speech may serve an important function in furthering the check on the government.

CORPORATE SPEECH AS A GOVERNMENTAL CHECK

The link between governmental performance and business performance cuts in both directions. Although the government may seek to assure that businesses perform fairly and effectively,[191] businesses must likewise assure that the government performs in a similar manner. There is no better way to achieve this goal than through the power of speech. The checking value demands protection for speech by "institutions outside of government with the resources, energy, and expertise to counter the government's messages" and actions.[192] The countervailing voices, according to Blasi, should be "well-organized, well-financed," and "capable of disseminating their information and judgments to the general public."[193]

Of many organized constituencies that fit this description, one of the potentially most effective is the profit-making corporation.[194] Early in the nation's history, Tocqueville recognized that government should not be the only active power. Rather, he argued, private "associations ought, in democratic nations, to stand in lieu of those powerful private individuals whom the equality of conditions has swept away."[195] The result is a political arena in which three powerful entities—the government, the press, and private organizations—provide competing views and messages, a broader range of information, and a check on one another.[196]

Corporate speech, precisely because of its power to disseminate widely its message and its obvious underlying motivating force of economic self-interest, can serve as an effective check on governmental excess. Often, corporations will not have to rely on the government for their information. They will formulate their own positions, usually according to the needs of their business, broadly defined. They likely will possess the resources, expertise, and economic incentive to disseminate broadly commentary and information on issues of social and economic policy.

Under the so-called "fourth estate" theory, it is primarily—if not exclusively—the institutional media that perform the checking function.[197] It is unclear, however, why the checking function should be viewed in so truncated a manner. As the Court noted in *Bellotti*, "the press does not have a monopoly on either the First Amendment or the ability to enlighten,"[198] or on the ability to check government. Indeed, expertise and incentive on certain issues may well enable corporations to perform the checking function much more effectively than the institutional media.[199] As one commentator has correctly observed, "[i]t simply is not clear that media speech contributes more significantly to the democratic dialogue than does non-media speech."[200]

Even if one were to assume, for the sake of argument, that the press is the most effective check on the government, it does not follow that other speakers are incapable of performing that function. Checking is a question of power, resources, and incentive to perform the function; corporations generally possess all three.

Most important, when the government and the media are allied on a particular issue—which has not been an infrequent occurrence—"the mass media are likely to magnify government's messages, thereby undermining the independence of the self-controlled citizen and increasing the tendency toward an authoritarian communications network."[201] The problem of a government–media alliance arguably reached its height during the Persian Gulf War, during which the media gave virtually no coverage to those who were critical of the decision to send troops into battle.[202] Thus, the public heard few, if any, strong dissenting voices from the media, the supposed check on the government.

The need to check the government, then, is too important to be entrusted to only one group of speakers. Returning to the separation-of-powers analogy, the more society subdivides power, presumably the smaller the danger of tyranny. In the context of the checking function, the greater the number of motivated and powerful private speakers, the smaller the danger of undue power centralization and unchecked governmental excess.

This conclusion, it should be emphasized, is in no way intended to imply that corporate speech always will be wise, persuasive, or motivated by good intentions. But the skeptical assumption underlying both separation-of-powers theory and the negative perspective of First Amendment theory is that one can never fully trust the motivations of any individual or institution, private or governmental.[203] It is for that reason that separation-of-powers theory seeks to disperse influence among a variety of interests and institutions. Modern society should recognize private corporate power as one of those interests. To the extent it does not, the inevitable result is that other societal and governmental institutions will dangerously accrete even more power than they already possess.[204]

Once society recognizes the important role that corporations may play in diffusing and checking societal power, governmental suppression of corporate speech takes on potentially ominous implications for avoiding the centralization of political power. One can never be sure whether restrictions on corporate expression are in reality nothing more than governmental attempts to curb or intimidate a potential rival for societal authority. Hence, excluding corporate speech from the First Amendment's reach would almost inevitably have a detrimental impact on the most fundamental values underlying the protection of free speech.

CORPORATE SPEECH RESTRICTIONS AS THOUGHT CONTROL

There are times when our system vests in private individuals or entities the right to challenge governmental action, not so much because we are concerned about the harmful impact of that action on that individual or entity but rather because we are troubled that the government would act in a particular manner. Further, we recognize that the affected party will have the greatest incentive to act as the equivalent of a private attorney general in seeking to check such governmental excess. The classic illustration of such a practice is the ability of concededly guilty criminals to challenge violations of their constitutional rights.[205]

In shaping modern constitutional law, corporations are often the beneficiary of the law's methodologies. For example, corporations affected by a federal regulation are deemed to have standing to challenge the regulation on grounds of constitutional federalism.[206] This is true even though the concern underlying the challenge is not so much that the government is mistreating the corporation (after all, the state government could probably impose the same regulation, consistent with governing principles of constitutional federalism) but rather that the federal government might be exceeding its constitutional powers within the federal system. Private corporations have this power to bring suit presumably because their economic interests will provide the incentive to present the most effective possible challenge.

Moreover, corporations can challenge governmental regulations as violations of procedural due process even though they are the same faceless, mindless, and robotic profit maximizers that they supposedly are for free speech purposes.[207] At least in part, this is probably due to the fact that we do not want our government behaving in certain ways, regardless of who the victim is.

The same analysis dictates free speech protection for corporations, at least against certain types of restrictions. The Court has recognized that "[o]ur whole constitutional heritage rebels at the thought of giving government the power to control men's minds."[208] The First Amendment forbids the government from commandeering people's thinking process in an effort to modify their behavior. Rather, behavioral choices and the information that guides them must remain free from governmental control or manipulation.[209] This prohibition on governmentally imposed thought control gives rise to the fundamental precept that the government may not restrict views or ideas merely because they are unpopular or deemed by the government to be unwise. The Court has stated that the "bedrock principle underlying the First Amendment . . . is that government may not prohibit the expression of an idea simply because society finds the idea itself offensive or disagreeable."[210]

In at least certain situations, governmental regulation of corporate speech is premised on grounds wholly inconsistent with this fundamental notion. Such regulation often reflects governmental mistrust of citizens' ability to make rational judgments on the basis of free and open debate. A classic illustration is the government's attempt to ban tobacco advertising: The government seeks to deal with expression that advocates an activity the government deems unwise—although lawful—not by encouraging counterspeech but rather by resorting to naked suppression because the government does not trust individuals to make proper choices on the basis of free and open debate.[211] Such governmental behavior is wholly inconsistent with First Amendment dictates. Because the principle that the government may not suppress expression due to its mistrust of its citizens focuses on the nature of the relationship between the government and the private citizen, the speaker's nature is rendered wholly irrelevant.

Viewed from this perspective, much of the Court's rationale in *Austin* takes on an Orwellian and counterproductive air. The *Austin* Court accepted as a rationale for governmental restriction of corporate expression an argument that manifests this mistrust of citizens' ability to judge competing contributions to public debate that is anathema to basic First Amendment principles. The Court took the unprecedented step of allowing the corporate speech restriction in order to ensure that the amount of expression by the corporation "reflect[s] actual public support for the political ideas espoused by [the] corporation[ ]."[212] The Court, however, did not explain why protection of expression should be calibrated to reflect the actual degree of public support, nor how, if such calibration were necessary, the idea's popularity could be measured if its expression were restricted beforehand. How, one might reasonably ask, can an idea "get itself accepted in the competition of the market"[213] if the state can restrict the idea at the source because of its presumed lack of support? The Court thus laid the groundwork for an interpretation of the First Amendment that counterproductively and circularly confines protection of expression on the basis of preexisting public support for that expression. The Court also ignored the fact that the expression of non-corporate, as well as corporate, interests could just as easily give rise to a false sense of support due simply to the intensity of non-corporate beliefs, even though the actual number of supporters is relatively small.

The *Austin* Court took the further puzzling step of labeling the presentation of ideas that, the Court assumed, lacked public support as "corruption,"[214] the mere potential for which apparently was sufficient to justify governmental suppression of corporate speech.[215] The Court's analysis is fundamentally flawed. The assumption that awareness of unpopular ideas or information inherently distorts or corrupts, rather than enhances, people's ability both to self-realize and to make personal and electoral choices is incompatible with basic notions of First Amendment theory.[216]

Wholly apart from this departure from fundamental precepts of First Amendment theory is the danger of abuse to which the Court's approach gives rise. Under the Court's reasoning, as Justice Scalia argued in dissent, "virtually anything [government] deems politically undesirable can be turned into political corruption—by simply describing its effects as politically 'corrosive.'"[217]

In any event, were one to accept the Court's reasoning, one could not logically confine its application to corporate speech. One could just as easily reason that an individual's amount of advocacy should not be disproportionate to the level of actual public support that currently exists for his position.[218] Employing the Court's logic, then, an individual who possesses unpopular political beliefs or who supports a fringe candidate could be restrained from financing expression beyond the existing level of support for that candidate's message. The explanation for this new concept of corruption might be, as L. A. Powe, Jr., has argued, that "[i]t is easy to defend speech we hate so long as it is ineffective, but it is much harder to do so when people actually respond positively."[219]

Powe's comment underscores the importance of a second precept derived from the First Amendment's prohibition on thought control, a precept that David A. Strauss labels the "persuasion principle."[220] This principle posits that the government may not suppress speech on the ground that it is too persuasive.[221] This position is a version of the First Amendment's "widely shared hostility to paternalism,"[222] which demands that "the government may not suppress speech on the ground that the speech is likely to persuade people to do something that the government considers harmful" or of which the government disapproves.[223] To permit the government to do so would constitute a "dangerous manifestation of governmental mistrust of citizens' abilities to absorb and judge the expression of competing viewpoints."[224]

Arguments against protection of corporate speech generally ignore these principles, relying instead on two basic paternalistic assumptions. The first assumption is that massive amounts of corporate speech are likely to persuade listeners, regardless of the merits of the ideas presented.[225] The second is that listeners may become overloaded with more information than they can process; thus, unless the government intervenes, listeners will be unable to make clear, rational decisions.[226]

These assumptions ignore the premises of individual dignity and rationality inherent in both democratic theory in general and free speech theory in particular.[227] No matter how often or loudly one disseminates expression, as David Shelledy has argued, "[i]f democracy is to have meaning, we must generally assume that speech affects voting behavior only when it persuades."[228] Indeed, neither the First Amendment nor the democratic system of which it is a part could function under any other premise.

The Case against Corporate Speech: A Response

Corporate Speech and the Profit Motive: The Role of Self-Interest in Free Speech Theory

Pursuant to Baker's liberty theory, free speech applies only to the voluntarily chosen, self-developmental expression of individuals or associations.[229] While the theory has implications for corporate speech protection, such a narrow approach to the values served by free expression improperly constricts the scope of the First Amendment.[230] Even if one were to reject this unduly truncated perspective of the liberty model, however, one might nevertheless oppose First Amendment protection for corporate speech simply on the grounds that narrow concerns of personal self-interest exclusively motivate such expression. The distinction between these two rationales for rejecting First Amendment protection for corporate speech is significant. One could conceivably accept—as the liberty model does not—that corporate expression is voluntarily chosen yet nevertheless seek to exclude it from the First Amendment's scope because it does not constitute an unselfish attempt to further the broad public interest.

Such opposition to self-interested speech is largely reflected in the theories of modern civic republican scholars who argue that "the motivating force of political behavior should not be self-interest, narrowly defined."[231] Civic republican scholars oppose purely "pluralist" activity that seeks selfishly and exclusively to promote the individual's private interests.[232]

As explained in detail elsewhere, under well-accepted First Amendment doctrine, a speaker's motivation is entirely irrelevant to the question of constitutional protection.[233] Motivation may be relevant in enabling the listener to evaluate the context of certain expression, and the listener's evaluation may well change based on the expression's motivation.[234] An individual is much more inclined to be skeptical of arguments against a product's regulation asserted by a profit-motivated manufacturer than similar arguments asserted by a completely objective observer. It does not follow, however, that self-interested speech is inherently valueless. Just as a lawyer representing a client can make persuasive arguments or present information important to an objective observer despite an obvious self-interest, a self-interested advocate also can make valuable contributions to public debate.

In addition, there is nothing necessarily immoral or illegitimate in using expression to further one's personal interests. Any theory of free expression that selectively reduces protection of self-interested expression is inconsistent with the historical and philosophical traditions of democracy, for these traditions recognize the centrality of an individual's right to contribute to the betterment of her personal welfare.

Many fully protected speakers do stand to gain financially or personally if listeners accept their speech. Some examples mentioned previously[235] include political candidates seeking elective office, consumer organizations seeking increased consumer protection, welfare recipients seeking increases in benefits, farmers seeking subsidies, and American auto workers seeking higher tariffs on foreign automobiles. Indeed, the incentives produced by self-interest are likely to significantly enrich the substance of public debate. These incentives are likely to spur the thoroughness, thoughtfulness, and breadth of distribution of such expression. To exclude all self-interested expression from the scope of the constitutional guarantee, then, would effectively gut free speech protection.

A speaker who is likely to gain or lose financially if some policy is implemented or a particular candidate is elected to public office possesses a strong incentive to devote the time, resources, and effort to creating and disseminating a particular message and to effectively advocating his position.[236] From the listener's standpoint, such self-interest may sharpen the disagreements among the several voices and illustrate the issues and positions on which the individual listener, like a court, ultimately must make decisions.

To use *Austin* as an example, the Michigan Chamber of Commerce advocated Richard Bandstra's election quite probably because the organization and its members believed they would gain financially from his election. This, of course, is not to say that financial interest provides a greater incentive to speak on political and social issues than would purely ideological interest; MCFL presumably has the same level of incentive to speak in support of pro-life candidates as the Chamber of Commerce has to speak in support of pro-business candidates. But that is the point: Both have similarly strong incentives. Speech should not lose its protection merely because the incentive is financial rather than ideological.

Shareholder Protection and the Preclusion of Forced Speech

A common argument made against the protection of corporate speech is that individual shareholders might oppose the message that the corporation disseminates; therefore, the government has a legitimate interest in protecting those shareholders from being forced to subsidize the expression of positions with which they disagree.[237] Normally, corporate shareholders do not have the power to veto individual decisions made by management.[238] A dissenting shareholder, for example, has no authority to halt management's decision to leave or enter a particular geographical market or to begin a new product line. At first blush, it might appear puzzling that the only corporate decision over which the state allows a dissenting shareholder to exercise a veto power is one concerning expression. As a prima facie matter, such gratuitous and selective inhibition on expressive activity would seem to contravene explicit Supreme Court statements rendering such actions invalid.[239] What at first appears to be a selective inhibition on expression, however, has been defended as a means to prevent the unique problem of compelled speech, which often has been characterized as a First Amendment violation, at least when the government compels the speech.[240] As Victor Brudney has argued, "government concerned with protecting First Amendment values could reasonably believe it important to free those citizens from bondage to management's political views."[241]

Closer examination reveals, however, that for several reasons, the forced speech rationale cannot justify excluding corporate speech from the First Amendment's scope. First, a parallel standard is not followed when it comes to associations other than profit-making corporations even though a similar problem could arise. Second, it is by no means obvious that shareholders automatically will be so identified with the corporations' expressed positions that the shareholders realistically can be deemed to have been forced to speak. Third, even assuming one can make such an identification, the relative cost of exit is not so high as to lead to the conclusion that the shareholder's expression actually has been forced. I will now explore each of these points in greater detail.

Attempting to Distinguish among Types of Associations

The theory underlying the "shareholder forced speech" argument is that because shareholders should not have their money used to promote messages with which they disagree,[242] a stockholder's money in the corporation's general treasury should not be used to support expression advocating a particular candidate or policy position.[243] This concern for dissenting members, however, never has been extended to nonprofit corporations, as the Court's decision in *MCFL* shows.[244] The Court there expressly recognized that contributors to a nonprofit corporation "are fully aware of its political purposes, and in fact contribute precisely because they support those purposes."[245] The Court reasoned that some entities, although assuming the corporate form, have "features more akin to voluntary political associations than business firms."[246] This argument turns entirely on a distinction between ordinary business and so-called ideological corporations in order to grant the latter type of organization greater free speech rights.[247] Such "advocacy" corporations are supposedly marked by a unanimity of positions among members and a desire to express common views.[248]

Supporters of this position are unclear, however, as to the specific matters on which unanimity must exist in order for this rationale to apply: ultimate goals, specific strategies, specific statements, or a combination of the three. To illustrate the point, consider MCFL, an organization whose members share a commitment to fostering respect for human life and defending the right to life of all human beings born and unborn.[249] Suppose the organization decides to advocate blockading abortion clinics as a means of stopping abortions. Suppose further that several members of the organization object to those statements and tactics. Has unanimity—or indeed, even commonality of interests—been lost? At some specific level, the answer has to be yes even though members likely continue to agree on the association's general pro-life policies. In such a scenario, either the *MCFL* Court's distinction no longer justifies protecting MCFL's expression or the distinction itself has been undermined. The latter conclusion is more reasonable. Just as members of an ideological association still agree on ultimate goals despite possible differences on specific strategies, so, too, do the shareholders of commercial corporations share the universal corporate goal of profit maximization even though they may disagree as to the best method to attain that result.[250]

Even at the most general level of ultimate goals, the *MCFL* Court's distinction fails because, as Rodney A. Smolla has correctly argued, "Americans who contribute to the ACLU are not likely to agree with every position in its platform, any more than the investor in General Motors agrees with all of its corporate positions."[251] The point may be illustrated by examining the actions and responses of organizations to the issue of First Amendment protection for hate speech.[252] Numerous advocacy organizations, expressly formed for the protection of First Amendment rights and whose members presumably joined for that purpose, came out in support of hate speech restriction while opposing other, similar speech restrictions.[253] Such inconsistencies, of course, are not in and of themselves problematic. What is problematic, however, is the view that First Amendment protection for the organization's speech should turn solely on a perceived absence of such inconsistencies. If such a standard were to be employed, the consistent protection of the speech of ideologically based associations would be at least as problematic as protecting the speech of profit-maximizing corporations. Indeed, General Motors is more likely to achieve general unanimity, because pursuing the ultimate goal of turning a profit is not only shared but actually required on threat of a shareholder suit.

One possible reason for distinguishing between profit-making and nonprofit, ideologically based associations turns on the difference between the incentives that are assumed to stimulate someone to join or support the two types of organizations. Many assume that the incentive for joining an ideologically based association is more effective advocacy while the incentive for investing in a profit-making corporation is the maximization of profits. This argument, however, ignores the fact that advocacy rarely is exclusively an end in itself but rather is a means to an end—political, ideological, personal, or economic. Individuals presumably did not join MCFL merely to speak about abortion and right-to-life issues; instead, they joined in order to achieve a goal, namely, changing existing government policies on right-to-life issues. They seek to achieve this result through a variety of activities, including speech. Similarly, individuals invest in General Motors in order to turn a profit as part of a socially and politically powerful entity through a variety of activities, including speech.[254] In each case, joining and speaking through an organization enhances one's ability to achieve certain ends through the vehicles of strong collective action and speech. Thus, the only difference between MCFL and General Motors lies in the two corporations' goals. Advocacy toward each organization's particular goal serves the same role for each organization and provides the same incentive for members to join.

Questioning the Cost of Exit

Yet another arguable basis of distinction between the two organizational types concerns the costs that dissenting members must incur in order to disassociate themselves from their respective organizations. Shareholders in profit-making corporations will have to sell their shares, while members of an ideological organization will be required merely to resign their membership. Thus, one might argue that shareholders will suffer more harmful consequences from such disassociation and, therefore, will have a disincentive to do so.[255] The argument, in essence, is that investors in a business corporation should not be "forced to choose between contributing to political or social expressions with which they disagree or foregoing opportunities for profitable investment."[256] Such a profit-oriented choice arguably is not at issue with an ideological or political corporation. Whether such reasoning justifies the view of the dissenting shareholder as a compelled speaker, however, is questionable.

This argument is derived from cases involving labor unions' expression in which the Court has held that mandatory union dues should not be used for political purposes, because to do so would force union dues-payers to fund messages with which they might disagree.[257] The union cases are distinguishable, however, on several key points. Initially, these cases all arose under situations in which the law permitted an agency shop arrangement. According to this arrangement, all employees either had to be members of the union or at least had to pay dues as an employment condition.[258] In these cases, individuals actually depended upon the organization for a job, income, and livelihood, thus rendering the option of exit unrealistic or at the very least, heavily burdensome.[259]

The same cannot be said, however, of investment in a profit-making corporation. At worst, the financial sacrifice that would follow from exiting a business corporation is impossible to determine, ex ante. Because shares of stock are presumably traded in efficient securities markets in which the stock and current market price likely are fungible, the shareholder probably will lose nothing in the transaction.[260] To the extent that the corporate speech somehow causes the stock's price to fall, the shareholder has other remedies, such as a shareholder suit for breach of fiduciary duty, as a means of obtaining redress.[261] The difference between labor unions and corporations, then, amounts to the difference between state-compelled membership as a prerequisite to earning a living and voluntary investment.[262] Because an investor dissatisfied with a corporation's speech generally may simply reinvest in another corporation, the element of forced speech in the union and corporate contexts is significantly different.[263] For purposes of determining the validity of governmental regulation of corporate speech, having to forego a particular investment opportunity—at least as an a priori matter—simply is not of the same magnitude as the obligation to find new employment.[264]

In any event, to the extent that one accepts the "compelled speech" rationale, it would be logically difficult to confine the rationale to the corporate context. Meir Dan-Cohen has demonstrated persuasively why the argument from economic choices cannot logically be so limited.[265] He posits a hypothetical in which a wealthy businessman who is a known fascist pays high interest on money he borrows from local individuals but uses the money to disseminate his unpopular political messages.[266] This scenario introduces ideological and political concerns into all business decisions; a potential lender is forced to choose between foregoing a profitable use of her money or contributing to a political message with which she disagrees. These are the exact choices that form the basis of this dissenting-shareholder argument against corporate speech, yet no one would suggest that the government could prevent the businessman from disseminating his message.[267] It is simply impossible to know, a priori, whether selling shares will harm, benefit, or have little economic effect on the shareholder. Therefore, it is impossible to draw such a distinction.

Gratuitous Inhibitions on Speech

An additional difficulty with the dissenting-shareholder argument is that dissenters' preferences are ignored freely in corporate decision-making contexts that do not involve speech. This is true even of the dissenters' ideological preferences. One could imagine numerous examples of corporations' non-expressive actions—such as investing in an apartheid-dominated South Africa, operating an abortion clinic, or employing low-wage foreign labor—that some shareholders might find politically or ideologically objectionable. Yet under governing corporation law, those dissenters would be largely powerless to stop such actions.[268] The use of corporate assets to support political causes that might be inconsistent with some shareholders' interests does not appear to differ significantly from any other type of management misbehavior.[269]

Targeting corporate speech as the sole method of protecting dissenting shareholders violates the principle wisely recognized by the Court in *Simon & Schuster, Inc. v. Members of the New York State Crime Victims Board*.[270] There the Court struck down a statute that served a state interest by burdening income derived by convicted criminals only from expressive activity.[271] The stronger version of this doctrine, suggested by Justice Kennedy in a separate opinion in the case, would invalidate, without further inquiry, any burdensome restriction that singles out protected speech.[272] Under this reasoning, the government cannot achieve even compelling interests by restricting only speech when non-speech activity gives rise to similar dangers. Thus, even assuming that there is a compelling state interest in protecting dissenting shareholders,[273] the government cannot serve that interest by burdening speech but leaving uncontrolled non-expressive conduct that continues to give rise to that very same concern.[274]

One could argue that expression does, in fact, present a unique danger in this context because of the state's legitimate interest in preventing compelled speech on the shareholders' part. The Court has held that such compulsion, when imposed by the government, violates the First Amendment.[275] The state, one might argue, properly may choose to prevent private entities from compelling their members' speech. By restricting corporate speech, the argument goes, the state is providing extra protection to these rights as investors in commercial corporations exercise them.[276]

At most, recognizing such a First Amendment–like interest on the shareholders' part results in a stand-off between dueling First Amendment rights. On the one hand are the free speech interests of corporate managers and majority shareholders who seek to utilize the corporate form's efficiencies for expressive purposes and of listeners who would benefit from the speech. On the other hand are the First Amendment interests of the dissenting shareholders who would be forced to subsidize the speech against their will.[277] Careful analysis reveals, however, that no such stand-off exists.

It is by no means clear that individual shareholders are widely identified with the positions taken in particular corporate expression.[278] This is especially so in light of the explicit legal dichotomy that traditionally has been drawn between corporate structure and individual shareholders.[279] In addition, such a choice exists in non-speech contexts as well: Potential investors must choose between foregoing a profitable investment or subsidizing non-expressive business conduct they might find disagreeable, such as using low-paid labor in foreign countries or operating an abortion clinic. Singling out speech for negative treatment violates the principle of the Court's decision in *Simon & Schuster*.[280]

From a certain perspective, profit-making corporations' expression represents the shareholders' common view, at least when that concept is defined broadly.[281] There may be disagreement as to the wisest strategies to accomplish the corporate goal, but shareholders have in common the basic goal of maximizing profits through the company's activities. Because a business corporation risks a shareholder suit if it expends corporate funds on any speech not plausibly tied to this goal, any political speech must support a candidate or position that, if adopted, will inure, in one way or another, to the corporation's financial benefit. In an important sense, then, such speech does reflect the shareholders' ultimate, common, and unanimously shared desire to enhance profits.

Seeking Less Invasive Means to Protect Shareholders

Assume, for purposes of argument, that some connection exists between shareholders and the corporation's speech and that the law therefore should recognize some governmental interest in protecting dissenting shareholders. The problem with the corporate speech prohibition is that such a remedy completely silences the majority of the shareholders who agree with the statement or position that the corporation wishes to express.[282] The remedy would prevent the majority or super-majority of shareholders, which ultimately determines a corporation's actions, from advocating political positions the shareholders wish to take through the corporate form. Moreover, completely excluding corporate speech from the First Amendment's scope would allow the government to prohibit corporate messages, even when shareholders unanimously authorized the expenditure for that expression.[283] This argument thus reaches the absurd conclusion that a nonexistent dissenting minority can restrict speech supported even by every investor in the corporation.

The Court sought to circumvent this problem in cases involving labor unions. Instead of categorically prohibiting union expenditures, the Court merely required unions to refund a percentage of the dues of a member who disagreed with specified speech expenditures.[284] Therefore, the union was allowed to speak in its own voice but without drawing on funds from any members who disagreed with the message being expressed. One scholar has suggested that this solution could work just as effectively in the corporate context.[285] Arguably, the segregated fund scheme recognized in *MCFL* and *Austin*—in which only those shareholders who support the speech are required to pay for it through donations to a separate fund—constituted a similar attempt to protect the dissenters while still permitting those who support a message to have their say.[286]

The problem with the segregated fund scheme is that when the dust settles, the corporation still does not have the right to speak. In effect, the scheme allows individuals to do exactly what they could have done even if the corporation had never existed. Unlike the union cases, in which the union itself still could present its own message when employing the refund procedure, the speech from the separate corporate fund is not that of the corporation because the corporation cannot put its money or its name toward its own political speech.[287] Rather, the speech is that of some subgroup of individuals, thus diffusing the corporation's message.[288]

Perhaps the greatest problem with the segregated fund scheme is that it effectively undermines the beneficial efficiency values of the corporate form solely in the context of expression. Laws establishing the structure of corporate decision making are designed to enable the corporation to function with the greatest degree of economic efficiency possible.[289] Requiring corporations to employ the cumbersome and inefficient method of the segregated fund for expression purposes would revoke those efficiency benefits only for expression purposes. The result quite likely would be a dramatic reduction in the effectiveness of the contributions made to public debate.

Brudney has suggested two additional ways in which dissenting shareholders may be protected. One is to restrict all wasteful corporate spending, defined as "expenditures from which the enterprise cannot reasonably be expected to benefit," including "speech not reasonably related to the corporation's business."[290] The second way is to structure the corporate decision-making process so as to require unanimous stockholder consent for all corporate expenditures.[291] Brudney then considers whether either restriction could be placed on only corporate speech or all corporate activities, and he concludes that the "First Amendment should not present an insurmountable obstacle to such a regulation," whether applied to all corporate activities (including speech) or solely to corporate political speech.[292]

If framed as speech-only regulations—prohibiting wasteful corporate speech or requiring shareholder unanimity for speech—these suggestions would be unconstitutional under *Simon & Schuster*. In such a situation, the government would be attempting to serve the general interest in protecting shareholders by burdening only corporate speech and leaving untouched non-expressive corporate conduct that implicates the same concern.[293]

Laws prohibiting waste in all corporate activities or requiring shareholder consent for all activities likely would survive First Amendment attack under the doctrine of *United States v. O'Brien*,[294] which established a lower level of scrutiny for generally applicable laws only incidentally burdening speech.[295] Assuming one accepts *O'Brien*,[296] Brudney's proposed laws aimed at all corporate waste or requiring shareholder consent across the board should satisfy that standard because any impact on speech would be incidental to a general law designed to serve a governmental purpose. Thus, there would be no gratuitous inhibition aimed at speech alone.

One could imagine, then, a constitutionally valid statute prohibiting all corporate activities "not reasonably related to the corporation's business."[297] This is not to suggest that the *Bellotti* Court was incorrect in striking down the state law that imposed a "materially affecting" speech restriction.[298] Rather, this recognizes an alternative ground on which the Court could have struck down the statute: It singled out speech from all other corporate activity for its ban.[299]

Pursuant to this analysis, assuming one accepts the state's asserted interest in protecting dissenting shareholders, one could modify the statute in *Bellotti* in order to simultaneously avoid unconstitutional interference with corporate speech and protect shareholders. The suggested law would prohibit all wasteful corporate activity, of which speech is merely one example. Thus, the distinction, for constitutional purposes, becomes one between an outright ban on all expression and a requirement that corporate managers simply use their best judgment in making all decisions involving the corporate funds' use, including decisions as to which messages the managers will disseminate.

The Equality Principle in Free Speech Theory: The Corporation as Power Surrogate

Another argument used to rationalize the exclusion of corporate speech from the First Amendment's scope is that because corporations have vast resources that enable them to disseminate a message more effectively and broadly than other speakers, the corporate message will unduly dominate the market, thereby "drowning out" competing expression as a practical matter.[300] The government, therefore, may restrict corporate speech in order to ensure that the public hears all competing expression equally.[301] This concept has been described as "proportional leveling" or "enhancement."[302] According to this argument, unequal expenditures for expression by candidates and by advocates in the public debate, including corporations, create an artificial barrier to the exercise of what the Court has described in a separate context as the "inalienable right to full and effective participation in the political process[ ]."[303] Judge J. Skelly Wright, for example, argued that accepting the ideals of "one person, one vote" and "all men are created equal" necessarily implies accepting that equality is part of the First Amendment's central meaning.[304] Cass Sunstein suggested that the concept of political equality dictates that "all individuals and groups have access to the political process; large disparities in political influence are disfavored."[305]

Although equality is certainly an important element of free speech theory, this rationale for the exclusion of corporate speech is seriously flawed in a number of respects. Most important, it significantly misstates both the scope and rationale of the First Amendment's equality principle. Moreover, even if one assumed that the rationale represented a legitimate application of the equality principle, its limitation to corporate speech artificially truncates the principle's reach and thus indefensibly confines its application in an irrationally underinclusive manner.

Misinterpreting the Concept of First Amendment Equality

The equality principle has a long and venerable tradition in First Amendment theory and doctrine.[306] When properly confined, the principle not only makes perfect sense but is actually essential to free speech theory's effective operation. The problem with the principle's use as a rationale for excluding corporate speech from the First Amendment's scope, however, is that such a use substantially misperceives the correct meaning and implications of the equality principle's proper role.

To understand the misreading of First Amendment equality that underlies this argument for excluding corporate speech from protection, it is necessary to conceptualize equality on two levels that can be called "first-order" and "second-order" equality. "First-order" equality, in the free speech context, is premised on the precept that "[u]nder the First Amendment there is no such thing as a false idea."[307] All viewpoints must have an equal opportunity to compete in the intellectual marketplace, free from selective governmental regulation, if the concept of free speech is not to be rendered totally meaningless. If the government is permitted to suppress the expression of a particular viewpoint that it deems wrong or offensive, there is no logical means of confining that power only to the suppression of certain positions. The only question would be which ideological viewpoint is held by those in power at the time.[308] Thus, properly understood, the equality principle dictates that the government must treat differing viewpoints' expression in an equal manner.

"Second-order" equality focuses on the need for an equality of resources among speakers at the pre-expression stage. Second-order equality is concerned not with the assurance of equal access of competing substantive viewpoints but rather with equality of the speakers' pre-speech economic resources. Not only is a concern with second-order equality not dictated by free expression values, a focus on second-order equality actually threatens to undermine those values.

Second-order equality can be achieved by one of two means: increasing the pre-speech resources of the economically inferior speakers or limiting the economically superior speakers' ability to employ their resources for expressive purposes. Whatever the constitutional implications of the former methodology,[309] the latter is in fundamental and inescapable tension with the First Amendment's premises. Whichever value or values one believes that free expression fosters, those values inevitably are undermined by a governmentally imposed reduction in the sum total of available expression. If one assumes that individuals self-realize on the basis of both the dissemination and receipt of expression or that making individual citizens more informed about the issues facing society facilitates the democratic process, at least as a prima facie matter a reduction in the sum total of expression undermines the achievement of those goals.

A hypothetical construct illustrates this tension: Imagine a society in which the government, motivated by concern about economic inequality among potential speakers, has brought about speaker equality simply by prohibiting expression of any kind. It would be impossible to deny that, in such a situation, the concerns of second-order equality have been fully satisfied because, after all, as a result of the government's action, no speaker has a resource advantage over any other. Yet it would be preposterous to suggest that such a scenario actually fosters free expression values: No one is saying or hearing anything. Although this construct is wholly hypothetical, it does underscore the key conceptual point that reliance on second-order equality as a rationale for restricting the use of economic resources for expression is in general tension with free expression values. Second-order equality effectively invites—indeed, absent realistic avenues for increasing the resources of the economically disadvantaged, logically dictates—a reduction of expression to the lowest common economic denominator. Instead of remaining in large part ignorant only of the views of those who lack economic resources, then, the public—because of governmental action—will remain "equally" ignorant of the views of those who do possess substantial economic resources. It is difficult to imagine that free expression interests could thrive in such a setting.

Even if a negative, second-order equality of silence were accepted as legitimate, however, it is unclear how it logically could be confined to the goal of remedying inequalities of economic resources. Numerous inequalities other than economic ones exist among competing speakers. Certain speakers—for example, former athletes, actors, or astronauts—are better known to the public than are others for reasons having nothing to do with their expression's subject, content, or persuasiveness.[310] If negative equality among speaker resources is the goal, why should the government not seek to counterbalance such extraneous built-in advantages? Indeed, given the potential existence of numerous other inequalities among speakers, it is quite conceivable that the use of superior economic resources actually could be employed to equalize other similarly unrelated but nevertheless effective inequalities. To allow the government to silence only the more economically powerful speakers, then, is inconsistent with the purposes and values of the free expression system.

Corporations do possess a number of statutorily granted economic advantages that may give them a competitive edge over other speakers. Thus, advocates of second-order equality might respond that restrictions on corporate expression are merely intended to counterbalance the undue corporate advantages that the state already artificially created. But it is important to recall that these advantages presumably were given in a wholly non-speech context; they were not specifically created to provide corporations with an expressive advantage. Similarly, inheritance laws ensure that heirs of large estates will retain most of the estate's corpus,[311] capital gains laws economically benefit successful investors, and patent laws give investors artificially created monopolies, thereby effectively providing all three groups with potential economic advantages in the expressive marketplace if they choose to exercise them. Moreover, the government has enacted statutes to provide not-for-profit corporations with significant benefits under the tax laws,[312] arguably resulting in parallel incidental expressive advantages. No one has seriously suggested that the expressive activity of these individuals or organizations can constitutionally be curbed as a result of their potential economic advantages.

To be sure, to the extent that the government has created any of these economic advantages solely for the purpose and effect of granting to certain groups or individuals an expressive advantage, it is conceivable that legitimate First Amendment equality problems would arise. If the government provides these advantages on a general basis, however, to revoke them exclusively in the limited context of expressive rights would undoubtedly run afoul of the wise and well-accepted doctrine that government may not selectively inhibit speech.[313]

This is not to suggest that the First Amendment somehow prevents the government from adjusting or revising the existing economic order, or from redistributing economic wealth. If, because of social policy or normative economic theory choices, the government decides to redistribute private economic wealth or to create new economic entitlement programs, it may do so without contravening free speech rights, even though the consequence of this action could well be effectively to reduce the power of the previously economically superior groups or individuals to express themselves. In such a case, the impact on expressive activity is wholly incidental to a broader, non-speech-related purpose.[314] But whether such economic reforms are morally or practically appropriate has long been a subject of great controversy—a subject that the First Amendment itself guarantees may be debated freely and openly. To employ concerns over second-order equality as a rationale for excluding corporate speech from the First Amendment's scope, then, would be to superimpose one side of this substantive economic debate on the very processes designed to air and resolve that debate.

Despite these obvious and severe difficulties inherent in the concept of second-order equality as a rationale for excluding corporate speech from the First Amendment's scope, both commentators and the Court have relied on this rationale—either explicitly or implicitly—as a basis for doing just that. The *Austin* Court, for example, seemed to adopt implicitly the second-order equality principle—while denying it was doing so—in the name of stopping corruption in the political arena. The Court defined corruption as "the corrosive and distorting effects of immense aggregations of wealth that are accumulated with the help of the corporate form and that have little or no correlation to the public's support for the corporation's political ideas."[315] Judge J. Skelly Wright similarly viewed such corporate spending as "corruption" because "the political arena is less healthy, and less likely to serve the public interest and democratic ideals, if the agenda and the discussion are dominated by those with ample financial resources."[316] The central assumption underlying such reasoning is that more of certain speech or speech from particular speakers harms, distorts, and corrupts the political process.[317]

This concept, if accepted, obviously is not logically limited to profit-making corporations' speech but must also apply to the speech of individuals or associations whose wealth enables them to better finance their message than less affluent individuals. Yet the Court rejected equality as applied to individuals as a rationale for a limitation on expressive expenditures in *Buckley v. Valeo*[318] and has shown no inclination to shift from that position.

The equality rationale effectively views corporations as surrogates for the broader concern about the dangers of economic power in general.[319] The fear is that the use of dominant economic power in the expressive marketplace will have the same effect that it usually has in the commercial marketplace. Under this theory, corporations are viewed, not unreasonably, as the rough equivalent of the feared concentration of economic power. This argument errs, however, in relying on economic power as the ultimate surrogate for political power, persuasiveness, and effectiveness. It certainly is true that money contributes to the depth and breadth with which a message is disseminated.[320] Experience demonstrates, however, that money alone does not make a message effective.[321]

Judge Wright completely ignored this fact in his analysis. He argued instead that "massive spending and sophisticated media campaigns . . . have swamped referenda that were initially favored by a majority of the voters."[322] He described several referenda campaigns in which initial polls had shown one side leading, but the electoral result, usually following spending by corporate interests, had been the opposite.[323] From these examples, he inferred that the corporate spending functioned to "distort[ ] the expressed will of the people by the sheer inequality of financial resources and the avalanche of campaign messages."[324] Judge Wright apparently assumed that the early poll results, not the electoral outcome, represented the electorate's true wishes and that the difference between the two was caused by the influx of corporate campaign messages that "used the big lie, the half truth, and the sly innuendo, amplified and repeated over and over again, to pervert the minds of the people."[325] This analysis cavalierly assumes—without reference to the slightest empirical support—that the existence of economic power necessarily implies the use of improper or deceptive substantive messages. Yet there is no reason to believe that economic power is either necessary or sufficient to create such problems.

Wright further assumed—again, without empirical support—that it was not the message's merits that convinced listeners to vote a certain way, but its sheer repetition that defeated "the very purpose of direct democracy."[326] The idea that "the expressed will of the people" is something other than the voluntarily chosen product of a popular voter referendum, however, is clearly inconsistent with the premises and operation of democracy.[327] Advocacy, even by entities that have amassed great wealth, will be effective "only to the extent that it brings to the people's attention ideas which—despite the invariably self-interested and probably uncongenial source—strike them as true."[328] Although Judge Wright argued that the *Bellotti* decision "placed the [F]irst [A]mendment squarely in opposition to the democratic ideal of political equality[,]"[329] in reality it is reliance on the second-order equality principle that creates such opposition by enabling the government to deny the voters the information and opinion that will inform their self-governing actions.

Judge Wright purported to expand upon Kenneth Karst's theory that the First Amendment's "central meaning" is the equal liberty of expression.[330] Karst's concern about equality, however, primarily revolved around limitations on governmental power to prohibit some speakers or some points of view and not others[331]—what has been described here as first-order equality.[332] When Karst wrote that "all speakers and all points of view are entitled to a hearing,"[333] he did not argue that the First Amendment requires the government to act in order to make a speaker heard. Rather, he argued only that the First Amendment prohibits the

government from preventing any of these speakers from being hea\
based on the content of a speaker's message.[334]

The Misperception of the Limited Pie: The "Drowning-Out" Concern

"The risk posed to freedom of speech," Fiss has argued, "occurs whenever speech takes place under conditions of scarcity, that is, whenever the opportunity for communication is limited. In such situations one utterance will necessarily displace another."[335] He believes that "in politics, scarcity is the rule rather than the exception," because "[t]he opportunities for speech tend to be limited, either by the time or space available for communicating or by our capacity to digest or process information."[336] He concludes that "[i]n a referendum or election . . . there is every reason to be concerned with the advertising campaign mounted by the rich or powerful, because the resources at their disposal enable them to fill all the available space for public discourse with their message."[337] Other commentators have expressed similar views. It has been asserted, for example, that "because of the wealth and power of corporations, 'their views may drown out other points of view.'"[338]

To the extent that guaranteeing economically powerful corporations' First Amendment rights would displace others' expression, the constitutional analysis advocated in the previous section[339] might require revision. No one, however, has made a persuasive argument—on intuitive or empirical grounds—that this is the case.[340] Indeed, the *Bellotti* Court rejected the drowning-out assumption, precisely because there had been "no showing that the relative voice of corporations has been overwhelming or even significant in influencing referenda in Massachusetts, or that there has been any threat to the confidence of the citizenry in government."[341]

It is doubtful that, as a practical matter, one could ever demonstrate this. Drowning out can occur only if there is a "limited pie" of speech, such as a situation in which one corporation buys up all the time and space in every mass media and speech outlet, thus preventing other speakers from ever reaching an audience or at least from reaching it to the extent that their desires and resources permit. Contrary to Fiss's wholly unsupported assumption,[342] however, it is by no means clear, as an empirical matter, that any such situation has occurred or, if it has, whether the situation has arisen with any meaningful frequency.

A milder version of the drowning-out argument suggests that some media reach larger audiences and tend to be more expensive. Therefore, wealth enables the corporation to access those media that less affluent advocates are unable to reach. Accordingly, the wealthy have access to more voters and more opportunities to persuade.[343] Alternatively, one scholar has argued, corporate speakers who consume a large amount of space and time will drive the price of all media beyond the means of less affluent advocates.[344] The former argument, it should be noted, is not really a "drown-out" scenario but rather merely a restatement of the competitive edge that economic superiority concededly creates. The latter argument, even if true, simply reflects the free market's operation. Assuming that any of these scenarios were true, however, there certainly would exist less restrictive means to avoid expressive drown-out than the heavy-handed elimination of the corporate voice in its entirety. These might include, for instance, setting price ceilings on media access, requiring media to provide access, or public financing.[345]

Beyond these unlikely scenarios of actual silencing, the drowning-out argument amounts to nothing more than a paternalistic and unverified assumption that at some unknown and unknowable point, so much expression has been disseminated that the consuming public has reached a desensitization point of "information overload." An example is Shelledy's description of a hypothetical message placed in a newspaper:

> Many people who receive those papers do not read them cover to cover. . . . When people receive more information than they can process, they process what they can and ignore the rest. . . . [A] competing advocate increases the likelihood that my views will be among the material readers will ignore. . . . [It is] also a competition for attention, in which material resources can provide a dispositive advantage.[346]

The reception model that Shelledy posits may or may not be empirically accurate. A message's frequency and volume and the money a speaker places behind that message certainly are elements—although not necessarily determinative ones—of influence.[347] It is an indisputable reality, however, that not everyone views the same medium at the same time. We do not know how, when, or where each person hears or processes particular information or why a particular message succeeds or fails. A person who has not driven by a billboard that takes a particular position may well see a political advertisement that takes the same position on television or in the newspaper. Therefore, it is impossible, and thus dangerous, to assume that at some point enough expression will have been disseminated to produce an informed public.

Even assuming that a point of public desensitization does exist, there is no empirical or intuitive support for the belief that the views of those with less economic power will fail to gain the public's attention. Except in the relatively unlikely scenario of total displacement,[348] less powerful interests would still have at least some degree of access to the public. Consequently, there is no a priori reason to believe that their messages are any less likely to reach the public before the public reaches the point of overload than are the messages of the economically more powerful interests. Indeed, by continually pounding the same message ad nauseam, the economically powerful interests might actually alienate the public—what could be described as the "Macarena" effect.

In short, one cannot construe the First Amendment to allow the government conclusively to determine either how citizens process information or when the fear of an information overload dictates a need for governmental intervention. Society can never be sure that such a point exists, much less that citizens have, in fact, reached it. The commitment to free speech clearly implies that too much information—if, indeed, there could ever be such a thing—always is preferable to too little. Moreover, it seems likely that the act of sifting through a range of information, selectively receiving some and ignoring the rest, is part of the exercise and development of human faculties. This exercise and development is an essential part of the self-realization process, and thus an essential part of free expression's purpose.[349]

The Exclusion of Corporate Speech as Viewpoint Regulation: The Ideological Rationale

If both sides of a political debate were likely to include powerful corporate interests, there probably would be little basis for the drowning-out concern; in such a scenario, no side of the debate necessarily would suffer in a relative sense from corporate speech protection. The assumption inherently underlying the second-order equality concern in general and the drowning-out concern in particular, then, must be that corporate speech likely will support only one side of a political debate.

This conclusion probably will be accurate in most cases. Not surprisingly, economically powerful corporate interests tend to favor such positions as less effective and pervasive governmental regulation, tort reform, and laissez-faire capitalism.[350] This, of course, will not always be the case. But it is probably accurate often enough to equate corporate speech with politically conservative free market advocacy. If this is the case, however, then attempts to exclude corporate speech from the First Amendment's scope are similarly likely to represent the rough equivalent of burdening only one substantive political-economic position. Given this, the objection to corporate speech ultimately amounts to little more than an indirect form of viewpoint discrimination. The benefits of banning corporate speech inhere entirely to those persons or groups who hold viewpoints that oppose or disagree with the particular corporate position because they no longer have to hear it, respond to it, or fear its persuasive impact.[351] A ban on corporate speech, therefore, does not equalize the debate but rather tilts the debate entirely in the other direction: The most effective contribution to one side of the public debate is effectively silenced. The viewpoint discrimination that appears to infect the debate over corporate speech is indicative of a larger scholarly debate over the issue of the First Amendment's "ideological drift."[352] Despite the general notion that fundamental First Amendment principles demand "neutrality for all political speech,"[353] some free speech theorists are alarmed that the First Amendment, formerly "sauce for the liberal goose[,] increasingly has become sauce for the more conservative gander."[354]

The paradigmatic example of the supposed appropriation of the First Amendment by conservatives is what Steven Shiffrin calls use of the First Amendment as "a banner for corporations seeking to dominate election campaigns."[355] It is not surprising that such First Amendment use would cause concern among scholars sympathetic to the political left. Several commentators have actually argued overtly that a reason to restrict corporate speech is that most corporations, benefiting as they do from laissez-faire economic policies, will present the politically and economically right-wing point of view.[356] The express goal, according to one scholar, is to "bring corporate power to heel."[357]

Scholars on occasion have suggested more subtle attempts to rationalize excluding corporate speech from the First Amendment. Shiffrin, for example, has advocated a free speech model that places the dissenting voice at the center of First Amendment concern, with a political tilt against the powerful.[358] On the basis of this analysis, Shiffrin concludes that corporations "have less of a claim to be at the heart of the First Amendment."[359]

In order to accept this argument, however, one first needs to define the "dissenting voice" concept. Surely economic power alone could not serve as the measuring rod, because—as the experience of the tobacco companies quite clearly illustrates—financial power does not always translate into widespread political popularity.[360] Even if one were to accept Shiffrin's dissenting-voice model, then, there is every reason to believe that the views of the economically powerful should trigger the need for First Amendment protection as easily as the expression of the economically disadvantaged. The availability of vast economic resources to disseminate views is of little assistance when the government has prohibited the dissemination of these views because it deems them offensive or unwise.

More fundamentally, there is something both puzzling and perverse in basing free speech theory on a reverse correlation between the expression's popularity and the degree of protection the speech is to receive. If a popularly elected and accountable government has banned expression, one would think that such expression cannot be characterized as either popular or powerful. If, on the other hand, certain speech is so powerful that it actually controls the political agenda,[361] then presumably the accountable and representative branches of government will never regulate it, and the First Amendment issue will remain forever a purely hypothetical one.

It is true, as Judge Wright argued, that the "core notion of the [F]irst [A]mendment remains the protection of diverse, antagonistic, and unpopular speech from restriction based on substance."[362] But acceptance of this relatively uncontroversial proposition in no way implies that what is normally non-diverse, non-antagonistic, or supposedly popular speech does not equally deserve protection, if and when the need for such protection actually arises. Otherwise, the principle of First Amendment equality would be rendered a truly bizarre concept. Indeed, if one took Shiffrin's logic seriously, then the legislative enactment of restrictions on corporate speech presumably would reduce the level of First Amendment protection to be given to expression by the opponents of corporations, since that expression would now represent the dominant rather than the dissenting view.

Although it would be presumptuous to attempt to speak for Shiffrin, it is highly doubtful that he would ever intend or accept such a preposterous result. If this is true, however, then the theory of greater protection for the dissenting voice is not really intended to protect all dissenting voices but rather amounts to little more than an indirect form of viewpoint discrimination.

For example, R. J. Reynolds' speech is today surely no less unpopular than that of someone burning a draft card; yet, Professor Shiffrin's dissent model would protect the latter but probably not the former.[363] The theory, therefore, cuts at the very heart of the First Amendment's true, first-order equality principle.[364] The fact that both Judge Wright and Shiffrin would deny protection to corporate speech while simultaneously claiming to protect unpopular voices indicates that their approach protects not all unpopular views but only those with which Judge Wright and Professor Shiffrin happen to agree.

The underlying—if largely unstated—viewpoint-based nature of free speech models that exclude protection for corporate speech should now be obvious. In the name of enhancing and broadening public debate and deliberations on policy questions, these models substantially restrict a central voice as a participant in that debate, quite probably because of substantive disagreement with the expressed views' merits.[365]

Conclusion: "Pay No Attention to the Man behind the Curtain"

"Pay no attention to the man behind the curtain," the Wizard of Oz futilely urges Dorothy, once she has discovered—much to her surprise—that the feared and powerful Wizard is nothing more than a human with an amplified voice and the benefit of special effects. Those who oppose extending full First Amendment protection to corporate speech similarly ignore the fact that, ultimately, corporations are entities formed by humans in order to further human interests.

As such, from the perspective of free speech theory, one should view corporations not as mindless, faceless organizations that are robotically driven by profit-maximization but rather as devices created and organized to facilitate human self-realization. Thus, corporate speech should be viewed no differently, for constitutional purposes, from the expression of other associations formed to foster or attain predetermined political, economic, or social goals.[366] Moreover, corporate speech may further the values of free expression by providing recipients with valuable information and opinion on issues facing them, both in their individual lives and as citizens within a collective democratic society.[367]

Although corporations are beneficiaries of special and artificial protections created by the state, these protections were developed in contexts wholly outside the expressive context, and their impact on expression is therefore wholly incidental. Much the same could be said of private individuals, not-for-profit corporations, and charitable institutions, all of whom may have benefited, in one way or another, from the largesse or financial protection of both federal and state laws. These facts have never disqualified the expression of these individuals or associations from the scope of constitutional protection[368]—nor could they, without dealing a virtually crippling blow to public debate's richness.

Corporations' economic resources do often provide them with a potentially significant advantage in the marketplace of ideas and information. But to exclude corporate speech from the First Amendment's scope in the name of equality would be to seriously misunderstand the equality concept's proper role in free expression theory. Correctly understood, the equality element in free speech thought dictates that the government must remain neutral among competing ideas in restricting the expression of private individuals and entities; all ideas must be treated equally.[369] It does not necessarily mean, however, that all speakers must enter the battle on totally equal terms.

Financial resources are only one of many conceivable advantages a speaker may bring to public debate, and any attempt to regulate solely the advantages of money for expressive purposes would give substantial and unequal strategic benefits to those possessing alternative advantages. Due either to the structural design of society or simply chance, different people will enter the public debate possessing different resources, talents, and advantages, none of which, experience has shown, guarantees ultimate success in the political arena. The government's attempt to equalize these relative advantages in public debate would be virtually impossible and, at the same time, would significantly harm the interests of free expression.

At the very least, equalization by reducing the sum total of available expression could only further impoverish the quality of debate and move us further away from the goal of an informed public. Despite wholly unsubstantiated warnings about the dangers of so-called information overload,[370] it is both dangerous and counterintuitive to proceed on the assumption that reducing the sum total of available information and opinion benefits the public.

Using what I have called second-order equality as a rationale for declining to protect corporate speech, therefore, would seriously endanger the values that widespread communication fosters, because it would inevitably result in a governmentally imposed leveling process, designed to reduce public debate to the lowest common denominator. Consequently, the populace would undoubtedly be deprived of potentially valuable communication, in direct contradiction of the essential premises of a free expression system.[371]

Commentators occasionally have expressed the fear that widespread corporate speech could drown out competing views due to its sheer volume.[372] But such a concept incorrectly presupposes a "limited pie" of expression—a presupposition that, for the most part, simply fails to comport with reality. Generally, the fact that one side of a debate widely disseminates its views in no way—either theoretically or practically—prevents the other side from speaking.[373] If and when such a situation ever arose—as when, for example, one side has purchased all available advertising time and space in the local media—more narrowly drawn methods for dealing with the situation may be developed.[374] This concern, even in the relatively rare instance in which it actually does arise, surely cannot justify the wholesale exclusion of corporate speech from the First Amendment's scope. Regulations that are so gratuitously sweeping in their reach clearly would exceed the limits of the First Amendment's overbreadth doctrine.[375]

Quite frankly, it is not all that difficult to comprehend the hostility that many commentators currently express toward corporate expression. Such speech is generally likely to advocate an anti-regulatory, free market philosophy that is widely unpopular among many academics today. At worst, then, one could view a governmental attempt to revoke the financial advantages the economically powerful hold in terms of public debate as an indirect—albeit no less ominous—form of viewpoint control. Viewed from this perspective, such efforts serve merely as a surrogate for the broader non-speech goal of reordering the distribution of economic wealth in society. This is an issue calling for ultimate moral choice and is, therefore, one that must itself be subject to free and open debate, protected by the First Amendment guarantee.

The danger of such reasoning should make us extremely hesitant to exclude corporate speech from the First Amendment's scope. To do so would amount to an indirect but nonetheless dangerous form of viewpoint regulation, premised on an unsupportable prediction as to the likely content and effectiveness of a particular type of speaker's expression. This manipulation of the First Amendment's scope is wholly inconsistent with the true equality principle that inheres in a free expression system: a belief that in choosing to restrict expression, the government is required to treat all ideas equally.

4

Free Speech and the Flawed Postulates of Campaign Finance Regulation

At least since the Supreme Court's 1976 decision in *Buckley v. Valeo*,[1] the constitutionality of campaign finance reform legislation has been among the most controversial and heated issues in First Amendment jurisprudence.[2] Those who believe in the necessity of reducing the importance of economic power in the political process have long argued that such reform actually fosters, rather than deters, free speech interests by opening political communication to those with less money.[3] They argue further that concerns of equality and systemic integrity more than justify whatever negative impact such reform may have on free speech interests.[4] Indeed, some have gone so far as to assert that, purely as a conceptual matter, the contribution or expenditure of money involves the non-expressive exercise of property rights, rather than the exercise of protected rights of expression.[5] In response, other commentators have argued that campaign finance and free expression are inherently intertwined, and that proposed and enacted reforms will inevitably and fatally invade First Amendment rights.[6]

To this point, it would be difficult to declare a clear winner. Indeed, the Supreme Court's decisions on the subject not only have failed to provide a coherent resolution of the competing and complex arguments, they have instead given rise to their own doctrinal and theoretical confusion. Purely on the level of social and political policy, at least, the Court's doctrinal framework may rightfully be accused of creating a pragmatic nightmare that not only refuses to permit establishment of a clear, consistent, and coherent campaign finance policy, but actually exacerbates the supposed social harms of the current system of finance regulation.[7]

In its 2000 decision in *Nixon v. Shrink Missouri PAC*,[8] the Court continued to operate in its severely confused doctrinal and theoretical state. There the Court upheld Missouri's highly restrictive limitations on campaign contributions, stubbornly adhering to the contorted and confused doctrinal framework it had adopted in *Buckley*.[9] The Court in *Nixon* even compounded the intellectually and pragmatically dubious aspects of that earlier opinion by giving it a grudgingly restrictive interpretation.[10] The two concurring opinions in *Nixon*, authored by Justices Stevens[11] and Breyer,[12] significantly added to the decision's problematic nature.[13]

The seemingly intractable problems of campaign finance reform can be attacked in a variety of ways. One strategy would be to provide a mercilessly detailed normative critique of all of the technical loopholes that currently plague campaign finance regulation, from "soft money"[14] to "bundling."[15] That, however, is not the approach I employ here. Given the generally confusing and unsatisfying nature of the Court's recent decision in *Nixon*, what the constitutional controversy over campaign finance reform needs most at this point is clarity and simplicity.

I believe this controversy can be clarified by carefully dissecting and deconstructing the case for the constitutionality of campaign finance regulation. That case may be reduced to a series of empirical or theoretical postulates that, taken together, provide the normative foundation for the argument that campaign finance regulation is consistent with First Amendment dictates. Detailed examination of these assertions reveals the serious conceptual, empirical, or logical flaws in the entire case for the constitutionality of campaign finance reform. By describing the postulates that underlie the campaign finance reform argument and simultaneously pointing out the fatal errors that plague each of them, we will be able to explain why most forms of campaign finance regulation—including both those which to this point have been held constitutional and those which have not–must be found to violate core notions of free expression.

Six key postulates can be discerned that, taken together, make up the essential elements of the argument in support of the constitutionality of campaign finance restrictions. This is not to suggest that all campaign finance reform advocates necessarily adhere to all six. Generally speaking, however, I believe it is accurate to assert that some combination or permutation of these six postulates provides the core case for the constitutionality of campaign finance regulation.

The postulates underlying the case for the constitutionality of campaign finance regulation are as follows:

1. The expenditure of money involves the exercise of property rights, not rights of free expression.

2. To the extent that one chooses to classify the expenditure of money as a form of protected expression at all, financial contributions to political campaigns at best represent only a marginally protected form of protected expression.
3. The judiciary should generally defer to legislative discretion in ruling upon the wisdom and/or necessity of campaign finance regulation.
4. The underlying rationale for extending full First Amendment protection to the use of money in political campaigns is improperly grounded in a narrowly based political theory of individualism.
5. Limitations on campaign expenditures and contributions are necessary to remove inequities among economically disparate groups and individuals, in furtherance of First Amendment–based principles of equality.
6. Limitations on campaign expenditures and contributions are necessary to prevent corruption of the political process, both real and perceived.

Each of these postulates can be shown to be seriously flawed from logical, empirical, or theoretical perspectives. Revealing these flaws demonstrates the serious constitutional defects in much of the existing structure of campaign finance regulation, as well as in most proposed reforms. If all— or even most—of these postulates can be shown to be false or misguided, then the foundation for the constitutional defense of campaign finance regulation will necessarily crumble.

The first section of this chapter briefly describes the current federal statutory framework of campaign finance regulation,[16] as well as the current state of Supreme Court doctrine concerning the constitutionality of campaign finance regulation.[17] It points out the hopeless state of practical and theoretical confusion that plagues the Court's decisions. The next section first attempts to describe the strongest case in support of each of the six postulates, and then proceeds to detail the serious flaws plaguing each one.[18]

Campaign Finance Regulation: The Existing Statutory Framework and Proposals for Reform

In response to growing concern over the role played by economic power in the political process, Congress passed and President Nixon signed into law the Federal Election Campaign Act (FECA) of 1971.[19] The act required disclosure of candidate and committee spending and placed limits on both expenditures in and contributions to congressional campaigns.[20] In reaction to the revelations of the Watergate scandal, in 1974 Congress enacted comprehensive amendments containing further restrictions.[21] Two years later, in *Buckley v. Valeo*,[22] the Supreme Court upheld contribution limits but not expenditure limits, effectively destroying the coherence of the legislative scheme.[23] By leaving expenditures unrestricted but upholding severe restrictions on campaign contributions, the Court effectively—if unintentionally—increased the practical importance of individual candidate wealth.

Today, the regulatory framework is largely the product of a synthesis of the 1971 Act, the 1974 legislation, and Supreme Court–dictated constitutional restrictions. Under that crazy-quilt framework, individuals may not contribute in excess of $1,000 (in aggregate) to any candidate or her authorized political committees for each election.[24] For purposes of contributions, primary elections for a party's nomination are distinguished from the general election for the office. Thus, an individual may contribute $1,000 to each.[25] A person may not contribute more than $20,000 in any calendar year to the political committees established and maintained by a national political party.[26] Moreover, an individual may not contribute more than $5,000 to any other political committee in any calendar year.[27] No individual may make campaign contributions aggregating more than $25,000 in any calendar year. Any contribution made to a candidate in a year other than the calendar year in which the election is held is considered to have been made during the calendar year of the election.[28]

Political action committees (PACs) may not make contributions in excess of $5,000 to any candidate or to her authorized political committee.[29] PACs may not contribute more than $15,000 to the national political committees in any calendar year, and may not contribute more than $5,000 to any other PAC in any calendar year.[30] These limitations do not apply to transfers of money between national, state, district, or local political committees of the same political party.[31]

A contribution made in cooperation or consultation with a candidate, his authorized political committee, or his agent, or any contribution made at the suggestion or request of the candidate, his authorized political committee, or his agent is considered to be a contribution to the candidate.[32] Contributions made for the benefit of a candidate for the office of vice president of the United States are considered contributions to the candidate of that party for the office of president.[33]

If a presidential campaign wishes to receive matching public funds, the candidate is limited to expenditures of $10 million in the primary campaign and $20 million in the general election.[34] The national committee of a political party may not make any expenditure in connection with the general election campaign of a candidate for president that exceeds an amount equal to two cents multiplied by the voting age population.[35] Neither the national committee nor the state committee of a political party may make any expenditure in connection with the general election campaign of a candidate for senator or representative of a state that is entitled to only one representative in excess of two cents multiplied by the voting age population of the United States or $20,000; if the candidate is running for representative, delegate, or resident commissioner, the limit is $10,000.[36] No more than $17,500 may be contributed to a senatorial candidate for a primary or general election during the year of the election by the Republican or Democratic Senatorial Campaign Committee, or the national committee of a political party, or any combination of the two.[37]

For the most part, recent efforts to fortify existing federal campaign finance regulation have stalled. The Bipartisan Campaign Reform Act of 1999 (commonly known as the McCain-Feingold legislation), which would heavily restrict parties and candidates from accepting so-called "soft money" contributions (see below) and strengthen disclosure laws,[38] was placed on the Senate calendar in October 1999 but has seen no recent movement. Senator John McCain has proposed an amended version of the bill[39] that calls for disclosure of expenditures and contributors from Section 527 groups, so-called "stealth PACs," which use a tax code provision to fund election work with undisclosed and unlimited contributions and claim exemption from federal taxation and election laws.[40] Section 527 provides a tax exemption to organizations that are primarily involved in elections, such as PACs, party committees, and campaign committees.[41] Currently, under the FECA, these groups do not need to report issue-advocacy contributions; according to Senator McCain, the groups "gain both the public subsidy of tax exemption and the ability to shield from the American public the identity of those spending their money to try to influence our elections."[42] The amendment requires Section 527 groups to file publicly available tax forms and to file with the IRS or make public reports specifying annual expenditures of over $500 and identifying those who contribute more than $200 annually to the organization.[43]

Notably, the amendment does not place restrictions on contributions or expenditures, but merely mandates disclosure.

The states generally have more lax campaign finance laws than the federal government. Twenty-four states have some provision for public funding of state legislative campaigns.[44] Eleven states, including California, Texas, and Virginia, have no limits on spending in campaigns.[45] Fifteen states have restrictions similar to federal election laws; five, including Florida, Maine, and Washington, have strict regulations involving public funding systems with corresponding restrictions on campaign expenditures.[46] Some states have enacted more limitations, which may flow from state cultures that are more supportive of the use of government to promote equality in participation.

The failure of significant reform efforts since the 1974 amendments to FECA is perhaps best explained by two factors. First is the significant roadblock imposed by the Supreme Court's 1976 decision in *Buckley v. Valeo*,[47] in which the Court effectively rendered futile any meaningful effort to control the importance of economic power in political campaigns. By simultaneously holding that expenditure limits violate the First Amendment while contribution limits do not,[48] the Court placed reform efforts between a rock and a hard place. To be sure, reformers may continue existing restrictions on campaign contributions and perhaps close up existing loopholes, such as bundling[49] or the use of so-called "soft money"—contributions made to political parties for purposes of grassroots "party-building" activities.[50] But in so doing they may actually be exacerbating the very economic inequities they purportedly seek to curb. According to one authority, "[t]oday's reform agenda is deeply set in the ideology of the Populism and Progressivism of the turn of the [twentieth] century." Pursuant to this philosophy, "[t]he task of regulation was to curb the influence of money and to legislate smallness."[51] Since, under *Buckley*, Congress lacks constitutional authority to limit campaign expenditures, continued or strengthened limitations on contributions will inevitably have the effect of increasing the importance of personal wealth. Individuals possessing personal fortunes will be able to spend at will on their own campaigns, while those with fewer personal resources will be unable to combat such massive use of money, because they will be severely restricted in their ability to raise funds. Because the Court has at no point indicated a willingness to reconsider its constitutional bar to expenditure limitations,[52] any reform efforts will necessarily reinforce whatever inequities may be caused by disparities in personal wealth.

The second reason that further reform efforts have largely failed[53] may come down to the simple fact of legislator self-interest—what has been referred to as "legislative entrenchment."[54] While modern public choice theory has long questioned the motivations of legislators in enacting laws,[55] the concern is quite probably at its greatest when legislative decisions directly impact upon the likelihood of a legislator's continuation in office. From this perspective, it is highly doubtful that legislators will enact laws that strengthen their opponents' chances of unseating them. A possible explanation for the general failure of further campaign finance reform, then, is legislators' concern that such reform would either weaken their own chances of reelection or strengthen their opponents' chances of unseating them.

While there has been relatively little movement on the legislative front, campaign finance reform has continued to capture the minds of scholars. For example, one scholar, pointing to the legislative entrenchment problem, has urged that state legislatures be given primary responsibility for imposing future regulations on the financing of federal campaigns.[56] Other scholars, proposing even more radical solutions, have "challenge[d] the conventional assumption that private financing of public election campaigns is consistent with the requirements of American constitutional democracy," and in its place "propose a replacement for this system in the federal context: Total public financing of congressional campaigns."[57] According to yet another scholar, "[e]xtending full public financing with attached spending limits from presidential to congressional campaigns would be the most obvious version of . . . reform, but is probably politically infeasible."[58]

Whatever one thinks of the advisability of proposed reforms, there can be little doubt that—at least in part due to the disruptive impact of the constitutional barriers imposed in *Buckley*—existing campaign finance regulation has not accomplished its stated goals. Between 1977 and 1992, spending for congressional campaigns increased by 347 percent. Contributions to congressional campaigns by PACs increased from $20.5 million in 1976 to $189 million in 1994. Since 1974, there has been an almost eight-fold increase in the number of federal PACs.[59]

The general failure of campaign finance regulation to accomplish its stated goals will no doubt lead to continued scholarly and political pressure to attain those goals. As noted at the outset, however, those who advocate such reform—to the extent that they consider the implications of the First Amendment guarantee of free expression at all—proceed on a number of core assumptions about both the nature of the First Amendment right and the harms caused by an unregulated system that purport to sustain campaign finance reform from First Amendment attack. If those core assumptions can be shown to be flawed on empirical or theoretical grounds, however, the First Amendment defense of campaign finance limitations crumbles. The purpose of the section that follows is to detail those core assumptions, and to explain the serious flaws in each.

The Flawed Postulates of Campaign Finance Regulation

Postulate 1: The Use of Money in Political Campaigns Implicates Property Rights, Not First Amendment Rights

While those who believe campaign finance regulation is constitutional often concede that at least on some level such regulation implicates rights of free expression, others refuse even to make that concession. Regulation of the use of money in political campaigns, Justice Stevens recently argued in his separate opinion in *Nixon v. Shrink Missouri PAC*,[60] implicates solely the exercise of constitutionally protected property rights. Because property rights are protected under the heavily diluted substantive due process protections of the Fifth and Fourteenth Amendments,[61] in enforcing them the courts defer broadly to legislative choices. Thus, viewing the use of money in political campaigns entirely from this perspective effectively disposes of any constitutional barrier to campaign finance regulation. As *Buckley*[62] and subsequent decisions[63] make clear, however, a majority of the Supreme Court has never accepted so narrow a constitutional perspective.

Those who believe that only property rights are implicated in campaign financing have suggested that *Buckley* and its progeny are reminiscent of the long-discredited line of cases associated with *Lochner v. New York*,[64] where the Court effectively substituted its own economic philosophy for that of the New York Legislature in holding the state's maximum hours laws to be an unconstitutional interference with the right of contract.[65] In equating the constitutional invalidation of campaign finance laws with the invalidation of the legislative regulation of economic conduct, these scholars ignore important expressive elements inherent in the campaign finance area.

Of course, it is not essential to adopt the property rights perspective in order to conclude that campaign finance regulation is constitutional. One could acknowledge that First Amendment rights are implicated by such regulation but nevertheless conclude that the interests served justify a restriction that otherwise would contravene the free speech guarantee.[66] But acceptance of the property rights view would significantly reduce the constitutional barriers to campaign finance regulation. Indeed, acceptance of the property rights perspective would almost certainly lead to a finding of constitutionality. Perhaps more importantly, even if one did not accept the property rights view completely, one could conceivably adopt it partially, reasoning that the presence of the financial element somehow dilutes the level of First Amendment protection involved. Thus, before we can hope to challenge the constitutionality of campaign finance regulation, we must respond to the property rights approach.

This is not a difficult task, at least not with regard to the extreme version of the property rights theory. To be sure, from a technical standpoint the expenditure and contribution of money for use in a political campaign do not involve the direct exercise of expressive powers. When viewed this myopically, the acts in question can be viewed as pure financial conduct. After all, people are merely transferring funds, not communicating. But so artificially truncated a view of the process completely misses the fundamental point, and in so doing seriously threatens core free speech values by ignoring their presence. The simple and obvious fact is that both expenditures and contributions are physical acts done as part of the facilitative or catalytic process, thereby making communication possible.

The point can best be understood by drawing analogies. Imagine the following laws: (1) one that prohibits the payment of money for books or newspapers; (2) one that prohibits publishers from paying their workers who print or distribute the final product; and (3) one that prohibits would-be picketers from purchasing material to be used in signs or sound amplification equipment. Assume that none of the hypothetical laws in any way prohibits or penalizes the specific acts of expression—for example, the distribution of the books or newspapers or the act of actually picketing. Nevertheless, there can be little doubt that the laws in question violate the First Amendment guarantee of free expression. Under these circumstances, protection of only the narrowly defined right of communication would be a hollow protection indeed. The expenditure of money in these situations is a precondition to the meaningful exercise of the expressive right. To restrict the use of money in those contexts is to render the expression extremely difficult, if not impossible. The same is obviously true of the use of money in the course of a political campaign. Given modern economic realities, the expenditure of money is essential to the ability of a candidate to convey her message to the electorate.

The property rights perspective focuses solely on the narrow act of financial transfer, and concludes that such an act involves exclusively the exercise of property rights. But both practical reality and First Amendment theory make clear that such a myopic focus dangerously distorts the First Amendment interests at stake in the use of money in a political campaign. The Supreme Court has readily extended full First Amendment protection to activity that is neither conceptually nor practically definable, in and of itself, as an act of protected expression, when to do so is necessary to protect the meaningful exercise of the right. The most obvious examples are the right of political association and the freedom of thought.[67] Under appropriate circumstances, the right to spend or give money quite clearly qualifies as just such an ancillary right. To focus exclusively on one element of the broader communicative process, as the property rights perspective does, ignores the extent to which that element is inherently intertwined with the ultimate fruits of that process: expression and communication.

Once one acknowledges the fatal flaws in the total property rights perspective, the logic of the partial property rights perspective becomes similarly suspect. The partial property rights perspective, it should be recalled, acknowledges that the use of money in political campaigns includes certain fully protected expressive elements, but posits that the presence of significant non-expressive elements dilutes or modifies the level of First Amendment protection given to such behavior.[68] As a result, government may regulate such behavior without satisfying the compelling interest standard normally employed when it encroaches on fully protected expression.

The Supreme Court held in *United States v. O'Brien* that when expression is intertwined with non-expressive elements, "a sufficiently important governmental interest in regulating the non-speech element can justify incidental limitations on First Amendment freedoms."[69] Thus, the partial property perspective reasons that the act of contributing to or spending in a political campaign constitutes a mixture of protected expression and unprotected conduct, and therefore is deserving of the reduced protection given to such hybrid forms of expression and conduct. But the Supreme Court's reasoning in *O'Brien* does not apply when the non-expressive activity is itself an essential catalyst to the exercise of a would-be speaker's expressive activity. Just as the First Amendment would extend full First Amendment protection to the non-speech financial activities in the analogous examples previously discussed because without them the expression itself could not survive, restriction on the use of money in a political campaign will inevitably reduce the candidate's ability to communicate effectively with the electorate. Both the full property rights perspective and the partial property view, then, unrealistically place form over substance. By taking so artificially narrow a view of the expressive process, both perspectives enable government to interfere significantly with fully protected expressive activities.

The unfortunate and puzzling irony of the property rights perspective is that the category of expression disrupted by its acceptance is core political speech. Scholars who believe that First Amendment protection extends exclusively or predominantly to such expression reason that the goal of speech protection is to facilitate the electoral process by providing the voter with information and opinion relevant to voting.[70] It has long been my belief that such a rationale unduly truncates the values served by the First Amendment guarantee.[71] But even the narrowest of First Amendment theories recognize the importance of political expression.[72] Yet by excluding the use of money in political campaigns from the scope of the First Amendment, scholars and jurists undermine this core value thought to be served by the free speech guarantee. The simple reality is that today, money is essential to communicate a candidate's message to the electorate. Indeed, one of the primary rationales for attempts to limit the role of economic power in political campaigns is presumably the desire to reduce the supposed communicative advantage that is assumed to flow from that economic superiority.[73] Those who seek to justify the constitutionality of campaign finance regulation cannot in the same breath deny First Amendment protection on the grounds that restricting the use of money in political campaigns does not interfere with expression.

Postulate 2: To the Extent the Use of Money Is Properly Characterized as Expression at All, Campaign Contributions Represent Only a Marginal Form of Protected Expressive Activity

Even advocates of campaign finance reform who concede that protected expressive activity is implicated at all in the use of money assert that contributions to political campaigns represent at best only a marginal form of such expression. For this reason, they argue, limitations on contributions may be more easily justified than limitations on direct expenditures. Their argument is premised on the view that however one wishes to characterize expenditures, contributions are simply not speech; they do not communicate to a third party the contributor's views. They are, rather, fundamentally a form of non-expressive conduct.

A somewhat similar dichotomy between expenditures and contributions was drawn by the Court in *Buckley*. There the Court reasoned that while contributions do represent an exercise of a form of associational rights protected under the First Amendment, that associational interest is fully vindicated when a contribution of *any* amount is permitted. The size of the contribution, the Court believed, is irrelevant to the nature of protected expressive activity involved.[74] It was largely on this basis that the Court distinguished restrictions on contributions from restrictions on expenditures.[75] It was also on this basis that the Court held that the highly restrictive federal limitations on contributions do not interfere with protected rights of expression: The contribution of $1,000 constitutes as much of an exercise of associational rights as the contribution of $50,000. Because the federal limitations on the amount of contributions did not substantially interfere with fully protected expression, then, government could more easily justify such limitations than it could if pure expression were involved.[76]

Such reasoning places form over substance, and in so doing ignores the vitally important role that campaign contributions play in furthering both the democratic process and the system of free expression. The conclusion that contributions are at best a marginal form of protected speech ignores two vital ways in which contributions fit within the framework of free speech protection. First, the very act of contributing constitutes a form of fully protected expression (what can be called "first party" expressive activity). Second, contributions help the candidate to communicate her message (what can be called "third party" expressive activity).

That contributions are themselves a form of pure expression can be seen by contrasting them to voluntary campaign activity. Those who volunteer on behalf of a candidate are exercising fully protected rights of expression, whether they deal directly with the electorate or aid indirectly through such activities as office work. By undertaking such activity, the individual demonstrates her political allegiance and thereby communicates a message concerning her beliefs. Moreover, she simultaneously exercises her First Amendment right to associate herself with a particular political position. However, today, according to one authority, "[c]andidates and parties . . . no longer use the participatory activity they once did. . . . Generally the decline in volunteered activity followed the decline in the parties' role in campaigns."[77] Thus, today "the defense of checkbook participation comes down to an assertion that the standards and avenues of citizen obligation change over time and that the giving of cash is a quintessential political activity for our era."[78]

Once the First Amendment nature of the act of political contribution is recognized, the *Buckley* Court's conclusion that whatever First Amendment rights this act implicates are vindicated by the making of a contribution of any size, no matter how small, can be seen to be fallacious. The conclusion is no more valid than would be the view that the First Amendment rights implicated by political activity in support of a candidate are fully satisfied, regardless of how much or little time the individual is allowed to devote to that activity. A $50,000 contribution can have a dramatically more significant impact on a candidate's campaign than a contribution of $1,000—a fact the contributor obviously knows when the contribution is made. The intensity of the commitment may be reflected in the size of the contribution.

Even if one rejects this "first party" perspective on campaign contributions, the facilitative role that contributions obviously serve in the exercise of protected rights of expression should not be ignored. Candidate communication costs money; to the extent that the candidate lacks the ability to pay, his ability to communicate is naturally reduced. Indeed, the *Buckley* Court recognized as much when it invalidated limitations on candidate expenditures. But if the candidate lacks her own funding, obtaining significant contributions naturally enables the candidate to communicate in ways that would be impossible otherwise. It does not require high-level mathematical analysis, then, to recognize that significant limits on the amount of contributions will hurt the candidate's ability to communicate her message. The result will be a decrease in voter awareness of the candidate's records and opinion. In this sense campaign contributions play a vitally important role as a catalyst in fostering political communication among the electorate.

It does not automatically follow from this analysis that limits on campaign contributions should be held unconstitutional.[79] Conceivably, one could recognize campaign contributions as fully protected expression, but nevertheless conclude that the social and political justifications for such limitations constitute sufficiently compelling interests to validate what are prima facie violations of free speech. That is a separate issue, considered later in this chapter. It does follow from this analysis, however, that if this conclusion is to be reached, it cannot be on the basis of a minimal level of judicial scrutiny of those justifications on the grounds that the First Amendment is only marginally implicated by restrictions on contribution levels.

Postulate 3: In Reviewing the Constitutionality of Campaign Finance Regulation, the Judiciary Should Give Significant Deference to Legislative Judgments

If, in reviewing the constitutionality of campaign finance regulation, one were to adopt either the exclusive property rights approach or the partial conduct analysis, some level of deference to legislative discretion would flow inexorably. Under the exclusive property rights model, courts would employ the highly deferential "rational basis" standard of review normally afforded alleged property rights violations, a standard that would almost certainly be satisfied. Under the partial conduct analysis, an intermediate standard of review would be employed.[80] In neither case would a reviewing court employ the strict scrutiny of a compelling interest standard normally utilized when legislation directly encroaches on rights of free expression. Similarly, if one were to conclude that contributions but not expenditures lack the qualities of fully protected expression, presumably one would significantly reduce the scope and intensity of judicial review at least for contribution restrictions.

There are some who believe that broad deference to legislative judgments is especially appropriate in the context of campaign finance regulation, even if fully protected expression is involved. The argument presumes that laws regulating campaign finance simultaneously further certain individuals' constitutional rights while diminishing the rights of others. As Justice Breyer reasoned in his concurring opinion in *Nixon v. Shrink Missouri PAC*, "by limiting the size of the largest contributions, [legislative] restrictions aim to democratize the influence that money itself may bring to bear upon the electoral process. . . . In doing so, they seek to build public confidence in that process and broaden the base of a candidate's meaningful financial support, encouraging the public participation and open discussion that the First Amendment itself presupposes."[81] When competing constitutional interests are implicated by legislation, Justice Breyer argued, "a presumption against constitutionality is out of place. . . . In such circumstances . . . the Court has closely scrutinized the statute's impact on those interests, but refrained from employing a simple test that effectively presumes unconstitutionality. Rather, it has balanced interests."[82]

On its face, Justice Breyer's argument does not appear to call for substantial deference to legislative choice. Rather, he purports merely to favor a neutral "balanc[ing of] interests" over an irrebuttable "presumption against constitutionality." But Justice Breyer's words must be read against the history and reality of the Supreme Court's prior First Amendment jurisprudence. At no point has the Court ever adopted an irrebuttable "presumption" of unconstitutionality. Instead, at most it has placed a heavy burden on government to justify its regulation.[83] On the other hand, when the Court has employed the language of "interest balancing" in its First Amendment jurisprudence, it has usually employed these words as a euphemism for all-but-total deference to legislative choices. Thus, Justice Breyer's reference to such interest balancing may reasonably be construed as a form of substantial legislative deference.[84]

That Justice Breyer was in fact urging the equivalent of substantial deference to legislative judgments is further evidenced by his subsequent analysis of the relative expertise of the judicial and legislative branches on issues of campaign finance reform: "Where a legislature has significantly greater institutional expertise, as, for example, in the field of election regulation, the Court in practice defers to empirical legislative judgments— at least where that deference does not risk such constitutional evils as, say, permitting incumbents to insulate themselves from effective electoral challenge." Justice Breyer expressed the view "that the legislature understands the problem—the threat to electoral integrity, the need for democratization—better than do we. We should defer to its political judgment that unlimited spending threatens the integrity of the electoral process."[85]

Justice Breyer immediately qualified this statement by noting that the Court "should not defer in respect to whether its solution, by imposing too low a contribution limit, significantly increases the reputation-related or media-related advantages of incumbency and thereby insulates legislators from effective electoral challenge."[86] But he summarily rejected this concern in the case before him, without any apparent meaningful investigation of the issue in light of the specific facts: "[A]ny contribution statute . . . will narrow the field of conceivable challengers to some degree. Undue insulation is a practical matter, and it cannot be inferred automatically from the fact that the limit makes ballot access more difficult for one previously unsuccessful candidate."[87] But if a clear case of challenger ballot exclusion, as was established in *Nixon,* does not meet Justice Breyer's criterion for establishing the requisite electoral insulation, then what evidentiary showing would *ever* satisfy it? In practical effect, then, Justice Breyer was concluding that deference should be imposed in *all* cases of campaign finance regulation. Respected commentators have similarly urged deference to legislative choices in the area of campaign finance regulation, on two related grounds: the presence of competing First Amendment interests, and the superiority of legislative expertise.[88]

In pointing out the serious flaws in the arguments in support of deference, one must distinguish between the two prongs of the rationale for such deference: (1) that competing constitutionally protected interests in the area of campaign finance regulation effectively creates a constitutional stalemate, thereby dictating deference; and (2) that the legislature's unique expertise on issues of the electoral process dictates deference. Analysis of each argument clearly demonstrates fatal inaccuracies.

The argument for deference premised on the assumption that laws regulating campaign finance simultaneously expand the First Amendment rights of some while undermining those of others is highly dubious on two levels. First, one may seriously question whether these laws in any way expand the constitutional rights of any one, for reasons to be explored in detail below.[89] And of course, if the very premise of the argument is empirically inaccurate, then the argument itself fails. But more importantly, even if one proceeds on an assumption of the premise's accuracy, it in no way follows that judicial deference is dictated. Indeed, when competing constitutional interests are simultaneously affected by legislative action, the need for the institutional independence and interpretive expertise of the judiciary assumes even greater importance. A law that simultaneously impacts conflicting constitutional provisions calls for careful, dispassionate, and experienced judicial analysis to insure that the balance struck by the legislative branch does not inordinately undermine one or the other of the constitutional interests involved. Thus, to assert that judicial deference is dictated because legislative regulation simultaneously implicates competing constitutionally protected interests amounts to a non sequitur.

Supreme Court precedent has not evinced the slightest indication that extraordinary judicial deference is called for when conflicting constitutional interests are implicated. For example, in cases pitting the First Amendment right of free press against the constitutional right of fair trial, the Court has painstakingly analyzed the competing interests and drawn its independent constitutional conclusions.[90] Similarly, when the First Amendment right of free expression has come into conflict with the quasi-constitutional interest in individual privacy, the Court has in no way shunned its ultimate responsibility to draw a constitutional balance.[91] Thus, the holding of *Marbury v. Madison,*[92] recognizing the necessity of judicial review in a constitutional democracy, still stands, especially when a decision calls for a careful structural analysis of competing constitutional provisions or interests.

Equally unpersuasive is the argument that special legislative expertise concerning the electoral process dictates deference to legislative choices in the area. Past instances of almost blind judicial deference to supposed legislative expertise have proven disastrous to the interests of liberty, as the Japanese exclusion cases[93] and the free speech cases during the McCarthy era[94] have proven all too clearly. In both of these instances, the Court blindly deferred to the supposedly superior expertise of government officials, in situations that most scholars would today recognize to have been severe miscarriages of justice that seriously undermined fundamental constitutional liberties.

Judicial deference to legislative judgments when First Amendment rights are at stake undermines the judiciary's central role as the counter-majoritarian check on the majoritarian branches of government.[95] It would, in Chief Justice Marshall's famous words in *Marbury*, provide to the legislative branch "a practical and real omnipotence" that is wholly inconsistent with the very nature of a counter-majoritarian, written constitution.[96]

The most important response to all of the arguments for deference to legislative judgment in the area of campaign finance regulation, however, is that appropriate skepticism of legislative motivation renders this the very last area in which judicial deference is dictated, for the simple reason that legislators' retention of office will often be affected by, if not determined by, the nature of restrictions on the financing of their own and their opponents' campaigns. This is a fact most assuredly not lost on sitting legislators.

That legislators' decisions are often influenced by factors other than a neutral assessment of the public interest is surely not a novel insight. For many years, public choice theorists have pointed to "the problems produced by the existence of interest groups . . . and their influence over the political process."[97] They have asserted that the legislative process "allows powerful private organizations to block necessary government action,"[98] and that as a result "the lawmaking process has been transformed into a series of accommodations among competing elites."[99] Public choice theory portrays politicians as "wealth-maximizing egoists"[100] who, when sitting in legislatures, "will produce too few laws that serve truly public ends, and too many laws that serve private ends."[101]

Public choice theory, in short, posits that legislation is often the product not of legislators' neutral assessment of the public interest but rather of narrow self-interest of the legislators themselves, their constituents, powerful private interests, or all three. While one may question whether the reality is as simple as public choice theory posits,[102] surely it would be naive to assume an unwavering purity of legislative motivation. As the theory of "legislative entrenchment" establishes,[103] the problem is aggravated when the legislator's own continuation in office is directly affected.[104]

The most obvious self-interested motivation for imposing restrictions on campaign expenditures or contributions is to preserve the advantages of incumbency. An incumbent possesses significant strategic advantages over a lesser-known challenger, due to past exposure, a built-in platform for drawing media attention, and, at least at the federal level, a franking privilege that enables the incumbent to communicate with her constituents at government expense. The best way for a challenger to counterbalance those competitive disadvantages is through the use of money to communicate his qualifications and message. In fact, the 1971 Federal Election Campaign Act has been referred to as "the Incumbents' Preservation Act."[105] The 1974 Act, not surprisingly, excluded the congressional franking privilege from its reach, "thereby preserving one of the incumbents' most powerful reelection tools."[106]

Some argue that today incumbency is actually furthered by unlimited campaign spending and contributions, since incumbents usually attract contributions at a much faster rate than their challengers.[107] But to the extent such a motivating force is at work, presumably no spending or contribution limits would be enacted in the first place. The only point at which the First Amendment comes into play, of course, is after legislative restrictions have been adopted. To the extent Congress or state legislatures do enact such restrictions, the theories of legislative entrenchment and public choice would seem to suggest that the individual legislators have concluded that they are personally helped more than hurt by the imposition of such limits.

It does not follow that campaign finance legislation should be assumed to be universally generated by improper motives, or that for these reasons such legislation should automatically be deemed unconstitutional. The point is that the very real possibility that campaign finance legislation has been motivated by questionable considerations renders absolute folly the idea that in reviewing First Amendment challenges to such legislation the judiciary should defer to the supposed legislative superiority in expertise.

Justice Breyer in *Nixon* recognized at least the theoretical possibility of such improper legislative motivation, and suggested that proof of such motivation in the individual case should dictate more searching judicial scrutiny.[108] But as already noted, Justice Breyer failed to make clear how such proof could ever be established. Nor did he consider the potentially serious friction, from either separation-of-powers or federalism perspectives, to which such a judicial inquiry into subjective legislative motivation could give rise.[109] In any event, none of the other jurists or scholars who have urged that courts provide such deference appears to have even acknowledged the possibility of such concerns.

As subsequent discussion will demonstrate, the level of judicial scrutiny may well determine the outcome in resolving the constitutional issues surrounding campaign finance regulation. Most of the arguments that have been amassed to establish the need for such legislation constitute largely conclusory and empirically unsupported assertions.[110] To the extent a reviewing court employs the highly deferential "rational basis" standard of judicial review, such laws would almost surely be upheld on the basis of what amounts to little more than a fig leaf of legislative justification. Were a reviewing court to demand that government justify blatant incursions into the rights of free expression, however, it is highly doubtful that the feeble empirical evidence that exists would suffice to support a finding of constitutionality.

Postulate 4: The Underlying Rationale for Extending Full
First Amendment Protection to the Use of Money in Political
Campaigns Is Improperly Grounded in a Narrowly Based
Political Theory of Individualism

Even if one were to concede both that the use of money in political campaigns is properly classified as purely expressive activity and that no basis exists for special judicial deference, one may nevertheless reject the extension of full First Amendment protection to campaign contributions or expenditures. Such a conclusion would be premised on the view that the argument for First Amendment protection is grounded in a misguidedly narrow perspective on the values fostered by the free expression guarantee. Defenders of campaign expenditure limitations have asserted that the *Buckley* Court "was incorrect in viewing freedom of expression as a negative right of the individual against the State. Rather, free speech should be understood in relation to its goal of furthering an informed electorate and promoting political participation."[111] As Kathleen Sullivan has written, "[a]rguments for greater limits on political contributions and expenditures typically suggest that any claims for individual liberty to spend political money ought yield to an overriding interest in a well-functioning democracy."[112]

Burt Neuborne is the leading advocate of this position. In his view, the Supreme Court in *Buckley* improperly "treated unlimited campaign spending as privileged autonomous behavior"[113] and while he believed it "possible to limit the spending of the super-rich within the confines of an autonomy-centered First Amendment,"[114] he recognized that "those confines are becoming increasingly difficult to maintain."[115] Neuborne has questioned whether the autonomy vision of the First Amendment actually represents a coherent theoretical view. He has suggested, however, that "[a]s it becomes increasingly difficult in an election context to maintain a coherent vision of a First Amendment that is exclusively designed to preserve autonomy, the question arises whether other possible visions exist that might supplant, or at least supplement, the traditional autonomy model."[116] That supplemental model, Neuborne asserts, should view free expression as playing "a democracy-enabling role" in which the First Amendment is deemed "democracy's safety net."[117] When viewed "as a bulwark of democracy (as well as a protection of individual autonomy), the First Amendment tells us that, when more than one candidate for First Amendment autonomy protection exists in a democracy case, the Court should privilege behavior that benefits democracy rather than behavior that saps its vitality."[118]

While Neuborne briefly acknowledges the possibility that "powerful arguments exist in favor of unlimited campaign spending," he notes that "[t]here are equally powerful arguments—rooted in democratic theory and our commitment to political equality—in favor of content-neutral, narrowly tailored restrictions on massive campaign spending by wealthy individuals."[119]

Free speech theorists have long debated the relative merits of competing individualist and communitarian models of free expression.[120] Some have suggested that the underlying normative rationale of First Amendment protection is a belief in the value of individual autonomy and development. Others have argued that the facilitation of democratic society, rather than the narrow and selfish concerns of the individual, provides the moral core of free speech protection. These issues have been examined in detail elsewhere in these pages. One may reasonably question, however, whether, in the campaign finance context, there is really any difference between the two normative models. Both theories proceed on an assumption of the value of self-determination, though one focuses on the self-determination of the individual while the other focuses on the self-determination of the society itself. But a democratic society is ultimately composed of its individual members, and if those individual members do not function as free thinking entities worthy of respect, the society as a whole will likely flounder.[121] Once that symbiotic intersection between individual and democratic society is recognized, the number of instances in which a free speech conflict exists between the two models will be relatively rare.

The primary fallacy in the critique of constitutional protection for campaign contributions and expenditures from the perspective of free speech theory, however, is that the strongest First Amendment arguments against campaign finance limitations are grounded not in an individualist view of the First Amendment but rather in a purely process-based, systemic rationale. Thus, Neuborne's premise—that the First Amendment attack against campaign finance regulation is grounded exclusively in an individualist model of free speech theory—is fundamentally flawed at the outset.

What renders campaign spending and contribution limitations so damaging to fundamental free speech values is the simple fact that money is generally necessary to communicate effectively, and a restriction on the availability or use of money in a campaign will therefore inevitably reduce the scope and amount of communication effectively disseminated to the voters.[122] Indeed, as already noted, it is the supposed communicative advantage gained from financial superiority that largely fuels the campaign finance reform movement in the first place. This result severely undermines free speech interests, not primarily because it interferes with an individual's autonomous decision to speak, but rather because it promotes voter ignorance, thereby undermining the effective operation of democracy.

A key fact apparently disregarded by advocates of campaign finance regulation is that restricting the power of a candidate with access to substantial funding in no way increases the public exposure of a candidate who lacks such funding. Assume that because candidate A has available substantial funds, he is able to communicate his message effectively to the electorate. Because candidate B lacks such funding, she is unable effectively to communicate her message. The goal of expenditure limitations and, at least indirectly, contribution limitations is to reduce candidate A's ability to communicate to a level roughly comparable to the lower capabilities of candidate B. But the inescapable result—indeed, the very goal—of campaign finance limitations is to create an equality in voter ignorance: The voters will now be just as ignorant about candidate A as they were—*and still are*—about candidate B.

This result is completely inconsistent with the "democratic process" goal of free speech protection. Alexander Meiklejohn, the leading democratic process free speech theorist, reasoned that the concept of free speech "springs from the principles of self-government."[123] Society's initial commitment to democracy logically dictates the guarantee of free expression, he reasoned, because voters need a broad and uninhibited range of communication of information and opinion relevant to their "self-governing" decisions in the voting booth.[124] The inescapable and intended impact of campaign financing limitation is that voters will have less information and opinion than they would have had available to them otherwise.

Meiklejohn's theory, it should be emphasized, did not turn on recognition of an individual autonomy value.[125] His concern, rather, was exclusively on the symbiotic relationship between free expression and the democratic process. Yet limits on a candidate's ability to raise or spend money inevitably undermine the core of the process values that Meiklejohn articulated. Thus, it is actually the systemic value of democratic facilitation, rather than a narrow autonomy-based value, that lies at the heart of the First Amendment challenge to restrictions on campaign expenditures or fundraising.[126] It is not surprising, then, that one of the leading scholarly advocates of the unconstitutionality of most forms of campaign finance regulation, Lillien Bevier, also rejects an individualist model of free speech theory.[127]

Postulate 5: Expenditure and Contribution Limits Are Necessary in Order to Remove Inequities among Economically Disparate Groups and Individuals, in Furtherance of the First Amendment Interest in Equality

Though the Supreme Court has uniformly rejected the argument,[128] perhaps the most widely used rationale among scholars and politicians to support the constitutionality of campaign finance limitations is that such restrictions are necessary to assure political equality among economically disparate groups and individuals. The argument is, basically, "that the Court has simply ignored the reality that wealth has tremendous power and influence over the political process and that this distorts political choice."[129] Chapter 3 devoted significant attention to this theory in the specific context of corporate political activity. However, it is also necessary to examine the equality argument in the context of general campaign finance regulation.

The equality argument can be explained in two ways. First, one could view the argument as a subset of equal protection, on a moral if not a constitutional level. Economic disparities are unfair, the theory assumes, because they result in an inequitable disparity in the ability to exercise fundamental expressive rights. In a certain sense, the argument is little more than a specific application of a broader normative theory of economic redistribution, viewed through a lens of equal protection.[130] In another sense, however, the equality rationale may be viewed predominantly through a free speech lens, as a means of bringing about equality among speakers. Those who articulate this approach seek to draw on the Supreme Court's recognition of an equal protection subset of free speech theory and doctrine.[131]

The equality rationale arguably gains strength when applied to so fundamental a constitutional interest as the right of free expression. Pursuing this fundamental rights perspective, scholars have sought to analogize campaign finance restrictions[132] to the Supreme Court's holding, grounded in equal protection, that legislative districts must be based on a principle of one person, one vote.[133] Just as the state may not, consistent with the constitutional requirement of equal protection, allow one voter to have more influence on an election than others, they argue, so, too, those with economic power should not be permitted to exert greater influence over the political process.[134]

The voting analogy, however, is both misguided and dangerous. It unwisely seeks to equate a formalized, single act—voting—with an expressive process that is clearly intended to be "uninhibited, robust, and wide open."[135] A logical extrapolation of the analogy would presumably require each speaker to have the opportunity to speak for the same amount of time, for anything more or less would destroy the equality that is constitutionally required as to voting. Such a result, however, would no doubt destroy the flow and spontaneity that is essential to the expressive system.

Moreover, if one really wanted to impose a rigid, formalized expressive equality analogous to the voting structure, presumably one could not limit oneself to economic differences. Some speakers are louder or more articulate than others, and the result of allowing such disparities to continue would be that some speakers would have more power and influence than others. Such disparities are surely unconstitutional in the voting context, and if we proceed on an assumption of a rigid analogy to the voting model, then these disparities must also be removed.

Such results would obviously be nonsensical, a fact that underscores the absurdity of the voting analogy in the first place. Though speech and voting are intertwined both practically and conceptually, they are very different acts with very different methods and requirements. A vote is an act with direct legal, non-expressive consequences. The act of voting is qualitatively different from an attempt to convince someone how to vote, just as advocating violent overthrow is different, for constitutional purposes, from actually attempting overthrow.

Those who make the voting analogy might respond, however, that it is just that—an analogy, not an identity. The point, they could assert, is not that the two processes are rigidly identical, but merely that they reflect roughly similar concerns and values. But the differences between the two are, in important ways, fundamental. By its nature, the one person, one vote rule represents a rigid, mathematically based equality in the performance of an act that instantaneously gives rise to legally enforceable, non-expressive consequences.

In any event, the voting analogy fails, for the simple reason that in the voting context governmental action has affirmatively given rise to the inequity, while in the expressive context no affirmative governmental action has directly caused the disparity in expressive power. More importantly, to focus exclusively on the equality aspect of the one person, one vote rule—as do those who analogize the rule to campaign finance—is to ignore the key differences in the respective underlying affirmative rights. If equality were the sole concern, one could satisfy that interest by prohibiting anyone from voting in the first place. There can be little doubt that the independently protected constitutional right to vote would not be satisfied by governmental creation of such an equality of electoral impotence. Yet those who urge limitations on campaign contributions and expenditures appear to be satisfied by—indeed, to be motivated by—the creation of an equality of voter ignorance about competing candidates. This is surely not a result consistent with the goals of free expression, whether viewed on systemic or individualist levels. Limiting the ability of those with economic power to spend on or contribute to political campaigns in no way expands the ability of those who lack such power to communicate their political message.[136]

Additionally, economic power may be used to offset other advantages that candidates may have, such as notoriety in other fields. In fact, as already noted,[137] the advantages of incumbency can usually be overcome only by a challenger's use of superior funds.[138] Thus, even if one were to accept the goal of equality in the abstract, it is quite possible that imposing equality of economic power would further distort other inequalities among candidates.

Perhaps the most ominous aspect of the equality argument is its likely—and arguably intended—disparate impact on political viewpoint. For the most part, it is evident at the outset which side of the political spectrum is most likely to possess economic power: the side that wishes to maintain that economic superiority. Invariably, this will include overwhelmingly those on the politically conservative side of that spectrum. This is a fact surely known to all those who seek to impose restrictions on the use of money in political campaigns.[139] One may therefore reasonably question the extent to which such limits are actually viewpoint-neutral. In an ironic twist, therefore, it is conceivable that limits imposed in the name of First Amendment equality actually undermine the true equality principle of the First Amendment: governmental equality in the treatment of the private expression of ideas.[140]

Postulate 6: Contribution Limits Are Necessary to Deter
Corruption and Maintain the Integrity of the Democratic Process

Though the point has long been disputed by campaign finance reform advocates, at least since *Buckley* the Supreme Court has steadfastly maintained that the goal of achieving political equality cannot, in and of itself, justify restrictions on campaign finance.[141] Rather, the only acceptable grounds for such regulation is the "prevention of corruption and the appearance of corruption."[142] Because the *Buckley* Court believed that direct expenditures by a candidate did not present this threat, it invalidated federal limits on expenditures.[143] However, the Court found that limits on contributions did further that legitimate interest, and therefore it upheld such limits.[144] The Court reasoned in the following manner:

> To the extent that large contributions are given to secure a political quid pro quo from current and potential office holders, the integrity of our system of representative democracy is undermined. . . . Of almost equal concern as the danger of actual quid pro quo arrangements is the impact of the appearance of corruption stemming from public awareness of the opportunities for abuse inherent in a regime of large financial contributions. . . . [In enacting contribution limits] Congress could legitimately conclude that the avoidance of the appearance of improper influence "is also critical . . . if confidence of the system of representative government is not to be eroded to a disastrous extent."[145]

The Court in *Nixon v. Shrink Missouri PAC*[146] recently reaffirmed its holding in *Buckley* that contribution limits may be justified by the desire to avoid corruption.

In critiquing this reasoning, it is at the outset necessary to understand exactly what the Court has meant by the dangers of "corruption" or the "appearance of corruption." As one commentator has correctly noted, in *Buckley* "the very concept of corruption was never clearly defined."[147] On one level, the term obviously extends to blatant acts of bribery: the corrupt provision of an officially ordained benefit in exchange for some type of quid pro quo. But while there can be little question that avoidance of such acts is a matter of legitimate government concern, there are serious problems with relying on this rationale as a justification for contribution limits.

Of course, if one were to begin—as the *Buckley* Court did—with the assumption that contributions only marginally implicate free speech interests, then presumably limits on contributions could be upheld on the basis of a considerably lesser showing of need than could a restriction on fully protected expressive activity.[148] To the extent this preliminary assumption explains the Court's approach to the review of the avoidance-of-corruption justification, the Court's lax examination of this justification may be understandable. For reasons already discussed, however,[149] the view that contributions are not fully protected expression is seriously flawed. Thus, my critique of the Court's scrutiny proceeds on the assumption that full First Amendment protection extends to campaign contributions. On the basis of that assumption, the Court's reliance on the avoidance-of-corruption rationale—at least when "corruption" is defined narrowly—is woefully inadequate to justify limits on contributions.

The constitutional inadequacy of the anti-corruption rationale derives from a synthesis of four factors. First, the Court has at no time pointed to evidence that corrupt quid pro quo political arrangements currently present a real problem facing the nation, or did so at the time of the contribution limits' enactment. Second, to the extent such a problem exists, there are no grounds on which to assume that all or even most contributions are made on such a basis, yet statutory limits apply across the board. Third, to the extent such a problem does exist, and to the extent that in individual cases particular contributions have been made on the basis of such a corrupt understanding, preexisting bribery statutes or other less invasive legislative alternatives adequately vindicate governmental interests. Fourth, even if we assume that contribution limits are necessary to deter the problem of corrupt quid pro quo arrangements, it is difficult to believe that limits as low as $1,000—the current federal limit—are required to avoid the harm. When taken together, these factors establish that contribution limits are significantly overbroad in their efforts to solve a problem that has never been established to exist in the first place.

There has never been an adequate empirical showing that corrupt quid pro quo arrangements present a serious and pervasive problem. The Supreme Court in both *Buckley* and *Nixon* was willing to assume that the political horrors of Watergate in 1972 justified such a concern.[150] But as a perceptive commentator has correctly noted, "for all the betrayal of public trust set out in the Watergate papers, there were no instances of quid pro quo for campaign contributions."[151] Even if there had been, however, surely what happened in 1972 cannot automatically be assumed to be true today throughout the nation. The Court in *Nixon* asserted that "*Buckley* demonstrates that the dangers of large, corrupt contributions and the suspicion that large contributors are corrupt are neither novel nor implausible."[152] But at no point has there ever been a careful judicial examination of this conclusion, nor did the Court in *Nixon* make anything more than a cursory inquiry into the available empirical evidence about the current national situation, much less the specific situation in Missouri, whose statute was challenged in that case.[153] Although the *Nixon* Court boldly asserted that the Court had "never accepted mere conjecture as adequate to carry a First Amendment burden,"[154] it is difficult to characterize the Court's unsupported assumption that corrupt quid pro quo practices are prevalent as anything but conjecture.

Even if we assume that the problem of corrupt quid pro quo arrangements is a real one, at no point has the Court ever demonstrated that all or most campaign contributions are made as part of such an improper arrangement. The Court in *Nixon* and *Buckley* appears to have proceeded on an analysis similar to the tort doctrine of *res ipsa loquitur*, which provides that in certain negligence cases a plaintiff's showing of the end result is enough to allow a jury to find it more likely than not that defendant's negligence caused that result.[155] In the context of political contributions, the Court appears to assume that the very act of contributing creates the likelihood of a corrupt quid pro quo arrangement. But there will often exist legitimate purposes for contributions, such as ideological compatibility. Individuals may choose to contribute to a candidate's campaign for no reason other than that they agree with the candidate's platform and therefore want the candidate to be elected. Given the serious First Amendment implications of contribution limits, it is at best unclear why the Court is so ready to assume the validity of the more incriminating inference.

More importantly, there is absolutely no reason that preexisting bribery statutes could not adequately handle whatever problem is in fact caused by such corruption. A corrupt quid pro quo arrangement, under which an officeholder employs official power to aid an individual in exchange for a benefit, would seem to be a classic example of illegal bribery.[156] Use of contribution limits to prevent such arrangements, then, is little more than a gratuitous inhibition on free speech rights. Moreover, to the extent it were decided that bribery statutes do not, for some reason, adequately protect against such illegal arrangements, there exist alternative measures that could prophylactically deal with the problem and that are considerably less invasive of First Amendment interests. For example, government could prohibit any contributor to a candidate from receiving a contract from that candidate once in office. Such a law would certainly invade free speech rights much less than a sweeping restriction on all contributions. Such "unlimited" limitations employ an axe, when the First Amendment demands use of a scalpel.

It should be recalled, however, that the *Buckley* Court made reference to concern over the *appearance* of corruption, as well as the actual existence of corruption, as a constitutionally acceptable justification for contribution limits. Presumably, this concern would lead a reviewing court to uphold such limits, even in the absence of any evidence either that corruption is a real concern or that contribution limits would avoid that concern more effectively than less invasive alternatives. All that would be required is presumably that the public perceive that such problems exist. Such an approach is problematic, for two reasons. First, at no point has there been an empirical showing that the public actually perceives such a problem to exist. Although scholars have pointed to "massive non-voting" as "[a] predictable consequence of a loss of faith in democracy,"[157] the reasons for non-voting are sufficiently complex that they render such an assumption overly simplistic.[158] Second, in no other case of speech regulation has the Court been willing to accept evidence of *public perception*, rather than of the existence of the interest itself, as a compelling justification for restrictions on expression. To pander to public perceptions, even when those perceptions are inaccurate, is to render the First Amendment hostage to the public's ignorance.

Ultimately, the most significant problem with the anti-corruption rationale for contribution limits is that no matter how restrictive those limits are, those who wish to circumvent them will be able to do so with relative ease. The limits will therefore be unable to achieve their goal. Would-be contributors who wish to curry influence with candidates may independently purchase advertising in support of the candidate, tacitly making sure that the candidate is aware of those efforts. As a practical matter, it would be impossible to regulate such private expenditures without all but destroying the First Amendment. Thus, contribution limits will almost definitely fail to prevent the danger of corrupt quid pro quo arrangements.

In *Nixon*, the Court noted that it had previously "recognized a concern not confined to bribery of public officials, but [one also] extending to the broader threat from politicians too compliant with the wishes of large contributors."[159] But at no point did the Court in either *Buckley* or *Nixon* fully explain in what sense, short of out-and-out bribery, contributions undermine American democracy. Scholars have sought to fill this void, by focusing on the concerns of "excessive or undesirable influence."[160] Neuborne articulates the concern in the following manner:

> A campaign financing system driven by extreme wealth disparity will inevitably reflect the needs and concerns of the persons who pay for the system, and it will ignore the needs and concerns of the persons who lack the means to participate in the funding process. . . . [T]he political agenda will inevitably be shaped by an estimate of the money that donors will spend to promote a particular idea. This means that issues of importance to the holders of great wealth are more likely to find themselves on the agenda than issues of importance to the poor.[161]

In the words of another commentator, "[t]he issues that animated reform and that animate reform now are the issues of healthy politics in the processes of representative democracy. These issues concern the concentration of political influence that money can buy, the undermining of competitiveness, and thus of meaningful choice, in our elections and the impoverishment of political debate and information."[162] The goal of reform, then, is to "return to the populist dream of grass-roots, direct political action by ordinary people."[163] The argument may be reduced to the following points: The undue influence of money in political campaigns simultaneously (1) fosters the implementation of the political program of the rich and hinders implementation of the political program of the poor; (2) alienates the common person from participation in the democratic process, and (3) ultimately impoverishes the quality of political debate.

This "undue influence" rationale for campaign finance regulation is extremely troublesome from the perspective of First Amendment theory, on several grounds. Initially, the argument is much too simplistic in its assumption that a speaker's superior economic power will automatically equate to greater political success for the speaker's platform and positions. If this were the case, it would be extremely difficult to explain all of the pro-labor, regulatory, or redistributive legislation enacted over the last seventy years.

One need not necessarily believe that legislators act out of well-intentioned assessments of the public interest to conclude that the economically powerful will not always get their way in the political process. Several alternative explanations also exist. First, one might reason that those without economic power have been sufficiently resourceful so as to counteract the political force of economic power. They may have done this through reliance on organizational skills, political effort, and the pooling of economic resources. For example, labor, environmentalist, and pro-choice groups have been able to influence legislative choices, despite the general lack of individual wealth on the part of their membership. Second, it is conceivable that legislators will seek to pressure economically powerful forces for contributions by adopting anti-capitalist or regulatory legislation.[164] This legislative incentive would be removed if the possibility of large economic support were taken away.

More importantly, the legitimacy of the very concern about the effect of speech regulation on the interests of the poor may be questioned, from the perspective of First Amendment theory. Such an approach views free expression as nothing more than a device to be manipulated in order to achieve predetermined normative political agendas. On this basis alone, then, the argument must be rejected because it contravenes the First Amendment's bar of viewpoint-based regulation.[165]

The concern that the dominant political influence of economic power has alienated significant portions of the electorate is, of course, a very different type of argument. However, the issue of alienation from the political sphere is complex and has been the subject of careful scholarly discussion for many years. It is impossible, on the basis of the existing literature, to explain the result by means of such a simplistic and single-minded rationale. In any event, to structure First Amendment protection to reflect the rising and falling emotional impact caused by expression effectively allows a heckler's veto, where the speaker's rights are determined by the extent to which the listeners are pleased with the substance of her speech. Surely, no meaningful First Amendment protection can survive under such a system. Yet the argument that expressive expenditures may constitutionally be limited because they alienate the voting public is not significantly different from such clearly unacceptable doctrinal framework.

Conclusion

The current state of doctrinal and theoretical confusion concerning the First Amendment limitations on campaign finance regulation did not come about over night. It arose as a result of the combination of years of poorly reasoned Supreme Court decisions and constitutional scholarship often influenced either by strategic political agendas or an underlying commitment to the value of economic redistribution.

The doctrinal and theoretical confusion that has plagued this area of First Amendment jurisprudence, however, can be eliminated by use of a process that combines logical reduction and political deconstruction. The constitutional defense of campaign finance regulation can, I believe, be reduced to six normative and empirical postulates. Careful analysis and critique of the logic and empirical assumptions underlying those postulates reveals their fundamental flaws. No amount of conceptual manipulation or empirical fudging can alter the key fact that the restriction of campaign spending and contributions inevitably causes a significant reduction in the extent and availability of expression concerning performance of the fundamental function of a democratic system: the electoral process.

To be sure, not all of that expression will be rational or well motivated. But the First Amendment does not permit government to suppress expression because of its judgment that the speech is harmful, irrational, or unwise. Moreover, limits on campaign finance in no way assure that the expression suppressed will be any more harmful or maliciously motivated than the expression that remains.

One may reasonably argue that basic considerations of fairness dictate the need for redistribution of economic resources. If government wishes to impose such a redistributive structure, nothing in the First Amendment will disrupt attainment of that socio-economic goal. But quite obviously not everyone agrees with such an economic philosophy. To restructure the expressive system on the basis of such a prior normative commitment would inevitably contravene the very value-neutrality that underlies that system.

Restrictions on campaign expenditures and contributions frontally assault the right of free expression, without a compelling, value-neutral justification. They therefore violate the First Amendment. When one steps back and examines the question free of the baggage of unsupported empirical assumptions, normative economic philosophy, and underlying political agendas, this conclusion is surprisingly easy to reach.

5

The Right of Expressive Access, Redistributive Values, and the Democratic Dilemma

Over the years, scholars or jurists have often analogized the right of free expression to a marketplace, in which contrasting ideas compete for acceptance among a consuming public.[1] Many have also questioned whether the analogy is an appropriate one.[2] But whether or not such a characterization was ever accurate or appropriate, respected scholars have in recent years suggested that the right of free expression does suffer from many of the inequities and inequalities that have historically been thought to plague the economic Darwinism of the capitalistic marketplace.[3]

No one could reasonably dispute that, for much of the latter half of the twentieth century, economic power and the ability to get oneself heard became significantly intertwined. The simple realities were—and, to a certain extent, may still be—that one must control or at least have meaningful access to institutionalized modes of communication in order to reach an extended audience. Yet for the large majority of individuals and organizations the costs of doing so have generally been prohibitive. Not surprisingly, then, most effective means of modern communication have been controlled largely by economically powerful entities or individuals. The result, some have argued, has been a harmful inequity in the relative ability of members of the populace to communicate their messages and a resulting impoverishment of the scope and substance of public debate.[4]

Certain scholars have further argued that control of expressive resources by economically powerful interests enables those interests to shape the modern political agenda and thereby heavily influence political decision making.[5] This strategic by-product of such concentration of expressive power, they suggest, circularly assures that government will refuse to adopt modes of economic redistribution that would allow change in the political agenda and, ultimately, readjust societal economic power more equitably.[6] The best means to break the cycle, these scholars contend, is to recognize some form of a governmentally enforced right of access on the part of private individuals and entities to existing privately owned sources of expression and information. Such a right of access, they assert, not only would fail to contravene the core values protected by the First Amendment, it would actually foster them.[7]

A right of expressive access could assume a variety of concrete forms. For example, it could require that broadcast licensees provide an opportunity for the expression of varying viewpoints on issues of public concern,[8] or that the print media provide an opportunity for reply to those whom they have criticized,[9] or that cable operators provide channels for local broadcasters.[10]

The arguments in support of a right of expressive access may at first appear intuitively appealing. But many of the empirical assumptions concerning the alleged link between financial resources and the ability to contribute meaningfully to public debate fail to take into account the impact of several relatively recent and important advances in communications technology, which may have ameliorated the communicative problems caused by financial concentration. Surely, the growth of both cable television (with its opportunities for both smaller and more specialized stations as well as for numerous public access channels) and the Internet (with its opportunity for immediate and inexpensive worldwide communications and information retrieval abilities) suggest the possibility of an explosion in the common person's ability to influence and communicate with her local community, as well as with broader national and international communities.[11]

Despite the potentially dramatic impact of such modern technological advances, the scope and substantive diversity of public debate arguably would be even further enriched by the extension of a right of expressive access to those who normally lack the opportunity to speak through institutional communicative sources. And, if one assumes that public debate would be enriched by such an extension, it is also reasonable to presume that the electorate's performance of the self-governing function would be improved correspondingly. Scholarly authorities have long recognized the positive intersection between a better informed electorate and the effective performance of the democratic process.[12]

While creation of an expressive right of access may well have the positive effect of enriching public debate,[13] it is also fraught with significant dangers to the values fostered by both the First Amendment right of free expression and the democratic system of which that right is an essential element.[14] For the most part, advocates of an expressive right of access have either completely ignored these dangers or dismissed them summarily.[15] Indeed, no commentator appears to have explored in detail the risks to the values of free expression to which creation of an expressive right of access gives rise. My goal in this chapter is to provide such an exploration.

In order to demonstrate the expressive harms caused by a creation of a right of access, we must first recognize the debate over expressive access as one part of a broader theoretical debate over the general redistribution of economic resources. Such a conceptualization of the right of access is appropriate because the governmental creation of a right of expressive access is, in reality, nothing more than the redistribution of a particular type of economic asset: the economic power to communicate. Thus, this chapter attempts to view the right of expressive access through the lens, not merely of general First Amendment theory, but also of what can be called "redistributive theory." That concept refers to the competing moral, social, and economic arguments concerning the value of the societal redistribution of privately owned economic resources.

Expressive redistribution has unique elements that arguably distinguish it in some important ways from other forms of economic redistribution.[16] However, conceptualizing the right of access as primarily a specific application of generalized redistributive theory gives rise to four extremely valuable insights, all of which aid substantially in grasping the true First Amendment implications of the creation of an access right.

The first insight to which the revised conceptual focus gives rise is the recognition that generally what is happening when a right of expressive access is created is, in fact, the *redistribution* of existing resources, rather than the *generation* of completely new expressive resources. In most contexts, then, from a redistributional perspective a right of access must be viewed as something approaching a zero sum game: Any extension of expressive power to A will automatically and correspondingly reduce the expressive power of B. Thus, the only way one can be sure that extension of a right of expressive access will actually "enrich" public debate—as its proponents have universally claimed—is to assume that public debate will be enriched more by the expression of those who have been granted access than by the expression that would have been disseminated by the expressive resource operator, but for the government's expressive redistribution.

It is difficult to ascertain, ex ante, whether this assumption is empirically accurate or not. Indeed, it is conceivable that on occasion the views and positions of the party seeking access will already have received considerably more public attention than those that would have been expressed by the expressive resource operator.[17] Moreover, no persuasive empirical evidence appears to support the contrary conclusion. It is thus questionable whether one should automatically assume that creation of a right of expressive access will necessarily enrich public debate.

The second insight one may derive from conceptualizing the right of access as a form of private resource redistribution flows readily from the first. While the primary goal of a right of access is the enrichment of public debate, recognition that such a right is merely a form of redistribution of expressive assets underscores the fact that government will need to fashion some basis on which to determine the nature and extent of such redistribution. Thus, as a practical matter, government will have to develop some substantive standard by which to operationalize the circumstances under which individuals or entities will benefit from a right of access. Short of completely mechanistic, content-neutral standards, some unit of government will be called upon to determine which private individuals or entities will benefit from, and which will be burdened by, the governmentally created expressive redistribution. Moreover, once that generalized standard has been chosen, some governmental agency will necessarily be called upon to apply it to ambiguous specific cases. It is virtually inevitable, then, that government will be placed in a position to manipulate the flow of private debate on the basis of predetermined substantive considerations.

Of course, if one believes—as certain respected scholars apparently do—that governmental intervention into the world of private expression is to be welcomed,[18] then there likely would exist no reason to mistrust the motivations behind either government's choice of a regulatory measure or the means by which it applies the chosen standards to the facts of complex cases. But such scholarly equanimity in the face of government's insertion of its regulatory power into the marketplace of private expression is grossly inconsistent with the venerable tradition of healthy skepticism of the governmental regulation of expression.[19] It is inconsistent as well as with much of the actual history of such regulation, which has more than justified such skepticism.[20] Indeed, it is ironic that at least one of the leading scholars who apparently welcomes government's regulatory entrance into the expressive marketplace as a positive influence for the advancement of public good has, in other contexts, expressed great mistrust of the motivations that dictate the outcome of the legislative process.[21]

The third insight that can be derived from the intersection between the right of access and principles of redistributive theory exacerbates the problems to which the second insight gives rise. This third insight focuses on the difficulty of separating the normative process-based arguments used to support the democratically grounded expressive redistribution normally associated with the right of access from the moral, social, and economic arguments traditionally relied upon to support more generalized economic redistribution. This difficulty in conceptually distinguishing between the process-based and substantive rationales underlying redistributive theory gives rise to serious problems for any principle of expressive redistribution, for several reasons.

As explained in prior chapters, it is standard First Amendment thinking that, in order to prevent the right of free expression from degenerating into nothing more than a tool of those in political power, it must be implemented on a completely value-neutral basis: Government may not selectively regulate expression on the basis of its judgment of the wisdom or offensiveness of the substantive views being expressed.[22] Because of the close conceptual connection linking the substantive and process-based redistributive theories, a real danger exists that a system of expressive redistribution could be adopted solely for the strategic purpose of achieving wider substantive redistribution of economic resources. But the morality, wisdom, and nature of such distribution are among the central issues reserved for decision, in a democratic system, to the polity, whether directly or through the representative process. Governmental manipulation of the competitive flow of the debate on this issue would thus seriously disrupt performance of the populace's democratic function. Such substantively motivated expressive redistribution would clearly violate the epistemological neutrality that stands at the core of the right of free expression.[23]

The final insight that flows from the reconceptualization of the right of expressive access as an outgrowth of more generally focused redistributive theory is the recognition that, as in all redistributive contexts, when one private party is benefited another party is necessarily burdened or deprived. Put simply, a process of "redistribution," as a definitional matter, requires the transfer of assets from one private party to another.

This fact alone has in modern times rarely deterred society from imposing various forms of non-expressive economic redistribution. However, we must take into account the unique impact of *expressive* redistribution. The First Amendment has wisely been construed to provide constitutional protection to the right of free expression beyond that given to individual rights of conduct and property.[24] The harms caused by expressive redistribution to the intellectual autonomy of the expressive resource operators, as well as to the quality and effectiveness of generalized public debate, can be significant.[25]

Such unique redistributive harms can be demonstrated by drawing upon a venerable and respected body of First Amendment doctrine that establishes the unconstitutionality of governmentally compelled expression.[26] Under this line of decisions, government is generally deemed to be constitutionally prohibited from requiring private individuals or entities to express a governmentally dictated message.[27]

Although the holding and current validity of the compelled expression line of cases are today beyond question,[28] only rarely has the Court attempted to provide any kind of coherent or sophisticated explanation of the doctrine's theoretical underpinnings.[29] I argue that such a theoretical analysis reveals a persuasive rationale underlying the compelled expression decisions that is, for the most part, equally applicable to situations in which government creates a private right of access.[30] Thus, the right of access undermines free speech values in much the same manner as the forced expression of a governmentally prescribed message.

Because a right of access represents a specific application of a broader conceptual category of governmental power to redistribute economic resources, to understand the constitutional implications of such a right one must grasp the essential norms and premises of modern redistributive theory. The first section of this chapter explores general redistributive theory, seeking to distinguish among various conceptual versions and explain which are appropriate as a conceptual and normative basis on which to ground a right of access.[31] While I seek to distinguish among these conceptually different versions of redistributive theory, it is important also to emphasize both the difficulty in drawing such distinctions and the inescapable overlap that results from that difficulty.[32]

I then examine the right of expressive access as a specific application of redistributive theory. Viewing the right in this manner underscores both the benefits and harms to the system of free expression to which a right of expressive access gives rise. I initially explore the right's beneficial impact on expressive interests, and then describe its dangers.[33] It is certainly conceivable that creation of a right of expressive access, either generally or in a narrower form, could enrich the quality of public debate. However, I ultimately conclude that the dangers far outweigh the limited and speculative benefits to the interests in free expression to which the right of access gives rise.[34]

I then examine possible narrower forms of the right of access that could avoid the expressive harms associated with the right of access and simultaneously enrich public debate. All such possibilities are rejected as either unworkable, incoherent, or insufficiently protective of free speech rights. Finally, I examine possible reasons why the need for the right of access may no longer be as strong as it once was.[35]

Theories of Redistribution

The Concept of Redistributive Theory: An Overview

Before one can understand the intersection between redistributive values and free speech theory, one must first comprehend the essential elements of redistributive theory itself. I thus begin by conceptualizing the different forms of economic redistribution. It should be emphasized that I approach this task, not from the perspective of political or economic theory, but rather from the perspective of free speech theory. Thus, my purpose here is not to engage in a detailed exploration of the moral, social, or political issues surrounding the questions concerning economic redistribution. It is, rather, to lay the groundwork for understanding the role that the right of expressive access plays within the broader framework of redistributive theory.

From this perspective, it is appropriate to divide redistributive theory into three subcategories which, while theoretically distinct, have substantial areas of overlap: substantive redistribution, democratic redistribution, and hybrid redistribution. *Substantive redistribution* refers to the basic arguments of morality, social policy, and economic efficiency that surround the heavily debated question concerning the nature of what economic redistribution, if any, society should impose. *Democratic redistribution* refers to the modern theory that it is impossible to attain the political equality required for democracy when significant economic disparities exist in society; therefore, economic redistribution is necessary, not because of the moral value of distributive justice in and of itself, but because absent such redistribution the democratic process will be unable to function effectively.

Though the rationale behind democratic redistribution may differ from that underlying substantive redistribution, the sought-after result in both situations is strikingly similar: the societal redistribution of privately owned economic resources. One could, however, fashion a form of democratic redistribution that is considerably narrower in scope than full democratic redistribution. This process-based subcategory of democratic redistribution would focus exclusively on the need to distribute only privately owned resources of expression and communication.

Hybrid redistribution refers to the attempt by several modern theorists to employ the process-based concept of democratic redistribution strategically, for the ideological purpose of achieving the normative goals of generalized substantive redistribution. These commentators initially make a normative judgment in favor of the value of economic redistribution throughout society. They also recognize, however, that given both the currently unequal distribution of economic power and the important relationship between economic power and political power, such dramatic economic redistribution is politically unrealistic. They reason that those who possess economic power also possess political power, and those who possess economic power are, for obvious reasons of self-interest, not likely to place issues of economic redistribution high on the political agenda.[36] These commentators therefore urge widespread democratic redistribution, with the hope and expectation that such a redistribution of *political* power will likely result ultimately in a significant redistribution of *economic* power.

Substantive Redistribution

The subject of substantive redistribution has provided the focus of many of the moral, economic, and political arguments made by scholars, commentators, and politicians over the years. Not surprisingly, these theorists have differed significantly over the proper role of the redistribution of private economic assets in society.

Capitalist theorists, for example, have opposed most or all forms of economic redistribution, on grounds of both economic efficiency and individual fairness.[37] They believe that the operation of the free market will inevitably produce the most efficient economic structure, and that therefore governmentally imposed departures from the effects of the market process will inevitably lead to inefficiency.[38] In addition, some defend a pure market system on the moral grounds of individual responsibility and just desserts: Individuals who have not earned economic benefits have no right to receive them from government. Moreover, capitalist theorists believe, government has no moral right to transfer the fruits of one's own efforts to another.[39] Finally, capitalist theorists may oppose economic redistribution on the grounds that it deters individual initiative and undermines individual freedom.

In opposition to such a narrowly based individualist perspective on redistributive issues stands a wide array of political and economic theories. Most starkly contrasted with the strict free market model is Marxist philosophy, which posits that "the capitalist economy, by virtue of its internal dynamics, inevitably produces systematic inequality and massive restrictions on real freedom."[40] According to Marxist theory, "[w]hat appears to the individual to be 'complete freedom' is really nothing but the free movement of 'his alienated life elements'—'in reality, this is the perfection of his slavery and his inhumanity.'"[41]

One need not adopt Marxist philosophy in order to accept the value of economic redistribution, however. Modern liberal political theory also rejects the strict free-market theorists' objections to economic redistribution, though without the Marxists' further rejection of liberal democratic theory's emphasis on the formal protection of individual rights and democratic values.[42] Several liberal theorists have sought to justify the need for economic redistribution on utilitarian grounds. In the words of one commentator, "[e]xtreme inequalities of income or wealth undermine the values of order and stability, communal harmony, liberty, self-fulfillment, and equal opportunity. Extreme inequalities reduce the overall happiness of mankind."[43] He notes that "inequalities breed resentment," and that such resentment "damages the sense of fellowship and solidarity essential to social harmony."[44]

To the extent that liberal theory is premised on a belief in the right of the individual to self-actualize,[45] one could fashion an argument favoring at least a certain degree of economic redistribution. After all, it is not unreasonable to believe that "[m]oney expands choices, and those deprived of money are deprived of liberty. . . . Creative thinking and aesthetic appreciation are not encouraged by an empty stomach or a desperate struggle for existence."[46] On the other hand, an alternative version of liberal theory would suggest that while economic redistribution may further the personal self-actualization of the recipients, it unduly disrupts the personal growth and self-development of the individuals whose assets have been redistributed.

When liberal theory is stripped of its utilitarian cast and replaced by a non-utilitarian concern with abstract normative principles of fairness and justice, the result—if not the reasoning—remains similar. For example, pursuant to John Rawls's so-called "difference principle," initial inequality in the distribution of income among social classes "is justifiable only if the difference in expectation is to the advantage of the representative man who is worse off."[47] To Rawls, this principle "represents, in effect, an agreement to regard the distribution of natural talents as a common asset and to share in the benefits of this distribution whatever it turns out to be."[48]

As already noted, I do not attempt here to provide anything approaching a detailed analysis of the comparative merits of the various theories of economic redistribution. My focus is solely on the impact of such theory on the scope of free speech protection. From that perspective, the actual merits of substantive redistributive theory are wholly inconsequential. Issues of free speech protection cannot be allowed to turn on the substantive merits of the speech in question. Otherwise, free speech protection would effectively degenerate into little more than a method by which to suppress the expression of views unpopular with those in power.[49] Such a result is, of course, wholly inconsistent with the nation's democratic traditions, of which free speech is so important a part.[50]

It does not necessarily follow, however, that redistributive concerns must play no role whatsoever in shaping free speech protection. One could conceivably conclude that existing forms of economic distribution are unacceptable, not merely because they are inconsistent with substantive moral precepts, but also because they effectively undermine the personal and/or process values associated with both free speech protection and the democratic process. But whether such process-based considerations can actually distinguish such a form of redistributive theory from classical substantive redistribution is open to question. It is therefore appropriate at this point to turn to the questions raised by the theory of democratic redistribution.

Democratic Redistribution

The theory of democratic redistribution posits that society must redistribute economic resources, not because of substantive moral concerns of fairness and justice, but rather because such redistribution is essential to the effective operation of the democratic process. Because the theory of democratic redistribution focuses on the need to preserve a vibrant democratic system, one need not accept—at least in the abstract—the moral or economic arguments behind the concept of substantive economic redistribution in order to approve of democratic redistribution.

To accept the theory of democratic redistribution, one need only accept the following normative and empirical premises: (1) Democracy represents the preferable form of government; (2) to be effective, democracy requires that the members of the polity be politically equal; (3) the modern realities are that political equality is impossible to achieve without some form of economic equality; and (4) such economic equality does not currently exist in our society. On the basis of these premises, the theory of democratic redistribution posits that the only means by which to achieve the requisite political equality is to redistribute private economic resources in some manner.

Those who advocate democratic redistribution[51] start from the premise that while democracy, as a definitional matter, requires equality in voting, the act of voting "stands at the end of a series of social processes which are themselves entirely permeated by substantial, material inequality, with consequences for the degree of political equality at the voting stage."[52] In light of the inequalities that pervade these pre-voting processes, those who advocate the theory argue, "the technical equality when we all come to vote can easily pale into insignificance."[53]

Democratic theorist Robert Dahl is the leading modern advocate of the theory of democratic redistribution.[54] Dahl argues that "when differences in political resources cause citizens to be politically unequal, then that inequality necessarily reveals itself by a violation of the criteria [for democracy]."[55] He further contends that for "real"—as opposed to merely "formal"—political equality to be attained, there must initially exist equality of income, wealth, and status.[56] Dahl believes that "both corporate capitalism and bureaucratic socialism tend to produce inequalities in social and economic resources so great as to bring about severe violations of political equality and hence of the democratic process."[57] As a possible remedy for such violations of political equality, Dahl suggests "an extension of the democratic process to economic enterprises."[58] By this he means creation of "a system of economic enterprises collectively owned and democratically governed by all the people who work in them."[59]

Obviously, Dahl is urging a dramatic restructuring of the nation's traditional system of private property ownership.[60] Recognizing this fact, he devotes significant attention to shaping a response to arguments grounded in concepts of private property rights.[61] This fact, however, merely highlights the significant—and perhaps inevitable—conceptual overlap between the substantive and democratic versions of redistributive theory. Although Dahl purports to frame the rationale for his redistributive proposal in the process-based terms of democratic theory, the end result of the remedy he advocates is a significant reshaping of our economic infrastructure. Yet in so doing, he indirectly preempts the very normative issues of morality, social policy, and economic theory implicated by the redistribution debate that the democratic process reserves to the polity as a whole. Thus, whether Dahl's suggested economic restructuring is truly grounded in process-based values, rather than the substantive normative premises underlying liberal, socialist, or Marxist theories of economic redistribution, is open to question.[62]

Because Dahl's analysis does not focus on issues of free expression, he need not distinguish between process-based and substantive rationales for economic redistribution in order to avoid violating the principle of epistemological humility central to the concept of free expression.[63] Indeed, Dahl can reasonably argue that process-based considerations merely supplement the substantive interests in fairness underlying the argument in support of economic redistribution. But once one adds a free speech focus, for reasons already discussed the distinction between substantive and process-based considerations becomes vital.[64] It is by no means clear that the concept of democratic redistribution allows such a distinction to be drawn.

Whatever the moral or social validity of the arguments in support of economic redistribution as an abstract matter, democratic theorists have not universally deemed economic equality to be the sine qua non of a democratic society. To the contrary, scholars have long propounded theories of democracy that contemplate operation of a democratic society in conjunction with a functioning capitalistic economic system. Yet economic redistribution is surely not a concept that normally characterizes the system of capitalism. Moreover, whether one attempts to rationalize the goal of economic equality through economic redistribution as a means of facilitating the democratic process or on purely substantive moral grounds, the end result will be the same. Thus, it is dubious whether any real difference exists between the liberal, socialist, or Marxist forms of substantive redistribution and the supposedly process-based redistributive theory propounded by democratic theorists such as Dahl.

Society could perhaps adopt a diluted form of democratic redistribution focused exclusively on a process-based redistributive model. This model would call, not for the full-scale redistribution of economic power advocated by Dahl, but rather only redistribution of resources intimately tied to the political process. In particular, this model would likely call exclusively for a redistribution of *expressive* resources. These are generally the resources used to contribute to public debate or to communicate with the populace. In short, this diluted form of democratic redistribution, by redistributing solely expressive resources, would amount to creation of a private right of access to existing institutionalized modes of communication, such as newspapers, broadcast outlets, cable television, or corporate advertising.[65]

It is this limited form of redistribution that effectively translates into the right of expressive access. Expressive redistribution may, upon first examination, appear satisfactorily to separate process-based redistributive rationales from substantive ones. But as the subsequent discussion of hybrid redistributive theory will demonstrate, it is not at all clear that substantive and process-based considerations can be so readily separated as rationalizations for expressive redistribution.

Hybrid Redistribution

Hybrid redistributive theory, as the name implies, represents a synthesis of the substantive and democratic redistributive models. It synthesizes them, however, not in a conceptual sense—it is, after all, difficult to distinguish the two on a conceptual level[66]—but rather on a purely strategic level. Simply put, the theory posits that (1) as a normative matter, for the reasons underlying the values of substantive redistribution, economic redistribution is both appropriate and advisable; but (2) because of widespread economic inequality and the inherent intersection between economic inequality and political inequality, those possessing political power will inevitably prove to be the same individuals and entities who also possess economic power; and (3) those who possess economic power are, not surprisingly, unwilling to place issues of economic redistribution on the political agenda. Therefore, in order to facilitate the political adoption of meaningful economic redistribution, society must initially redistribute the resources of political power.[67]

It is important to distinguish the concept of hybrid redistribution from the seemingly overlapping concepts of substantive and democratic redistribution.[68] Of course, if those two theories were identical in everything but name and rationale, then hybrid redistribution, as a separate concept, would be rendered moot. However, to the extent that democratic redistribution applied only to the expressive context, one could choose to adopt this mode of redistribution, not because of its supposedly beneficial impact on the democratic process, but rather solely for the strategic purpose of facilitating the ultimate goal of substantive economic redistribution.

In a number of ways, the theory underlying hybrid redistribution is seriously flawed. From a purely strategic perspective, it appears to suffer from a serious form of pragmatic circularity. If, under existing political structures, society will not even place the issue of substantive economic redistribution on the political agenda because those in political power are the very same individuals and entities who currently possess economic power, why are those very same power centers any more likely to place the issue of democratic redistribution on the political agenda? The only conceivable answer is that those employing the strategy of hybrid redistribution hope that because purely process-based redistributive values, when stated in the abstract, have more universal public appeal than the controversial claims of substantive redistribution, their exclusive emphasis on process-based redistributive values will sufficiently cloud the nature of public debate to enable them to achieve their seemingly more limited process-based goals. But if the assumptions of hybrid redistributive theorists[69] are empirically accurate, their ability even to place the issue of expressive redistribution on the political agenda would seem to be severely limited.

Moreover, from a purely conceptual perspective, hybrid redistributive theory suffers from fatal analytical flaws. The use of normative substantive factors as support for a process-based redistribution effectively turns the democratic process on its head. The issue of substantive redistribution is both morally and economically controversial, and by its very nature the democratic process assumes that the electorate will make substantive political choices, if only indirectly through the selection of accountable representatives.[70] The electorate must therefore be permitted to make a substantive policy choice against economic redistribution on the basis of free and open debate. In a democratic society, government may not impose an externally derived normative choice on the populace. If government is unable to preempt substantive choices of social policy, then it logically follows that government may not control or manipulate private expression in order to attain a predetermined moral, social, or political result. To structure the debate in a manner designed to achieve a preordained policy conclusion would therefore violate this basic premise of both democratic theory and the system of free expression.[71]

The Right of Expressive Access as an Application of Redistributive Theory: Implications for First Amendment Analysis

The Positive Case for Expressive Redistribution

OVERVIEW

At the most fundamental level, the arguments in support of the proposition that a right of access to privately owned modes of communication is consistent with, if not dictated by, the First Amendment right of free expression can be viewed from two distinct perspectives. On the one hand, employing the reasoning of redistributive theory,[72] one may defend the proposition that a right of access is consistent with the First Amendment right of free expression[73] purely on grounds of political equality. Because expression is so critically intertwined with one's ability to influence the political process, the argument proceeds,[74] meaningful—as opposed to merely formalistic[75]— political equality cannot exist absent something at least approaching a state of equality in public access to expressive resources. This reasoning could be characterized as the "equality" rationale for the right of access.

A right of access could alternatively be defended on the basis of an "enrichment" rationale. This rationale turns on the assumption that whatever value or values one believes that the right of expression is designed to foster, the extent to which those values are actually fostered generally will be in direct proportion to the number of opportunities that diverse groups or individuals have to engage in meaningful expressive activities. The more opportunities people have to express themselves in a meaningful manner, the more the values served by free speech protection will be advanced. Correspondingly, the fewer the individuals with opportunities for such expression, the less these values will be advanced.

Of course, even without creation of a right of access to existing communicative resources, individuals could simply stand on a street corner and attempt to speak to whoever happened to pass by. Proponents of a right of access have argued, however, that such a romantic perspective on the exercise of free speech rights no longer comports with the modern realities of our communications system, if in fact it ever did. In order to have a *meaningful* opportunity to contribute to public discussion, they contend, individuals must be given access to preexisting expressive resources.[76]

This rationale for creating a right of access may be labeled the "enrichment" perspective, because it posits that the existence of such a right is necessary in order to enrich public debate. Such enrichment, the argument proceeds, will foster either the individual's ability to self-develop, society's ability to govern itself, or both.

The two conceivable rationales for a right of expressive access are by no means identical, though scholars appear on occasion to have significantly confused the two.[77] As the name implies, the "equality" perspective turns exclusively on a measure of the *relative* ability of potentially competing speakers to reach their intended audience. Pursuant to this reasoning, the equality perspective has no concern with the *absolute* amount of available expressive activity, but rather solely with the comparative expressive power of private speakers. The "enrichment" perspective, in contrast, deems such competitive equality among speakers to be neither necessary nor sufficient for advancement of the goals of free expression. Its focus, rather, is on the importance of increasing the amount and diversity of publicly available expression, in order to better inform the populace in preparation for performance of its self-governing function.

While the enrichment perspective presents at least an arguable basis on which to ground acceptance of a right of access, the equality perspective fundamentally misperceives the proper role that the concept of political equality plays in democratic theory. Moreover, its application could actually undermine the values sought to be fostered by the guarantee of free expression.

THE EQUALITY PERSPECTIVE

The concern motivating the equality perspective is the fear that, due to disparities in citizens' abilities to communicate their messages, those private individuals and entities who possess greater expressive power will have an undue advantage over those who lack similar power. Because one can reasonably assume that such disparities in expressive power invariably derive from disparities in economic power, these inequalities could presumably be solved by imposing a system of fundamental economic redistribution.[78] A less sweeping means to alter such inequalities in communicative power, however, would be to redistribute only expressive resources, by the creation of a private right of access to preexisting privately owned sources of communication, such as broadcast stations, cable outlets, the print media, or corporate advertising.

Because the sole focus of this rationale is on equality concerns, however, presumably its goal could be attained as easily by *reducing* the expressive capacities of the speakers who possess greater expressive power as by *expanding* the expressive capabilities of those possessing less expressive power. Proposals to limit campaign expenditures represent an attempt to produce political equality by reducing the permissible scope of expression to something approaching the lowest common denominator among competing candidates. Commentators who advocate creating a right of access solely in order to bring about expressive equality would logically be just as satisfied by suppression of the speech of the powerful as by an increase in the expressive opportunities of the unempowered.[79] They rationalize such suppression on the basis of the wholly unsupported and counterintuitive theory that, by utilizing their expressive resources, the powerful "drown out" the existing speech of the less powerful. This argument assumes—without empirical support—either that there exists some sort of universal physical scarcity of opportunities for expression, or that listeners have only a limited attention span that would somehow automatically be consumed only by the speech of the powerful. Such a transparently ideologically based analysis must be readily dismissed by anyone who believes in the necessity of ideological neutrality in the shaping of free speech protection.[80]

Reliance on the equality perspective is not as easily dismissed when the issue concerns the extension of expressive opportunities to the powerless, rather than suppression of the speech of the powerful. Even in this context, however, the equality perspective misperceives the proper scope of the concept of political equality. That concept demands governmental neutrality in the restriction of private expression. As previously explained, under the principle of epistemological humility, which lies at the heart of the systems of democracy and free expression,[81] all ideas are allowed to compete freely for adherence. Any departure from such neutrality would inescapably undermine the essential democratic premise of societal self-determination and render the scope of protected expression nothing more than the subject of a political power struggle.[82]

The concept of political equality does not mean, however, that every speaker must enter public debate with equal means of contributing to that debate. Not only would it be impossible to structure an expressive system in which all views are equally represented, or in which all speakers possess equal means of communication, any such attempt would also prove harmful to the interests of free expression by leading to a reduction to the lowest common denominator of expressive power. This is because ultimately, economic equality among speakers can be attained only by suppressing the speech of the economically powerful. The myopic pursuit of economic equality among speakers would inescapably undermine the goals sought to be fostered by the guarantee of free expression—namely, the facilitation of the self-governing function through the provision of information and opinion.[83]

Finally, expressive redistribution imposed out of concern for economic equality could lead to the indirect adoption of a substantive philosophy favoring the values associated with economic redistribution. Thus, much like the theory of hybrid redistribution, this approach would improperly superimpose on the substantively value-neutral system of free expression a preordained, externally derived substantive value structure.

The fact that a right of expressive access cannot properly be grounded in the equality perspective, however, does not necessarily mean that recognition of such a right is inconsistent with the First Amendment right of free expression. It means merely that recognition of such a right cannot be justified by a misguided appeal to a concept of equality that is measured without regard to its impact on other free speech concerns. To determine whether a right of expressive access may be grounded in justifications other than equality, it is necessary to examine the reasoning underlying the enrichment perspective.

THE ENRICHMENT PERSPECTIVE

Unlike the equality perspective, which focuses exclusively on a comparative assessment of speaker power measured in a vacuum, the enrichment perspective focuses on the need to expand the diversity and the sum total of available expressive activity. Thus, unlike its equality counterpart, the enrichment perspective could not possibly be satisfied by governmental imposition of an equality of silence among competitive speakers. Such suppression would inevitably undermine the goals sought to be attained by the protection of free expression, because it would reduce the sum total of information and opinion available to the populace and thereby significantly impoverish public debate.

The enrichment perspective posits that whatever ultimate value or values one believes the system of free expression was designed to foster, those values would be furthered by an increase in the opportunity of private speakers to communicate their views effectively. For example, if one accepts the facilitation of the self-governing process as either the primary or exclusive goal of free speech protection, much as Owen Fiss[84] and Alexander Meiklejohn have,[85] one can quite easily conclude that the more individuals who have expressive opportunities to reach the public at large, the stronger the basis the electorate will have on which to make self-governing decisions.[86]

In contrast, Stephen Gardbaum argues that a right of access is justified, not out of concern for the development of society as a whole but rather because the self-realization of the individual members of the society will be facilitated by an expansion of the dissemination of information and opinion available to them.[87] He asserts that while autonomy of the individual represents a fundamental value, it is important to recognize that protection of such autonomy solely against governmental incursion will often prove inadequate, because privately imposed constraints on individual autonomy can be equally harmful. Thus, government may be called upon to affirmatively intervene in order to remove such constraints.[88]

The reasoning underlying the enrichment rationale in support of a right of expressive access proceeds as follows. At least since the communications explosion at the beginning of the twentieth century, the idea that providing individuals with the freedom to speak will enable them to make meaningful contributions to public debate has been rendered largely unrealistic. An individual's right to speak on a street corner simply cannot match the power to communicate instantaneously to large population concentrations.[89] Thus, the only means to provide speakers with an effective opportunity to reach the populace is to open the privately owned institutional centers of communicative power to those who would otherwise lack the means to have their views widely disseminated. Absent such access, the argument proceeds, the scope and substance of public debate will remain truncated and the democratic process will suffer.[90] Ever since the scholarly inception of the right-of-access theory in the late 1960s, its proponents have contended that "if ever there was a self-operating marketplace of ideas, it has long ceased to exist. The mass media's development of an antipathy to ideas requires legal intervention if novel and unpopular views are to be assured a forum."[91]

Under this view of modern communicative realities,[92] governmental protection of an individual's right to speak cannot alone accomplish all of the goals sought to be achieved by the free speech guarantee. This problem, commentators have argued, has been exacerbated by the significant concentration of media ownership in the hands of relatively few,[93] combined with the apparent efforts by those in charge of the media—at least in certain instances—to exclude or severely restrict the expression of unpopular views on controversial issues.

The impact of a right of expressive access on the scope of public debate, however, is open to question. The view that redistribution of expressive resources will, in fact, enrich public debate necessarily relies on two key assumptions: first, that an insufficient diversity of opinion exists among those who currently control or have access to the means of nationwide communications; and second, that those provided with such access will, in fact, provide information or opinions that would otherwise not receive widespread distribution.[94] The empirical basis for both assumptions is uncertain at best.

No one could realistically deny that, at least under certain circumstances, the former assumption is accurate. For example, political scientist Benjamin Page has documented the all-but-total uniformity among the media on the wisdom of the Persian Gulf War in 1991, as well as the almost total exclusion of anti-war opinion and information detrimental to the pro-war position.[95] Existence of some form of right of expressive access might well have resulted in an increase in the diversity of relevant opinion and information available to the public and therefore in an enrichment in the scope and nature of public debate on the issue of the war's wisdom and morality. It is by no means empirically established, however, that a similar lack of diversity plagues other issues of public concern that are not so consumed by public emotion. It is quite conceivable that on most issues, an empirical survey of the national media would already produce a fairly wide spectrum of opinion. At the very least, it appears that advocates of the enrichment rationale have produced no systematically prepared empirical evidence to the contrary. Thus, the empirical case for expressive redistribution remains largely speculative.

Indeed, if one were to rely—ironically, to be sure—on the reasoning of many of the very same scholars who have urged creation of a right of access on enrichment grounds in other contexts, one might seriously question whether creation of such a right would not substantially impoverish, rather than enrich, the scope of public debate. These commentators have argued that the speech of economically powerful interests should be curtailed, in part because of the limited attention span of the public, which is in danger of being overwhelmed by a flood of confusing and distracting communication.[96] But if this argument is accurate,[97] then there presumably exists a danger that allowing access to those who may make rambling or unreasonable statements or arguments would result in exactly the same type of confusion. One may wonder, then, whether we can be sure, ex ante, that creation of a right of expressive access would actually enrich, rather than impoverish, the substance of public debate.

In any event, viewed in light of the enrichment perspective, the benefits of such expressive extension are uncertain, because it would be difficult to guarantee that those who would benefit from a right of access will have views, opinions, or information that have not already been widely disseminated to the public. In most cases, the creation of a right of expressive access actually functions as a form of redistribution, by taking away a certain portion of expressive opportunity from the operator of the expressive resource. In these cases, every time the right of access is exercised just as much expression will be lost as gained. In order to accept the enrichment rationale, then, one would have to assume that the replacing expression is more likely to enrich debate than the replaced expression would have. While this may often be the case, it is surely difficult to guarantee such a result.

Arguably illustrative of this danger are the so-called "must-carry" provisions of the Cable Television Consumer Protection and Competition Act of 1992.[98] These provisions require cable television systems of various sizes to set aside a certain percentage of their cable channels for commercial broadcast stations that request carriage.[99] The Supreme Court upheld these provisions against First Amendment attack by the cable industry,[100] and jurists and commentators have applauded the statutory provision as a form of right of access that enriches public debate.[101]

Yet one may reasonably question whether the result of the must-carry provisions was actually to enrich, rather than to impoverish, public debate. If one assumes a limited number of available cable channels—probably no longer a technologically realistic assumption, but one that may well have been accurate at the time of the provisions' enactment[102]—then for every broadcast station a cable operator is required to carry, the cable operator would have to exclude a cable station that it would otherwise have included.

Is it necessarily the case that the scope and substance of public debate will be enriched more by the expression of the broadcast outlet than by an excluded cable channel? Surely, no one could reasonably guarantee such an empirical result, and in fact such a conclusion may actually be counterintuitive. Broadcast outlets traditionally have often been bland and uncontroversial in the substance of their expression. Indeed, local broadcast affiliates of the major networks are, for the most part, conveying much the same mental pablum that those powerful networks have long conveyed to the public. It hardly seems likely that providing these affiliates a right of access to cable programming will enrich public debate;

much more likely is that it will do little more than enrich executives of the networks and their affiliates, while simultaneously restricting the expressive options open to the cable operator.

In contrast, many of the excluded cable stations would probably have provided significantly new and different perspectives and emphases, rarely heard otherwise. Indeed, given the triage decision that the must-carry provisions may force on cable operators, it is likely that any cable stations discarded as a result of those provisions were those with the smallest level of mass market appeal. It is surely not unreasonable to presume that these stations were likely to be those that have a limited appeal for the very reason that they are controversial or unique. Thus, until cable technology expanded to include a virtually unlimited number of available channels (and Congress does not appear to have assumed such a situation when it enacted the must-carry provisions), ironically the impact of these provisions was likely to have been the very opposite of that assumed by the provisions' many advocates.

Another context in which creation of a right of access would just as likely impoverish as enrich public debate is a forced-right-of-reply statute.[103] On the surface, of course, creation of a right of reply would appear to enrich public debate by providing those criticized by the print media an opportunity to communicate an alternative perspective to the populace. However, the legal requirement that the print media provide an opportunity for reply to those whom it has criticized or defamed could just as easily lead to an impoverishment of public debate by chilling the print media from making controversial statements about individuals in the first place.[104]

Despite the speculative impact of access rights on the scope of public debate, one might nevertheless consider its use in the hope that it would, in fact, further the goals of the system of free expression and the democratic process. But creation of a right of expressive access threatens important First Amendment interests. Indeed, viewing free speech theory from the perspective of redistributive theory reveals significant dangers to expressive values created by adoption of a system of expressive redistribution. The next section describes and explains those dangers.

Expressive Access as Redistribution: The Ominous Implications

As the previous section demonstrated, the only even arguably legitimate characterization of the right of access is as an enrichment-based form of democratic process redistribution.[105] Viewed from this perspective, the right of access would have as its goals the facilitation of both the democratic process and individual listener autonomy, by providing the public with a greater diversity and breadth of public debate.[106] It would accomplish these goals by supposedly providing an opportunity to those who would express information and opinion not likely to have been otherwise widely disseminated, thereby enriching public debate and making the electorate more informed and thoughtful.

As the previous section also demonstrated, however, whether such beneficial impact on either public debate or the democratic process would actually result from creation of a right of access is generally speculative. Rather, the insight that the right of access is for the most part an application of redistributive theory casts doubt on the assumption—so readily engaged in by proponents of access rights—that the provision of a right of access will likely enrich public debate. Application of this insight casts further doubt on the constitutional validity of an expressive access right, by highlighting serious harms to the interests of free expression to which creation of such a right may give rise.

The Right of Expressive Access as Political Strategy: Epistemological Humility and the Twilight Zone of Redistributive Theory

I have already described the difficulty of drawing clear conceptual distinctions between process-based democratic redistribution and substantive redistributive theory. I have also described the concept of hybrid redistributive theory, which views process-based redistribution merely as a strategic means to attain a political end—namely, substantive economic redistribution.[107] Although not all commentators who have urged the creation of a right of access appear to advocate a seemingly process-based expressive redistribution as little more than a procedural means to achieve the substantive end of economic justice,[108] some prominent theorists who advocate a right of access arguably can be described as proponents of a hybrid redistributive model.

One example is Cass Sunstein, who has advocated what he calls a "New Deal" for free expression in which private expressive power would be redistributed in much the same way that the New Deal dictated a redistribution of economic resources.[109] It is interesting to note that on other occasions he has argued that, pursuant to the principle of "universalism," there exist "substantively right answers" to basic issues of moral and political choice facing the polity.[110] On still other occasions, he has urged that free speech protection for pornographic expression be shaped in light of a set of predetermined substantive moral positions concerning acceptable treatment of women.[111] Thus, it is conceivable that Sunstein's process-based analysis of the right of access spills over into predetermined substantive considerations of economic justice.

Similarly, Owen Fiss advocates various forms of expressive redistribution, at least in part[112] because, absent such redistribution, those with economic power will continue to control—and thereby effectively exclude issues of redistributive justice from—the political agenda.[113] In making this argument, Fiss relies on the insights of economist Charles Lindblom, who fashioned what he described as "the circularity principle" previously discussed in Chapter 3: Those who possess political power will keep from the political agenda issues concerning the morality of their very possession of that power. Lindblom concludes that because of the principle of circularity, powerful corporate interests have been able to prevent meaningful political consideration of the moral and social need for the widespread redistribution of economic resources.[114]

In order to circumvent the problem created by the principle of circularity, Fiss argues both that the expression of economically powerful interests be strictly limited and that their expressive power be partially redistributed to those who currently lack access to expressive sources.[115] To the extent that Fiss's support for expressive redistribution can properly be characterized as an attempt to avoid the political implications of the circularity principle, his rationale would appear to blend process-based and substantive redistributive considerations, much in the manner of hybrid redistributive theory.[116]

Reliance on such hybrid redistributive considerations in an expressive context breaches the fundamental wall of epistemological humility that separates process-based from normative factors in shaping the structure of free speech.[117] When those currently in power are able to shape controlling precepts of free speech protection selectively on the basis of their own preordained moral value structure, they breach this principle of epistemological humility, and thereby skew the operation of the democratic process.[118] As previously noted, it is this reasoning that underlies the Supreme Court's unwavering constitutional condemnation of all viewpoint-based regulations of expressive activity.[119]

In viewing the debate over the right of expressive access through the lens of redistributive theory, one can thus discern an ominous substantive moral gloss on the arguable process-based rationale for such expressive redistribution.[120] When viewed from the perspective of traditional First Amendment analysis, this application of hybrid redistributive theory must be rejected.

"We're from the Government and We're Here to Help You": Expressive Redistribution and the Danger of Governmental Intervention

When one describes the right of expressive access in the abstract, it appears to have only positive effects: Individuals who are otherwise unable to disseminate their views widely are given the opportunity to do so. As a result, public debate is enriched and both individual growth and the operation of the democratic process are facilitated. Indeed, advocates of the right of access have, for the most part, described the right exclusively in such positive terms; harms to the system of free expression that may result are either ignored[121] or summarily dismissed.[122] But when one fully comprehends the redistributive nature of the right of expressive access, one will also recognize that in implementing this right government must establish some workable standard by which such redistributive decisions are to be made. To the extent that those standards turn on substantive considerations both established and interpreted by government officials, there will inevitably arise a serious danger of improper governmental manipulation of the private expressive marketplace.

Sunstein and Fiss have summarily dismissed concern over governmental intervention into the world of private expression. Both believe that, just as government over the last half of the twentieth century did much to improve the balance of distributive justice in the economic realm,[123] so, too, should it be trusted to intervene in the private expressive marketplace.[124] Such an argument, however, makes significant normative assumptions about the moral validity of economic redistribution, thus further underscoring the troubling mixture of substantive and process-based considerations underlying the rationale for the right of expressive access.

Moreover, the eagerness with which access advocates view the possibility of governmental intervention into the expressive marketplace appears to contradict the heavy skepticism with which public choice theorists have viewed the operation of the modern legislative process. These theorists see the modern legislative process as nothing more than the mechanistic sale of legislative goods to the highest bidding private interest group.[125] Indeed, Sunstein himself has, in other contexts, expressed a similar degree of mistrust of the motivations underlying the legislative process.[126] Given Sunstein's own skeptical view of legislative motivation, his equanimity—indeed, enthusiasm—in the face of direct legislative interference with private expressive interchange is mystifying. For if legislative actions are truly motivated solely by the desire to further certain private interests at the expense of others, the danger of legislative intervention into the expressive sphere should be obvious.

While public choice theory's extreme characterization of the legislative process appears to have little empirical support,[127] it would surely be naive to doubt the significant impact of interest groups and other questionable influences on the legislative process. Although legislatures will generally characterize their actions in public interest terms, in reality their motives often focus more on advancement of one interest group at the expense of competing groups.[128]

There is no reason to believe that such cynical considerations will motivate legislative choices in shaping the scope of a right of expressive access any less than they have been widely assumed to do in the allocation of other private legislative goods. Indeed, the must-carry provisions imposed by Congress on the cable industry,[129] which have been applauded by access proponents such as Sunstein,[130] may well constitute just such a cynical sale of legislative goods to one competitor at the expense of another. While access advocates glorify the provisions as an effort by Congress to enrich public debate,[131] as previously explained it is questionable whether their impact actually enriches rather than impoverishes such debate.[132] More importantly, though no one can be certain, the must-carry provisions could give rise to all of the concerns about the danger of private interest group influence on the legislative process universally feared by scholars of public choice theory. The immediate impact of the law, after all, was simultaneously to inhibit the growth of one communications provider while benefiting another. Viewed from a public choice perspective, then, the must-carry provisions arguably do little more than burden one competitor (the cable industry) in order to promote the interests of another competitor (the broadcast industry).

Wholly apart from the insights of public choice theory, the nation's long and well-documented history of speech suppression renders folly the naive acceptance of governmental motivations at face value in the regulation of expression. One need only recall the Alien and Sedition

Acts,[133] the suppression of anti-war speech during World War I,[134] the Communist scares of the 1920s and 1950s,[135] and congressional prohibition of draft-card burning for the thinly veiled purpose of suppressing dissent[136] to realize that the history of governmental intervention into the expressive marketplace is largely one of openly avowed or thinly disguised suppression. It is therefore difficult to understand how one can view the prospect of significant governmental tinkering with the expressive balance with such enthusiasm. For the First Amendment to perform its function effectively, those who enforce it must begin their constitutional analysis with a healthy skepticism of the government's motives.[137] Such skepticism is missing, however, in the writings of the scholars who advocate creation of a right of access.

Of course, if government were to establish a right of access on the basis of completely value-neutral considerations, arguably the danger of improper governmental motivation and veiled manipulation of expression would be significantly reduced. Whether such totally value-neutral grounds for invocation of the right of access are realistically available, however, is dubious.

When government creates a right of access, some standard or point of reference must be adopted by which it can determine exactly who is to benefit from such a right. If government were to impose a first-come-first-served standard for invocation of a right of access, or alternatively chose by lot who would receive access, then possibly the danger of disguised suppression could be avoided. But use of such standards would, in most contexts, be extremely unhelpful. In most instances it is unlikely that government would, as a practical matter, find that such value-neutral criteria provided a satisfactory basis on which to determine invocation of a right of access.

It does not necessarily follow, of course, that the criteria ultimately selected will be overtly viewpoint-based. Instead, the standards chosen by government may focus on such twilight zone–type distinctions as the right of reply[138] or fairness considerations.[139] Alternatively, the standards may focus on more categorical distinctions, such as the one drawn by the must-carry provisions between broadcast outlets and cable operators. However, whether such criteria are appropriately characterized as value-neutral is by no means clear. Right of reply, for example, could easily serve as a means by which government may harass the press, even though government does not, ex ante, pick and choose among the viewpoints to be granted access. Similarly, the considerations of fairness implicated by the Federal Communications Commission's fairness doctrine[140] are so vague and manipulable that they easily could be employed as a covert means of suppression, insulated from effective judicial review. Presumably this will not always be the case. But anyone who believes that government is unlikely to employ such vague criteria selectively for improper purposes ignores the long tradition of suppression that marks prior governmental involvement in the world of private expression.[141]

While government's use of broadly framed standards will not automatically signal the existence of a surreptitious motivation of suppression, it is doubtful that the judicial review process will be able effectively to separate the improperly motivated instances from legitimate legislative categorizing efforts. The Court's complete failure—or, perhaps, refusal—to see through Congress's thinly veiled effort to suppress anti-war dissent by criminalizing draft card burning[142] certainly does not augur well for the effectiveness of the judicial process in ferreting out indirect or furtive legislative attempts to suppress or intimidate. The Court has made clear, rightly or wrongly, that it does not consider itself in a position to question possible hidden motivations underlying what on its face appears to be content-neutral governmental action.[143]

Even if the judiciary were aggressively to seek out such ulterior legislative or regulatory motivations, it would be dangerous to assume that the courts would be successful in each case. Usually, the criteria employed will be sufficiently vague that, absent some unlikely evidentiary smoking gun, it would be all but impossible practically to distinguish valid attempts to apply the generalized legislative standard from secretive motivations of suppression.[144] Legislative creation of a variety of access rights thus provides government with new tools by which to harass or punish selected private speakers, and to do so without the realistic possibility of effective judicial review.

Expressive Redistribution as Expressive Burden: Drawing an Analogy to the Compelled Speech Cases

Overview

When the right of expressive access is placed within the broader framework of redistributive theory, one can see that the right is actually a two-edged sword: When one party is benefited, another is burdened. Although the benefits to the democratic process that derive from such expressive redistribution are speculative,[145] the harms it would cause to the values sought to be fostered by the free expression guarantee are relatively clear.

In order to understand the nature of these harms, it is helpful to contrast them to the evils caused by a related form of governmental intervention into the world of private expression: governmentally compelled speech. This concept includes situations in which the government has required private individuals or entities—under penalty of criminal or civil punishment—to express a substantive message prescribed by the government.

The Supreme Court has long held that most forms of governmentally compelled expression violate the First Amendment.[146] However, the Court has provided little in the way of a theoretical rationale for such a conclusion. Moreover, at least as a prima facie matter one might reasonably question the extent to which compelled speech violates the right of free expression, because such compulsion does not itself automatically restrict the ability of the speaker to say what she wishes to say. Yet closer analysis reveals a number of important ways in which governmentally compelled speech undermines significant free speech values.

Though the two forms of expressive intervention by government are not identical,[147] compelled speech and compelled access are nevertheless similar in important ways.[148] Thus, once one comprehends the theoretical nature of the expressive harm caused by governmentally compelled speech, one will be in a better position to understand the nature of the First Amendment harm caused by creation of a right of access.

The Harms of Compelled Expression

Compelled speech undermines the interests fostered by protection of free expression by giving rise to four distinct but related harms: confusion, dilution, humiliation, and cognitive dissonance. To elaborate, compelled speech harms the interests of free expression by (1) confusing the populace as to the actual strength and popularity of substantive positions advocated by the government; (2) diluting the force of the speaker's persuasiveness in the eyes of his listeners; (3) publicly humiliating the speaker, thereby possibly demoralizing him and undermining his resolve to maintain his own positions; and (4) risking the harm of cognitive dissonance, a psychological process whereby an individual who has been forced to express a view contrary to her own eventually rationalizes her actions by subconsciously adopting the positions she has been forced to express.[149] Each of these harms undermines the collective's performance of its self-governing function, disrupts the individual's ability to persuade the collective, or interferes with the autonomy of the individual's mental processes. Each therefore breaches the wall between government and the mentally autonomous private individual—a central tenet of any democratic system of government.

To illustrate these dangers, consider the following two hypotheticals. First, imagine Martin Luther King, Jr., prior to conducting a civil rights march in Alabama, being required to express a governmentally authored defense of the morality of segregation. Second, imagine the federal government requiring the leaders of the anti-war movement in the 1960s, prior to every anti-war rally at which they appear, to articulate the government's position in support of the war. In both instances, we can readily assume that the speakers were in no way restricted in what they were allowed to say after proclaiming the government-authored positions, and that they were permitted to make clear to their audiences that they had been required to make these statements by the government. The harms to the interests of the democratic process are nevertheless evident.

First, there is a serious risk that, despite the opening disclaimers, the audience members would be confused over the actual positions held by the speakers. Second, even if the audience members were not confused as to the speaker's actual views, surely there would exist the serious risk that the impact of the speaker's utterance of her own views would be diluted as a result of the publicly degrading experience of having to mouth a position that she finds abhorrent. Third, while perhaps such dedicated and intelligent activists as Dr. King and the anti-war leaders of the 1960s would not suffer the personal demoralization or cognitive dissonance usually caused by governmentally compelled speech, undoubtedly many other speakers would. If government is allowed to disrupt the democratic processes by which private individuals either seek to shape public opinion or make their own personal choices in such a manner, the fact that as a technical matter individuals remain "free" to say whatever they wish provides only hollow protection to the values of free expression.

That compelled speech is inimical to the interests of democracy and free expression can be demonstrated by noting that such speech has traditionally played a vital role as a tool for totalitarian regimes first to obtain and then to maintain public compliance. In its attempt to solidify its power, the totalitarian state seeks to destroy its citizens' mental autonomy and personal identity. In its place, the state seeks to create a completely integrated population of like-thinking citizens. Totalitarian states are distinguished from earlier autocratic regimes in their goal of complete subjugation of individual personality.[150] These states create atomized individuals who have intentionally been linked emotionally to the state.[151] This atomization of the individual is created through a disruption of effective communication among individuals, which, in turn, leads to a breakdown in the social relations among the citizens.[152] In order to preempt potentially disruptive exercises of individual will, a totalitarian system must destroy the mental integrity of the individual citizens, so that they can be transformed into nothing more than mindless sub-units of the state.

By disseminating propaganda and creating an educational training system, the totalitarian state seeks to mold its citizens into an integrated population of unthinking automatons. The success of totalitarian propaganda lies in its constant repetition.[153] As the same phrases are repeated over and over again, even citizens opposed to the regime will often succumb to the state's message. "A general pattern of thought, almost a style of thinking, proves increasingly irresistible as the regime continues in power."[154] For example, interviewers of former Soviet citizens have noticed that these citizens, even if they had been determined opponents of the Soviet regime, nevertheless tended to employ words laden with "propaganda-derived value judgments."[155]

Under a totalitarian regime, the educational system functions as a long-range arm of the state propaganda machine. In the schoolrooms, students learn by rote rituals and propagandistic formulas. For example, students in fascist Italy would time and again sing the theme song of Mussolini's regime: "The School is life, and Italian life is enthusiasm of faith and Fascist discipline."[156] Such forced repetition of predetermined political messages destroys the mental autonomy of the individual citizen, thereby facilitating the citizen's ultimate mental subjugation to the state's will. Thus, the totalitarian state seeks to create a type of *tabula rasa* in its citizens, and then seeks to fill the void with the pervasive, all-consuming reach of its ideological message.

In a totalitarian regime, then, forced speech can serve as an essential tool employed by the government in its strategic effort to destroy the individual's mental autonomy. Destruction of individual mental autonomy is exactly the result that a totalitarian state must achieve in order to effect and solidify its power. This is because autonomy of the mind is anathema to the totalitarian state. With its monopoly on mass communications, the state seeks to coopt the process of public debate for its own purposes. There can only be one perspective in the totalitarian state. There is no ongoing dialectic, just the incessant dissemination of the state's propaganda. Forced speech can readily serve as the mechanism by which the state makes its propaganda ubiquitous, completely preempting all other perspectives.

This description of totalitarian strategy is not intended to suggest that a democratic government's resort to methods of compelled speech automatically transforms that government into a totalitarian state. The totalitarian model is utilized, rather, purely as an analogous analytical construct, from which one can derive the true harms to democratic values caused by compelled speech. Using this perspective, one reasonably can conclude that the fact that totalitarian societies, quite understandably, find both that it is necessary to destroy the mental integrity of their citizens and that compelled speech may prove an effective strategy in achieving that end demonstrates the harms to democratic values caused by government's use of compelled speech.

CONTRASTING COMPELLED EXPRESSION WITH EXPRESSIVE REDISTRIBUTION

Four possible arguments could be advanced to attempt to show that expressive redistribution does not pose the same threats to free speech as compelled speech. First, one might argue that the dangers of humiliation, personal degradation, and cognitive dissonance are substantially reduced when the speaker is merely required to provide a platform for another to speak, rather than to mouth the words of others. Second, one could argue that as a practical matter, if not a legal one, the only speakers who will be required to provide a forum for the expression of others as a result of the creation of a right of access will be large corporate interests, who are in any event incapable of exercising the type of personal autonomy that is traditionally exercised by individuals and that is threatened by the personal degradation and cognitive dissonance associated with compelled speech. Third, one could reasonably suggest that the primary danger of compelled speech derives from the intentional promotion of the particular substantive viewpoint, adopted by those in power, and that the neutral creation of a right of access does not have the same effect.

Finally, one could argue that the primary distinction between the two forms of expressive regulation is that the right of access has the intended beneficial effect of substantially furthering important First Amendment values. Compelled speech, on the other hand, has an exclusively negative impact on the interests of free expression. This difference could be thought to alter the free speech cost–benefit analysis sufficiently to justify simultaneous acceptance of a right of access and rejection of compelled speech. Indeed, Fiss has argued that the significant enrichment of public debate to which the right of access gives rise more than counterbalances whatever interference with personal autonomy its recognition might cause.[157]

Although neither the burdens nor the benefits of the right of access are identical to those of compelled speech, many of the significant threats to the values of free expression to which compelled speech gives rise are abundantly present in the right-of-access context as well. Moreover, while creation of a right of access, at least in theory, might significantly benefit the interests of free expression,[158] ultimately the substantial dangers that such a right would cause render the cure considerably worse than the disease it is attempting to eradicate. In any event, both technological developments and alternative governmental strategies could produce many of the expressive benefits brought about by the right of access without many of its risks.[159]

HUMILIATION, COGNITIVE DISSONANCE, AND EXPRESSIVE REDISTRIBUTION

Differences between compelled speech and forced private access do exist, but whether those differences actually rise to a constitutional level is subject to doubt. When one is forced to provide a forum for the expression of views that differ from one's own, the risks of personal demoralization and public humiliation are considerable. To return to earlier hypotheticals,[160] imagine a requirement that at every civil rights march, Martin Luther King, Jr., were required to provide a forum for the expression of segregationist views, or that prior to every rally anti-war activists are required to provide a platform for the American Legion or Veterans of Foreign Wars to lecture about the advisability and morality of war. One can hypothesize countless additional illustrations—for example, the *Jewish News* being required to print a column by the head of the American Nazi Party, or a newspaper published primarily by and for African Americans being required to print a column by the Grand Dragon of the Ku Klux Klan.

The publicly humiliating and personally degrading effects may be even greater when private individuals are called upon to mouth words and thoughts they find abhorrent. But that fact does nothing to minimize the substantial expressive harm that is likely caused by forced private access.[161] The very act of providing a platform for the public expression of views one despises or even simply rejects, and doing so solely because of governmental compulsion, can have serious humiliating and demoralizing effects. For example, the publishers of the *Jewish News* will suffer public humiliation and personal demoralization, whether they are forced to print that the holocaust never happened or merely forced to provide space to private individuals to write that the holocaust never happened.

Moreover, to the extent that compelled speech threatens to bring about cognitive dissonance, being required to provide a platform for the expression of a particular viewpoint gives rise to a similar danger. In both cases, a private party is required to facilitate the expression of a viewpoint he finds abhorrent and would not otherwise facilitate in any way.

Of course, it could be argued that the threats of cognitive dissonance, public humiliation, and personal demoralization are minimal when the operator of the expressive resource is a large media outlet. But the individuals or interests who operate large media companies are no less likely than smaller operators to have clearly defined political, moral, or social views.[162] In any event, it is by no means clear that the right of access can reasonably be confined to such media behemoths. Many operators of printed publications and even many broadcast licensees are of considerably smaller stature. Where a smaller media operator is constantly forced to provide a forum for the expression of views it would not otherwise have chosen to express, the danger of cognitive dissonance appears as great as when such media operators are required to convey governmentally prescribed substantive positions.

EXPRESSIVE REDISTRIBUTION AND CORPORATE SPEECH

No more persuasive is the contention that recognition of a right of access would fail to undermine free speech interests because virtually all of the speakers to be negatively affected are corporate entities. Such entities, the arguments proceeds, are incapable of personal development through the exercise of expression and are therefore undeserving of First Amendment rights in the first place. Several scholars have argued that because they are nothing more than slavish, robotic profit maximizers, corporations are incapable of engaging in the type of voluntary expressive activity to which the First Amendment right of free expression is properly confined.[163] But as demonstrated elsewhere in these pages, this argument improperly ignores the significant expressive interests furthered by corporate speech.[164] Thus, if one rejects—as the analysis employed here does—the arguments for excluding corporate expression from the scope of the First Amendment in the first place, then this argument for distinguishing the right of access from compelled speech must also be rejected.[165]

In any event, the argument against protection of corporate speech ultimately proves too much, because if taken to its logical conclusion it would eventually lead to the complete exclusion of the corporate-run press from the scope of the First Amendment. One could, perhaps, somehow exempt the institutional press from the category of excluded corporate speech.[166] Since most operators of existing expressive resources would fit within the concept of "the press," one could perhaps rely on the argument that corporate speech should be excluded from the scope of First Amendment protection solely for the purpose of requiring nonpress private corporations to submit to a right of access. However, when limited in this manner, the right of access would have precious little effect as a means of providing meaningful expressive opportunities to those who otherwise could not reach the public, because it would have no impact on the institutional communications media, which naturally control a substantial segment of the nation's sources of expression.

COUNTERVAILING BENEFITS

Perhaps the most obvious distinction between directly compelled speech and creation of a right of access is that in the latter case, right-of-access proponents contend, there is a strong countervailing benefit— namely, the enrichment of public debate. In contrast, compelled speech generally fails to give rise to a similar benefit. Whatever contribution to public debate that could conceivably be made through compelled speech can usually be made as or more effectively through direct government speech.[167] Fiss, for example, has dismissed the harms that might result to the operator of the expressive resource as little more than an interference with personal autonomy, a harm he believes to be readily outbalanced by the substantial enrichment of public debate to which creation of a right of expressive excess would give rise.[168]

It is doubtful, however, that the expressive harms caused by creation of a right of access can be so summarily dismissed, for several reasons. First, as prior discussion has demonstrated,[169] the harms caused to the expressive resource operator by the right of access interfere with more than merely the unrestrained power of personal choice that only the most extreme libertarians find to be morally vested in the individual. Rather, the harm to which forced access gives rise extends to the autonomy of the mind of those speakers who are forced to provide a platform for those with whom they may disagree. Such interference results from the creation of public humiliation, personal demoralization, and cognitive dissonance, described previously.[170]

These externally imposed disruptions of intellectual autonomy may make it extremely difficult for the individual—or the individuals who have joined together in the associational enterprise that operates the expressive resource[171]—to exercise the mental autonomy that is both essential to the operation of a viable democracy and clearly protected by the First Amendment.[172]

Fiss apparently believes that whatever the cost of a right of access to personal autonomy, the benefit such a right provides to the collective's interest in enriching public debate and thereby facilitating the democratic process more than justify the imposition of such individualized harm. Fiss apparently chooses the communitarian value of collective self-determination over the individualist value of personal intellectual autonomy. In so doing, however, he neglects the reasons why a society chooses to employ a collective democratic process in the first place.[173] As a result, Fiss counterproductively undermines the very democratic process he believes the right of expressive access is designed to advance.

It is impossible to separate the value of the collective democratic process from the value of personal intellectual autonomy, for the simple reason that personal intellectual autonomy is widely recognized as central to the effective operation of democracy. Absent the existence of personal intellectual autonomy, the individual members of society cannot make truly free choices. Absent the individual citizens' ability to make such free choices, the concept of a democratic society is rendered incoherent. It is thus not surprising that democratic theorists have long recognized the vital intersection between personal mental autonomy and the maintenance of a viable democratic process.[174]

Moreover, as even certain modern civic republican theorists have recognized, it is highly questionable whether a democratic society in which government is authorized to disrupt autonomous individual mental processes could perform its self-governing function with any level of real effectiveness. For example, Frank Michelman has noted that if the exercise of collective self-will is to be effective, the mental processes of the individual members of society must not be allowed to atrophy.[175]

One might respond that even if all of these points are assumed to be true in the abstract, they do not alter the ultimate balance in favor of a right of access. One could concede the harms to personal intellectual autonomy caused by a right of access, the argument proceeds, but nevertheless conclude that on balance the democratic process would benefit more from the resulting enrichment of public debate than it would suffer from the resulting interference with personal autonomy. Such a conclusion should be rejected, however, on several grounds.

To this point, in attempting to choose between the harms and benefits of the right of access, my analysis has proceeded on the assumptions that (1) creation of a right of access would significantly enrich public debate, and (2) the expressive harms to which a right of access gives rise are solely to the interests in personal intellectual autonomy of those who are in some way involved in the operation of an expressive resource. Even under these assumptions, one should have relatively little trouble in concluding that the right of access cannot withstand First Amendment scrutiny. But it is also appropriate to question the accuracy of both assumptions.

I have already raised serious doubt concerning the truly "enriching" impact of a right of access on public debate. It is by no means clear that the expression of those provided access would be more likely to provide a diversity of views, opinions, and information than the expression it replaces. It also remains an open question whether, as a result of the creation of a right of access, the expressive resource operator will be chilled or demoralized into saying less than he would have absent creation of the right of access.[176]

Moreover, it is by no means clear that the harm to expressive interests caused by creation of a right of access would necessarily be limited to the negative impact on the personal intellectual autonomy of the speakers. As previously noted,[177] the harms caused by compelled speech may also include the dilution of the impact of a private message due to the public humiliation caused by the governmentally imposed requirement that the speaker either mouth a governmentally dictated message or provide a platform for the expression of views with which she strongly disagrees.[178] By imposing expressive burdens on speakers, then, government may artificially alter public perceptions of those speakers and their views. In addition, government may skew public debate through use of forced speech mechanisms, by confusing the public as to the actual views of the speaker who has been forced to provide access. Thus, creation of a right of access may just as likely impoverish public debate as enrich it, and just as likely undermine the democratic process as facilitate it.

Finally, a serious danger of abuse arises any time government is provided a weapon by which selectively to pressure, punish, or harass private speakers—especially those who are historically charged with the responsibility of checking government, as is the institutional press.[179] Complicating matters even further is the fact that such abuses will be extremely difficult to discern in the course of the judicial review process.[180]

Thus, one is left with a situation in which we are asked to allow government the constitutional power to create a right of access, despite the resulting interference with the personal intellectual autonomy of speakers, despite the risks to the viability and clarity of public debate, and despite the serious risks of undetectable governmental abuse to which it clearly gives rise. All of these harms are to be risked, in the name of an empirically unproven and largely speculative benefit to public debate. To the extent one judges the right of access purely from the process-based perspective of the First Amendment (rather than from the more strategic, substantively oriented goal of economic resource redistribution),[181] the conclusion that governmental creation of a right of access is unconstitutional appears a relatively easy one to reach.

Seeking a Compromise Solution: The Possibility of a Limited Right of Access

To this point, the chapter has examined the right of expressive access in a generic sense. Government, however, need not adopt a generalized, unfocused right of access. Indeed, when government has created a right of access in the past, the right has always been confined to specific circumstances, such as the FCC's fairness doctrine or the must-carry provisions imposed on cable operators. While in the abstract the right of access gives rise to prohibitive First Amendment difficulties, there also exists the possibility that its advocates are correct in their assumption that its creation would expand the diversity of available opinion and thereby enrich public debate.[182] Hence, it is worth inquiring whether a compromise solution may be fashioned in which the First Amendment dangers would be so significantly reduced that its beneficial impact on the scope of public debate would clearly outweigh its possible harms.

Although a number of limited forms of a right of access are conceivable, ultimately none presents a coherent basis for distinguishing among them on First Amendment grounds. This is because none effectively reduces the First Amendment threats posed by the right of access sufficiently to avoid the overwhelming constitutional harms to which creation of such a right gives rise. In this section, four possible bases on which to fashion a more limited right of access are considered: (1) The broadcast dichotomy, (2) the "expressive addition" dichotomy, (3) the "gatekeeper" dichotomy, and (4) the "ideological commitment" dichotomy. Each, for its own reasons, fails to provide a legitimate basis on which to ground a constitutionally valid form of access right.

The Broadcast Dichotomy

Best known of the conceivable limitations on the reach of the right of access is the supposed dichotomy between the broadcast and print media. The Supreme Court has effectively adopted such a dichotomy, initially upholding the FCC's imposition of the fairness doctrine's access obligations on broadcast licensees in *FCC v. Red Lion Broadcasting Co.*[183] and subsequently holding unconstitutional a state's imposition of a right-of-reply obligation on the print media in *Miami Herald Publishing Co. v. Tornillo.*[184] Puzzlingly, at the time of its decision in *Tornillo* the Court made absolutely no mention of the arguable inconsistency between the two decisions. Indeed, in *Tornillo*—the decision in which the Court invalidated the imposition of a right-of-reply obligation on the print media—the Court failed even to cite its earlier decision upholding the fairness doctrine.

Nevertheless, a number of possible grounds of distinction between the two contexts exist. First, unlike the print media, broadcasters are issued licenses by the government providing them the exclusive privilege to utilize a frequency on the governmentally owned airwaves. Because government need not grant to private individuals or entities the exclusive privilege to utilize national resources in the first place, the argument proceeds, it may logically take the lesser step of imposing conditions on the extension of the privilege to those private beneficiaries. This argument can be summarily rejected, however, because it completely ignores the sound constitutional limitations imposed on governmental power by the so-called "unconstitutional conditions" doctrine.[185] Pursuant to that doctrine, government may not condition the award of a privilege on the required waiver of the right of free expression.

That the logic of the privilege theory proves too much can be seen simply by positing a case in which government conditions the award of a broadcast license on the licensee's agreement not to criticize the government, or to play patriotic music and speeches twenty-four hours a day. If one accepts the logic of the greater-includes-the-lesser principle, then presumably the greater power not to grant the license would subsume the lesser power to condition the grant on any basis the government wishes. Such an obviously unacceptable result makes clear that if there is some basis on which validly to distinguish between the broadcast and print media, it must be something other than the fact that broadcasters may function only when granted a license by government.

Another possible basis of distinction is that the broadcast media, unlike the print media, are characterized by a scarcity of resources. Only a finite number of broadcast frequencies are available, and only one licensee may broadcast on each frequency. In contrast, according to this argument, there exists no finite limit on the number of possible participants in the print media. Thus, the argument concludes, government may properly require a broadcast licensee to provide access to the many who are physically unable to acquire a broadcast license.

While in dicta in more recent decisions the Supreme Court has expressly adopted this scarcity rationale to explain the distinctive treatment given to the broadcast industry,[186] even the Court itself has acknowledged the questionable technological support for this conclusion.[187] Whether an assumption of broadcast scarcity made any sense at the time the Court first drew a distinction between the broadcast and print media in the 1970s, it surely does not today. The wide availability of FM and UHF frequencies demonstrates that technical scarcity is not the reason that a broadcast license is denied. At the same time, the enormous practical difficulties that face an entrant into the print market create at least as great a practical barrier to the establishment of new publications as faced by would-be entrants into the broadcast market.

One scholar a number of years ago suggested that while no rational basis exists on which to distinguish the broadcast from the print media for purposes of the right of access, it is nevertheless appropriate to draw such a distinction for the simple reason that it makes practical sense to limit the reach of the right of access.[188] Under this reasoning, it would have been equally appropriate for the Court to have flip-flopped its holdings, by upholding imposition of the right of access on the print media but not the broadcast media.[189] Although one may sympathize with the yearning for some intermediate solution to the right-of-access problem, surely a solution so intellectually bankrupt as this must be rejected.

Many of the leading proponents of the right of access have understandably disdained the broadcast distinction. Instead, they believe that the right of access should apply, regardless of the medium of communications.[190] If one accepts the arguments that have been advanced in support of the right of access, the right's proponents are absolutely correct in believing that there would exist no legitimate basis on which to distinguish between the print and broadcast media.

The "Expressive Addition" Dichotomy

A possibly more legitimate basis on which to limit the right of access is the "expressive addition" dichotomy. On the basis of this distinguishing criterion, a right of access would be deemed constitutional when and only when the expression made available through creation of such a right would actually add to the sum total of available expression, rather than merely replace expression that would otherwise have been disseminated by the expressive resource operator. For example, under this standard the must-carry provisions would be constitutional if and only if, but for their obligation to carry the broadcast outlets, the cable operators would have had available unused channels.

This dichotomy might also apply to such situations as the attempt to distribute leaflets in the privately owned mall involved in *Pruneyard Shopping Center v. Robins*[191] or the attempt by gay groups to participate in the privately operated Boston St. Patrick's Day Parade in *Hurley v. Irish-American Gay, Lesbian & Bisexual Group*.[192] In both cases, the expression sought to be disseminated through provision of the right of access presumably would not replace expression that would otherwise have been disseminated by the expressive resource operator—the mall owner in *Pruneyard* or the parade organizers in *Hurley*. Rather, such expression would be added to whatever expressive activity the resource operator had planned.

The rationale for the expressive addition dichotomy is based on the assumption that the goal of the right of access is to increase the scope, extent, and diversity of the sum total of available expression. While proponents of the right of access automatically assume that the expression made available through the provision of access rights would add more diversity than the expression that it replaces, the empirical basis for this assumption may be subject to some doubt. At the very least it remains unproven.[193] If, however, one were to limit the right of access solely to situations in which one could be assured that the sum total of expression would be increased as a result of the right's creation, one would not need to deal with the empirical uncertainty raised by the replacement situation.

Of course, one cannot assume that an addition to the sum total of expression will necessarily augment the diversity of available information and opinion. But in the addition context one can at least be assured that one will not lose the benefits to public debate of whatever expression has been replaced by the newly disseminated expression, for the simple reason that there would be no expression replaced.

Nonetheless, centering the constitutional defense of the right of access exclusively on the expressive addition factor fails to solve many of the significant First Amendment problems to which the right of access gives rise. For example, in the *Hurley* context, providing forced access to gay rights groups would risk all of the personal demoralization and public humiliation to the private individual or entity required to provide that governmentally compelled speech always risks creating.[194] Additionally, the dangers that flow from vesting the government with the selective power to force access to privately owned communicative sources[195] remain, even when the right of access is confined to the expressive addition context. Thus, while the expressive addition dichotomy is both more coherent than the broadcast dichotomy and constitutionally preferable to an unlimited right of access, it is highly doubtful that it provides a constitutionally valid basis on which to confine the access right.

The Gatekeeper Dichotomy

A third possibility is the limitation of the right of access to situations in which the expressive resource operator is appropriately characterized as nothing more than a "gatekeeper" for the expression of others, rather than a speaker himself. In such contexts, one might reasonably believe that the harms of demoralization, humiliation, and cognitive dissonance often associated with directly compelled speech[196] are irrelevant when the expressive resource operator does nothing more than neutrally facilitate the expression of others.

Under the gatekeeper standard, it is arguable that cable operators could be constitutionally subjected to the must-carry provisions, because the cable operators do not themselves engage in expressive activities.[197] Even if one could properly distinguish so-called gatekeepers from pure speakers, however, many of the systemic harms caused by creation of a right of access—including the danger of surreptitious governmental skewing of public debate—would remain under this dichotomy.

More importantly, one may question whether it is possible to conceptualize a distinction, for First Amendment purposes, between gatekeepers and speakers. The very act of selecting which speakers will be heard is often inherently intertwined with the desire to convey a particular message. For example, when liberal Chicago radio talk show host Studs Terkel brings on to his show a series of guests who share his general political outlook, he is properly viewed as both a gatekeeper *and* a speaker. Thus, a governmentally imposed obligation to include politically conservative speakers would give rise to all of the First Amendment harms traditionally associated with compelled speech, even though such an obligation would technically interfere only with Terkel's gatekeeper function. The same description would quite probably apply to the parade organizers in *Hurley*.

Of course, a gatekeeper could conceivably have no substantive message to convey through the choice of speakers and instead be interested primarily or exclusively in maximizing profits. The goal of profit maximization, however, has never disqualified expression from the scope of the First Amendment.[198] Moreover, regardless of the gatekeeper's underlying motivation, free speech interests are inherently implicated by the conduct of the editorial selection process.[199] Thus, adoption of the gatekeeper dichotomy would not avoid the serious First Amendment problems to which the right of access gives rise.

The "Ideological Commitment" Dichotomy

A variation on the gatekeeper dichotomy can be called the "ideological commitment" dichotomy. This dichotomy avoids the conceptual difficulty caused by the attempt to distinguish between a gatekeeper and a speaker, since it assumes, if only for purposes of argument, that the expressive resource operator subjected to a right of access is always a speaker. Instead, the dichotomy turns solely on whether the speech of those granted a right of access would convey a substantive message that would be ideologically offensive to the expressive resource operator. Where the expression that the expressive resource operator is required to allow conveys an ideological message that operator finds offensive, the harms of public humiliation and personal demoralization and the danger of the artificial skewing of public debate are at their greatest.[200] Therefore, under the reasoning of the ideological commitment dichotomy, the constitutional prohibition on the right of access should be confined to these core departures from the values of free expression.

Ironically, accepting the ideological commitment dichotomy would logically lead to a reverse form of viewpoint regulation. Whereas the First Amendment has universally been construed to prohibit the government from regulating expression on the basis of the speaker's viewpoint,[201] the ideological commitment dichotomy effectively construes the First Amendment to protect an expressive resource operator only when the operator does, in fact, object to the viewpoint sought to be expressed through exercise of the right of access.

The ideological commitment dichotomy preserves the assumed enrichment resulting from creation of the right of access, at least to a limited extent, while avoiding the extremely troubling effects caused by forcing a private party to provide a platform for the expression of views it finds offensive. Under this dichotomy, presumably the *Jewish News* would not have to provide access to the local chapter of the American Nazi Party, nor would the African-American-oriented *Chicago Defender* newspaper have to allocate space to the Ku Klux Klan's Grand Dragon.[202] From the perspective of right-of-access advocates, the dichotomy would also have a comparative advantage in that it would presumably extend the right of access to many situations than beyond the extremely limited reach of the gatekeeper dichotomy.

It is highly doubtful, however, that the ideological commitment rationale provides a workable standard on which to fashion a limited right of access. First, one may reasonably wonder whether a reviewing court could realistically distinguish between those cases in which the expressive resource operator finds the expression in question substantively offensive and those in which it does not. Second, the rationale for adopting the right of access in the first place is the desire to enrich public debate by diversifying the information and opinion available to the public.[203] Thus, allowing the expressive resource operator to exercise an ideological veto over the views sought to be expressed through the right of access would not appear to provide the desired effect on the nature of public debate. Ultimately, then, none of the conceivable compromise solutions satisfactorily resolves the dilemma to which the right-of-access issue gives rise.

Enriching Public Debate: Seeking Less Invasive Alternatives

To this point, we have established three points: (1) The right of expressive access gives rise to significant First Amendment difficulties, both on individual and systemic levels; (2) while it is possible that creation of a right of expressive access would in certain instances have the desired impact of enriching public debate, such a result as a general matter is both empirically and intuitively speculative, and in any event would not justify the sweeping and pervasive threats it poses to the values of free expression;

and (3) no coherent, limited version of the right of access may be fashioned in a manner that avoids First Amendment difficulties.

It does not necessarily follow, however, that one must abandon all hope of enriching public debate by including the expression of those who normally lack communicative access to the public at large. A number of important technological developments have been made since right-of-access advocates first warned of the dangers of expressive scarcity caused by the concentration of media control in the hands of only a few, economically powerful interests.[204]

Chief among these technological developments is the rapid growth of the Internet. As one court has described it, "[t]he Internet is not a physical or tangible entity, but rather a giant network which interconnects innumerable smaller groups of linked computer networks."[205] It is "a decentralized, global medium of communication that links people, institutions, corporations and governments around the world," and that enables communications to take place "almost instantaneously." These communications can be directed either "to specific individuals, to a broader group of people interested in a particular subject, or to the world as a whole."[206] The Internet has been compared to a "highway, consisting of many streets leading to places where a user can find information."[207] Individuals may place a Web page on the Internet that may include messages, names, sounds, and pictures.[208] Any individual possessing a personal computer, a telephone modem, and the proper software may gain access to the Internet, allowing him to retrieve any of the many Web pages that have been created.

The ability to retrieve information and instantaneously to communicate with others through the Internet is truly staggering. A Web site "can be visited repeatedly by any number of users on a given day, making the information on a Web page even more accessible to a greater number of people than other forms of publication or advertisement."[209] In addition, Internet users may "participate in surveys, play games, or communicate with the host of a particular home page by e-mail."[210] Moreover, the number of individuals possessing access to the Internet has grown dramatically in recent years. "In 1981, fewer than 300 computers were linked to the Internet, and by 1989, the number stood at fewer than 90,000 computers. By 1993, over 1,000,000 computers were linked. [By 1996], over 9,400,000 computers [had] capability to access the Internet."[211] The Internet, then, could properly be described as the new marketplace of expression.

The implications of the Internet's rapid development for the function sought to be performed by an expressive access right should be obvious. The Internet provides private individuals with the opportunity to circumvent the institutional media as both a source of communicative power and as a method of information retrieval. Although an individual's power to reach the public through the Internet does not match that of a national television network, the power instantaneously to convey her message to a wide audience has grown significantly in recent years.

Even absent the Internet, one should have found that the speculative benefits of a right of expressive access were clearly outbalanced by the serious threats to both systemic and personal interests in free speech. But if one had qualms about reaching this conclusion before the Internet's development, surely the Internet's rapid growth acts as at least a partial safety valve for the need to enrich public debate, as well as the concern over undue concentration of information resources in the hands of a few.

The development of cable television has performed a similar safety valve function. Cable television reduces the concerns that underlie the creation of a right of expressive access on several levels. First, the development of such national cable giants as CNN has provided legitimate competition with and an alternative source of information to the traditional broadcast networks. Second, the substantial number of available cable channels has allowed the growth of numerous, highly specialized national cable networks that enable viewers across the nation to access an abundance of information and opinion about many narrow issues that was previously difficult to access. Third, the availability of local access channels substantially facilitates the ability of the so-called "common person" to reach potentially large audiences.

The development of cable may not have solved all of the conceivable problems of impoverished debate that some have thought dictate the need for a right of expressive access to institutionalized sources of communication. But it is not clear, ex ante, that creation of a right of access is more likely to lead to enrichment of public debate than to an increased impoverishment due either to personal chilling or improper governmental manipulation of the flow of public debate. Thus, it is essential that those who have drawn the constitutional calculus in favor of the right of expressive access add to their computation the continuing technological growth of communicative methods that provide significant opportunities for enrichment without governmental intrusion into private expressive interchange.

Conclusion

Determining the constitutionality of a governmentally created right of expressive access gives rise to a troubling dilemma: Such a right simultaneously appears to foster yet threaten the viability of the democratic process. As its proponents have argued, creation of a right of expressive access could perhaps expand the diversity of public debate, thereby bringing about a more thoughtful and better informed electorate.

Yet, when one recognizes that creation of a right of expressive access is actually a specialized application of a more generalized theory of economic redistribution, the assumed benefits of such a right become more speculative and the dangers it causes to the values of free expression become more clear. Viewing the right of access as the redistribution of resources underscores the fact that providing an expressive opportunity to one private party will usually lead to a corresponding reduction in expressive opportunity for another.

One might assume that such redistribution would naturally increase the diversity of views and information expressed, since the party operating the expressive resource would continue to have available the opportunity to communicate its views. But it is difficult to be assured, ex ante, that this will be the case. As the must-carry provisions arguably show, it is possible that it is the views of the party operating the expressive resource—or of the speakers to whom that party chooses to provide a forum—that have not previously received wide dissemination, and the views of the party seeking access which have in the past received far reaching distribution.

Moreover, the redistribution of expressive resources may well threaten both the systemic and individual values sought to be fostered by the right of free expression. To require the operator of an expressive resource to provide a forum for the expression of views it deems offensive may skew the flow of public debate, either by confusing the public as to the operator's actual views or diluting the impact of the operator's substantive message in the eyes of the listeners. Such a requirement may also give rise to the many threats to the individual's mental autonomy normally associated with governmentally compelled expression, including humiliation, demoralization, and cognitive dissonance.

While one might argue that such dangers are unrealistic when the speaker is a large corporate entity such as a broadcast licensee, a newspaper owner, or a large corporation, common experience proves this point to be incorrect. A private corporation is both organized and operated by human beings, and the corporation may well have a political or economic identity or ideology that those individuals have chosen to adopt in conjunction with the operation of the corporation. For example, those who run a religiously based broadcast outlet no doubt would be highly demoralized by the requirement that they provide a forum for advocates of free love or abortion, just as the publishers of the *Jewish News* would be both humiliated and demoralized by the requirement that they provide space to the head of the American Nazi Party. This is true, though in both cases the expressive resource operator is presumably a corporate entity. Perhaps not all expressive resource operators have such clearly held substantive views. But it would be extremely difficult to fashion a workable right of expressive access that could effectively pick and choose among such operators to avoid these difficulties.

Finally, accepting a right of expressive access would necessarily invite a dangerous governmental intrusion into the process of private expressive interchange. Although it would probably be unwise to accept the extreme negative perspective of many of the modern public choice theorists concerning the motivations of the legislative process, our nation's long and infamous history of governmental suppression of views with which it disagrees should at the very least give one considerable pause before one rushes to welcome such additional governmental involvement. The dangers of disguised governmental suppression become even greater when one recognizes the generally vague and flexible nature of the operational standards by which most forms of access rights will necessarily be implemented. Indeed, recognition of the conceptual difficulties incurred in attempting to separate the redistributive rationales grounded in the needs of the democratic process from those grounded in a particular substantive moral value structure underscores the danger that expressive redistribution will prove to be nothing more than a strategic means by which to implement particular moral and social redistributive goals of those in power. Such a strategic use of the right of expressive access would pervert the fundamental epistemological humility inherent in society's protection of free expression.

One need not, however, totally abandon the goal of enriching public debate merely because one is forced to conclude that creation of a right of access to private expressive resources violates the constitutional protection of free expression. The dilemma of the democratic process is best avoided by recognizing the significant positive impact of dramatic advances in communications technology on the scope and nature of public debate.

The rapid development of such technologies as cable television and the Internet have already expanded the amount and diversity of public debate, and they will no doubt do so to an even greater extent in the future. More importantly, these developments have benefited public debate without simultaneously giving rise to the ominous threats to free expression that are all too clearly associated with the governmental creation of a right of expressive access.

6

Government Subsidies and Free Expression

Solving the Subsidies Dilemma

To this point, the book has focused exclusively on the positive intersection between private economic resources and the individual's rights of free expression. However, government, too, may employ financial power to dramatically affect the balance of expressive power within society, either by selectively subsidizing different forms or subjects of private expression or by making expenditures to support direct government expressive activity.

Determining the constitutionality of government subsidization of expression is one of the most frustrating tasks facing First Amendment scholars. One may legitimately ask whether courts should ever deem government subsidization to violate the right of free expression. One might reasonably argue that as long as government in no way affirmatively restricts or punishes expression, it does not violate the First Amendment guarantee. While this position, originally well accepted, wisely has been rejected by more modern decisions, the conclusion that selective governmental subsidization of expression implicates the First Amendment ultimately raises more questions than it resolves.

The primary difficulty is that a reasonable observer will probably have very different intuitive reactions concerning the constitutionality of various conceivable examples of government subsidy. Furthermore, a reasonable observer will have no self-evident method of articulating a coherent, principled rationale to explain those different reactions. For example, one could reasonably accept the government's "subsidization" of the vice president's trip to speak in favor of a proposed political program, even though the government refuses to subsidize the speech of the program's leading opponent.[1] Yet, most constitutional observers would find very troubling the government's decision to provide funding only to those scholars who agree with its positions. Similarly, many constitutional observers have vehemently criticized the Supreme Court's decision in *Rust v. Sullivan*[2] upholding the government's refusal to subsidize clinics that inform their patients about the availability of abortion.[3] Presumably none of those critics, however, would hold unconstitutional the cancellation of a contract with the printer of the *Congressional Record* because the printer insisted on including additional pro-abortion material in the *Record*.

The task at hand is to develop an analytical structure that simultaneously provides coherent, generalized criteria by which to measure the constitutionality of governmental decisions whether or not to subsidize expression, and to do so in a manner that effectively fosters the values underlying the free speech guarantee. To date, none of the judicial or scholarly attempts to provide such a structure has been successful. The Supreme Court's hopelessly incoherent analysis in *Rust*[4] sadly underscores the confusion and futility of its current approach. While the efforts of commentators are perhaps not deserving of the criticism appropriately leveled at the Court's insufficient analytical attempts, they, too, ultimately fail. This is because either they choose to focus on what are largely tangential or irrelevant factors, or because they lump issues of free expression together with other constitutionally protected interests.[5]

This chapter proposes an analytical structure that substantially advances the inquiry. The proposed structure is designed to categorize and conceptualize different forms of government subsidy on the basis of their respective impacts on the normative theoretical values underlying the constitutional guarantee of free speech. Incorporated into the analysis—developed by means of a form of ex ante categorical balancing—are commonsense practical limitations on constitutional restriction of subsidization, designed to prevent the free speech guarantee from counterproductively undermining the values it protects.[6] Put most simply, the approach seeks to allow government subsidization when it promotes the values underlying the free expression guarantee and to prohibit it when it undermines those values.[7]

The structure initially draws a distinction between what are appropriately referred to as "negative" subsidies and "positive" subsidies.[8] Negative subsidies—the subsidies given to a private individual or entity in order to induce that individual or entity to remain silent—are presumptively unconstitutional. Only if the government can establish a compelling governmental interest and show that the negative government subsidization is narrowly tailored to meet this interest may the government provide a negative subsidy. In short, the structure permits negative subsidies only when current First Amendment jurisprudence would allow the direct infringement of free speech.

The approach I advocate here divides positive government speech subsidies—subsidies expended to encourage entities or individuals to speak—into two groups: "policy" subsidies and "auxiliary" subsidies.[9] Policy subsidies include situations in which the government either funds the speech of "core" policymaking government employees or makes a political appointment at least in part on the basis of that appointee's prior expression. Such subsidies should be deemed constitutional. The analysis of auxiliary subsidies, on the other hand, is more complicated. It is appropriate to divide these subsidies into three subcategories: "categorical" subsidies, "viewpoint-based" subsidies, and subsidies of "judgmental necessity."[10] The government grants a categorical subsidy of speech when it makes a viewpoint-neutral choice to fund a particular category, subject, or class of expression. Such subsidization of expression, the analysis suggests, is constitutional. The government grants a viewpoint-based subsidy of speech when it chooses to fund a speaker on the basis of the viewpoint espoused by that speaker, such as when the government chooses to fund the work of a particular artist because she produces art glorifying the Republican Party. My approach generally deems this type of subsidy unconstitutional.[11]

Finally, the government provides a subsidy of "judgmental necessity" when it selects among applicants for funding within a categorical subsidy of speech—for example, when the government chooses between two artists applying for government funding, or between two researchers in similar areas seeking governmental support of their research. The approach adopted here considers these types of subsidies to be conditionally constitutional. The choice of one speaker over another should be deemed constitutional if it is based on criteria "substantially related" to the prescribed viewpoint-neutral purpose of the subsidy.[12]

In essence, subsidies of judgmental necessity allow for a narrow group of necessarily content-based funding decisions and an even narrower group of inevitably viewpoint-based subsidies to be made by the government. As such, subsidies made of judgmental necessity should not be seen as an *alternative* to categorical and viewpoint-based subsidies. Rather, in certain instances, they constitute narrow *exceptions* to the general unconstitutionality of viewpoint-based subsidies.

The structure advocated here would allow courts to calibrate the constitutionality of government subsidies simply by locating the challenged subsidy within the model's established structural framework.[13] While legitimate disputes may arise over exactly where a particular type of subsidy should be placed,[14] whatever doctrinal and conceptual difficulties to which the structure might give rise pale in comparison to the overwhelming confusion that plagues the approaches previously suggested by commentators or utilized by the judiciary.[15] More importantly, the structure advocated here possesses the distinct advantage of tailoring constitutional regulation to foster widely accepted free speech values.[16]

Before more fully articulating the rationale for and implications of the suggested structure, we must first examine the logically prior question of why government subsidy decisions *ever* violate the First Amendment. Unless one concludes that a refusal to subsidize constitutes a prima facie abridgement of constitutionally protected expression, no need arises to calibrate the constitutionality of different types of subsidization. In addition, exploring exactly how governmental refusals to subsidize may undermine the values underlying free speech protection will help us devise a structure that most effectively fosters those values. Hence, the first portion of the chapter focuses on this preliminary inquiry. The second portion explains the structure and rationale of the approach. The third portion applies the proposed structure to several of the most troubling and frustrating examples of government subsidy. The chapter's final section critiques alternative attempts to frame analytical models for determining the constitutionality of government subsidy decisions.

No analytical structure is free from doubt or question; any time generalized standards are applied to specific, concrete facts the possibility of uncertainty and ambiguity exists. But when properly crafted, such models can help assure that judicial decision making fulfills the underlying normative values the law is designed to serve. No area of law requires greater assurance of this than the convoluted area of governmental subsidization of expression.

Denial of Subsidization as Abridgement: Government Funding and the Value of Free Expression

The Right–Privilege Distinction and the Concept of "Unconstitutional Conditions"

Writing for the Massachusetts Supreme Judicial Court in *McAuliffe v. Mayor of New Bedford*,[17] Judge Oliver Wendell Holmes succinctly described the traditional view concerning the constitutionality of the government's denial of subsidy because of expression: "The petitioner may have a constitutional right to talk politics, but he has no constitutional right to be a policeman."[18] In other words, government's denial of a subsidy because of a private individual's expression does not violate the First Amendment because the individual had no right to the subsidy in the first place.

The logical support for this position derives from two premises. First, by definition, a government subsidy is a matter of governmental largesse, and the greater governmental power to completely deny the subsidy logically includes the lesser power to grant the subsidy conditionally on the waiver of a constitutional right. Second, if the individual chooses to exercise her right instead of receiving the subsidy, she is in no worse position than she would have been had the subsidy never been offered in the first place.

Modern scholarship and doctrine have, for the most part,[19] rejected this deceptively simple logic, under the terms of the so-called "unconstitutional conditions" doctrine.[20] The fallacy of the traditional analysis is evident in the context of equal protection.[21] The government may constitutionally deny welfare to all citizens. It does not logically follow, however, that this "greater" power to deny welfare includes the "lesser" power to grant welfare to whites only. The right of equal protection constitutes its own freestanding right to equal treatment. No comparable independent constitutional right to receive welfare exists.[22] Thus, the Constitution does not view the power to deny welfare as "greater" than the power to deny welfare to non-whites. Outside of areas doctrinally subjected to strict scrutiny under the Equal Protection Clause, however, the logic behind the unconstitutional conditions doctrine's modern rejection of the traditional right–privilege distinction is uncertain.

According to Kathleen Sullivan, the unconstitutional conditions doctrine has traditionally been justified on three grounds.[23] The first rationale "locates the harm of rights-pressuring conditions on government benefits in their coercion of the beneficiary."[24] Sullivan asserts, however, that "[n]either the Court nor the commentary . . . has developed a satisfying theory of what is coercive about unconstitutional conditions. Conclusory labels often take the place of analysis."[25]

Her second rationale focuses on the legislative impropriety in engaging in such activities.[26] This explanation, however, begs the initial question: Unless the practice is defective in the first place, how can there be any legislative impropriety? Finally, Sullivan notes, the doctrine could be justified on the basis of the essential inalienability of constitutional rights.[27] Unfortunately, this answer suffers from the problem of fatal circularity, asserting only that constitutional rights are inalienable because they are constitutional. Such reasoning also runs contrary to a considerable body of established constitutional doctrine recognizing a citizen's ability to waive constitutional rights.[28]

Various commentators have suggested alternative theoretical rationales to explain the unconstitutional conditions doctrine. Sullivan, for example, has proposed an approach that "focuses not on the individual beneficiary, the legislative process, or the alienability of a right, but rather on the systemic effect of conditions on the distribution of rights in the polity as a whole."[29] She argues that unconstitutional conditions implicate three distinctive concerns:[30] (1) "they permit circumvention of existing constitutional restraints on direct regulation";[31] (2) they undermine "the maintenance of government neutrality or evenhandedness among rightholders";[32] and (3) they foster "discrimination among rightholders who would otherwise make the same constitutional choice on the basis of their relative dependency on a government benefit."[33]

The validity of Sullivan's suggested rationale for the unconstitutional conditions doctrine, as well as others that have been suggested by commentators,[34] is the appropriate subject of debate.[35] One could also examine the Supreme Court's puzzlingly (and unexplained) selective use of the doctrine.[36] For present purposes, however, it is not really necessary to explore these issues. Regardless of the validity of the unconstitutional conditions doctrine's constitutional basis, the difficulties caused by expressively based conditions on the dispensation of government subsidies become easy to comprehend when viewed from the more limited perspective of the theory of free expression.

Constitutional Text: Subsidy Denials as "Abridgements"

By its terms, the First Amendment prohibits "abridgements" of free speech.[37] Thus, the constitutional inquiry, at least as an initial matter,[38] must always be whether or not the challenged governmental action "abridges" the free speech right. Courts have not construed the concept of "abridgement" to require that government actually physically prevent a private individual or entity from speaking.[39] Issuance of an injunction, for example, does not physically halt the expression; no one, as a result of an injunction, places tape over the mouth of the would-be speaker. Rather, it merely means that if the subject of the injunction does engage in the prohibited expression she will be subject to a contempt citation.[40] In a sense, then, under such circumstances a court gives the individual the option of not speaking and avoiding contempt, or speaking subject to the imposition of the contempt penalty. Yet courts have established that such injunctions constitute classic illustrations of presumptively unconstitutionally abridgements.[41]

Similarly, one who has been sentenced to prison because of his expression has not been physically prevented from speaking.[42] The government instead has offered him the "option" of not speaking and staying out of jail, or speaking and receiving a prison sentence. Most people presumably would agree that imposition of a prison sentence constitutes a prima facie "abridgement" of protected expression.

When government ties subsidies to expression, then, the mere fact that the government's actions do not actually physically prevent expression but rather leave the would-be speaker with a type of choice does not necessarily imply that such actions fail to "abridge" the free speech right. The textual question ought to be whether the government's actions penalize protected expression. Contempt citations, prison sentences, and civil and criminal fines constitute prima facie abridgements because they penalize speech. In other words, such penalties abridge the First Amendment guarantee even though they technically leave the speaker with the "choice" to speak, because they represent clear deterrents to the exercise of individuals' expressive rights.

At first glance one might think that government subsidies directly tied to expression present a different situation, since unlike the previous examples, with such subsidies the government does not affirmatively impose a new burden on the speaker because of his expression. At worst, the government merely is denying the citizen a benefit to which he had no overriding right in the first place. In a sense, then, following the denial or revocation of a government subsidy the speaker is arguably in no different position than he was before the subsidy became available. The same could not be said, of course, of the speaker sent to prison or subjected to a fine. The proper question, however, is not whether, because of his expression,[43] the government placed the speaker in a worse position *than if it had granted no benefit at all*, but whether the speaker has been placed in an unambiguously worse position *than if he had not spoken at all*. If so, the government has "penalized" him for his expression, in much the same sense as when he has been fined or imprisoned because of his expression. From a purely linguistic perspective, then, his right of expression is "abridged" by the denial of a subsidy, much as it is when he is fined or imprisoned.

One can argue, of course, that the severity of the penalty is considerably greater when the government fines or imprisons a speaker than when the it merely denies the speaker a subsidy. Although this point may be accurate in the majority of cases, however, it is not always true. One could conceive of a government subsidy so central to an individual's well-being[44] that the denial of it will, as a practical matter, have at least as much adverse impact as would a fine or prison sentence.

In any event, the point is irrelevant to answering whether a subsidy denial potentially constitutes a prima facie violation of the First Amendment. To be sure, the extent or severity of the abridgement may influence the outcome of a pragmatic judicial calculus in an individual case.[45] However, at least as a prima facie matter, any abridgement—no matter how small—may trigger a First Amendment inquiry. A fine of fifty dollars may "abridge" an individual's free speech right in the same manner as a $50,000 fine or a twenty-year prison sentence.

Government Subsidies and Free Speech Theory

When a normative theoretical perspective is added to the analysis, it is easy to see how denial of a subsidy may undermine the value or values sought to be fostered by the protection of free expression. The important point to note is that this is true, regardless of which side one takes in the numerous debates over the proper course of First Amendment theory.

As more detailed discussion in earlier chapters has already shown, the theories underlying the First Amendment's protection of freedom of expression can be placed in two broad categories: communitarian and individual autonomy.[46] Supporters of the former argue that free speech constitutes a necessary ingredient of the processes of community and self-government and protects "the common needs of all the members of the body politic."[47] Alternatively, the latter theories contend that free speech is "protected not as a means to a collective good but because of the value of speech conduct to the individual."[48] For present purposes, we need not proclaim one of these theories superior, because it matters little which normative approach one prefers. Regardless of whether one espouses a communitarian theory or an autonomy theory of the First Amendment, the government's decision to fund the expression of some individuals or entities but not others can amount to an abridgement of speech, because that decision may undermine the fundamental principles underlying either theory. This is due to the simple fact that the grant or denial of a subsidy may have the effect of deterring individual expression, artificially skewing the nature of public debate, or both.

Selective award of governmental subsidies on the basis of the recipient's expression seriously risks undermining the autonomy values served by free speech protection, because the government's action may well influence a private individual either not to say anything at all or not to say what she would have said absent the government's influence. Thus, the threat of a subsidy denies, or at the minimum stunts, whatever self-development or actualization the individual would have gained as a result of genuine (i.e., non-subsidization influenced) expressive activity.

One might argue that denying a government subsidy does not violate the First Amendment autonomy/self-development value because the ultimate choice not to speak remains with the individual. As explained above, however, one could say the same of any governmental penalty for expression, short of arresting the speaker prior to her speaking. In almost every instance, the individual may choose to speak, as long she is willing to accept the consequences.

Of course, one can also persuasively contend that when imprisonment or a heavy fine is the alternative to remaining silent, the individual's decision not to speak is not "free" in any meaningful sense of the term. The same can be said, however, when the government links a valuable subsidy to the individual's choice not to speak or to the individual's message. In neither case does the individual make a truly "free" decision.

Similarly, a communitarian theorist (at least a democratic communitarian theorist),[49] who presumably cares little about negative effects on individual development, should find troubling the potential impact of government subsidy decisions on the political and societal values fostered by free expression. A democratic communitarian theorist values free expression, because unrestrained expressive activity facilitates performance of the self-governing function by providing the electorate with information and opinion about the issues that require community decisions. Through this process, members of the electorate become more effective "governors" by becoming better informed and aware voters.[50]

To the extent that government subsidy decisions chill expression, the electorate will be deprived of whatever information or opinion that the chilled speaker would have expressed. To the extent that the subsidy decisions cause individuals to assert viewpoints that they would not have asserted of their own free will, they artificially skew the tenor and direction of public debate. As a result, by selectively denying subsidies on the basis of expression the government might preclude the expression of opinion or information important to the electorate from reaching that audience. The subsidy denial therefore harms the public's decision-making process.[51] Thus, whatever one's broad perspective on the value of free expression, one can perceive that linkage between government subsidies and either the existence or content of expression potentially presents a substantial threat to those values.

Calibrating the Constitutionality of Government Subsidization: A Proposed Analytical Structure

An Overview of the Structure

On the basis of the analysis in the preceding sections, one might at first be tempted to conclude that *any* linkage of government subsidies to protected expression[52] violates the First Amendment, much as imposition of a fine or prison sentence does. The First Amendment issue, however, is considerably more complex. In certain cases, not only do government subsidies of expression not present the aforementioned dangers to First Amendment interests, they affirmatively foster the values served by free expression. For example, government funding of the arts and scientific research likely promotes both autonomy and communitarian values. Although courts generally do not construe the Constitution to impose on the government an affirmative obligation to support individuals,[53] surely it would be Orwellian to prohibit the government totally from facilitating expression in the name of the First Amendment. Both scholars and jurists, then, face the dilemma of fashioning an analytical structure that will guide the courts in deciding when government subsidy decisions overstep constitutional boundaries.

In shaping an approach to this dilemma, the analysis here draws a distinction between "negative" and "positive" subsidies. A negative subsidy is one that conditions receipt on a potential speaker's decision either to refuse to speak or to cease speaking. A positive subsidy, on the other hand, requires the recipient to engage in expression in order to receive the governmental benefit.

Under the structure adopted here, negative subsidies are presumptively unconstitutional. They are constitutional only in those cases in which current First Amendment jurisprudence would uphold an affirmative imposition of a burden on expressive activity, such as when the government imposes a fine or prison sentence for expression falling outside the scope of the First Amendment[54] or when competing social interests outweigh the need for free expression.[55] Analysis of positive subsidies, on the other hand, requires a more detailed inquiry.[56]

Negative Subsidies

With the philosophical foundations of the First Amendment's protection of free expression in mind,[57] it should not be all that difficult to see that negative subsidization of speech, such as the government's provision of a subsidy to an individual on the condition that she remain silent, constitutes a significant abridgement of free speech. Negative subsidization of speech undermines the underpinnings of both communitarian and autonomy rationales of First Amendment protection. Under a communitarian view, negative subsidization reduces the sum total of speech available to facilitate wise collective self-government and therefore impedes the community's ability to govern itself effectively. Similarly, under an autonomy view, government inducement not to speak reduces not only the development of the speaker, but also that of her would-be listeners, readers, or viewers.

Since negative subsidizations of speech undermine the values served by the First Amendment, they should be presumptively unconstitutional. Indeed, negative subsidization of speech closely resembles direct, content-based, government restrictions on speech, which are almost never constitutionally permissible.[58] For all the reasons that courts strictly scrutinize content-based government restrictions on speech, so, too, should they subject negative subsidies to a presumption of unconstitutionality.[59]

Positive Subsidies

It is tempting to believe that the government does not abridge the freedom of speech when it funds expression in a positive manner. After all, as long as it does not impose a penalty or otherwise discourage the exercise of free expression, it would seem reasonable to conclude that government does not violate the First Amendment. Unlike negative subsidies, positive subsidies do not reduce the sum total of expression, and no one is placed in a better position as a result of not speaking. The speaker who is denied a positive subsidy because her views differ from those of the government is placed in no better position by saying nothing than by saying what she had intended to say in the first place. Moreover, the government is wholly neutral as to this speaker's initial choice whether to speak or to remain silent. The government cares only what the speaker will say if and when she does choose to speak.

Nevertheless, the government's decision to subsidize an entity may still constitute an abridgement of speech because it may artificially skew a public debate by inducing some who otherwise would have taken a contrary position (or would have chosen not to speak at all) to support the government's views. Such a result undermines both the communitarian and the autonomy values conceivably underlying the First Amendment guarantee. It does so from a communitarian perspective by artificially and misleadingly distorting the level of public support for positions advocated by the government. It does so from an autonomy perspective, since it leads to expression that does not represent the truly free choice of the individual speaker. The goal, therefore, is to construct an analytical framework that allows the government to subsidize speech positively when such subsidization promotes First Amendment values, but precludes the government from subsidizing speech positively when such subsidization undermines those values.

The Costs and Benefits of Government Subsidization of Speech

To establish a structure for gauging the constitutionality of positive government subsidization of speech, one must first examine the conceivable benefits and costs of such subsidization.[60] This examination confirms the contention that positive subsidization of speech may both foster and undermine First Amendment values.

THE BENEFITS OF GOVERNMENT SUBSIDIZATION

On both practical and theoretical levels, a democratic society must permit the government on occasion to communicate with the populace, both with its own voice and through the voices of others.[61] Commentators have recognized that the government is uniquely situated to inform directly and to teach the populace.[62] In addition, indirect government subsidization of private speech may provide a voice to an entity that, without the aid of government funding, would not be heard.[63]

Thomas Emerson noted that

> [p]articipation by the government in the system of freedom of expression
> is an essential feature of any democratic society. It enables the government
> to inform, explain and persuade—measures especially crucial in a society
> that attempts to govern itself with a minimum use of force. Government
> participation also greatly enriches the system; it provides the facts, ideas,
> and expertise not available from other sources. In short, government ex-
> pression is a necessary and healthy part of the system.[64]

Perhaps the most zealous scholarly advocate in support of the government's subsidization of speech in order to teach and inform was Joseph
Tussman, who argued "not only that government has authority in the
realm of the mind, but also that its responsibilities there are among the
most important that it has."[65] Tussman recognized that the government
serves a crucial function in supporting "knowledge-creating and trans-
mitting institutions,"[66] and that "[t]he teaching power is the inherent
constitutional authority of the state to establish and direct the teaching
activity and institutions needed to ensure its continuity and further its legitimate general and specific purposes."[67] Tussman argued that because
the government functions, in part, by teaching, persuading, and informing the populace, it therefore must be able to subsidize speech.[68]
Zechariah Chafee argued that the government must be able to communicate with the public in order to explain the statutes and regulations it
promulgates,[69] and must be able to inform those who are governed of potential dangers to their well-being.[70]

In addition to directly teaching and informing the public, government
subsidization of speech may indirectly enable private individuals or entities that would have difficulty being heard without the government's assistance to speak, thereby allowing them to reach their intended audience
more effectively than would be possible absent subsidization. Indeed, it
has been persuasively argued that "government speech often offsets the
vast communications resources controlled by corporate or wealthy interests,"[71] insofar as it "can amplify the voices of the local populace that seek
to participate in debates dominated by mass institutions."[72]

THE DANGERS OF GOVERNMENT SUBSIDIZATION

The impact of government subsidization on free speech interests is not
uniformly beneficial. Countless commentators have expressed the fear
that, by subsidizing speech, the government might artificially skew the

debate on a particular issue and thereby artificially shape public attitudes.[73] Mark Yudof, for example, expressed concern over the government's ability to "shape public attitudes" through communication.[74] "The obvious danger," Yudof asserted, "[was] that government persuaders [would] come to disrespect citizens and their role of ultimate decider, and manipulate them by communicating only what [made] them accede to government's plans, policies and goals."[75] Yudof expressed the fear that government communications might be used to "falsify consent," that is, that the government would "attempt to fashion a majority will through uncontrolled indoctrination activities."[76] Yudof believed that this eventuality became more likely as the "expansion of government at all levels had increased its opportunity to communicate with the populace."[77]

Thomas Emerson and David Haber concurred with Yudof's position:

> The penetration of government into more and more aspects of modern life, including the field of mass communication; the increasing dependence of higher education and scientific research upon government support; the many forms of pressure toward political, intellectual and social conformity—these and other factors raise grave issues as to the proper role of government in controlling communication and molding thought and expression in a democratic society.[78]

Perhaps the concerns of the aforementioned scholars were most effectively summarized by Robert Kamenshine, who contended that "[t]he government has the potential to use its unmatched arsenal of media resources and legislative prerogatives to obtain political ends, to nullify the effectiveness of criticism, and, thus, to undermine the principle of self-government."[79]

Subdividing Positive Subsidies

When the government positively subsidizes speech such that the hazards of the government-sponsored communication outweigh its benefits to the values and interests of free expression, it improperly undermines First Amendment values, and courts must deem the subsidization unconstitutional. The obvious task, then, is to conceptualize and categorize positive subsidies in a manner that enables a reviewing court to distinguish the beneficial positive subsidies from the detrimental ones with reasonable accuracy and efficiency. Recognizing the need for such a dichotomy, of course, is considerably easier than fashioning one.

With this admonition in mind, it is possible to divide the category of positive subsidies into two broad subcategories: "policy" subsidies and "auxiliary" subsidies. Policy subsidies consist of both the funding of "core" government employees—for example, those who are responsible for directing governmental policy[80]—when they engage in expression about and in support of government activities and initiatives. This funding may be described as "limited government employee subsidies." Policy subsidies also include the selection of political appointees when decision makers base their selection at least in part on the viewpoints expressed by the appointed individuals. These subsidies are termed "appointment subsidies." The approach presumptively deems both types of policy subsidies constitutional. Auxiliary subsidies, on the other hand, consist of all positive government subsidization of the expression of private individuals or entities except appointment subsidies, and subsidization of the speech of non-core government employees.[81]

POLICY SUBSIDIES

Limited Government Employee Subsidies

The first type of policy subsidy is the limited government employee subsidy, which should be deemed constitutional. Society must permit government employees who participate in directing governmental policy to speak, supported by government funding, about and in favor of government policies and initiatives.[82] From the perspective of democratic theory, it is essential that these government employees inform the populace of the government's policies and initiatives. Because the government informs the populace about its functioning through these subsidies, it facilitates self-government by providing members of the community with information and data on which to judge the performance of its political leaders. As a result, the electorate is better able to check elected officials and hold them accountable.[83]

Permitting core government employees to speak on matters regarding the functioning of the government does present the risk that government could artificially skew a debate by overwhelming the opposition due to the sheer volume of government speech, and thereby undercut First Amendment principles. The fact that listeners may readily identify the government speaker as such, however, mitigates the likelihood of this potentiality. As a result, the speech of a core government employee is unlikely to skew substantially the marketplace of ideas, since the populace remains free to evaluate the message with an eye toward the messenger.[84] Any remaining possibility that the government might undermine First Amendment principles by skewing a debate with limited government employee subsidies must, as a categorical matter, be deemed to be substantially outweighed by the practical and theoretical benefits that derive from allowing core government employees to speak on issues of importance to the government.

A classic example of a limited government employee subsidy is government funding of the travels of the vice president of the United States in order to allow him to speak in favor of a policy supported by the administration. Certainly, the Constitution permits the vice president to travel the country, at government expense, to speak in favor of an administration proposal, even though the administration quite naturally declines to fund the expression of the proposal's opponents. This type of subsidization is constitutional for the simple reason that it fosters First Amendment values: The public is better informed as a result.[85]

Appointment Subsidies

The approach being advocated here also permits the government to make hiring decisions of policymaking, non-civil-service employees based on the candidates' previously expressed viewpoints. Few would argue that the Constitution does not permit the government to consider the writings, speeches, and other public statements of a scholar in considering whether to appoint that scholar to the cabinet. Precluding the government from engaging in such a positive subsidization of speech could result in the appointment of an individual whose ideas are incompatible with those of the government. As a result, prohibiting this positive subsidy would hinder elected government officials in their efforts to implement the policy choices they were presumably elected to bring to fruition. Such a result would undermine fundamental notions of representative democratic theory.

Permitting the government to provide appointment subsidies does potentially allow the government artificially to skew debate. Moreover, an individual might alter her expression in order to be appointed to some position by the government. Despite this possibility, considerations of governmental efficiency and democratic theory lead to the conclusion that appointment subsidies, like limited government employee subsidies, are constitutional.[86]

Auxiliary Subsidies

Auxiliary subsidies are positive subsidies that the government grants to entities or individuals other than core government employees and to government appointees to encourage and facilitate their expression. They include such subsidies as a government grant to an organization to allow it to produce a study examining the effects of smoking on human beings, government funds given to a private library in order to purchase books, and a government grant to support completion of a particular private artistic or literary work.

Under the approach advocated here, the government may constitutionally provide auxiliary subsidies only in certain instances. Auxiliary subsidies allow the government to teach, inform, or provide a voice to a relatively silent entity and therefore may well promote First Amendment values. Once again, however, allowing the government to act as a benefactor to third parties creates the danger that the government may artificially skew public debate or impede an individual's exercise of free will in fashioning her expression. Moreover, auxiliary subsidies, unlike policy subsidies, do not always assist the government in performing essential functions. Therefore, the proposed structure significantly circumscribes, but does not entirely curtail, the government's ability to dispense auxiliary subsidies.

Auxiliary subsidies are divided into three not entirely segregated subcategories: "categorical" subsidies, "viewpoint-based" subsidies, and subsidies of "judgmental necessity." The government provides categorical subsidies of speech when it makes viewpoint-neutral choices to fund particular categories, subjects, or classes of speech. The government generally makes categorical subsidies both because of the public's need for information and because such subsidization is unlikely to come from other sources.[87] For example, the government makes a categorical subsidy when it funds a study on the physical effects of smoking or when it subsidizes the purchase of history books or new African fiction for a public library. The proposed structure here deems such subsidies to be presumptively constitutional.

The government establishes a viewpoint-based subsidy of speech when it chooses to fund speakers on the basis of their viewpoints. The proposed structure deems these subsidies presumptively unconstitutional.[88] If we permit the government to make viewpoint-based subsidies, the government could choose to fund only those viewpoints with which it agreed, thereby dramatically skewing public debate and undermining First Amendment principles. The greatest fears attendant to government subsidization of speech result from this kind of subsidy.

Before accepting the proposed structure's suggested bar against viewpoint-based positive auxiliary subsidies, we must answer three questions. First, why are viewpoint-based auxiliary subsidies thought to be more harmful to First Amendment values than are categorical auxiliary subsidies? Second, why does the proposed structure deny government the power to do indirectly through auxiliary subsidies what it permits government to do directly through policy subsidization of the expression of core government employees and appointees?[89] Finally, even if one were to accept, as a theoretical matter, the validity of a viewpoint-categorical dichotomy for purposes of positive auxiliary subsidies, how, as a practical matter, is a court to decide whether a subsidy, labeled superficially as a categorical subsidy, is in reality a disguised viewpoint subsidy?

The distinction that the proposed structure draws between viewpoint-based and categorical subsidies represents a well-established precept of First Amendment doctrine in other areas of speech regulation.[90] While this dichotomy is by no means free of risk in areas of direct governmental regulation,[91] in the context of government subsidies the justification for the distinction is compelling. In a case of direct governmental regulation, it is difficult to understand why the fact that a prohibition is categorically based, rather than viewpoint-based, somehow implies that the prohibition need not be subjected to a compelling interest standard; the sum total of expression is reduced as a result of the regulation in any event, and whatever values free speech protection serves are thereby harmed.[92] In the case of government subsidies, however, complete denial of government power has the effect, not of *preserving* expression but of actually *reducing* the sum total of expression. Thus, those interested in fostering First Amendment values should be quite hesitant to deny such power to the government.

Although categorical regulations may on occasion be harmful to First Amendment values,[93] surely they are not as harmful as viewpoint-based regulations. Categorical distinctions do not skew public debate in the same manner, nor do they present as great a danger of stark governmental suppression of political opinion as viewpoint-based regulations. Thus, given the potentially beneficial impact of positive subsidies, it is appropriate to draw a line that allows government to subsidize speech in a categorical manner but simultaneously denies it the power to subsidize on the basis of viewpoint.

Under the proposed structure, government is permitted to subsidize the speech of its own core policy employees on a viewpoint basis.[94] It does not necessarily follow, however, that the same standards should apply to auxiliary subsidies. The justification for policy subsidies is considerably stronger than the asserted justification for viewpoint-based auxiliary subsidies, and the risk of harm of such subsidies is simultaneously considerably less than the potential harm caused by viewpoint-based auxiliary subsidies. It is difficult to imagine how government could operate effectively without having the opportunity to communicate its positions and programs to the public, or without the opportunity to select its policymaking employees on the basis of their previously expressed viewpoints. It is equally difficult to understand, however, why efficient representative government somehow requires the opportunity to control the flow of debate among private parties through the selective use of viewpoint-based subsidies. At least as a general matter, government should be able to operate effectively without the need to "deputize" private parties to foster government views and positions.[95]

Moreover, auxiliary viewpoint-based subsidies to private parties present a danger of defrauding the public in a manner not present in the case of policy subsidies. When a government officer speaks, much as when a political candidate or a commercial advertiser speaks, the listener is able to "discount" the expression on the basis of the speaker's evident self-interest.[96] However, when government fosters dissemination of its positions by funding private-party expression, the danger arises that the public will be misled into failing to appropriately discount the views expressed. Even if it were somehow feasible to require the private parties to identify the existence of their government funding, the risk of "consumer confusion" on the part of only partially or casually attentive members of the public is very real. Thus, drawing a distinction between auxiliary viewpoint-based subsidies and policy subsidies makes perfect sense from the perspective of both free speech theory and the practical needs of governmental operations.

Government may on occasion seek to disguise what are in reality viewpoint-based subsidies under the shield of the label of permissible categorical subsidies. This problem has long plagued efforts to draw a conceptual or doctrinal distinction between viewpoint-based and content-neutral regulations of expression. Although this danger is impossible to avoid completely, at least two tactics can mitigate the likelihood of its arising. Initially, courts must prohibit the government from defining categorical subsidies in a viewpoint-laden manner, such that the very contours of the category effectively exclude viewpoints with which government disagrees. For example, government cannot define the category as "the evils of abortion," thereby effectively excluding any expression that advocates freedom of choice. A reviewing court should generally be in a position to resolve this issue on the four corners of the governmentally established category, without the need to resort to a separate factual inquiry.

In certain situations, however, courts must still undertake a separate factual inquiry. Such a case would arise when an unsuccessful applicant for a categorical subsidy asserts that in reality the government based its denial on the applicant's underlying viewpoint. For example, assume that the government chooses to fund studies on the presumably viewpoint-neutral category of the social effects of abortion. An unsuccessful applicant, however, claims that the government based its denial of his application entirely or predominantly on the fact that he intended to describe those social effects as positive.

Under the proposed structure, in order to challenge a facially "neutral" funding decision as viewpoint-based a plaintiff must follow the procedure set out by the Supreme Court in *Mt. Healthy City School District Board of Education v. Doyle*.[97] This procedure dictates that the entity challenging the funding decision must show, by a preponderance of the evidence, that in reality the government impermissibly based its decision on the recipient's viewpoint.[98] The burden then shifts to the government to show, by a preponderance of the evidence, that it would have reached the same funding decision absent the viewpoint-based consideration.[99] If the government fails to meet this burden, the challenged subsidization fails.

There are costs to this procedure. Some viewpoint-based subsidies likely will go unchallenged because of the transaction costs that inevitably accompany litigation. Even with these costs in mind, however, the *Mt. Healthy* procedure should adequately protect against the hazards of surreptitious viewpoint-based government subsidization.

Subsidies of Judgmental Necessity

Once the government decides to award a categorical subsidy, it naturally must choose among different candidates for funding within that category. For example, once the government decides to fund a study on breast cancer, it must choose Firm X or Firm Y to undertake the study. In making this funding choice, one cannot require the government arbitrarily to pick names out of a hat. Rationality requires that the government examine and judge the content of the various competing applications or proposals. Thus, while one can require the government to eschew virtually all viewpoint-based factors in the initial establishment of its subsidized categories,[100] one cannot entirely preclude the influence of normative value judgments in the actual selection among competing applicants for the subsidy.

It would be unwise to conclude that, as a result of the dangers inherent in such an approach, one should constitutionally deny government the opportunity to provide positive auxiliary subsidies. The general societal and First Amendment values served by such subsidies are simply too great.[101] The task, then, is to engage in a form of constitutional damage control. We probably cannot avoid all dangers of abuse. We can, however, fashion certain flexible and comprehensible ex ante guidelines that will enable a reviewing court to determine whether the substantive normative criteria employed by government officials in selecting among competing applicants are unconstitutional.

Under this structure, the government's selection is constitutional as long as it is based on criteria "substantially related" to the prescribed goals and purposes of the program pursuant to which the category of speech is funded. For example, if the government chooses to award a categorical subsidy to fund a study on breast cancer, the government may choose among competing applicants provided that its decision is based on criteria "substantially related" to the prescribed purposes of the funded program. Assuming that the government's program is designed to fund the study that will reveal the most thorough, accurate, and reliable results, it may choose to fund one firm's research to the exclusion of the other's if it finds that the former firm's study is more likely to meet these predetermined criteria.

Thus, the government may fund Firm X's study to the exclusion of Firm Y's because it concludes that the former will employ superior or more advanced technology or because its primary researchers are better qualified. The government may not fund Firm X's study to the exclusion of Firm Y's because Firm Y is comprised of a higher percentage of Democrats than Firm X. The political leanings of the members of the firm are unrelated to the predetermined scope of the program for which the subsidy is provided.

This requirement of "substantial relationship," coupled with the requirement that the category of subsidized expression itself be defined in a viewpoint-neutral manner,[102] ensures, to the degree possible, that the government is not in reality engaging in viewpoint-based subsidization when it makes subsidies of judgmental necessity. This, in turn, precludes the government from undermining First Amendment values by means of viewpoint-based subsidies.[103]

Applying the Proposed Structure

Thus far I have described the elements of the structure proposed here in abstract terms. Because difficulties naturally will arise in application of the structure to specific situations, it is helpful to consider how the structure operates in real circumstances. This section, therefore, examines the use of the approach in three highly controversial cases of government subsidization: federal funding of family planning programs, governmental subsidization of the arts, and government selection of public school textbooks.

Federal Funding of Family Planning Programs: Rust v. Sullivan Revisited

In *Rust v. Sullivan*,[104] the Supreme Court upheld Health and Human Services Department (HHS) regulations concerning federal funding of family planning services promulgated pursuant to Title X of the Public Health Services Act.[105] According to the Act, the Secretary of HHS was directed to promulgate regulations, pursuant to which she would make grants and contracts.[106]

In 1988, the Secretary promulgated the regulations in question. As the Supreme Court indicated, these regulations "attach[ed] three principal conditions on the grant of federal funds for Title X projects."[107] First, the regulations prohibited a Title X clinic from providing "counseling concerning the use of abortion as a method of family planning or [from] provid[ing] referral for abortion as a method of family planning."[108] Second, the regulations prohibited a Title X project from "encourag[ing], promot[ing], or advocat[ing] abortion as a method of family planning."[109] Finally, the regulations required that a Title X project be organized in a way that ensured that "it [was] physically and financially separate" from activities prohibited in the regulations.[110] In essence, by means of the new regulations, the Secretary attempted to erect "a wall of separation between Title X programs and abortion as a method of family planning."[111]

In concluding that the regulations were constitutional, the Court relied heavily on its interpretation of the unconstitutional conditions doctrine. The petitioners had argued that "the restrictions on the subsidization of abortion-related speech contained in the regulations [were] impermissible because they condition[ed] the receipt of a benefit . . . on the relinquishment of a constitutional right, the right to engage in abortion advocacy and counseling."[112] The argument did not persuade the majority. Rather, the majority concluded that the government was not "denying a benefit to anyone, but [was] instead simply insisting that public funds be spent for the purposes for which they were authorized."[113] The Court found that the regulations govern the scope of the Title X project's activities, leaving the grantee unfettered in its other activities. The Title X grantee can continue to perform abortions, provide abortion-related services, and engage in abortion advocacy; it simply is required to conduct those activities through programs that are separate and independent from the project that receives Title X funds.[114]

The Court concluded that since the regulations placed a condition on the program pursuant to which funds were received, and not on the grantee receiving the funding, the condition did not qualify as an unconstitutional condition. In other words, because the regulations did not dictate what a Title X grantee could do outside the boundaries of the program, those regulations were constitutional.

Viewed from the perspective of the unconstitutional conditions doctrine, the Court's analysis has a superficial appeal. But closer examination reveals the conceptual limitations of the unconstitutional conditions doctrine[115] more than it demonstrates the correctness of the Court's decision. The Court properly reasoned that in order to violate the unconstitutional conditions doctrine, the government must be linking the receipt of a subsidy either to the recipient's assumption of a particular viewpoint or to the recipient's refraining from asserting a particular viewpoint. The Court, however, viewed the Secretary's regulations not as constituting subsidies forcing the recipient's assumption or rejection of a particular viewpoint, but rather as the very structural description of the scope and purpose of the subsidy. The government established the subsidy for the purpose of fostering family planning methods other than abortion. It therefore would be absurd to hold unconstitutional the government's choice not to fund pro-abortion counseling. Thus, in the Court's view, the regulations constituted not an improper government "carrot" designed to silence expression of a particular viewpoint, but rather a self-defined governmental program whose inherent purpose was to deter abortions, or at least solely to promote alternatives to abortion.

The problem with unconstitutional conditions analysis is that it allows the government to define its subsidization programs in a wholly unchecked, self-referential[116] manner.[117] Although such an analysis may enable the government to escape the conceptual strictures imposed by the unconstitutional conditions doctrine, its failure to view the government's initial funding choice itself from the restraints imposed by the perspective of the First Amendment enables the government to employ subsidies in a manner that seriously threatens core values of free expression.

Viewed from the perspective of the proposed analytical structure, the Secretary's regulations are clearly unconstitutional. In the Court's view, from its inception the funding program had as its primary purpose the dissemination of information about alternatives to abortion. Although the contours of the unconstitutional conditions doctrine allow the Court to satisfy the constitutional inquiry without questioning the legitimacy of the government's program, the structure adopted here, premised exclusively on considerations unique to First Amendment policy and theory, does not. For reasons previously discussed,[118] the First Amendment cannot allow government to employ subsidies as a means of skewing the expression of private parties. The regulations at issue in *Rust* established a positive auxiliary viewpoint-based subsidy, which is unconstitutional under the proposed structure.[119] The very description of the subsidy program as a means of disseminating information concerning family planning methods other than abortion inescapably reveals the viewpoint-based selective nature of the subsidy[120] and makes the program unconstitutional under the approach advocated here.[121]

The fallacy of the *Rust* Court's self-referential approach to government subsidization programs becomes clear if one visualizes the subsidization of private expression exclusively in favor of such ideas as a free-market economic philosophy, or the political theories of Mao Zedong or Rush Limbaugh. In such situations, the Court could reason under an unconstitutional conditions approach—as it did in *Rust*—that exclusion of funding for those opposed to the political viewpoints sought to be disseminated makes perfect sense in light of the program's own purposive description. It does not follow, however, that such initial decisions as to scope are themselves constitutional. The proposed structure demonstrates that they are not.

Government may appropriately choose neutrally to fund works on family planning, on the viability of free market economic philosophy, or on the wisdom of Mao Zedong's or Rush Limbaugh's political thought. Each of these subsidies would foster First Amendment values by adding to the public's knowledge and facilitating the self-realization of those engaged in the particular expressive activities as well as those listening to or watching them. For reasons already discussed, however, government may not foster public acceptance of its own viewpoints by means of manipulation of private expression.

Government Subsidization of the Arts

Robert O'Neil has posed the crucial dilemma caused by government subsidization of the arts:

> [I]f government cannot fund all artists or all works, how must it choose? If it makes choices, it must adopt and apply standards. And if those standards are not simply broad and bland categories—for example, fund only oil paintings but not water colors . . . —then there is inevitable potential for content differentiation. The difficulty is in deciding when that differentiation abridges or inhibits freedom of expression in ways the First Amendment will not allow.[122]

Indeed, while few would argue that the government is not constitutionally permitted to fund works of art,[123] much disagreement has arisen over the way in which the government may constitutionally make its funding decisions.[124]

In part to answer this question, Congress in 1965 established the National Endowment for the Arts (NEA).[125] The NEA was designed as a mechanism for funding the "best" works of art for which artists had requested grants. Congress intended that the choice was to be "insulated from partisan political considerations."[126] Only artwork that was of "substantial artistic or cultural significance" would receive funding.[127]

Legislators have, at times, attempted to narrow the definition of "best" by either defining out of consideration or restricting application of the definition to specified types of art. For example, in 1990, the NEA's reauthorization bill contained what became known as the "decency clause."[128] Under that clause, the NEA chairperson was to ensure that all works funded by the NEA comported with "general standards of decency and respect for the diverse beliefs and values of the American Public."[129] The question arising out of this provision was whether attempts to make content-based distinctions among works of art, such as the decency clause, are constitutionally permissible.

Determining the constitutionality of the decency clause probably presents the most difficult test for the standard proposed here.[130] At least in the abstract, the government is entitled to fund the arts: Such a subsidy represents a positive auxiliary categorical subsidy.[131] Within this categorical subsidy, pursuant to the principle of "judgmental necessity,"[132] the government must make content-based distinctions. The government cannot be expected either to fund every one of the applicants for funding or to make its selections arbitrarily. As discussed earlier, the choice of one applicant over another is properly deemed a constitutionally valid subsidy of judgmental necessity if it is based on criteria "substantially related" to the program pursuant to which the category of speech is funded.[133] Thus, since by creating the NEA Congress intended to fund on the basis of artistic excellence, it may choose between applications only by means of criteria designed to determine excellence.

There appears to be no basis on which a reviewing court could objectively determine that considerations of "decency" are inherently unrelated to the quality of the art. To be sure, one could quite reasonably argue that such considerations should be deemed to have no connection to quality. This, however, seems to be a purely subjective judgment, one which a court has no more ability to make than it does the initial quality determination. As a result, if a particular applicant is denied on the grounds that his art is unduly gross or offensive, it would be effectively impossible for a reviewing court to conclude, for constitutional purposes, that such a judgment was substantially unrelated to the work's artistic quality.

Arguably a different situation is presented when, rather than influencing a determination of whether particular artwork meets standards of excellence, decency considerations are employed ex ante to exclude entire categories of work that deal with certain subjects or employ certain words or visual images. In such a case those in authority could be making a good faith, broadly based judgment concerning artistic quality. A reviewing court, however, could reasonably be suspicious of any such mechanistic approach. It is doubtful that true artistic judgments could be so broadly and crudely made. It is much more likely in such a case that those in power are superimposing onto the selection process normative content-based judgments that are wholly unrelated to considerations of quality. This likelihood is even greater when this a priori decency limitation is imposed, not by those experts designated to make the individual funding selections, but by Congress itself. While it is difficult and dangerous for a reviewing court to question asserted congressional motivations,[134] in such a situation a court could properly conclude, as a matter of law, that Congress's concern is not with issues of artistic quality but with wholly extraneous normative moral, social, and lifestyle judgments.[135] The decency clause, in that case, would therefore not qualify under the "judgmental necessity" exception, because the criteria employed to make the choice are not "substantially related" to the legitimate viewpoint-neutral perimeters of the subsidy program.

One might respond that Congress should not be forced to fund expression with which its members or those they represent disagree or find morally repugnant, and of course, Congress cannot be forced to do so. Congress could decide that it will fund absolutely no art. It does not follow, however, for reasons already discussed,[136] that it may choose indirectly to manipulate both public opinion and private speech through the use of viewpoint-based auxiliary subsidies.

In *National Endowment for the Arts v. Finley*,[137] the Supreme Court adopted a constitutional analysis that, upon first examination, appears to be directly opposite to the analysis suggested here. There the Court rejected a facial constitutional challenge to the decency clause. Justice O'-Connor, speaking for the Court, initially construed the provision to "impose[] no categorical requirement."[138] Rather, it contained only "advisory language" that "stands in sharp contrast to congressional efforts to prohibit the funding of certain clauses of speech."[139] So construed, the Court reasoned, the statute did not present "a realistic danger" that it would compromise First Amendment values.[140]

In rejecting the facial attack, the Court pointed to a number of potential applications of the decency clause that would clearly be constitutional.[141] However, the Court did not completely foreclose the possibility that the decency clause could be applied unconstitutionally in a specific instance.[142] In contrast to the Court's approach, the position taken in the proposed structure suggests that the ex ante categorical application of criteria that are unrelated to the substance of the subsidy is considerably more suspect, under the First Amendment, than the use of multi-factor judgmental criteria in a particular instance.

However, the decision in *Finley* might arguably be distinguishable on the basis of the Court's reliance on the procedural elements of the First

Amendment overbreadth doctrine.[143] That doctrine prohibits facial constitutional challenges brought by litigants whose own behavior may constitutionally be regulated, unless the number of potentially unconstitutional applications of the statute far exceeds the number of constitutional applications.[144] Under the overbreadth analysis, then, the Court could be procedurally barred from considering the provision's constitutionality. But in effect, the Court did rule on the merits of the facial constitutional challenge, finding the statute constitutional in most of its applications.[145] Thus, while the *Finley* Court did employ an analysis similar to the "judgmental necessity" standard developed here,[146] ultimately the decision is flawed, because it ignores the reasoning that renders the decency clause constitutionally suspect at its core.

Selecting Public School Texts

Public schools give rise to a unique First Amendment conundrum. On the one hand, public schools play an important, indeed vital, role in socializing and inculcating values in students.[147] On the other hand, government, in its efforts to socialize and inculcate, "may cast a pall of orthodoxy over the classroom," thereby undermining the First Amendment rights of students.[148] Commentators have often argued that the role of the school as indoctrinator and the First Amendment rights of the students are in direct conflict.[149] As a result of this conflict, the power of the school to indoctrinate often violates the First Amendment rights of students.[150]

How are we to negotiate the conflict between the authority of government as indoctrinator in public schools and the rights of students as private autonomous human beings? A number of scholars have addressed this question. Mark Yudof and Stanley Ingber have argued that the Supreme Court's inability to resolve this conflict makes clear that the primary restraints on the government as indoctrinator in the public schools must be "political, social and attitudinal."[151] Other scholars take a stronger position against governmental indoctrination in the public schools, arguing that society has no legitimate interest in inculcating students. Some of these scholars argue that attempting to inculcate "political values" is inappropriate because there are no "uniformly acceptable" political values.[152] Others argue that attempting to indoctrinate students is inappropriate generally because the government is so ineffective at inculcating that which it seeks (or ought to seek) to inculcate that it has no compelling interest to justify its attempts to indoctrinate students.[153] A number of these scholars have advocated adoption of a "fairness doctrine" in public schools.[154] Such a doctrine would require "that schools expose students to different viewpoints on controversial issues."[155]

Perhaps the clearest area of conflict in the public schools is in the selection of history textbooks. Commentators have noted that the purpose of history texts is "not to explore but to instruct—to tell children what their elders want them to know about their country."[156] Two studies of American textbooks have confirmed this view, concluding that these textbooks generally "minimize the role of dissent in our history."[157] This likely stems from the desire of "elders" that their children not be made fully aware of the potential effectiveness of dissent. Is such a presentation of history constitutionally permissible? That is, may a school board select a textbook although in doing so it inaccurately minimizes the role of dissent in our history?

Two points are particularly relevant to this question. First, it is almost impossible to choose the "best" textbook if to do so is to choose the textbook that objectively contains the "correct" account of history. It is simply impossible to conclusively make such a determination. Rather, selecting the "best" textbook more likely means selecting the textbook that best accords with the view of history espoused by those charged with selecting texts. Second, in selecting a textbook, a school board need not merely select the best transmitter of facts. Rather, as the Supreme Court and many commentators have recognized, the Constitution permits a school board, within certain boundaries, to attempt to inculcate values in its students.[158] Some of this inculcation appropriately occurs through textbooks selected by the school board.

With these points in mind, we can now turn to the question of what factors, under the proposed structure, a school board may properly consider in selecting a history textbook. Consider the hypothetical case of a school board that indicates that it will select only a textbook that portrays history as accurately as possible. Moreover, the school board believes accuracy requires that Christopher Columbus be portrayed as a racist. Pursuant to the board's requirements, although the text might tell of Columbus's arrival in North America, it must also tell of his allegedly savage treatment of Native Americans. According to the structure advocated here, the school board may employ such selection criteria.

In deciding to purchase textbooks, the government makes a viewpoint-neutral choice to fund a particular study or class of speech, what amounts to a constitutionally valid categorical subsidy. Within this category of speech, a school board may select a particular textbook for use in its schools. The First Amendment does not require that the board make a choice through a process of random selection.

Under the proposed structure, the board's choice falls within the "judgmental necessity" exception, as long as it makes that choice on the basis of criteria "substantially related" to the predescribed purpose of the program pursuant to which textbooks are funded. The job of the school board, presumably, is to select the textbook that will provide students with the most complete and accurate description and understanding of history. If a particular school board believes that Christopher Columbus was a racist, then it is likely that, all other things being equal, this school board will choose a textbook that describes Columbus as a racist over one that ignores his treatment of Native Americans. Insofar as subjective viewpoint is inextricably linked to the board's judgment of textbook quality, it is difficult to argue that a school board cannot make the decision based on the competing textbooks' treatment of Columbus.[159]

The more troubling situation concerns a case in which the school board selects a textbook that it openly believes to be inferior in its picture of history but superior insofar as it inculcates values that the school board desires to inculcate. While inculcation of values is an inescapable function of the educational process,[160] surely the First Amendment imposes outer limits on this power.[161] A school board could not, for example, constitutionally require instructors to teach that the New Deal never took place, simply because the board wished to inculcate only free-market values in its students. Similarly, one should not deem acceptable the government's conscious falsification or manipulation of historical fact and analysis for the avowed purpose of indoctrinating students.[162] Because of the obvious proof problems in establishing such blatantly improper conduct on the part of the school board, however, cases in which such a showing could be made convincingly are likely to be extremely rare.

Rejecting Alternative Structures

Before the groundwork for accepting the proposed structure is complete, we must explore the comparative merits of alternative structures previously suggested for measuring the constitutionality of government subsidization of expression. The Supreme Court's opinion in *Rust* all too effectively illustrates the inherent defects of the non-speech-specific "unconstitutional conditions" approach.[163] Moreover, none of the other structures previously put forward by scholars adequately resolves the difficult constitutional issues surrounding subsidy decisions.

The "Spheres-of-Neutrality" Approach

David Cole has proposed a structure for gauging the constitutionality of government subsidization of speech.[164] Although Cole purports to consider the benefits and dangers of government subsidization of speech,[165] his structure fails sufficiently to accommodate either of these considerations. As a result, his approach would allow the restriction of government subsidization of speech even when that subsidization would actually foster First Amendment values, while simultaneously permitting government subsidization of speech when those subsidies would threaten these values.

In establishing his structure for gauging the constitutionality of governmental subsidization of speech, Cole initially recognizes that the government's direct restriction of speech is very similar to the its selective subsidization of speech.[166] He notes that, with regard to direct government restriction of speech,[167] courts generally enforce "a strict neutrality mandate."[168] That is, "government generally must remain neutral as to the content and viewpoint of speech, absent a compelling justification."[169] Cole then questions whether this neutrality mandate is "transferable to selective government funding of speech."[170] He contends that the mandate is not perfectly transferable, because of the nature of government speech. He recognizes that "[w]e cannot mandate neutral funding across the board, because such rule would disable government as we know it."[171] However, Cole believes that the neutrality mandate should not be completely rejected. He argues that "[i]f government were allowed unfettered discretion to support speech that it favors, public debate would be subject to substantial co-optation."[172]

To accommodate these concerns, Cole proposes a "structural accommodation, attuned to the role that certain institutions play in maintaining a robust public debate and an autonomous citizenry."[173] This accommodation "draw[s] on the neutrality principle that governs selective government prohibitions on speech, but [applies] it only to certain spheres of government funding."[174] Therefore, Cole proposes that:

> [w]here neutrality is consistent with . . . an institution's function, strict neutrality should be required; where some non-neutral content decisions

must be made, the First Amendment should guarantee a degree of independence for the decision-maker. Where, on the other hand, the institution does not play an important role in furthering public dialogue or individual autonomy, or where non-neutral government speech is necessary to further an important government function or First Amendment values, government should be free to support speech non-neutrally.[175]

Under Cole's structure, when "government non-neutrality does not pose a substantial risk of skewing or indoctrinating, it should be permitted."[176] Cole believes that this risk is unacceptably high only in certain predetermined institutional settings or expressive contexts. He refers to his approach as a "spheres-of-neutrality" approach.[177] Indicating that the Supreme Court has recognized them as such, Cole initially identifies public fora,[178] public education,[179] and the press[180] as such "spheres of neutrality."[181] He suggests a three-pronged approach for determining whether other settings qualify as "spheres of neutrality":

> First, the Court should ask whether government control of the content of speech in the institution would be threatening to a vigorous public debate or to the autonomy of listeners; second, the Court should ask whether the internal operation of the institution is consistent with a neutrality mandate; and third, where non-neutrality poses a threat to free speech values, but strict neutrality would impede the institution's internal functioning, the court should ask whether the independence of speakers can be structurally accommodated in some intermediate fashion.[182]

With this approach as his guide, Cole finds that the arts[183] and professional fiduciary counseling[184] also qualify as spheres of neutrality.

Cole's approach has many flaws. First, it is unclear under his analysis whether *any* forum exists in which non-neutral funding should be permitted. Indeed, Cole never suggests one. In any event, if settings exist that do not qualify as "spheres of neutrality," Cole's approach does not clearly explain why the government should be permitted to fund them in a non-neutral manner to any degree that it desires. Indeed, government non-neutrality in any setting may undermine First Amendment values.[185]

An examination of his classification of the arts as a sphere of neutrality underscores the problem with Cole's approach. While it is incontrovertible, as Cole notes, that art "is a forum for dissent and opposition"[186] and therefore that government control over the arts would "be threatening to a vigorous public debate,"[187] it is far less clear that one could not say the same of every other forum or subject of expression. Although Cole correctly notes the historical importance of the arts as a forum for dissent and opposition,[188] this history is not dispositive of whether an institution today serves as such a forum. The logical question to be posed to Cole, then, is whether there exists any forum over which government control does not threaten vigorous public debate.

The "Condition-of-Public Discourse" Approach

Owen Fiss has objected to a "criterion-based" examination of government subsidization of the arts, such as the one proposed here. Fiss argues that examinations that rely on an inquiry into the criteria on which the government bases its funding decisions are suspect for three reasons. First, he argues that "[w]hile in the discrimination context it might be possible to construct a finite and rather well-understood list of forbidden criteria . . . in the free speech context, no such list readily suggests itself."[189] Second, he argues that even if forbidden criteria could be located, "often the real reason for an allocative decision cannot be authoritatively ascertained."[190] Finally, Fiss contends that the criterion approach is particularly inappropriate under the First Amendment because such an approach focuses on individual fairness, while the "First Amendment is a guarantee of collective self-determination."[191]

As an alternative to the criterion approach, Fiss proposes that the focus of a system gauging the constitutionality of NEA grants "should be on the condition of public discourse, not the process by which that condition was created."[192] Fiss argues that the judiciary "should keep the focus on effects, specifically the effect the exercise of state power has on public debate. . . . Such a judgment requires a sense of the public agenda, a grasp of the issues that are now before the public and what might plausibly be brought before it, and then an appraisal of the state of public discourse . . . to see whether all the positions on the issue are being fully and fairly presented so that the people can make a meaningful choice."[193] For example, Fiss concludes that Robert Mapplethorpe's art would require funding because the denial of a grant "would impoverish public debate" by preventing a voice that counters the prevailing orthodoxy regarding homosexuality from reaching the marketplace.[194]

Serious flaws exist in both Fiss's criticism of the criterion-based approach and his suggested alternative. Whatever one thinks of his criticisms of a criterion-based approach, one should have considerable difficulty in accepting his suggested "condition-of-public-discourse" alternative. Ironically, while Fiss criticizes a criterion-based approach because of its inability to fashion workable and principled criteria, his suggested alternative suffers from a complete lack of workable or predictable standards by which to determine its applicability. How can a reviewing court possibly decide whether, absent public funding, the ideas in question would not reach the public?

Even if one were to accept Fiss's first two criticisms of a criterion-based analysis, his conclusion flowing from these criticisms is suspect. Fiss assumes that it is more difficult under the First Amendment than it is under the Fourteenth Amendment to identify forbidden criteria, and even if one locates forbidden criteria, it will be difficult to know when the NEA has relied on these criteria in allocating scarce resources. Although these may be valid observations, the difficulties they present do not invalidate an inquiry into these factors. Certainly one can point to criteria on which the NEA may not constitutionally rely. Under the approach adopted here, for example, the NEA may not make subsidization decisions based on the unrelated viewpoints of those applying for funding. The government thus may not refuse to fund an artist simply because that artist produces art advocating liberal political principles. Moreover, once forbidden criteria are identified, the possible difficulty of determining whether these criteria have been employed in a particular case should not preclude a court from attempting to make this determination.

Fiss's third criticism is also misplaced. He argues that a criterion-based methodology is particularly inappropriate under the First Amendment because it focuses on individual fairness, while "the First Amendment is a guarantee of collective self-determination." The approach proposed here does not rely exclusively on notions of individualism. Quite to the contrary, it takes into account notions of communitarian interest in addition to elements of individual self-development. Indeed, the approach deems certain criteria unconstitutional because of their potential effect on both community self-government and individual self-realization.[195] The decision not to fund a work of art because of the political viewpoint the work espouses is suspect because such a decision might allow the government to skew artificially the marketplace of ideas and therefore undermine both autonomy and communitarian values that arguably underlie the First Amendment.[196]

Finally, Fiss's approach all but eliminates the power of those making an award to consider the inherent artistic merit or quality of a work, the criterion on which NEA funding was intended to be based in the first place.[197]

Presumably, under Fiss's structure, a monochromatic crayon drawing that voices a viewpoint that is otherwise insufficiently represented in the marketplace of ideas should logically be chosen for funding over a painting universally deemed a superior work of art, if that painting espouses a viewpoint that reinforces the prevailing orthodoxy. Fiss's approach thus places significant restraints on the ability of government to foster individual self-realization and human flourishing by promoting and encouraging literary or artistic excellence.[198] The structure proposed here avoids these two problems by allowing government to fund art regardless of the political viewpoint it expresses while enabling government to adhere to the statutory objective of the NEA to fund the highest quality art.

Conclusion

In proposing an analytical structure to determine the constitutionality of government subsidization of expression, this chapter has employed a methodology that has in the past been described in other contexts as a priori balancing.[199] I have attempted to fashion broadly phrased, flexible guidelines, chosen because I believe that these categories best fulfill the purposes served by the protection of free expression. These selections are by no means free of doubt or controversy. Moreover, application of these abstract categories to specific situations may not always be obvious. As the chapter has shown, however, alternatives that other commentators have suggested fail to provide a viable method for sorting out the complex constitutional issues inherent in the review of subsidy decisions.

The proposed structure focuses on an effort to tame the "Jekyll–Hyde" nature of speech subsidization by government. By selectively subsidizing speech, government may artificially skew public debate, thereby undermining the effective operation of the democratic process. Selective subsidization also may deter an individual's freely chosen expressive activity, thereby threatening autonomy and self-realization values. Yet a complete denial of governmental power to subsidize expression would also significantly undermine First Amendment values by precluding government from facilitating the communicative and expressive activities of private individuals and entities. This chapter's proposed structure seeks to reconcile these competing strains.

One may believe that the analytical structure proposed here is vulnerable to criticism from opposite perspectives. On the one hand, it might be argued that the approach overly complicates and confuses the constitutional inquiry because it provides neither a single, yes-or-no answer to the question of the constitutionality of expressive subsidies nor a single, workable criterion by which to separate constitutional subsidies from unconstitutional ones. On the other hand, one might criticize the structure for seeking mechanistic, easily applied solutions to what are in reality difficult and subjective value choices.

Both criticisms should be rejected. That difficult and subjective value choices are involved cannot alter the basic fact that somehow those choices must be made. The structure adopted here attempts to balance the competing interests, ex ante, by fashioning guiding categorical precepts designed to implement universally accepted principles of free-speech theory. While they are far from mechanistic or automatic in their application, neither do they suffer from total malleability or turn substantially on the subjective judgment of the individual implementing them. As a result, they represent a significant advance over previously suggested approaches.

7

Conclusion
Free Expression and the Sound of Money

Because money talks, there are many who wish to silence it. The goal of this book has been to establish that for the very reason that money does talk, its use for expressive purposes is central to the successful operation of both the nation's democratic system and the free speech guarantee. To restrict the expressive use of money, or the use of expression for the purpose of making money, dramatically reduces the flow of information and opinion that forms the lifeblood of democracy. Hence, such restriction contravenes core values served by the First Amendment's guarantee of free expression.

Government may attempt to interfere with the expressive use of economic power in a number of ways. First, it may seek to regulate or suppress the use of expression for purposes of promoting commercial sale—so-called "commercial speech." Second, it may seek to regulate or suppress the use of economic power for purposes of expression about traditionally protected subjects, such as political expression by corporations or campaign contributions or expenditures by private individuals or entities. Third, it may choose to redistribute existing private communicative power, by creating rights of access to privately owned print or broadcast media. Finally, it may attempt to manipulate private expression by selectively funding private expression that takes positions the government advocates. Though each of these regulatory options gives rise to complex and unique constitutional problems and issues, with only limited exception each of these strategies should be found to violate the First Amendment's guarantee of free expression.

Several of these options constitute frontal assaults on private expression because they directly restrict the flow of information and opinion. This is true of restrictions on commercial speech, restrictions on corporate expression, and restrictions on campaign contributions and expenditures. Such efforts strike at the heart of both private self-realization and the functioning of the democratic process. By reducing the flow of information and opinion, they expand public ignorance—a result in prima facie conflict with both of these core free speech values.

On a more subtle level, restrictions on commercial speech, corporate political expression, and campaign finance indirectly but nevertheless ominously tend to favor one political viewpoint over another. Invariably, each of these categories of expression will favor politically conservative, anti-redistributive positions. This fact is not lost on many of the scholars and jurists who have urged their restriction. Yet nothing undermines First Amendment values more than selective governmental regulation of expression on the basis of disagreement with the viewpoint expressed. Careful deconstruction of the arguments used to justify such restrictions reveals that in many instances that is exactly what they are. They therefore should trigger the full force of the First Amendment's protection.

The remaining strategies for interfering with the expressive exercise of economic power do not—at least on their face—directly reduce the flow of private expression. To the contrary, they appear actually to expand that flow, and therefore may be thought to give rise to less troubling First Amendment difficulties than do affirmative restrictions on expression. To a certain extent, that is true. Governmentally created private rights of access on one level actually expand expressive power, by providing individuals with an opportunity to communicate that they otherwise would not have had. Government subsidization of private expression similarly creates opportunities for private communication and expression that would not otherwise exist. In this sense, both of these regulatory options appear at the very least to present a diluted First Amendment problem, if indeed they present a First Amendment problem at all.

It would be a serious mistake, however, to ignore the troubling free speech issues to which these supposedly expansive forms of regulation may give rise. The power to establish private rights of access carries with it a virtually uncontrollable governmental power to burden speakers in invidious ways. A requirement that a private communicator provide access to those advocating views the communicator finds offensive presents most or all of the problems to which forced expression has been found to give rise: demoralization, skewing, and humiliation of private individuals or entities. Rights of access give rise to such dangers, without any assurance that the quality of public debate will be enriched as a result of their creation. For in most situations rights of access will amount to a zero sum game: A requirement that access be provided correspondingly curtails the speaker's options.

The dangers of selective or manipulative governmental subsidization of private expression are similarly great. By supporting only private speakers with whom it agrees, government penalizes those with competing viewpoints. Moreover, government may skew the nature of public debate in invidious ways. It most certainly does not follow that the First Amendment imposes a blanket bar to governmental subsidization of private communication. Such a rigid barrier would be counterproductive to the very values the First Amendment is designed to foster. However, much as when humankind first discovered fire, it is vitally important to recognize and distinguish between the potentially positive and negative uses of the process, lest we be consumed by a device originally designed to aid us. In these pages, I have attempted to develop a complex but understandable construct to distinguish the beneficial uses of governmental subsidization from those that are more invidious than helpful.

In putting forth my theories concerning the intersection between free speech and economic power, it is of utmost importance that I emphasize a number of clarifying or qualifying points. First, to suggest that governmental restriction of the use of money for purposes of expression contravenes the First Amendment in no way implies a belief that, absent such restriction, all speakers and viewpoints will have identical opportunities to convey their message. Economic reality today is—and probably always has been—that those with greater economic resources will be able to purchase greater opportunities to communicate. But this is equally true of the ability to purchase countless other services, commodities, and opportunities. The simple fact is that those with more money will be in a position to purchase more than those with less money.

Nothing in the First Amendment prevents government from redistributing economic power or resources, even though a possible result would be that those from whom that power has been taken will have a reduced ability to purchase opportunities for expression. Such an incidental negative impact on expressive power is simply a necessary adjunct to government's general power to regulate non-expressive activity. However, when government singles out use of economic resources for purposes of expression for regulation, the resulting gratuitous inhibition on expression clearly contravenes the First Amendment.

Second, I must emphasize that to advocate full First Amendment protection for commercial speech does not in any way dictate a similar view favoring the constitutional protection of economic liberties in general. Indeed, one of the fatal flaws in the theories of those who oppose full protection for commercial speech is their reliance on a mistaken equation between commercial speech protection and substantive economic due process. The First Amendment protects expression, not conduct. This is certainly true in the context of political speech: To conclude that one has a First Amendment right to advocate or consider the possibility of certain behavior does not necessarily imply that one has an equally powerful constitutional right to engage in that behavior. To be sure, scholars have long debated the legitimacy of the distinction between speech and conduct for purposes of constitutional protection. I have always found the distinction quite easy to understand and support, though admittedly there will exist close cases of definition at the margins. But the key point for present purposes is that whatever one believes about the viability of that distinction, there is no reason to deem the problem unique to the protection of commercial speech. If those who advocate full constitutional protection only for political expression may draw a speech–conduct dichotomy, I fail to see any logical basis for denying me the ability to draw the very same distinction in the context of commercial speech protection.

Finally, and perhaps most importantly, it is necessary to emphasize that one who advocates full First Amendment protection for the role of money in the free expression system does not automatically endorse the substantive views that are expressed as a result. It is standard operating procedure in First Amendment scholarship that an important distinction must be drawn between a belief in an individual's or entity's right to speak on the one hand and substantive agreement with the normative positions being expressed, on the other. One who defended the First Amendment rights of Communists in the 1950s was not necessarily a Communist, any more than one who defended the First Amendment rights of Nazis in the 1970s necessarily agreed with their political positions. To defend the rights of powerful economic interests to contribute to the expressive marketplace by no means signals automatic agreement with everything they might say.

This caveat underscores the fundamental point of my entire analysis. All too often, the constitutional arguments that have been mounted against the role of money within the system of free expression have focused on—or been openly motivated by—the likely offensive or politically harmful nature of the views that will be expressed as a result of the widespread use of economic power. These arguments have often been framed in terms of an appeal to equality. In reality, however, the equality to which these arguments appeal is simply a belief in a type of economic redistribution. Yet the very notion of value neutrality that underlies any commitment to free expression is inescapably violated by a protective structure grounded in a selective favoring of one particular political or economic philosophy. Just as Justice Holmes once warned that "[t]he 14th Amendment does not enact Mr. Herbert Spencer's Social Statics,"[1] which advocated a stark form of economic Darwinism, neither does the First Amendment prohibit the enactment of such a free market philosophy through the democratic process.

Ironically, the appeal to economic equality, used as a justification for suppressing the speech of the economically powerful, violates the real equality principle that is a necessary condition to any meaningful system of free speech. Absent government's commitment to an equality of ideas in regulating expression, the First Amendment is rendered at best useless and at worst a harmful and manipulative political tool.

One may of course reasonably believe that the harms caused by "big money" must be stopped. But whether or not this is true as a social, political, or moral matter, there can be no doubt that manipulating the First Amendment to achieve this end will give rise to a cure that is considerably more dangerous than the disease.

Notes

NOTES TO CHAPTER 1

1. See, e.g., Ronald Collins & David Skover, The Death of Discourse 83–105 (1996); Owen Fiss, Liberalism Divided (1996); Cass R. Sunstein, Democracy and the Problem of Free Speech (1993); Steven Shiffrin, The Politics of the Mass Media and the Free Speech Principle, 69 Ind. L.J. 689 (1994); Mark Tushnet, Corporations and Free Speech, in The Politics of Law 253 (David Kairys ed., 1982); J. Skelly Wright, Money and the Pollution of Politics: Is the First Amendment an Obstacle to Political Equality?, 82 Colum. L. Rev. 609 (1982).

2. See, e.g., C. Edwin Baker, Human Liberty and Freedom of Speech (1989); Fiss, supra note 1.

3. See, e.g., Baker, supra note 2.

4. See Chapter 2, infra.

5. See Chapter 4, infra.

6. See, e.g., Wright, supra note 1.

7. See, e.g., Fiss, supra note 1; Sunstein, supra note 1.

8. See, e.g., Fiss, supra note 1.

9. Fiss, supra note 1, at 13–15.

10. In certain narrow circumstances, such as reasonable time-place-manner restrictions where there exists a strong competing interest in the public's safety, comfort or egress, government may be forced to draw such lines. However, absent such competing and powerful needs, government has no authority to draw such arbitrary lines.

11. Alexander Meiklejohn, Political Freedom (1960). It should be noted that even in the specific context of the town meeting this argument is fallacious. A particular view may be supported in different ways, and in any event the sheer weight of opinion might itself be deemed probative.

12. See generally Martin H. Redish, Freedom of Expression: A Critical Analysis (1984); Baker, supra note 2.

13. See, e.g., Meiklejohn, supra note 11; Robert Bork, Neutral Principles and Some First Amendment Problems, 47 Ind. L.J. 1 (1971).

14. It should be noted that in a *constitutional* democracy, certain moral or political choices have been insulated from simple majoritarian control. However,

even these choices are subject to super-majoritarian control through the amendment process. Moreover, the substance of these constitutional choices was originally shaped through some form of representative process, so they cannot be characterized as externally imposed and unchangeable moral choices.

15. Cf. Frank Michelman, Law's Republic, 97 Yale L.J.1493 (1988).

16. For more detailed discussion, see Chapter 3, infra.

17. The concept of the equality of ideas, it should be emphasized, in no way requires acceptance of an epistemological principle of total moral relativism, nor one of complete governmental neutrality on issues of normative concern. Indeed, as I argue in Chapter 6, government itself should be deemed to have every opportunity to contribute to these normative debates. The point is, simply, that government must not be allowed to suppress expression of private individuals and entities selectively on the basis of its own normative judgments. And such a principle derives, not from any formalistic acceptance of a particular theory of epistemology, but rather as a necessary corollary to a society's initial normative commitment to the process-based value of democracy.

18. The point is examined in more detail in Chapters 3 and 5, infra.

NOTES TO CHAPTER 2

1. See generally Ronald Rotunda, The Commercial Speech Doctrine in the Supreme Court, 1976 U. Ill. L.F. 1080.

2. 316 U.S. 52 (1942).

3. Id. at 54: "This Court has unequivocally held that the streets are proper places for the exercise of the freedom of communicating information and disseminating opinion and that, though the states and municipalities may appropriately regulate the privilege in the public interest, they may not unduly burden or proscribe its employment in these public thoroughfares. We are equally clear that the Constitution imposes no such restraint on government as respects purely commercial."

4. See Rotunda, supra note 1; Martin H. Redish, Freedom of Expression: A Critical Analysis 60–61 (1984).

5. 425 U.S. 748 (1976).

6. Ohralik v. Ohio State Bar Ass'n, 436 U.S. 447, 456 (1978).

7. Compare id. at 464 (attorney's in-hospital solicitation of tort plaintiff may constitutionally be restricted) with In re Primus, 436 U.S. 412 (1978) (civil rights attorney's solicitation of potential plaintiffs in public interest litigation is constitutionally protected); see also Friedman v. Rogers, 440 U.S. 1, 13 (1979).

8. 447 U.S. 557 (1980).

9. Id. at 564.

10. See, e.g., NAACP v. Button, 371 U.S. 415, 438 (1963) (employing "compelling interest" test).

11. 447 U.S. at 567–68.

12. 478 U.S. 328 (1986).

13. See 44 Liquormart v. Rhode Island, 517 U.S. 484 (1996).

14. 478 U.S. at 340.

15. See John M. Blim, Comment, Free Speech and Health Claims Under the Nutrition Labeling and Education Act of 1990: Applying a Rehabilitated Central Hudson Test, 88 Nw. U. L. Rev. 733, 751 (1994): "[I]nterpretations that see *Posadas* as materially reducing the constitutional protection afforded commercial speech by the *Central Hudson* test tend to misread or exaggerate the case's result. . . . *Posadas* . . . largely toed the *Central Hudson* line."

16. 478 U.S. at 340.

17. See, e.g., West Coast Hotel Co. v. Parrish, 300 U.S. 379 (1937) (use of rational basis test as standard of substantive due process in the regulation of private commercial activity).

18. See, e.g., Rubin v. Coors Brewing Co., 514 U.S. (1995) (federal statute restricting beer labeling held unconstitutional because regulation failed to directly advance substantial interest); Peel v. Attorney Registration & Disciplinary Comm'n of Illinois, 496 U.S. 91 (1990) (state may not categorically prohibit attorney from advertising his certification as a trial specialist on his letterhead).

19. 517 U.S. 484 (1996).

20. See id. at 496 (finding that false or misleading commercial speech falls outside of First Amendment protection).

21. 517 U.S. at 495.

22. Id. at 498.

23. Id. at 501.

24. Id. at 511.

25. Id. at 518 (Thomas, J., concurring).

26. Id. at 517–28 (Thomas, J., concurring).

27. Id. at 512.

28. Id. at 528 (O'Connor, J., concurring in the judgment).

29. See discussion supra text at notes 23–24.

30. See discussion supra text at note 24.

31. 517 U.S. at 529.

32. See discussion supra text at notes 23–24.

33. See discussion supra text at notes 1–17.

34. See, e.g., Bad Frog Brewery, Inc. v. New York St. Liquor Auth., 134 F. 3d 87 (2d Cir. 1998).

35. See, e.g., Thomas H. Jackson & John Calvin Jeffries, Commercial Speech: Economic Due Process and the First Amendment, 65 Va. L. Rev. 1 (1979); Ronald Collins & David Skover, The Death of Discourse (1996); R. George Wright, Selling Words: Free Speech and Commercial Culture 7 (1997).

36. See generally Martin H. Redish, Tobacco Advertising and the First

Amendment, 81 Iowa L. Rev. 589 (1996); Martin H. Redish, The First Amendment in the Marketplace: Commercial Speech and the Values of Free Expression, 39 Geo. Wash. L. Rev. 429 (1971).

37. It has been noted that the definition of commercial speech is "unsettled," with "'commonsense differences' and a variety of slogans for identification," leading to "an astonishing variety of interpretations." Todd F. Simon, Defining Commercial Speech: A Focus on Process Rather Than Content, 20 N. Eng. L. Rev. 215, 216 (1984). Compare Bolger v. Youngs Drug Prod. Corp., 463 U.S. 60, 68 (1983) (unsolicited direct-mail pamphlet describing the risks of venereal disease and the advantages of condoms in preventing venereal disease constituted commercial speech where the pamphlet mentioned a specific brand of condom) with In re Primus, 436 U.S. 412, 431 (1978) (letter from ACLU attorney offering to represent recipient not commercial speech).

38. See Redish, supra note 36, 39 Geo. Wash. L. Rev. at 429.

39. In the words of one group of critics of commercial speech protection, "Whatever else it may mean, the concept of a first amendment right of personal autonomy in matters of belief and expression stops short of a seller hawking his wares." Jackson & Jeffries, supra note 35, at 14.

40. Alexander Meiklejohn, Political Freedom (1960); Robert Bork, Neutral Principles and Some First Amendment Problems, 47 Ind. L.J. 1 (1971).

41. See Meiklejohn, supra note 40, at 27: "The principle of the freedom of speech springs from the necessities of the program of self government. . . . It is a deduction from the basic American agreement that public issues shall be decided by universal suffrage."

42. See Virginia St. Bd. of Pharmacy v. Virginia Citizens Consumer Council, Inc., 425 U.S. 748, 762 (1976) (defining commercial speech at that which "proposes a commercial transaction"); Bolger v. Youngs Drug Products Corp., 463 U.S. 60, 66 (1983) (describing the core notion of commercial speech as "speech which does no more than propose a commercial transaction"). In Central Hudson Gas & Electric Corp. v. Public Service Corp., 447 U.S. 557, 561 (1980), the Court defined commercial speech as expression tied to the economic interests of the speaker. Such a definition broadens the concept beyond the narrow scope of pure commercial advertising. However, in *Bolger* the Court returned to the "propose-a-commercial-transaction" approach. See Steven Shiffrin, The First Amendment and Economic Regulation: Away from a General Theory of the First Amendment, 78 Nw. U. L. Rev. 1212, 1222 (1983). For present purposes, nothing turns on this disparity. Either form of the definition penalizes expression because of the presence of an economic motivation.

43. See note 42, supra.

44. See Bose Corp. v. Consumers Union of United States, Inc., 466 U.S. 485 (1984).

45. For the best description of this position, see Vincent Blasi, The Pathological Perspective and the First Amendment, 85 Colum. L. Rev. 449 (1985).

46. See, e.g., Police Dep't v. Mosley, 408 U.S. 92, 96 (1972) (First Amendment requires that all viewpoints enjoy equal opportunity to be heard); Schacht v. United States, 398 U.S. 58 (1970) (holding unconstitutional a congressional ban on the unauthorized wearing of American military uniforms in a manner calculated to discredit the armed forces). See also Geoffrey Stone, Restrictions of Speech Because of Its Content: The Peculiar Case of Subject-Matter Restrictions, 46 U. Chi. L. Rev. 81, 103 (1978) (government lacks power to restrict speech because it disapproves of the message conveyed).

47. Compare Meiklejohn, supra note 40 (First Amendment designed solely to facilitate self-governing process); Bork, supra note 40 (First Amendment protects only political expression advocating lawful conduct); with C. Edwin Baker, Scope of the First Amendment Freedom of Speech, 25 UCLA L. Rev. 964 (1978) (free speech guarantee designed to foster individual liberty); Redish, supra note 4, at 9–86 (free speech designed to foster self-realization).

48. See Vincent Blasi, The Checking Value in First Amendment Theory, 1977 Am. B. Found. Research J. 521 (First Amendment designed to check governmental excesses and abuses).

49. See Meiklejohn, supra note 40.

50. See Baker, supra note 47; Redish, supra note 4. See also Thomas Scanlon, A Theory of Freedom of Expression, 1 Phil. & Pub. Aff. 204 (1972) (advocating "autonomy" rationale for free speech protection).

51. See Daniel A. Farber & Philip P. Frickey, Practical Reason and the First Amendment, 34 UCLA L. Rev. 1615 (1987).

52. I have discussed these issues in Martin H. Redish, The Constitution as Political Structure 4–6 (1995).

53. See Frank Michelman, Law's Republic, 97 Yale L.J. 1493 (1988) (arguing that protection of individual rights is required so that individuals can be active participants in process of collective self-rule).

54. John Stuart Mill recognized this intersection in On Liberty, where he argued:

> The worth of a State, in the long run, is the worth of the individuals composing it; and a State which postpones the interests of their mental expansion and elevation, . . . a state which dwarfs its men, in order that they may be more docile instruments in its hands even for beneficial purposes—will find that with small men no great thing can be accomplished.

John Stuart Mill, On Liberty 68 (1913).

55. The "pluralist" view of democracy conceptualizes the process as one of decentralized bargaining among competing interest groups. See, e.g., David Truman,

The Governmental Process (1951). See also Cass R. Sunstein, Interest Groups in American Public Law, 38 Stan. L. Rev. 29 (1985).

56. Thomas Spragens, Reason and Democracy 148 (1990).

57. Id. at 148–49. For a critical discussion of the "rational choice" school of democratic theory, which is premised on the assumption of the individual's mechanical pursuit of his or her self-interest, see Jane Mansbridge, Self-Interest in Political Life, 18 Pol. Theory 132 (1990).

58. David Held, Political Theory and the Modern State 13 (1989).

59. See sources cited in note 55, supra. See also Robert Dahl, A Preface to Democratic Theory 63–123 (1956).

60. Held, supra note 58, at 13.

61. The point can best be illustrated by reference to the writings of Hillel, the famed Jewish rabbi and philosopher. Hillel rejected a concept of mutual exclusivity between the pursuit of individual interests and a communitarian concern for the interests of others: "If I am nothing to myself, who will be for me? And if I am for myself only, what am I?" Quoted in Chapters of the Fathers 17 (R. Hirsch ed. 1967).

In accompanying commentary, Professor Hirsch explains the quotation:

> It is only through his own efforts that a man can attain spiritual fitness and moral worth, which are the most essential attributes to which he can aspire. Similarly, it is primarily upon himself, his own diligence, his own efforts and his own good sense that man must depend in the process of acquiring and certainly of preserving the worldly goods he needs. . . . But even though he may have become who and what he is solely by dint of his own efforts, a man must never say: "Since it is solely by my own efforts that I have become what I am, I will use my attainments for myself alone." For it is only when, in selfless devotion, he actively works to create, to establish and to increase the happiness and prosperity of his fellow man that a man begins to become truly human in the image of his God.

Id. at 16–17 n. 14

62. Held, supra note 58, at 176.

63. Carole Pateman, The Problem of Political Obligation: A Critique of Liberal Theory 17 (1985).

64. Held, supra note 58, at 176 (emphasis omitted).

65. Id. at 177.

66. See, for example, the Civil Rights Act of 1964, 42 U.S.C. § 2000, prohibiting most discrimination on the basis of race in public accommodations or employment.

67. See Linda Hirshman, The Virtue of Liberality in American Life, 88 Mich. L. Rev. 983, 1011–22 (1990) (describing impact of poverty on participation in political life).

68. "[I]t has been said that democracy is the worst form of Government ex-

cept all those other forms that have been tried from time to time." Winston Churchill, Speech to the House of Commons (Nov. 11, 1947), reprinted in The Oxford Dictionary of Quotations 150 (3d ed. 1979).

69. See David Easton, The Political System 223 (1953) (defining democracy as "a political system in which power is so distributed that control over the authoritative allocation of values lies in the hands of the mass of the people").

70. See John Rawls, A Theory of Justice 136–42 (1971).

71. U.S. Const. Art. V (authorizing super-majoritarian process for enacting constitutional amendments).

72. See discussion infra at 000–000.

73. See Meiklejohn, supra note 40. Meiklejohn began with the premise that "[g]overnments . . . derive their just powers from the consent of the governed. If that consent be lacking, governments have no just powers." Id. at 9. Because the citizens perform the governing function in the voting booth, they need a free flow of information and opinion relevant to the political decision-making process. Hence, "[t]he principle of the freedom of speech springs from the necessities of the program of self government. . . . It is a deduction from the basic American agreement that public issues shall be decided by universal suffrage." Id. at 27.

74. Gertz v. Robert Welch, Inc., 418 U.S. 323, 339 (1974).

75. See sources cited in note 46, supra.

76. Abrams v. United States, 250 U.S. 616, 630 (1919) (Holmes, J., dissenting).

77. See, e.g., R. Wolff, The Poverty of Liberalism 11–12 (1968) (criticizing the marketplace-of-ideas theory of John Stuart Mill); Baker, supra note 47, at 967 (same).

78. See, e.g., Brandenburg v. Ohio, 395 U.S. 444 (1969) (per curiam) (under First Amendment, state may forbid advocacy of use of force when and only when such advocacy is directed toward inciting or producing imminent lawless action and is likely to produce such action).

79. See, e.g., Bethel School Dist. No. 43 v. Fraser, 475 U.S. 675 (1986) (schools); Greer v. Spock, 424 U.S. 828 (1976) (military).

80. See generally Stone, supra note 46.

81. See, e.g., New York Times Co. v. Sullivan, 376 U.S. 254, 280 (1964) (full First Amendment protection extends even to defamation said out of motivation of revenge or hatred, as long as speech was not uttered with knowledge of falsity or reckless disregard of truth). The same principle applies to noncommercial speech uttered for purposes of financial gain. See id. at 265–66 ("That the Times was paid for publishing the [challenged] advertisement is as immaterial in this connection as is the fact that newspapers are sold."). See also Consolidated Edison Co. v. Public Serv. Comm'n, 447 U.S. 530 (1980) (holding that profit-motivated corporations have a fully protected First Amendment right to contribute to debate on public issues).

82. See New York Times Co. v. Sullivan, 376 U.S. 254 (1964). See also Meiklejohn, supra note 40.

83. See, e.g., Cohen v. California, 403 U.S. 15, (1971): "[M]uch linguistic expression serves a dual communicative function: it conveys not only ideas capable of relatively precise, detached explication, but otherwise inexpressible emotions as well. In fact, words are often chosen as much for their emotive as their cognitive force. We cannot sanction the view that the Constitution, while solicitous of the cognitive content of individual speech, has little or no regard for that emotive function which, practically speaking, may often be the more important element of the overall message sought to be conveyed." In *Cohen,* the Court held unconstitutional the conviction of an individual for wearing a jacket in public with the words "Fuck the Draft" on it. See also Texas v. Johnson, 491 U.S. 397 (1989) (prohibition on flag-burning as form of political protest held unconstitutional).

84. See, e.g., Erznoznik v. City of Jacksonville, 422 U.S. 205 (1975) (manner regulation aimed at content of expression is subject to compelling interest review).

85. Virginia Board, 425 U.S. at 772, n. 24.

86. Id.

87. 44 Liquormart v. Rhode Island, 517 U.S. 484 (1996).

88. 376 U.S. 254 (1964).

89. Id. at 279–80.

90. Id. at 265–66.

91. See discussion infra text at notes 121–22.

92. See, e.g., United States v. O'Brien, 391 U.S. 367, 376 (1968) ("We cannot accept the view that an apparently limitless variety of conduct can be labeled 'speech' whenever the person engaging in the conduct intends thereby to express an idea.").

93. See Friedman v. Rogers, 440 U.S. 1, 10, n. 9 (1979).

94. For a variant of this argument, see Daniel A. Farber, Commercial Speech and First Amendment Theory, 74 Nw. U. L. Rev. 372 (1979).

95. Even at the point of sale, it should be noted, speech promoting the sale is arguably still sufficiently distinct from the actual sale as to remain fully protected expression.

96. See Brandenburg v. Ohio, 395 U.S. 444 (1969) (per curiam), discussed in note 78, supra.

97. To the extent the speaker is not a corporation, of course, this rationale is wholly irrelevant.

98. See, e.g., C. Edwin Baker, Realizing Self-Realization: Corporate Political Expenditures and Redish's "The Value of Free Speech," 130 U. Pa. L. Rev. 646 (1982).

99. Bolger v. Youngs Drug Products Corp., 463 U.S. 60, 68 (1983). See also Pacific Gas & Elec. Co. v. Public Utilities Comm'n, 475 U.S. 1 (1986) (corporation has First Amendment right not to be required to mail newsletter with utility bill);

First Nat'l Bank v. Bellotti, 435 U.S. 765 (1978) (corporation's political expression fully protected under First Amendment). For a more detailed discussion of these issues, see Chapter 3, infra.

100. Austin v. Michigan Chamber of Commerce, 494 U.S. 652 (1990) (statute prohibiting corporations from making expenditures from their general treasuries held constitutional). For a detailed analysis of this decision, see Chapter 3, infra.

101. See generally Chapter 3, infra.

102. See Chapter 3, infra.

103. See Baker, supra note 98; Chapter 4, infra.

104. See Meiklejohn, supra note 40.

105. See Chapter 3, infra.

106. Jackson & Jeffries, supra note 35, at 14 ("Whatever else it may mean, the concept of a first amendment right of personal autonomy in matters of belief and expression stops short of a seller hawking his wares.").

107. Ronald Collins & David Skover, Commerce and Communication, 71 Tex. L. Rev. 697, 745 (1993) (footnote omitted).

108. See, e.g., First Nat'l Bank v. Bellotti, 435 U.S. 765 (1978).

109. See Spragens, supra note 56 , at 4: "The burden of the communitarian position is that a healthy liberal society is not an aggregation of rights-protecting and interest-maximizing individuals but rather a community of public-spirited citizens oriented towards the common good. Some communitarians, as a consequence, identify with the tradition of civic republicanism, which they contrast with what they see as the rampant individualism of the liberal tradition." See also Cass Sunstein, Beyond the Republican Revival, 97 Yale L.J. 1539, 1541 (1988), referring to the "republican belief in the subordination of private interests to the public good."

110. David Held, Models of Democracy 56 (2d ed. 1996).

111. Jean Jacques Rousseau, The Social Contract (1912).

112. Held, supra note 110, at 58.

113. See sources cited in note 109, supra.

114. According to Sunstein, "[r]epublicans . . . reject ethical relativism and skepticism, and believe that different perspectives are sometimes subject to mediation both in theory and in the real world." Sunstein, supra note 109, at 1554. See also id., at 1541, describing the republican principle of "universalism, exemplified by the notion of a common good, and made possible by 'practical reason.'" Sunstein adds that "[t]he republican commitment to universalism, or agreement as a regulative ideal, takes the form of a belief in the possibility of settling at least some normative disputes with substantively right answers." Id. Demonstrating how subjective normative premises influence the shaping of the "external objective" model of civic republicanism, Sunstein argues that while in general people should not act out of their own private interests, certain "social groups—especially the disadvantaged—should not . . . be prevented from invoking their private interests in the political

process." Id. at 1572. Professor Fallon has written that classical republican theory posited that "there exists an objective public good apart from individual goods." Richard H. Fallon, What Is Republicanism and Is It Worth Reviving?, 102 Harv. L. Rev. 1695, 1698 (1989).

115. As Professor Michelman explains civic republicanism, "[w]hat distinguishes politics, as Arendt and Aristotle said, is . . . the possibility of a shared, collective, deliberate, active intervention in our fate, in what would otherwise be the by-product of private decisions. Only in public life can we jointly, as a community, exercise the human capacity to 'think what we are doing,' and take charge of the history in which we are all constantly engaged by drift and inadvertence. . . . [T]he distinctive promise of political freedom remains the possibility of genuine collective action, an entire community consciously and jointly shaping its policy, its way of life. . . . A family or other private association can inculcate principles of justice shared in a community, but only in public citizenship can we jointly take charge of and responsibility for those principles. From Frank Michelman, Law's Republic, 97 Yale L.J. 1493, 1503–4.

116. The term is used by Sunstein, supra note 109, at 1554.

117. See discussion supra text at notes 47–73.

118. See note 114, supra. Scholars have also employed the concept of practical reason as a means of enabling courts, under the guise of statutory interpretation, to ignore or override normative legislative policy choices. See William N. Eskridge, Jr. & Philip P. Frickey, Statutory Interpretation as Practical Reasoning, 42 Stan. L. Rev. 321 (1990).

119. See discussion supra text at notes 74–84.

120. See note 109, supra.

121. See generally Sunstein, supra note 109.

122. See, e.g., Alexander MacIntyre, After Virtue 137–53 (1981) (discussing the Aristotelean idea that *eudaimonia*, or "human flourishing," is the end that society should seek); Margaret Radin, Market Inalienability, 100 Harv. L. Rev. 1849, 1877–87 (1987) (rhetoric of free markets and pluralism does violence to conception of "human flourishing"). But see John Finnis, Natural Law and Natural Rights 23, 88–89, 192 (1980) (arguing that "human flourishing" is only practically achieved when individual autonomy is respected).

123. In this sense, one can trace modern civic republicanism to its theoretical origins in the democratic theory of the Greek city-state, where "[a] purely private moral code without reference to the state was inconceivable." W. Jaeger, 1 Paideia: The Ideals of Greek Culture 326 (2d ed. 1945). According to Professor Sartori:

> The ancients did not, and could not, recognize the individual as a person and, concurrently, as a "private self" entitled to respect, for the obvious reason that this conception came with Christianity and was subsequently developed by the Renaissance, by Protestantism, and by the modern school

of natural law. What the Greek individualistic spirit lacked, then, was the juridical projection of the single human person. Therefore, the Greek experience of political freedom did not and could not signify an individual liberty based on personal rights.

G. Sartori, The Theory of Democracy Revisited 286 (1987) (footnote and emphasis omitted)

Sartori notes that Greek democracy "did not respect the individual; rather, it tended to suspect him." Id.

124. James G. March & John P. Olsen, Democratic Governance 5 (1995). March and Olsen, it should be noted, further assert "that individualism and exchange theories of democracy provide incomplete bases for thinking about governance." Id. at 6. However, their criticism is aimed primarily at the narrow and mechanistic pluralist version of democratic theory.

125. Sartori, supra note 123, at 286.

126. See Michael Walzer, The Communitarian Critique of Liberalism, 18 Pol. Theory 6, 7–8 (1990) (describing one communitarian vision of liberalism):

[C]ontemporary Western societies (American society especially) are taken to be the home of radically isolated individuals, rational egotists, and existential agents, men and women protected and divided by their inalienable rights. . . . The members of liberal society share no political or religious traditions. . . . [Each individual] imagines himself absolutely free, unencumbered, and on his own—and enters society, accepting its obligations, only in order to minimize his risks.

127. Jane Mansbridge, Beyond Adversary Democracy (1980).

128. Id. at 16–17.

129. Stephan Landsman, The Adversary System: A Description and Defense 45 (1984).

130. Valley Forge Christian College v. Americans United for Separation of Church and State, Inc., 454 U.S. 464, 472 (1982) ("At an irreducible minimum, Art. III requires the party who invokes the court's authority to 'show that he personally has suffered some actual or threatened injury as a result of the particularly illegal conduct of the defendant.'").

131. See Sierra Club v. Morton, 405 U.S. 727 (1972) (purely ideological plaintiffs lack standing in federal court pursuant to Article III).

132. See, e.g., Antonin Scalia, The Doctrine of Standing as an Essential Element of the Separation of Powers, 17 Suffolk L. Rev. 835 (1983).

133. Martin H. Redish, The Federal Courts in the Political Order: Judicial Jurisdiction and American Political Theory 101 (1991): "The theory behind the asserted connection [between injury-in-fact and standing] is, basically, a rationale premised on greed: the assumption that an individual who has something personally to gain

or lose as the result of a litigation will take that litigation more seriously, and therefore prepare and conduct the litigation more effectively than one who is motivated either by concern for the interests of others or by purely ideological factors." See also Lea Brilmayer, The Jurisprudence of Article III: Perspectives on the "Case-or-Controversy" Requirement, 93 Harv. L. Rev. 297 (1979).

134. See discussion supra text at notes 7–46.

135. See discussion supra text at notes 49–84.

136. Herbert Wechsler, Toward Neutral Principles of Constitutional Law, 73 Harv. L. Rev. 1 (1959).

137. Mark Tushnet, Following the Rules Laid Down: A Critique of Interpretivism and Neutral Principles, 96 Harv. L. Rev. 781, 805 (1983).

138. R. George Wright, Selling Words: Free Speech in a Commercial Culture 7 (1997).

139. Id. at 6.

140. See, e.g., Richard Delgado, The Ethereal Scholar: Does Critical Legal Studies Have What Minorities Want?, 22 Harv. C.R.–C.L. L. Rev. 301, 303–4 (1987): "The [Critical Legal Studies] critique of legal rules and reasoning is well known. Rules, since they are indeterminate and manipulable, can generate practically any result in a given situation. . . . Rights, Crits argue, are never promulgated in genuinely important areas such as economic justice. They protect only ephemeral things, like the right to speak or worship. When even these rights become threatening, they are limited."

141. Thomas Hobbes, The Leviathan 97 (Clarendon Press 1909).

142. Ronald K. L. Collins & David M. Skover, Commerce & Communication, 71 Tex. L. Rev. at 739 (1993).

143. Id. at 699.

144. Amy Guttmann & Dennis Thompson, Democracy and Disagreement 1 (1996).

145. Id. at 2.

146. Deliberative Democracy: Essays on Reason and Politics xiii (James Bohlman & William Rehg, eds. 1997).

147. John Stuart Mill argued that democracy is necessary in order to facilitate the mental and personal development of the individual. See John Stuart Mill, Considerations on Representative Government 62–63, 69–80 (1882).

148. Joshua Cohen, "Deliberation and Democratic Legitimacy," in Bohlman & Regg, supra note 146, at 67, 75–78.

149. Id. at 80 (discussing relevance of "[v]iews of the good" to deliberative democracy).

150. Bohlman & Regg, supra note 146, at xxi.

151. Sunstein, supra note 109.

152. Jonathan R. Macey, The Missing Element in the Republican Revival, 97 Yale L.J. 1673 (1988).

153. See discussion supra text at notes 74–84.

154. See Mill, supra note 54; Mill, supra note 147.

155. See, e.g., Vincent Blasi, The Checking Value in First Amendment Theory, 1977 Am. B. Found. Research J. 521.

156. See generally Blasi, supra note 45.

157. As Professor Posner has noted, much of public choice theory "asserts that legislation is a good demanded and supplied much as other goods, so that legislative protection flows to those groups that derive the greatest value from it, regardless of overall social welfare." Richard A. Posner, Economics, Politics, and the Reading of Statutes and the Constitution, 49 U. Chi. L. Rev. 263, 265 (1982). See also William N. Eskridge, Politics Without Romance: Implications of Public Choice Theory for Statutory Interpretation, 74 Va. L. Rev. 275, 277 (1988) ("Public choice theory indicates that the legislature will produce too few laws that serve truly public ends, and too many laws that serve private ends."); Jonathan R. Macey, Promoting Public Regarding Legislation Through Statutory Interpretation: An Interest Group Model, 86 Colum. L. Rev. 223, 223 (1986) ("Too often the legislative process seems to serve only the purely private interests of special interest groups at the expense of the broader public interests it was ostensibly designed to serve.").

158. Daniel A. Farber, Commentary: Free Speech Without Romance: Public Choice and the First Amendment, 105 Harv. L. Rev. 554, 566 (1991).

159. Central Hudson Gas & Electric Corp. v. Public Service Corp., 447 U.S. 557, (1980) ("The First Amendment's concern for commercial speech is based on the informational function of advertising. Consequently, there can be no constitutional objection to the suppression of commercial messages that do not accurately inform the public about lawful activity. The government may ban forms of communications more likely to deceive the public than to inform it.").

160. Id. at 562.

161. 517 U.S. 484 (1996).

162. Id. at 502.

163. See discussion supra text at notes 22–31.

164. One such exception, at least prior to his confirmation hearings, would have been Judge Robert Bork, who wrote that "[t]here is no basis for judicial intervention to protect any . . . form of expression [other than political speech], be it scientific, literary or that variety of expression we call obscene or pornographic." Bork, supra note 40. Robert Nagel is another scholar who would provide only very limited protection to speech of any kind. See Robert Nagel, Constitutional Cultures: The Mentality and Consequences of Judicial Review 27-59 (1989). He appears to make no special mention of scientific expression, however.

165. The Federal Trade Commission's authority derives from Section 12 of the Federal Trade Commission Act, 15 U.S.C. § 52, which provides: "It shall be

unlawful for any person, partnership, or corporation to disseminate, or cause to be disseminated, any false advertisement . . . [b]y any means, for the purpose of inducing, or which is likely to induce, directly or indirectly, the purchase in or having an effect upon commerce of food, drugs, devices, or cosmetics." In addition, § 5 of the Act, 15 U.S.C. § 45, which applies to advertising for more than merely foods, provides that "unfair or deceptive acts or practices in or affecting commerce, are declared unlawful." According to one group of authorities, "A central principle in FTC law is that if advertising claims are not adequately substantiated they will be regarded as deceptive or unfair." J. Calfee & J. Pappalardo, How Should Health Claims for Foods Be Regulated? An Economic Perspective 7 (1989).

166. J. Calfee & J. Pappalardo, supra note 165, at 5 (footnote omitted): "FDA authority over disease prevention claims in food marketing arises from the Food Drug and Cosmetic Act . . . which prohibits the sale of misbranded foods or drugs in interstate commerce." Section 403(a) of the Food Drug and Cosmetic Act provides that "[a] food shall be deemed to be misbranded [if] its labeling is false or misleading in any particular." 21 U.S.C. § 343. See generally Hutt, Government Regulation of Health Claims in Food Labeling and Advertising, 41 Food Drug Cosm. L.J. 3 (1986).

167. An example is the proceeding brought in Texas state court by the State of Texas against the Quaker Oats Company. The state alleged that "Quaker has embarked upon a campaign of deception, designed to entice Texans who are concerned about their cholesterol levels and the risk of heart attack to buy and consume Quaker's oatmeal and oat bran products . . . as a substitute for traditional medical treatment" and that Quaker is "motivated solely by the base purpose of selling as much of Quaker's products as possible." Plaintiff's Original Petition at 3, Texas v. Quaker Oats Co. (Dist. Ct., Dallas County, Texas, Sept. 7, 1989) (No. 89-10762-M).

168. Virginia State Board of Pharmacy v. Virginia Citizens Consumer Council, Inc., 425 U.S. 748, 772 n. 24 (1976).

169. See, e.g., New York Times Co. v. Sullivan, 376 U.S. 254, 279–80 (1964).

170. Constitutional issues may arise concerning the accuracy of government's characterization of the commercial statement as "false." However, this problem is no greater in the context of fraudulent commercial speech than it is in the context of fraudulent political speech.

171. See Consolidated Edison Co. v. Public Serv. Comm'n, 447 U.S. 530, 536 (1980) (quoting Niemotko v. Maryland, 340 U.S. 268, 282 (1951) (Frankfurter, J., concurring)): "[W]hen regulation is based on the content of speech, governmental action must be scrutinized more carefully to ensure that communication has not been prohibited 'merely because public officials disapprove the speaker's views.'"

172. Geoffrey R. Stone, Content Regulation and the First Amendment, 25

Wm. & Mary L. Rev. 189, 213 (1983) ("The point, rather, is that the government ordinarily may not restrict the expression of particular ideas, viewpoints, or items of information because it does not trust its citizens to make wise or desirable decisions if they are exposed to such expression. This 'highly paternalistic' view, as the Court has recognized, is at odds with the notion of free expression. The Court's antipaternalistic understanding of the first amendment, therefore, seems well-founded in the philosophical and historical underpinnings of the constitutional guarantee.").

173. See discussion supra text at note 13.

174. Whitney v. California, 274 U.S. 357, 377 (1927) (Brandeis, J., concurring).

175. It has been argued that tobacco advertising is inherently deceptive because

> [N]o cigarette advertising gives adequate warning of the wide range of serious and life threatening diseases induced by the ordinary use of the product. Quite to the contrary, the effect of this advertising is to conceal or to minimize these facts. Smoking is portrayed as not harmful, by associating it with traditionally young, healthy, athletic, and virile activities. . . . Moreover, no cigarette advertising gives even the remotest suggesting that cigarettes are strongly addictive. Quite to the contrary; smoking is portrayed as not the product of addiction, but rather as an exciting activity that, like mountain climbing, is freely undertaken by "real" men and women.

Vincent Blasi & Henry P. Monaghan, The First Amendment and Cigarette Advertising, 256 JAMA 502, 506

176. It should be emphasized that the tobacco industry has long asserted that its advertising does not urge individuals to take up smoking, but rather only that existing smokers choose a particular brand. Even under this view of tobacco advertising's role, however, it is clear that the advertising at the very least proceeds on the assumption that smoking is a legitimate activity.

177. See Robert D. Richards & Clay Calvert, Counterspeech 2000: A New Look at the Old Remedy for "Bad" Speech, 2000 B.Y.U. L. Rev. 553, 574–77, for a discussion of the effectiveness of countering cigarette advertising.

178. 517 U.S. 484 (1996).

NOTES TO CHAPTER 3

1. Wilson made this statement before the Senate Armed Services Committee during his confirmation hearing for the position of Secretary of Defense. See Excerpts from "Two Wilson Hearings Before Senate Committee on Defense Appointments," N.Y. Times, Jan. 24, 1953, at 8.

2. Cf. Herbert Hovenkamp, Enterprise and American Law, 1836–1937, at 3 (1991) ("Classical political economy purported to develop rules for evaluating a legal regime's justice or fairness without regard to how its wealth happened to be

distributed. As a political and legal doctrine, classicism identified the best regime as the one that maximized total wealth.")

3. See infra notes 106–9 and accompanying text.

4. Charles E. Lindblom, Politics and Markets 179 (1977).

5. See, e.g., C. Edwin Baker, Realizing Self-Realization: Corporate Political Expenditures and Redish's "The Value of Free Speech," 130 U. Pa. L. Rev. 646, 652 (1982) (asserting that corporate speech is undeserving of protection because it "does not derive from the values or political commitments of any individuals"); see also infra notes 126–30 and accompanying text.

6. See Victor Brudney, Business Corporations and Stockholders' Rights Under the First Amendment, 91 Yale L.J. 235, 294–95 (1981); Charles R. O'Kelley, Jr., The Constitutional Rights of Corporations Revisited: Social and Political Expression and the Corporation After First National Bank v. Bellotti, 67 Geo. L.J. 1347, 1382–83 (1979); David Shelledy, Autonomy, Debate, and Corporate Speech, 18 Hastings Const. L.Q. 541, 576–77, 584 (1991).

7. See infra notes 126–49, 196–198 and accompanying text.

8. 435 U.S. 765 (1978).

9. See id. at 777; infra notes 29–41 and accompanying text.

10. See, e.g., Pacific Gas & Elec. Co. v. Public Utils. Comm'n, 475 U.S. 1, 8 (1986) (plurality opinion) ("Corporations . . . contribute to the discussion, debate, and the dissemination of information and ideas that the First Amendment seeks to foster." [internal quotation marks omitted]).

11. See, e.g., id. at 8–9 (holding that a corporate newsletter receives the full protection of the First Amendment); infra notes 43–45 and accompanying text. In the context of commercial speech protection, it should be noted, the Court routinely has extended First Amendment protection to corporations without any discussion of the point. See, e.g., City of Cincinnati v. Discovery Network, Inc., 507 U.S. 410, 430–31 (1993); Central Hudson Gas & Elec. Corp. v. Public Serv. Comm'n, 447 U.S. 557, 657–60 (1980). Traditionally, however, such protection has been at a somewhat reduced level. See Discovery Network, 507 U.S. at 422; Central Hudson, 447 U.S. at 563.

12. See Austin v. Michigan Chamber of Commerce, 494 U.S. 652, 657–60 (1990).

13. See C. Edwin Baker, Human Liberty and Freedom of Speech 219 (1989) (asserting that corporate political speech is unprotected because the "speech cannot be attributed to the choice of a free agent"); Randall P. Bezanson, Institutional Speech, 80 Iowa L. Rev. 735, 739 (1995) (defining corporate speech as "institutional speech," undeserving of First Amendment protection because it lacks a speaker); infra notes 124–28, 168–70 and accompanying text.

14. See, e.g., Meir Dan-Cohen, Rights, Persons, and Organizations 179–84 (1986); Owen Fiss, Liberalism Divided 15–16 (1996); infra notes 340–54 and accompanying text.

15. See Brudney, supra note 6, at 268.

16. See infra notes 229–352 and accompanying text.

17. See infra notes 81–228 and accompanying text.

18. See infra notes 129–47 and accompanying text.

19. See infra notes 147–49 and accompanying text.

20. See infra notes 124–49 and accompanying text.

21. See infra notes 149–77 and accompanying text.

22. See infra notes 191–94 and accompanying text.

23. See infra notes 197–202 and accompanying text.

24. See infra notes 194–203 and accompanying text.

25. The concept is drawn, by analogy, from John Rawls, A Theory of Justice 136–42 (1971). For a more detailed discussion of the relevance of Rawls's "veil of ignorance" theory, see Chapter 2, supra at 000–000.

26. See Martin H. Redish & Gary Lippman, Freedom of Expression and the Civic Republican Revival in Constitutional Theory: The Ominous Implications, 79 Cal. L. Rev. 267, 279–80 (1991).

27. See infra notes 353–68 and accompanying text. Although this critique may be appropriate when applied to academic attacks on corporate speech's protection, it would be difficult to suggest that many of the current members of the Supreme Court are guilty of ulterior, left-wing ideological motivations for their hesitancy to extend full protection to corporate speech. In light of this, the inescapable conclusion must be that the Court's approach is wholly defenseless, even on the basis of ulterior ideological motivations, and can therefore be attributed simply to an insensitivity to important free speech values. See infra notes 208–28 and accompanying text.

28. See, e.g., Linmark Assocs. v. Willingboro, 431 U.S. 85, 97 (1977) (striking down a restriction on posting "For Sale" signs); Miami Herald Publ'g Co. v. Tornillo, 418 U.S. 241, 258 (1974) (striking down a state law requiring newspapers to print replies to editorials); New York Times Co. v. United States, 403 U.S. 713, 714 (1971) (per curiam) (striking down an injunction against newspaper publication of government documents); Kingsley Int'l Pictures Corp. v. Regents of the Univ., 360 U.S. 684, 688–90 (1959) (finding unconstitutional the denial of a permit to show a non-obscene movie); Grosjean v. American Press Co., 297 U.S. 233, 240, 251 (1936) (striking down a state law requiring a license tax on all publishers, including corporations, that had publications with circulations over 20,000).

29. See First Nat'l Bank v. Bellotti, 435 U.S. 765, 777, 784 (1978); infra text at notes 30–41.

30. 435 U.S. 765 (1978).

31. Id. at 768. The statute also provided that no question submitted to voters dealing with taxation could materially affect the corporation. See id.

32. See id. at 778, 784.

33. See id. at 769.

34. Id. at 777.

35. Id.

36. Id at 783.

37. Id. at 785; see also id. at 784 (noting that it is impermissible to prohibit speech based on the identity of the speaker's interests).

38. See id. at 789–90. The Court also rejected the state's paternalistic belief that it had to suppress advocacy that might persuade the voters. See id. at 791–92 & n. 31.

39. Id. at 791 (citing Buckley v. Valeo, 424 U.S. 1, 48–49 [1976] (per curiam)) (internal quotation marks omitted).

40. See id. at 792–93.

41. See id. at 793.

42. 475 U.S. 1 (1986) (plurality opinion).

43. See id. at 5–6. The utility company had long distributed its own monthly newsletter called "Progress" with its monthly statements. See id. at 5.

44. See id. at 6.

45. See id. at 8.

46. Id.

47. See id. at 12.

48. See id. at 13.

49. See id. at 18. The Court relied on this point in Miami Herald Publishing Co. v. Tornillo, 418 U.S. 241 (1974), in which the Court struck down a state law granting a right-of-reply to newspaper editorials. See id. at 258. The Court emphasized that First Amendment concerns, such as protection from forced speech, applied to all corporations, not only the institutional press. See id.

50. 479 U.S. 238 (1986).

51. See id. at 241. MCFL was incorporated as a nonprofit, non-stock corporation to perform educational, political, and other activities to "foster respect for human life and to defend the right to life of all human beings, born and unborn." Id. (citation omitted).

52. See id.

53. See id. at 243–44.

54. Id. at 252.

55. See id. at 254.

56. Id. at 255; see also id. at 254 (noting the disincentive for organizations to engage in political speech).

57. See id. at 257–58.

58. See id. at 259.

59. See id.

60. See id. at 241.

61. Id. at 263.

62. See id. at 263–64.

63. 494 U.S. 652 (1990).

64. See id. at 656.

65. See id. at 714 (appendix to opinion of Kennedy, J., dissenting).

66. See id. at 654–55.

67. See id. at 657.

68. Id.

69. See id. at 658.

70. Id. at 660; see also id. at 666 (describing the state's interest in "eliminating from the political process the corrosive effect of political 'war chests'").

71. See id. at 658–59.

72. See id. at 660.

73. See id. at 661.

74. See id. at 662.

75. See id. at 662.

76. See id. at 662–63.

77. See id. at 663.

78. See Rebecca L. Brown, Separated Powers and Ordered Liberty, 139 U. Pa. L. Rev. 1513, 1515–16 (1991).

79. See generally Vincent Blasi, The Checking Value in First Amendment Theory, 1977 Am. B. Found. Res. J. 521 (emphasizing the value of free speech in checking abuse of power in a democratic society).

80. See id. at 538–43.

81. See, e.g., Vincent Blasi, The Pathological Perspective and the First Amendment, 85 Colum. L. Rev. 449, 449–50 (1985) (positing a "pathological perspective" to adjudicating First Amendment disputes that protects the integrity of "core" speech from societal intolerance).

82. See generally Martin H. Redish, The Role of Pathology in First Amendment Theory: A Skeptical Examination, 38 Case W. Res. L. Rev. 618, 621, 627 (1988) (rejecting Blasi's pathological perspective and explaining that the decision whether to protect speech is related to the values served by free speech).

83. Id. at 627.

84. The First Amendment provides in relevant part: "Congress shall make no law . . . abridging the freedom of speech." U.S. Const. Amend. I, cl. 1.

85. See, e.g., Baker, supra note 13, at 3 (focusing on the liberty value that free speech protection fosters); Thomas I. Emerson, Toward a General Theory of the First Amendment 3 (1963) (recognizing a combination of four values that free speech fosters); Alexander Meiklejohn, The First Amendment Is an Absolute, 1961 Sup. Ct. Rev. 245, 263 (recognizing how free speech benefits the democratic process).

86. See Chapter 2, supra.

87. Martin H. Redish, Freedom of Expression: A Critical Analysis 21 (1984).

88. See id. at 22.

89. For criticism of the self-realization theory, see Robert H. Bork, Neutral Principles and Some First Amendment Problems, 47 Ind. L.J. 1, 25 (1971) (noting that the benefits of self-realization do not distinguish speech from other freedoms); Frederick Schauer, Codifying the First Amendment: New York v. Ferber, 1982 Sup. Ct. Rev. 285, 312 (highlighting the lack of predictability in using the self-realization principle to foster free speech protection).

90. See, e.g., Alexander Meiklejohn, Political Freedom 27 (1960) (asserting that freedom of speech originated from self- government); Bork, supra note 89, at 26 (stating that speech functions to deal with politics and government).

91. One of the key arguments used against corporate speech protection is that corporations are incapable of personal self-realization. Under a communitarian model, however, even if this is true, it would be irrelevant because corporate speech is consistent with the democratic political process. See discussion infra text at notes 149–77.

92. See, e.g., C. B. MacPherson, The Life and Times of Liberal Democracy 51 (1977) ("Democracy would . . . make people more active, more energetic."); Jack L. Walker, A Critique of the Elitist Theory of Democracy, 60 Am. Pol. Sci. Rev. 285, 288 (1966) ("The most distinctive feature, and the principal orienting value, of classical democratic theory was its emphasis on individual participation in the development of public policy. . . . [A]bove all else they were concerned with human development, the opportunities which existed in political activity to realize the untapped potentials of men.").

93. For a more detailed explanation of this intersection, see Chapter 2, supra.

94. See id.

95. See supra note 92.

96. See infra notes 106–9 and accompanying text.

97. See Lindblom, supra note 4, at 172–73 (noting that "economic distress can bring down a government").

98. See David Millon, Theories of the Corporation, 1990 Duke L.J. 201, 252.

99. See id. at 201 (recognizing that "corporate activity has broad social and political ramifications"); see also James Willard Hurst, The Legitimacy of the Business Corporation in the Law of the United States 162 (1970) (recognizing the "idea that the corporation's utility served the general economy"); Lindblom, supra note 4, at 175 (viewing businesses as performing "indispensable" functions).

100. See supra note 1 and accompanying text.

101. See Hurst, supra note 99, at 58–59 (arguing that performing socially useful and responsible functions legitimizes corporations' use of the facilities that the law provides).

102. Peter Bachrach, The Theory of Democratic Elitism: A Critique 80 (1967). Professor Bachrach cites United States Steel Corporation's response to the civil rights struggle in Birmingham in 1963: "Under pressure, it declared its neu-

trality and thus was forced to admit to itself and to the nation that it is a separate political institution." Id.

103. Adolf A. Berle, Jr., The 20th Century Capitalist Revolution 60 (1954); see also id. at 181 (asserting that "the corporation, almost against its will, has been compelled to assume in appreciable part the role of conscience-carrier of twentieth-century American society").

104. Morton S. Baratz, Corporate Giants and the Power Structure, 9 W. Pol. Q. 406, 413 (1956).

105. See Lindblom, supra note 4, at 201–21.

106. Fiss, supra note 14, at 10.

107. See, e.g., S. 5148, 104th Cong. s 671 (1995) (discussing a later-rejected proposal on punitive damages); H.R. 161, 104th Cong. (1995) (discussing a later-rejected proposal to reform product liability law); 21 C.F.R. § 897.1–.34 (1997) (regulating the sale, distribution, advertising, and labeling of tobacco).

108. See generally Geoffrey R. Stone, Content Regulation and the First Amendment, 25 Wm. & Mary L. Rev. 189, 231–33 (1983) (distinguishing between content-based and content-neutral restrictions on speech and emphasizing the unique risks inherent in viewpoint-based restrictions); see also infra notes 355–70 and accompanying text. It should be emphasized that Professor Lindblom did not purport to draw First Amendment implications from his observation. Professor Fiss, however, does appear to do so. See Fiss, supra note 14, at 10–12.

109. See Lindblom, supra note 4, at 178–79. Actually, Professor Lindblom emphasizes business officials' role in public policy. See id. at 179. Because the official does not necessarily speak or act on the corporation's behalf, however, we can extend Lindblom's idea to the corporation. Cf. Henry N. Butler & Larry E. Ribstein, The Corporation and the Constitution 63–64 (1995) (explaining that regulation of officials' speech creates First Amendment concerns because such speech is seen as the individual manager's speech); Manuel F. Cohen, The Corporation Within the Community, in The Corporation in a Democratic Society 28, 34 (Edward J. Bander ed., 1975) (address to the Economic Club of Detroit) (noting that the "corporation as an institution is, in fact, invested with political powers").

110. See Austin v. Michigan Chamber of Commerce, 494 U.S. 652, 694 (1990) (Scalia, J., dissenting) (noting the significance of the fact that private associations owning and operating much of the state's business believe that a particular candidate is important to the state's prosperity).

111. Cf. Meiklejohn, supra note 85, at 255–56 (stating that the First Amendment dictates absolute protection of expression that aids the citizenry in making governing choices).

112. Lindblom, supra note 4, at 172.

113. See, e.g., Dun & Bradstreet, Inc. v. Greenmoss Builders, Inc., 472 U.S. 749, 762 (1985) (plurality opinion) (asserting that speech damaging to a corporation's reputation does not warrant special protection).

114. See Hurst, supra note 99, at 162.

115. See Bose Corp. v. Consumers Union of United States, Inc., 466 U.S. 485, 489–90 (1984) (adopting a district court finding that the corporation was a public figure) (citing New York Times Co. v. Sullivan, 376 U.S. 254, 279 [1964]); see also Snead v. Redland Aggregates Ltd., 998 F.2d 1325, 1329 (5th Cir. 1993) (applying a three-part analysis to determine whether a corporation is a public or private figure). But see Dun & Bradstreet, 472 U.S. at 753 (plurality opinion) (treating action involving a plaintiff corporation as governed by the standards for a private individual).

116. New York Times, 376 U.S. at 279–80 (setting the fault standard for a suit by a public official). The Court later extended this standard to so-called "public figures." See Curtis Publ'g v. Butts, 388 U.S. 130, 164 (1967) (Warren, C.J., concurring); see also Gertz v. Robert Welch, Inc., 418 U.S. 323, 336 n. 7 (1974) (noting that a majority of Justices in *Curtis Publishing* agreed that the New York Times test applies to public figures as well as public officials).

117. New York Times, 376 U.S. at 270.

118. See Patricia Nassif Fetzer, The Corporate Defamation Plaintiff as First Amendment "Public Figure": Nailing the Jellyfish, 68 Iowa L. Rev. 35, 85 (1982) (asserting that "[f]ew would dispute . . . that a Ford Motor Company or an IBM command at least the same name recognition" as most public figures); Norman Redlich, The Publicly Held Corporation as Defamation Plaintiff, 39 St. Louis U. L.J. 1167, 1172 (1995) ("[A] corporation that has become a 'household name' in the relevant community will be deemed an 'all purpose' public figure.").

119. 418 U.S. 323 (1974).

120. Id. at 344. The second reason for the distinction between public and private plaintiffs in Gertz was the fact that public officials and public figures voluntarily had sought to enter the public eye and thus ran the risk of closer public scrutiny and possible defamation. See id. at 345; see also Redlich, supra note 118, at 1173 (noting that advertising may "thrust" a corporation into some controversy).

121. Fetzer, supra note 118, at 54. This ability to respond to a falsehood is derived from the decision in *Bellotti* and the expansive protection given to commercial speech. See id. at 54–55; see also Bolger v. Youngs Drug Prods. Corp., 463 U.S. 60, 69 (1983) (holding that mailing contraceptive advertisements is "clearly protected by the First Amendment"); Central Hudson Gas & Elec. Corp. v. Public Serv. Comm'n, 447 U.S. 557, 561–62 (1980) (reasoning that commercial speech is protected because it "furthers the societal interest in the fullest possible dissemination of information"); Virginia Bd. of Pharmacy v. Virginia Citizens' Consumer Council, Inc., 425 U.S. 748, 770 (1976) (rejecting the argument that the flow of price information on prescription drugs is not protected by the First Amendment).

122. See O'Kelley, supra note 6, at 1360 (arguing that corporations possess "the constitutional rights necessary to protect their business[es]"); cf. Austin v.

Michigan Chamber of Commerce, 494 U.S. 652, 678 (1990) (Stevens, J., concurring) (noting the vast difference between political campaigns and other speech).

123. See Lindblom, supra note 4, at 172–75; discussion supra at 000–000.

124. See generally Baker, supra note 13, at 219 (arguing that corporate speech "does not depend on either individual or collective visions about what humanity should be" and "need not reflect anyone's substantive political views"); Bezanson, supra note 13, at 739 (asserting that "institutional speech . . . has nothing to do with liberty and no necessary relationship to freedom").

125. See Baker, supra note 13, at 218 (arguing that "business considerations may dictate the content of the company's political speech").

126. See id. at 219; Bezanson, supra note 13, at 755–56.

127. Bezanson, supra note 13, at 779.

128. For a detailed critique, see Redish, supra note 87, at 29–36.

129. See, e.g., NAACP v. Alabama ex rel. Patterson, 357 U.S. 449, 466 (1958) (holding that forced disclosure of the association's membership list would violate the First Amendment's guarantee of freedom of association); id. at 460 ("[I]t is beyond debate that freedom to engage in association for the advancement of beliefs and ideas is an inseparable aspect of the 'liberty' assured by the Due Process Clause of the Fourteenth Amendment, which embraces freedom of speech.").

130. 2 Alexis de Tocqueville, Democracy in America 130 (Henry Reeve trans., 1862).

131. Id. at 129; see also id. at 140–41 (discussing the link between the existence of political and other civil associations).

132. See id. at 140–41; see also id. at 130 (describing the American view of association as "the only means they have of acting").

133. See Redish, supra note 87, at 20.

134. See Hurst, supra note 99, at 32 (describing the corporation as historically "a useful instrument of regular business.").

135. Cf. Tocqueville, supra note 130, at 129 (noting that almost all Americans took part in commercial and manufacturing companies).

136. According to one commentator, the Jacksonian period was marked by "the transfer of economic primacy from an old and conservative merchant class to a newer, more aggressive, and more numerous body of business men and speculators of all sorts." Bray Hammond, Sovereignty and an Empty Purse: Banks and Politics in the Civil War (1970), reprinted in Conflict and Consensus in Early American History 216, 218 (Allen F. Davis & Harold D. Woodman eds., 1984). Hammond notes that the period "produced a dazzling democratic expansion experienced nowhere else," and that "the Jacksonian revolution signified that a nation of democrats was tired of being governed, however well, by gentlemen from Virginia and Massachusetts." Id. at 217. Jacksonianism, he states, "opened economic advantages to those who had not previously had them." Id.

137. Ronald E. Seavoy, The Origins of the American Business Corporation,

1784–1855, at 256 (1982). According to Professor Hovenkamp, "[c]lassical political economy in the United States is a Jacksonian phenomenon. . . . Andrew Jackson was an entrepreneurial president. His terms of office—or, in political economic terms, his regime—stood for economic growth, unobstructed by 'artificial' constraints. The two greatest classical legal institutions in the United States—the modern business corporation and the constitutional doctrine of substantive due process—are both distinctively Jacksonian products. The modern business corporation had its origin in the general corporation acts, one of the most important legal accomplishments of a regime bent on democratizing and deregulating American business." Hovenkamp, supra note 2, at 2 (emphasis added).

138. Hurst, supra note 99, at 32.

139. Id.; see also Seavoy, supra note 137, at 256 (arguing that general incorporation laws "helped equalize the opportunities to get rich").

140. See Hurst, supra note 99, at 120 (citing the common example of the New York constitutional convention of 1846); see also Seavoy, supra note 137, at 255 (noting that Connecticut was the first state to adopt a policy of granting charters to any legitimate business).

141. Hurst, supra note 99, at 120; see also id. at 32 (noting that the "individualistic egalitarian objection passed out of [the] Jacksonian [arguments] against corporations"). Professor Hovenkamp asserted that "[t]o be a classicist was to be opposed to state intervention on behalf of the rich and the politically powerful. Classicism achieved its popularity in the United States in a political movement, Jacksonianism, that was heavily supported by society's disfavored classes. The issues were not welfare and subsidized education. Rather, they were special corporate charters or licenses that gave unique privileges to engage in business to certain favored people, while denying access to others. When Federalists intervened in the market, the immediate beneficiaries were generally people of property." Hovenkamp, supra note 2, at 4.

142. Milton Friedman & Eli Goldston, The "Responsible" Corporation: Benefactor or Monopolist?, Fortune, Nov. 1973, at 56, reprinted in The Corporation in a Democratic Society, supra note 109, at 43, 44 (statement of Goldston).

143. See id. (statement of Goldston) (describing large publicly held corporations as "social aggregations of talent"); cf. Pembina Consol. Silver Mining & Milling Co. v. Pennsylvania, 125 U.S. 181, 189 (1888) (noting that "corporations are merely associations of individuals united for a special purpose").

144. Cf. Tocqueville, supra note 130, at 131–32 (reasoning that individuals gain power and independence from the ability to form associations).

145. See NAACP v. Alabama ex rel. Patterson, 357 U.S. 449, 460 (1958) ("Effective advocacy . . . is undeniably enhanced by group association.").

146. See generally Mullane v. Central Hanover Bank & Trust Co., 339 U.S. 306 (1950) (describing the common trust fund concept).

147. See NAACP, 357 U.S. at 460; see also Mark G. Yudof, When Government Speaks 161–62 (1983) (asserting that organizations represent the mass of individuals who rarely can provide a powerful voice on their own); Victor Brudney, Association, Advocacy, and the First Amendment, 4 Wm. & Mary Bill Rts. J. 1, 79 (1995) ("[A]ssociations are essentially amplifiers ... or in any event communicators, of individual expressive interests."); Meir Dan-Cohen, Freedoms of Collective Speech: A Theory of Protected Communications by Organizations, Communities, and the State, 79 Cal. L. Rev. 1229, 1249 (1991) (arguing that individuals speak through organizations knowing that their "views will gain greatly in audibility").

148. See Chapter 2, supra.

149. But see supra notes 142–48 and accompanying text.

150. See supra notes 90–95 and accompanying text; see also Meiklejohn, supra note 85, at 256–57 (describing how the enjoyment of art, literature, and education cultivates citizens' values, independence, and wisdom); id. at 263 (arguing that novels, dramas, paintings, and poems enhance people's ability to vote).

151. Redish, supra note 87, at 30; see id. at 50; see also Meiklejohn, supra note 90, at 27 (arguing that the result will be "ill-considered, ill-balanced planning for the general good" if citizens must decide an issue with less than complete information).

152. See David A. Strauss, Persuasion, Autonomy, and Freedom of Expression, 91 Colum. L. Rev. 334, 371 (1991) (arguing that "freedom of expression is designed to protect the autonomy of potential listeners").

153. Meiklejohn, supra note 90, at 26; see id. ("It does not require that, on every occasion, every citizen shall take part in public debate. Nor can it even give assurance that everyone shall have opportunity to do so."). This is not to endorse entirely this aspect of Professor Meiklejohn's theory because in many ways his theory is too limiting, most notably in his argument that the same message should not be repeated (see id.) and his limitation of speech protection only to public, or political, speech. See id. at 83; Redish, supra note 87, at 14–15 (critiquing the Meiklejohnian approach).

154. Meiklejohn, supra note 85, at 255.

155. Id.; see also id. at 263 (arguing that the "judgment-making of the people must be self-educated in the ways of freedom").

156. Meiklejohn, supra note 90, at 27; see also Meiklejohn, supra note 85, at 256–57 (arguing that the spreading of information and ideas must be unabridged).

157. See Meiklejohn, supra note 90, at 27; Meiklejohn, supra note 85, at 256–57.

158. Board of Educ. v. Pico, 457 U.S. 853, 867 (1982) (plurality opinion); see also Stanley v. Georgia, 394 U.S. 557, 564 (1969) (stating that "[i]t is now well established that the Constitution protects the right to receive information and ideas"); Lamont v. Postmaster Gen., 381 U.S. 301, 308 (1965) (Brennan, J., concurring) ("The dissemination of ideas can accomplish nothing if otherwise willing addressees are not

free to receive and consider them."); Burt Neuborne, Speech, Technology, and the Emergence of a Tricameral Media: You Can't Tell the Players Without a Scorecard, 17 Hastings Comm. & Ent. L.J. 17, 30–31 & n. 58 (1994) (stating that "[e]ntire categories of speech arose where the principal justification for First Amendment protection was the hearer's right to know," including corporate and commercial speech); Strauss, supra note 152, at 371 ("[F]reedom of expression is designed to protect the autonomy of potential listeners.").

159. See Pacific Gas & Elec. Co. v. Public Utils. Comm'n, 475 U.S. 1, 8 (1986) (plurality opinion) ("First Amendment protects the public's interest in receiving information."); see also Dan-Cohen, supra note 14, at 109 (arguing that business corporations have a right to speak derived from the public's right to listen); Dan-Cohen, supra note 149, at 1245 (protecting corporate speech because the corporation is a "source of communication to which the public is entitled to listen"); Shelledy, supra note 6, at 571 (arguing that corporate speech can add to the "limited range of views given widespread dissemination").

160. First Nat'l Bank v. Bellotti, 435 U.S. 765, 783 (1978); see also Austin v. Michigan Chamber of Commerce, 494 U.S. 652, 706 (1990) (Kennedy, J., dissenting) (rejecting the suggestion that government has an interest in shaping debate by insulating the electorate from certain views); id. at 695 (Scalia, J., dissenting) ("The premise of our system is that there is no such thing as too much speech."). But see J. Skelly Wright, Money and the Pollution of Politics: Is the First Amendment an Obstacle to Political Equality?, 82 Colum. L. Rev. 609, 641 (1982) (arguing that Bellotti "paid only lip service to the rights of listeners" and really was more concerned with protecting "the privileged few who can spend unlimited amounts of money to purchase political effectiveness").

161. City of Ladue v. Gilleo, 512 U.S. 43, 56 (1994).

162. See Bellotti, 435 U.S. at 791–92 (stating that the people in a democracy "may consider . . . the source and credibility of the advocate"); Rodney A. Smolla, Free Speech in an Open Society 235 (1992) ("The effectiveness of speech is often connected to the identity of the speaker."); see also Austin, 494 U.S. at 684 (Scalia, J., dissenting) (arguing that listeners will consider the "self-interested and probably uncongenial source" in evaluating a message); Yudof, supra note 147, at 161 (arguing that sources of information must have "high claims to legitimacy in the public mind"); C. Edwin Baker, Turner Broadcasting: Content-Based Regulation of Persons and Presses, 1994 Sup. Ct. Rev. 57, 65. ("Many listeners find that the identity of the source affects the worth or at least their evaluation of the speech.").

163. Gilleo, 512 U.S. at 56–57. "A sign advocating 'Peace in the Gulf' in the front lawn of a retired general or decorated war veteran may provoke a different reaction than the same sign in a 10-year-old child's bedroom window." Id. at 56.

164. See Bellotti, 435 U.S. at 782 n. 18 ("Certainly there are voters . . . who would be as interested in hearing appellants' views on a graduated tax as the

views of media corporations that might be less knowledgeable on the subject.");
see also Austin, 494 U.S. at 699 (Kennedy, J., dissenting) (noting that "corporations . . . [may] have unique views of vital importance to the electorate" that
should not be muted).

165. Cf. Austin, 494 U.S. at 684 (Scalia, J., dissenting) (arguing that listeners
will consider the corporate source of the message and might find it uncongenial).

166. See infra notes 303–52 and accompanying text.

167. New York Times Co. v. Sullivan, 376 U.S. 254, 270 (1964).

168. See Baker, supra note 162, at 73; Bezanson, supra note 13, at 739; see also
id. at 740 (calling the First Amendment the "guarantee of individual freedom to
speak"). But see Meiklejohn, supra note 85, at 255 ("The First Amendment does
not protect a 'freedom to speak.'").

169. See Bezanson, supra note 13, at 739.

170. See Baker, supra note 162, at 73 ("[W]ithout speakers, listeners' autonomy is irrelevant. . . . [T]he listener's desire to hear something seldom gives her
the right to hear it unless some speaker has both the right (or bureaucratically
defined duty) and desire to talk."); id. at 78 (arguing that "listener autonomy of-
fers very little protection without prior invocation of speaker autonomy"); Brudney, supra note 147, at 68 ("If there exists a right to hear, it is only the right to
hear what others can and wish to say."); id. at 72–73 (arguing that where no
speaker exists, "the audience has lost nothing to which it is entitled"); Brudney,
supra note 6, at 247 (arguing that the listener's interests are not independent of
the speaker's ability and desire to speak).

171. See supra note 43 and accompanying text; cf. Wooley v. Maynard, 430
U.S. 705, 714 (1977) (recognizing a First Amendment right against governmentally compelled speech); West Va. Bd. of Educ. v. Barnette, 319 U.S. 624, 633–34,
642 (1943) (holding a compulsory flag salute unconstitutional under the First
Amendment).

172. See supra notes 124–29 and accompanying text.

173. Baker, supra note 162, at 78 (citations omitted).

174. See, e.g., Turner Broadcasting System, Inc. v. FCC, 512 U.S. 622, 641
(1994) (stating that decisions about what expressions to make, hear, or adopt rest
with each individual); R.A.V. v. City of St. Paul, 505 U.S. 377, 414 (1992) (White,
J., concurring in the judgment) ("The mere fact that expressive activity causes
hurt feelings, offense, or resentment does not render the expression unprotected."); Texas v. Johnson, 491 U.S. 397, 418 (1989) (upholding flag burning as
protected speech, because although national unity is a proper official end, the
government may not achieve this end by arresting those who express disagreement); Hustler Mag., Inc. v. Falwell, 485 U.S. 46, 55 (1988) (rejecting the "outra-
geousness" standard as the boundary of actionable political speech); Cohen v.
California, 403 U.S. 15, 25 (1971) ("[O]ne man's vulgarity is another's lyric.").

175. See Chapter 1, supra (discussing the "epistemological humility" concept);

Redish & Lippman, supra note 26, at 281 (connecting the Court's prohibition of viewpoint regulation with the construct of epistemological humility).

176. Baker, supra note 13, at 55.

177. See Baker, supra note 162, at 78–79.

178. See supra notes 84–95 and accompanying text.

179. See Blasi, supra note 79, at 527.

180. See Stanley v. Georgia, 394 U.S. 557, 565 (1969) ("Our whole constitutional heritage rebels at the thought of giving government the power to control men's minds.").

181. Blasi, supra note 79, at 527.

182. Id.

183. Id. at 541.

184. Id. at 525; see Martin H. Redish & Elizabeth J. Cisar, "If Angels Were to Govern": The Need for Pragmatic Formalism in Separation of Powers Theory, 41 Duke L.J. 449, 463 (1991) (arguing that separation of powers requires that each branch of government possess the "formal tools necessary to limit the excesses of its rivals").

185. The Federalist No. 51, at 160 (James Madison) (Roy P. Fairfield ed., 2d ed. 1966).

186. Id.

187. See Redish & Cisar, supra note 184, at 462.

188. Compare id. at 476 (arguing that separation of powers must operated before one branch has acquired an undue amount of power), with Blasi, supra note 79, at 541 (calling for "well-organized, well-financed, professional critics to serve as a counterforce . . . to pass judgment on the actions of government").

189. For a detailed critique of Professor Blasi's explication of the checking function, see Redish, supra note 128, at 41–45.

190. Blasi, supra note 79, at 538.

191. See Lindblom, supra note 4, at 173.

192. Yudof, supra note 147, at 161; see also id. (stating that checking institutions must be "establishment organizations," with "high claims to legitimacy in the public mind").

193. Blasi, supra note 79, at 541.

194. See Yudof, supra note 147, at 161; Shelledy, supra note 6, at 573 (arguing that the "existence of distinct corporate views and the ability of corporations to compete with government and press for public attention support the conclusion that corporate speech can enrich public debate").

195. Tocqueville, supra note 130, at 133; see also Austin v. Michigan Chamber of Commerce, 494 U.S. 652, 693–94 (1990) (Scalia, J., dissenting) (quoting larger passage of Tocqueville's argument).

196. See Shelledy, supra note 6, at 571 ("[C]ompetition among three loud voices will provide a more diverse discourse than a debate dominated by two.");

cf. Redish & Cisar, supra note 184, at 463 (describing the separation of powers in which each of the three branches possesses the tools to restrict the other two in a prophylactic manner).

197. See Baker, supra note 13, at 231–33 ("[T]he role of the press in exposing abuses of power is likely to be central."); Floyd Abrams, The Press Is Different: Reflections on Justice Stewart and the Autonomous Press, 7 Hofstra L. Rev. 563, 585 (1979) (arguing that the ability to be an independent check on government is "unique to the press"); id. at 592 ("[T]he press is the only institution that can serve on a continuing basis as an open eye of the public."); Randall P. Bezanson, The New Free Press Guarantee, 63 Va. L. Rev. 731, 735 (1977) (asserting that the press is a "check on government that no other institution could provide").

198. First Nat'l Bank v. Bellotti, 435 U.S. 765, 782–83 (1978); see also Abrams, supra note 199, at 587 (arguing that recognizing the press's unique role and status is not inconsistent with granting broad First Amendment protections to others).

199. See Bellotti, 435 U.S. at 782 n. 18.

200. David Lange, The Speech and Press Clauses, 23 UCLA L. Rev. 77, 103 (1975).

201. Yudof, supra note 147, at 37.

202. See Steven Shiffrin, The Politics of the Mass Media and the Free Speech Principle, 69 Ind. L.J. 689, 708–9 (1994) (noting that during the first month of the war's coverage, *Nightline* failed to feature any guest who opposed the government's actions). Political scientist Benjamin Page has documented this charge. His empirical study demonstrates that the actual level of opposition to the war was never accurately reflected in news or in editorial coverage. See Benjamin I. Page, Who Deliberates? Mass Media in Modern Democracy 26–37 (1996).

203. See Martin H. Redish, The Constitution as Political Structure 99–113 (1995).

204. Cf. Yudof, supra note 147, at 164 ("[I]t is incumbent upon the courts to cultivate the ability of all institutions to counter government and one another.").

205. See, e.g., Miranda v. Arizona, 384 U.S. 436, 448 (1966) (allowing defendants to challenge improper custodial interrogation procedures as violative of their Fifth Amendment privilege against self-incrimination). Another example is the First Amendment's overbreadth doctrine. Cf. Henry P. Monaghan, Overbreadth, 1981 Sup. Ct. Rev. 1, 4 (stating that, in arguing a statute's overbreadth, "claimant is asserting his own right not to be burdened by an unconstitutional rule of law, though naturally the claim is not one which depends on the privileged character of his own conduct" [footnote and internal quotation marks omitted]).

206. See, e.g., Heart of Atlanta Motel, Inc. v. United States, 379 U.S. 241, 262 (1964) (allowing, but rejecting on the merits, a corporation's challenge to the 1964 Civil Rights Act on Commerce Clause grounds).

207. See, e.g., Ohio Valley Water Co. v. Ben Avon Borough, 253 U.S. 287, 289

(1920) (allowing a corporation to present a procedural due process challenge to the fixing of maximum rates chargeable without an independent judicial determination).

208. Stanley v. Georgia, 394 U.S. 557, 565 (1969) (recognizing a right to possess obscene materials in the home).

209. See Redish, supra note 87, at 47; Strauss, supra note 152, at 355–56; see also 44 Liquormart, Inc. v. Rhode Island, 517 U.S. 484, 517–19 (1996) (Thomas, J., concurring in part and concurring in the judgment) (stating that the First Amendment rejects any attempt to keep people "ignorant in order to manipulate their choices").

210. Texas v. Johnson, 491 U.S. 397, 414 (1989); see also Forsyth County v. Nationalist Movement, 505 U.S. 123, 134–36 (1992) (striking down a law that allowed higher permit fees for speech likely to arouse public hostility); Cohen v. California, 403 U.S. 15, 21 (1971) (placing the burden on unwilling listeners to "avert[ ] their eyes" to avoid objectionable or offensive speech); Abrams v. United States, 250 U.S. 616, 630 (1919) (Holmes, J., dissenting) ("[W]e should be eternally vigilant against attempts to check the expression of opinions that we loathe."); Stone, supra note 108, at 214–15 & n. 98 (citing cases in arguing that the First Amendment does not permit government to prohibit unpopular views).

211. See Chapter 2, supra; see also Martin H. Redish, Tobacco Advertising and the First Amendment, 81 Iowa L. Rev. 589, 590–92 (1996).

212. Austin v. Michigan Chamber of Commerce, 494 U.S. 652, 660 (1990); see also FEC v. Massachusetts Citizens for Life, Inc., 479 U.S. 238, 258 (1986) ("The availability of these resources may make a corporation a formidable political presence, even though the power of the corporation may be no reflection of the power of its ideas.").

213. Abrams, 250 U.S. at 630 (Holmes, J., dissenting).

214. See Austin, 494 U.S. at 659–60; see also MCFL, 479 U.S. at 257 (expressing concern over the "corrosive influence of concentrated corporate wealth").

215. See Austin, 494 U.S. at 661; see also Paul S. Edwards, Defining Political Corruption: The Supreme Court's Role, 10 BYU J. Pub. L. 1, 21 (1996) (arguing that the Austin Court's view of corruption may be understood as reflecting a Rawlsian view of political equality according to which corporations should not be permitted to control the course of public debate).

216. See Austin, 494 U.S. at 706 (Kennedy, J., dissenting) (stating that insulating voters from access to ideas is incompatible with the First Amendment); see also Redish, supra note 87, at 113 (arguing that decreasing the flow of available information undermines important First Amendment values).

217. Austin, 494 U.S. at 684 (Scalia, J., dissenting).

218. See id. at 685 (Scalia, J., dissenting); cf. Cass R. Sunstein, Democracy and the Problem of Free Speech 238 (1993) (arguing that some individual speech does not reflect popular support).

219. L. A. Powe, Jr., Mass Speech and the Newer First Amendment, 1982 Sup. Ct. Rev. 243, 283; see also id. (illustrating that unpopular "mass speech" reaches a wider audience and thus is potentially more effective than unpopular speech on a soapbox).

220. See Strauss, supra note 152, at 334.

221. See id.; see also First Nat'l Bank v. Bellotti, 435 U.S. 765, 790 (1978) ("[T]he fact that advocacy may persuade the electorate is hardly a reason to suppress it.").

222. David L. Shapiro, Courts, Legislatures, and Paternalism, 74 Va. L. Rev. 519, 519 (1988); see also id. at 542–43 (discussing the Supreme Court's emphasis on the idea that the First Amendment "outlaws a paternalist[ic] approach to the messages a person may receive"); Stone, supra note 108, at 212 ("The Court has long embraced an 'antipaternalistic' understanding of the first amendment."). This antipaternalism concept is clearest in the Court's commercial speech cases. See Chapter 2, supra.

223. Strauss, supra note 152, at 335; see also Redish, supra note 87, at 47 (arguing that because the government may not determine what life-affecting decisions an individual can make, it cannot suppress the information on which those decisions are based); Stone, supra note 108, at 213 ("The point, rather, is that the government ordinarily may not restrict the expression of particular ideas, viewpoints, or items of information because it does not trust its citizens to make wise or desirable decisions.").

224. Redish, supra note 211, at 636.

225. See Austin v. Michigan Chamber of Commerce, 494 U.S. 652, 659 (1990) (restricting corporate speech because "the power of the corporation may be no reflection of the power of its ideas" [citation omitted]); see also Frederick Schauer, The Political Incidence of the Free Speech Principle, 64 U. Colo. L. Rev. 935, 949 (1993) (suggesting that "resources have more explanatory power than truth in determining which propositions a population will accept and which it will reject"); Wright, supra note 160, at 638 (stating that government regulation is necessary "so that the wealthiest voices may not dominate the debate by the strength of their dollars rather than their ideas").

226. See Owen M. Fiss, Free Speech and Social Structure, 71 Iowa L. Rev. 1405, 1412 (1986) (noting that opportunities for speech are "limited . . . by our capacity to digest or process information"); Shelledy, supra note 6, at 575–76 (arguing that "selective reception of messages" limits the amount of information that individuals can process, thus enabling the wealthy advocate's views to exert greater influence).

227. See supra notes 86–95 and accompanying text.

228. Shelledy, supra note 6, at 574; see also Austin, 494 U.S. at 684 (Scalia, J., dissenting) (arguing that speech is effective only to the extent it strikes someone as true).

229. See supra notes 124–27 and accompanying text.

230. See supra notes 128–33 and accompanying text.

231. Cass R. Sunstein, Beyond the Republican Revival, 97 Yale L.J. 1539, 1550 (1988) ("[I]n their capacity as political actors, citizens and representatives are not supposed to ask only what is in their private interest.").

232. See id. at 1564–65.

233. See, e.g., Hustler Mag., Inc. v. Falwell, 485 U.S. 46, 53 (1988) (arguing that, although relevant for tort liability, motive is irrelevant for First Amendment purposes).

234. Chapter 2, supra; see also Austin v. Michigan Chamber of Commerce, 494 U.S. 652, 684 (1990) (Scalia, J., dissenting) (noting that corporate advocacy's effectiveness is impacted by considering the "invariably self-interested and probably uncongenial source").

235. See Chapter 2, supra.

236. See First Nat'l Bank v. Bellotti, 435 U.S. 765, 782 n. 18 (1978).

237. See Dan-Cohen, supra note 14, at 108–9 (discussing the argument that shareholders are forced to contribute to the expression of views they do not hold); Brudney, supra note 6, at 247 ("A's right to receive information does not require the state to permit B to steal from C the funds that alone will enable B to make the communication."); see also Austin v. Michigan Chamber of Commerce, 494 U.S. 652, 675 (1990) (Brennan, J., concurring) ("[the] State surely has a compelling interest in preventing a corporation it has chartered from exploiting those who do not wish to contribute to the [corporation's] political message."); Bellotti, 435 U.S. at 812 (White, J., dissenting) (discussing the overriding governmental interest in "assuring that shareholders are not compelled to support and financially further beliefs with which they disagree").

238. See infra note 271 and accompanying text.

239. See, e.g., Simon & Schuster, Inc. v. Members of the N.Y. Crime Victims Bd., 502 U.S. 105, 120 (1991) (rejecting selective application of state's compelling interest); infra notes 275–78 and accompanying text.

240. See supra note 173 and accompanying text.

241. Brudney, supra note 6, at 238; see also Bellotti, 435 U.S. at 814 (White, J., dissenting) ("States have always been free to adopt measures designed to further rights protected by the Constitution even when not compelled to do so."); id. at 813–14 (discussing cases protecting individuals from forced speech).

242. See supra note 240 and accompanying text.

243. See Austin v. Michigan Chamber of Commerce, 494 U.S. 652, 670 (1990) (Brennan, J., concurring); Bellotti, 435 U.S. at 812 (White, J., dissenting) (arguing for protecting shareholders if the issue does not materially affect business of the corporation).

244. See FEC v. Massachusetts Citizens for Life, Inc., 479 U.S. 238, 260–61 (1986); see also supra notes 50–58 and accompanying text.

245. MCFL, 479 U.S. at 260–61.

246. Id. at 263.

247. See id. at 263–64 (describing three features of such political organizations); see also Baker, supra note 13, at 220 (arguing that modern corporations are not oriented toward "associative value goals"); Bezanson, supra note 13, at 778–81 (distinguishing types of organizations based on the degree of connection between an organization's members and the corporate statements); Brudney, supra note 147, at 74 (distinguishing business corporations from other voluntary associations); Dan-Cohen, supra note 147, at 1248 (distinguishing the type of speech rights held by business corporations as opposed to other organizations).

248. See O'Kelley, supra note 6, at 1365–66 (describing the "associational rationale" for protecting some corporate speech); see also Brudney, supra note 147, at 75 (describing individuals who join organizations in order to support their advocacy activities).

249. See MCFL, 479 U.S. at 241–42 (explaining the corporate purpose).

250. Cf. Glickman v. Wileman Bros. & Elliott, Inc., 521 U.S. 457, 462 & n. 3 (1997) (finding that fruit growers share the same basic aim as government-controlled advertising campaign—namely, increasing sales—even though they might differ over specific strategies as to how to accomplish that goal).

251. Smolla, supra note 162, at 239; see also Austin v. Michigan Chamber of Commerce, 494 U.S. 652, 687 (1990) (Scalia, J., dissenting) ("Would it be any more upsetting to a shareholder of General Motors that it endorsed the election of Henry Wallace (to stay comfortably in the past) than it would be to a member of the [ACLU] that it endorsed the election of George Wallace?"). But see Dan-Cohen, supra note 147, at 1249 (arguing that members maintain affiliation with expressive organizations precisely because of the communicative activity and despite potential disparity between the organization's views and the individual's views on some issues).

252. See, e.g., R.A.V. v. City of St. Paul, 505 U.S. 377, 391 (1992) (striking down an ordinance banning racially motivated hate speech).

253. See, e.g., Edward J. Cleary, Beyond the Burning Cross: The First Amendment and the Landmark R.A.V. Case 96 (1994) (describing People for the American Way's positions supporting the hate speech ordinance but opposing efforts to ban violent rap songs); see also id. at 199–200 (discussing the positions of the ACLU, which had defended the Nazis' right to march in Skokie, Illinois: lukewarm opposition to the hate speech ordinance and support for sentence enhancement for racially motivated crimes).

254. See Friedman & Goldston, supra note 142, at 44; see also supra notes 129–48 and accompanying text.

255. See Brudney, supra note 147, at 58–60 (discussing the need to protect individual shareholders).

256. Brudney, supra note 6, at 268; see also First Nat'l Bank v. Bellotti, 435

U.S. 765, 818 (1978) (White, J., dissenting) (noting a state interest in ensuring that "citizens are not forced to choose between supporting the propagation of views with which they disagree and passing up investment opportunities").

257. See, e.g., Abood v. Detroit Bd. of Educ., 431 U.S. 209, 235–36 (1977) (requiring that expenditures for political expression be financed from dues "paid by employees who do not object to advancing those ideas"); Pipefitters Local 562 v. United States, 407 U.S. 385, 414–15 (1972) (holding that political funds must be separate from union dues and must indicate their political purpose); International Ass'n of Machinists v. Street, 367 U.S. 740, 768–69 (1961) (denying unions, "over an employee's objection, the power to use his exacted funds to support political causes which he opposes").

258. See Abood, 431 U.S. at 212 (requiring union-shop and "service charge" by nonmembers); Street, 367 U.S. at 746–47 (providing an example of federal law permitting union-shop agreements).

259. See FEC v. Massachusetts Citizens for Life, Inc., 479 U.S. 238, 260 (1986) (distinguishing union cases from corporations); Cohen, supra note 109, at 33 ("Individuals are increasingly dependent upon memberships and participation in organizations such as labor unions . . . to practice their trades.").

260. See Butler & Ribstein, supra note 109, at 65; see also Austin v. Michigan Chamber of Commerce, 494 U.S. 652, 687 (1990) (Scalia, J., dissenting) (arguing that selling stock "does not ordinarily involve the severe psychic trauma or economic disaster that Justice Brennan's opinion suggests").

261. See Butler & Ribstein, supra note 109, at 65–66; see also Austin, 494 U.S. at 691 (Scalia, J., dissenting) ("General Motors, after all, will risk a stockholder suit if it makes a political endorsement that is not plausibly tied to its ability to make money for its shareholders.").

262. See First Nat'l Bank v. Bellotti, 435 U.S. 765, 794–95 n. 34 (1978); cf. Austin, 494 U.S. at 710 (Kennedy, J., dissenting) (stating that "[o]ne need not become a member of the Michigan Chamber of Commerce or the Sierra Club in order to earn a living").

263. See Austin, 494 U.S. at 709–10 (Kennedy, J., dissenting); Brudney, supra note 6, at 270 ("[T]he freedom to refrain from working is not equally as exercisable as the freedom to refrain from investing.").

264. But see Bellotti, 435 U.S. at 818 (White, J., dissenting) (arguing that employees in the union cases were free to seek other employment); Brudney, supra note 6, at 270 (arguing that the "freedom of investors to go elsewhere would be costly, if not wholly illusory").

265. See Dan-Cohen, supra note 14, at 108–9.

266. See id. at 109.

267. Obviously an individual is free to reach a private agreement with the businessman stating that the businessman not use the loan for his fascist speech. Likewise, one can employ private shareholder agreements to restrict the corpora-

tion's speech. Neither implicates the First Amendment because the government does not compel the restriction. See Butler & Ribstein, supra note 109, at 65 (arguing that such private contracts restricting corporate speech "do not raise significant First Amendment concerns").

268. Cf. Austin v. Michigan Chamber of Commerce, 494 U.S. 652, 686–87 (1990) (Scalia, J., dissenting) ("[M]anagement may take any action that is ultimately in accord with what the majority . . . of the shareholders wishes, so long as that action is designed to make a profit."); cf. Fred D. Baldwin, Conflicting Interests 3–4 (1984) (discussing corporate governance reform and the controversy surrounding the "proper relation between private business interests and other social concerns").

269. See Butler & Ribstein, supra note 109, at 59–60.

270. 502 U.S. 105 (1991). The Court invalidated New York's "Son of Sam" law, which required anyone convicted of a crime to surrender to the state, and then to the victim or victim's family, any income earned from books relating to the crime. See id. at 123.

271. See id. at 116 (classifying law as "content-based").

272. See id. at 124 (Kennedy, J., concurring in the judgment). The weaker version, from the majority opinion, is that such a direct burden is subject to strict scrutiny, requiring a compelling state interest and narrow tailoring of the law. See id. at 120–21. The majority opinion recognized a compelling state interest in compensating crime victims but held that the statute was not narrowly tailored as required by strict scrutiny. See id. at 120–23.

273. See Austin, 494 U.S. at 675 (Brennan, J., concurring); First Nat'l Bank v. Bellotti, 435 U.S. 765, 812 (1978) (White, J., dissenting); see also Brudney, supra note 6, at 256–57 (discussing how political science and economic theory justify state interest as compelling).

274. See Bellotti, 435 U.S. at 794–95 n. 34 (stating that no one has explained "why the dissenting shareholder's wishes are entitled to such greater solicitude in this context than in many others where equally important and controversial corporate decisions are made").

275. For a detailed discussion of the compelled speech issue, see Chapter 5, infra.

276. See supra notes 242–45 and accompanying text.

277. See Austin, 494 U.S. at 676–77 (Brennan, J., concurring); see also Neuborne, supra note 158, at 31 (noting that there is no metric to determine who wins when the interests of speaker and listener diverge).

278. See Hovenkamp, supra note 2, at 42 ("The doctrine that a corporation is a constitutional person meant that the corporation's directors or managers had the power to assert the corporation's constitutional claims. The far less cited corollary was that the shareholders lacked standing to assert these rights.").

279. See generally Stephen B. Presser, Piercing the Corporate Veil § 1.01

(1991) (discussing the distinction between the corporate entity and individual shareholders for purposes of liability).

280. See supra notes 270–76 and accompanying text.

281. The Court, in fact, has construed broadly the "common view" concept. See Glickman v. Wileman Bros. & Elliott, Inc., 521 U.S. 457, 471–73 (1997).

282. See First Nat'l Bank v. Bellotti, 435 U.S. 765, 794–95 n. 34 (1978) (expressing concern that the majority will be completely silenced because a "hypothetical minority might object").

283. See id. at 794.

284. See Abood v. Detroit Bd. of Educ., 431 U.S. 209, 240 (1977).

285. See Brudney, supra note 6, at 271 (discussing "least restrictive means" of furthering compelling state interest). But see Bellotti, 435 U.S. at 818 (White, J., dissenting) (suggesting that such a refund system is unworkable for corporations and does not solve the problem of investors who are deterred from investing).

286. See Austin v. Michigan Chamber of Commerce, 494 U.S. 652, 660 (1990) (holding that the law is narrowly tailored because it eliminates distortion of wealth while allowing corporate views to be expressed); id. at 669 (Brennan, J., concurring) (noting that the law is not an "across-the-board prohibition on political participation by corporations"); see also Sunstein, supra note 218, at 238 (distinguishing the "mere segregation requirement" of *Austin* from the "flat ban" of *Bellotti*); Brudney, supra note 6, at 272 (suggesting a segregated fund as an acceptable alternative); Shelledy, supra note 6, at 577 (arguing in favor of restrictions that "leave some outlet for corporate points of view," as did the segregated fund in *Austin*).

287. See Smolla, supra note 162, at 236–37; see also Austin, 494 U.S. at 681 n.* (Scalia, J., dissenting) ("Just as political speech by [John D. Rockefeller's] association is not speech by John D. Rockefeller, so also speech by a corporate PAC ... is not speech by the corporation itself."); Butler & Ribstein, supra note 109, at 63–64 ("[P]olitical speech by managers of publicly held firms can generally be considered the expression of the individual managers from whom the speech originates.").

288. See Austin, 494 U.S. at 709 (Kennedy, J., dissenting); see also Dan-Cohen, supra note 14, at 108 (arguing that individuals cannot produce speech that is "irreducibly 'corporate' in nature").

289. According to Hurst, "corporation law early favored business arrangements which centralized decision making, gave it considerable assurance of tenure, and armed it for vigorous maneuver. Shareholder decisions, it was soon established, should normally be by simple majority. Active management should be concentrated in a board of directors; stockholders did not have owners' rights over the particular assets of a going corporate enterprise; unless exhibiting gross abuse of power or breach of faith, directors' decisions governed the regular course of the business. [Furthermore, corporate law] favored strong central di-

rection of pooled assets; capacity for indefinite life, uninterrupted by change of shareholders. . . . A board of directors must do its business as a body, not as individuals. Hurst, supra note 99, at 25.

290. Brudney, supra note 6, at 243–44; see also O'Kelley, supra note 6, at 1362 (arguing that the corporation must assert its rights "in connection with a form of expression that is a part of the corporation's business").

291. See Brudney, supra note 6, at 254; see also Baldwin, supra note 268, at 112 (discussing a different suggestion for a unanimity requirement). Note, of course, that this would virtually halt all corporate operations because any individual or group could purchase a veto in the form of one share of stock. See id. at 112; Brudney, supra note 6, at 272 (noting that a unanimous shareholder requirement for corporate political speech "would effectively prohibit political speech by the corporation").

292. Brudney, supra note 6, at 254.

293. See supra notes 270–76 and accompanying text.

294. 391 U.S. 367 (1968) (upholding law prohibiting burning of draft cards).

295. See id. at 376–77. The Court reasoned that "[G]overnment regulation is sufficiently justified if it is within the constitutional power of the Government; if it furthers an important or substantial governmental interest; if the governmental interest is unrelated to the suppression of free expression; and if the incidental restriction on alleged First Amendment freedoms is no greater than is essential to the furtherance of that interest." Id. at 377. Professor Stone refers to this as a "no gratuitous inhibition approach." Stone, supra note 108, at 190–91 n. 5 (internal quotation marks omitted).

296. But see Redish, supra note 128, at 100–101 (describing *O'Brien* as the "most troubling illustration of the Court's modern approach to content-neutral restrictions"). The Court has continued to employ the *O'Brien* test. See, e.g., Barnes v. Glen Theatre, Inc., 501 U.S. 560, 566–68 (1991) (plurality opinion) (holding a public indecency statute valid under *O'Brien*, "despite its incidental limitations on some expressive activity"); id. at 582 (Souter, J., concurring in the judgment) (agreeing with the plurality opinion's use of the *O'Brien* test to determine the required degree of First Amendment protection).

297. Brudney, supra note 6, at 244.

298. See First Nat'l Bank v. Bellotti, 435 U.S. 765, 768 (1978) (internal quotation marks omitted); see also id. at 785 (rejecting legislature's requirement that corporation "stick to business").

299. See supra notes 270–76 and accompanying text.

300. See Dan-Cohen, supra note 147, at 1245–46 (criticizing the *Bellotti* Court for rejecting the concern that "corporate wealth and power may be used to 'drown out other points of view'" [citation omitted]); Shelledy, supra note 6, at 575 ("[W]ealth gives some advocates exposure to more voters and thereby gives them an opportunity to persuade a larger part of the electorate . . . as a result of

selective reception of messages."); Wright, supra note 160, at 637 ("Unchecked political expenditures . . . may drown opposing beliefs.").

301. See Wright, supra note 160, at 637 ("Limiting the amount that wealthy interests may spend to publicize their views enhances the self-expression of individual citizens . . . furthering the values of freedom of speech.").

302. Smolla, supra note 162, at 237 ("proportional leveling"); Powe, supra note 219, at 267 ("enhancement").

303. Reynolds v. Sims, 377 U.S. 533, 565 (1964) (discussing the Equal Protection Clause's dictate of "one person, one vote").

304. See Wright, supra note 160, at 610, 642.

305. Sunstein, supra note 231, at 1552.

306. See Kenneth L. Karst, Equality as a Central Principle in the First Amendment, 43 U. Chi. L. Rev. 20, 20–23 (1975); see also Police Dep't v. Mosley, 408 U.S. 92, 96 (1972) (articulating the equality principle).

307. Gertz v. Robert Welch, Inc., 418 U.S. 323, 339 (1974).

308. See Chapters 1 & 2, supra.

309. I ultimately conclude that such a right of access violates the First Amendment. See Chapter 5, infra. However, at least relatively speaking, it is preferable to direct restriction.

310. Perhaps one could argue that a speaker's prior success and public notoriety—no matter how unrelated to her expression's subject—conceivably might provide a listener with a distinct rational basis for giving that speaker's expression greater weight. Even if one were to accept such reasoning, one could fashion a similar argument about wealth's advantages: The very fact that the speaker has had the ingenuity to access or retain such financial resources arguably may provide greater legitimacy to the speech, at least in certain recipients' minds.

311. See generally §§ 26 U.S.C. §§ 2001, 2010 (establishing rules for taxes and tax credits on estates).

312. See id., § 501 (exempting certain corporations from taxation).

313. See supra notes 270–76 and accompanying text.

314. See United States v. O'Brien, 391 U.S. 367, 377 (1968).

315. Austin v. Michigan Chamber of Commerce, 494 U.S. 652, 660 (1990); see FEC v. Massachusetts Citizens for Life, Inc., 479 U.S. 238, 258 (1986) (arguing that resources make a corporation formidable "even though the power of the corporation may be no reflection of the power of its ideas").

316. Wright, supra note 160, at 631; see also Austin, 494 U.S. at 660–61 ("Corporate wealth can unfairly influence elections . . . and present[s] the potential for distorting the political process."); MCFL, 479 U.S. at 257 ("Th[e] concern over the corrosive influence of concentrated corporate wealth reflects the conviction that it is important to protect the integrity of the marketplace of political ideas."); Sunstein, supra note 218, at 239 (arguing that equality of speech is a legitimate goal, but the state should not be selective by limiting corporations with-

out limiting the speech of others); id. at 235 (arguing that restricting corporate speech alone cannot achieve political equality).

317. See Sunstein, supra note 218, at 20–21 (arguing for a theory of the First Amendment based on the ideal of "deliberative democracy," including a commitment to equality and diversity of views); Wright, supra note 160, at 636 ("[T]he truth-producing capacity of the marketplace of ideas is not enhanced if some are allowed to monopolize the marketplace by wielding excessive financial resources.").

318. 424 U.S. 1, 48–49 (1976) (per curiam).

319. See Sunstein, supra note 218, at 238 (suggesting it is improper to restrict only the speech of wealthy corporations but not of wealthy individuals).

320. See Powe, supra note 219, at 275 (noting the privilege of wealth in purchasing more of a consumption item—media advertisements); Carl E. Schneider, Free Speech and Corporate Freedom: A Comment on First National Bank of Boston v. Bellotti, 59 S. Cal. L. Rev. 1227, 1280 (1986) (arguing that the power to purchase access to the media is "not a fair test of either an argument's truth or its innate popular appeal" [citation omitted]); Shelledy, supra note 6, at 575 ("[W]ealth gives some advocates exposure to more voters."); J. Skelly Wright, Politics and the Constitution: Is Money Speech?, 85 Yale L.J. 1001, 1019 (1976) (arguing that money is merely the idea's intensity, not the idea itself); id. at 1019 n. 70 ("[J]ust as the volume of sound may be limited by law, so the volume of dollars may be limited, without violating the First Amendment.").

321. See Bezanson, supra note 13, at 778 ("[D]ominant economic power has at best an uncertain relationship to persuasion of the electorate through advertisements."); Shelledy, supra note 6, at 574 ("[I]t is not so readily apparent how a corporation's advocacy could exert an influence on elections that exceeds public support for its ideas."); see also Austin, 494 U.S. at 684 (Scalia, J., dissenting) (arguing that corporate advocacy will be accepted only to the degree that the message strikes voters as true).

322. Wright, supra note 160, at 623.

323. See id. at 623–24.

324. Id. at 624–25.

325. Id. at 625.

326. See id.

327. See Shelledy, supra note 6, at 574; supra notes 86–95 and accompanying text.

328. Austin v. Michigan Chamber of Commerce, 494 U.S. 652, 684 (1990) (Scalia, J., dissenting) (emphasis omitted); see also Shelledy, supra note 6, at 574 ("[W]e must generally assume that speech affects voting behavior only when it persuades.").

329. Wright, supra note 160, at 632.

330. Karst, supra note 306, at 21–23. This theory, based on the Court's decision in Police Department v. Mosley, 408 U.S. 92, 94 (1972), in which the Court

struck down a law permitting all picketing except labor picketing outside a school, provides a possible theoretical justification for the First Amendment's content distinction.

331. See Karst, supra note 306, at 29; Mosley, 408 U.S. at 96 (stating that the First Amendment requires "an equality of status in the field of ideas" and that all viewpoints be heard equally [internal quotation marks and citation omitted]).

332. See supra notes 306–9 and accompanying text.

333. Karst, supra note 306, at 28.

334. See id. at 35.

335. Fiss, supra note 14, at 15.

336. Id. at 15–16.

337. Id. at 16.

338. Dan-Cohen, supra note 14, at 109 (citation omitted); see Dan-Cohen, supra note 147, at 1245–46 (criticizing the *Bellotti* Court for rejecting this argument); Shelledy, supra note 6, at 576 ("[C]oncentrated wealth may enable corporations to reduce the likelihood that individual voices will be heard."); Wright, supra note 160, at 625 ("Regardless of their message, [corporations] simply drown out their opponents when they have the wherewithal to outspend them by margins of up to fifty to one."); id. at 637 ("Unchecked political expenditures . . . may drown opposing beliefs.").

339. See supra notes 309–37 and accompanying text.

340. See Powe, supra note 219, at 280 (noting the absence of proof that counterspeech to economically powerful interests' expression will not be forthcoming).

341. First Nat'l Bank v. Bellotti, 435 U.S. 765, 789–90 (1978); see also Austin v. Michigan Chamber of Commerce, 494 U.S. 652, 706 (1990) (Kennedy, J., dissenting) ("[E]ven were we to assume that some record support . . . would make a constitutional difference . . . [t]he majority provides only conjecture."); Shelledy, supra note 6, at 576–77 (requiring record evidence or legislative findings that corporate speech was dominating and therefore impoverishing public debate, and arguing that such evidence was lacking in both *Bellotti* and *Austin*).

342. See Fiss, supra note 14, at 15 (asserting that "in politics, scarcity is the rule").

343. See Shelledy, supra note 6, at 575.

344. See id.

345. These proposals, of course, raise their own First Amendment issues. See Chapter 5, infra.

346. Shelledy, supra note 6, at 575–76; see also Fiss, supra note 226, at 1412 (noting that opportunities for speech are limited "by our capacity to digest or process information"); Schneider, supra note 320, at 1283 (noting that the *Bellotti* statute restricted only media advertisements, which present no information at all).

347. See supra notes 313–17 and accompanying text.

348. See supra notes 338–45 and accompanying text.

349. See supra notes 86–95 and accompanying text; see also Redish, supra note 87, at 21–22 (arguing that free speech fosters self-realization by promoting the development of one's "uniquely human faculties" and by facilitating one's ability to make life-affecting decisions); Wright, supra note 322, at 1020 ("The play of ideas, the sifting of good ideas from bad, of truth from falsehood, of justice from injustice—all these are essential parts of our system as well.").

350. See Schauer, supra note 225, at 938 (providing an example of alcohol and tobacco industries opposing "encroaching restrictions or outright prohibitions on advertising their products"); Shiffrin, supra note 202, at 689–90 (discussing the conservative position taken by corporations).

351. See Pacific Gas & Elec. Co. v. Public Utils. Comm'n, 475 U.S. 1, 13–14 (1986) (plurality opinion).

352. J. M. Balkin, Some Realism About Pluralism: Legal Realist Approaches to the First Amendment, 1990 Duke L.J. 375, 383.

353. See Austin v. Michigan Chamber of Commerce, 494 U.S. 652, 701 (1990) (Kennedy, J., dissenting).

354. Balkin, supra note 352, at 384.

355. Shiffrin, supra note 202, at 689.

356. See id. at 712 (noting that it is "relevant that the [corporate] owners of the press are largely conservative" and that it is natural for their speech "to reflect their general view"); Mark Tushnet, Corporations and Free Speech, in The Politics of Law 253, 259 (David Kairys ed., 1982) (noting that "nominally independent expenditures are made with a heavy tilt toward the right wing"); see also Fiss, supra note 14, at 10–11 (assuming that allowing unlimited speech of economically powerful interests will "impoverish rather than enrich public debate"); Lindblom, supra note 4, at 201–21 (expressing concern over the principle of "circularity," i.e., that the very corporate interests that the state is supposed to regulate dominate the political agenda); Wright, supra note 160, at 636 (assuming that the expression of economically powerful interests will be dominated by lies, half-truths, and innuendos). Professor Fiss openly advocates the use of viewpoint-based discrimination to determine the First Amendment's reach when he argues that the "program advanced by Ralph Nader and other consumer advocates might have a First Amendment basis, because in fighting 'agency capture' we might be increasing the independence of the state from the market and thus enhancing its capacity to correct for the constraints that social structure imposes on public debate." Fiss, supra note 14, at 44.

357. Tushnet, supra note 356, at 260.

358. See Shiffrin, supra note 202, at 719.

359. Id.

360. See 21 C.F.R. §§ 897.1–.34 (establishing regulations applicable to the tobacco industry).

361. See Lindblom, supra note 4, at 201–6; supra notes 105–9 and accompanying text.

362. Wright, supra note 160, at 636; see also Tushnet, supra note 356, at 257 (noting that the First Amendment normally is a vehicle to give power to the powerless).

363. Professor Shiffrin has argued that speakers in cases such as United States v. O'Brien, 391 U.S. 367, 369 (1968), in which an individual burned a draft card to protest the war, and FCC v. Pacifica Foundation, 438 U.S. 726, 729–30 (1978), in which comedian George Carlin made obscenity-laced social commentary, are at the center of constitutional protection. See Steven H. Shiffrin, The First Amendment, Democracy, and Romance 80–81 (1990).

364. See supra notes 309–37 and accompanying text.

365. Similar free speech problems inhere in the arguments of civic republican scholars such as Professor Sunstein, although he never singles out corporate speech for special negative treatment. See Sunstein, supra note 218, at 239. His theory relies on a belief, however, that "[d]ramatic differences in wealth and power are . . . inconsistent with the underlying premises of a republican polity," Sunstein, supra note 231, at 1552, combined with a general opposition to individuals acting in their private interests, see id. at 1550. Logically, this would eliminate the corporate speaker, which is often powerful and usually motivated by economic self-interest. This theory fails, because of the same problem of viewpoint bias, by suggesting the possibility of an objective common good that overrides individual self-interest. See Redish & Lippman, supra note 26, at 295. If we imagine a candidate with strong anticorporate views, the result under Professor Sunstein's theory is that those who possess the most powerful incentive to support that candidate may speak in support, but those who oppose him—including corporations whose business might be harmed, a clear example of private interest—cannot voice their opposition.

366. See supra notes 133–48 and accompanying text.

367. See supra notes 149–77 and accompanying text.

368. See supra notes 129, 247–57, 314 and accompanying text.

369. This does not mean, it should be emphasized, that in its own expression the government must be neutral among competing philosophies and ideas.

370. See supra notes 351–54 and accompanying text.

371. See Chapter 2, supra.

372. See supra notes 338–52 and accompanying text.

373. Although several commentators have argued that at some point the sum total of available expression could amount to an information overload on the populace, there exists neither empirical support for such a notion nor any workable means for determining whether such a point had ever been reached.

374. One could say the same for the argument that corporate sp⟨
terfere with the free speech rights of dissenting shareholders.

375. See generally New York v. Ferber, 458 U.S. 747, 771 (1982) (
a statute may be invalidated as overbroad when it "reaches a substar
of impermissible applications"); Monaghan, supra note 205, at 4 (d⟨
overbreadth doctrine as protecting the plaintiff's right not to be bu⟨
unconstitutional rule of law).

NOTES TO CHAPTER 4

1. 424 U.S. 1 (1976).

2. There were some of us who recognized the troubling implications of campaign finance reform for the First Amendment right of free expression long before the decision in *Buckley*. See, e.g., Martin H. Redish, Campaign Spending
Laws and the First Amendment, 46 N.Y.U. L. Rev. 900 (1971); Ralph K. Winter,
Campaign Financing and Political Freedom (1973); Robert A. Bicks & Howard I.
Friedman, Regulation of Federal Election Finance: A Case of Misguided Morality,
28 N.Y.U. L. Rev. 975 (1953).

3. Burt Neuborne, Is Money Different?, 77 Tex. L. Rev. 1609, 1622–25 (1999);
J. Skelly Wright, Money and the Pollution of Politics: Is the First Amendment an
Obstacle to Political Equality?, 82 Colum. L. Rev. 609, 625–42 (1982).

4. See, e.g., Burt Neuborne, Toward a Democracy-Centered Reading of the
First Amendment, 93 Nw. U. L. Rev. 1055, 1071–73 (1999); John Rawls, Political
Liberalism 358–63 (1993).

5. See, e.g., Nixon v. Shrink Missouri PAC, 120 S. Ct. 897, 910 (2000) (Stevens,
J., concurring); Cass R. Sunstein, Political Equality and Unintended Consequences, 94 Colum. L. Rev. 1390, 1398–99 (1994).

6. See, e.g., Nixon v. Shrink Missouri PAC, 120 S. Ct. 897, 910 (2000) (Stevens,
J., concurring); Cass R. Sunstein, Political Equality and Unintended Consequences, 94 Colum. L. Rev. 1390, 1398–99 (1994).

7. See discussion infra notes 53–59 and accompanying text.

8. 120 S. Ct. 897 (2000).

9. See discussion infra notes 53–59 and accompanying text.

10. 120 S. Ct. at 908–9.

11. 120 S. Ct. at 910 (Stevens, J., concurring).

12. Id. at 910 (Breyer, J., concurring).

13. See discussion infra notes 60–70, 80–110 and accompanying text.

14. The term "soft money" refers to unlimited sums that may be given by
individuals, PACs, corporations, and labor unions to political parties for purposes of grass-roots and "party-building" activities. Kathleen Sullivan, Political
Money and Freedom of Speech, 30 U.C. Davis L. Rev. 663, 668 (1997).

15. Id. (Bundling occurs when one person collects several individual contributions of one thousand dollars each and gives the entire sum to a candidate, PAC, or party, thus receiving credit for a larger amount than he or she personally contributed).

16. See discussion infra notes 19–46 and accompanying text.

17. See infra notes 47–59 and accompanying text.

18. See infra notes 60–162 and accompanying text.

19. Federal Election Campaign Act of 1971, Pub. L. No. 92–225 (1972).

20. See Robert K. Goidel, Donald A. Gross, and Todd G. Shields, Money Matters: Consequences of Campaign Finance Reform in U.S. House Elections 2 (1999).

21. Federal Campaign Act Amendments of 1974, Pub. L. No. 93–443 (1974).

22. 424 U.S. 1 (1976).

23. See discussion infra notes 53–59 and accompanying text.

24. 2 U.S.C. § 441a (2000).

25. 2 U.S.C. § 431(1) (2000).

26. 2 U.S.C. § 441a.

27. Id.

28. Id.

29. Id.

30. Id.

31. Id.

32. Id.

33. Id.

34. Id.

35. Id.

36. Id.

37. Id.

38. S. 1593, 106th Cong. (1999). The similar Shays-Meehan legislation in the House is still in committee. H.R. 417, 106th Cong. (1999).

39. S. 2549, 106th Cong. (2000).

40. 146 Cong. Rec. S4656 (daily ed. June 7, 2000) (statement of Sen. McCain).

41. Political organization is defined as "a party, committee, association, fund, or other organization (whether or not incorporated) organized and operated primarily for the purpose of directly or indirectly accepting contributions or making expenditures, or both, for an exempt function." 26 U.S.C. § 527(e)(1) (2000). An exempt function is "the function of influencing or attempting to influence the selection, nomination, election, or appointment of any individual to any Federal, State, or local public office or office in a political organization, or the election of Presidential or Vice-Presidential electors, whether or not such individual or electors are selected, nominated, elected, or appointed." 2 U.S.C. 527(e)(2).

42. 146 Cong. Rec. 4657 (daily ed. June 7, 2000) (statement of Sen. McCain).

43. S. 2549.

44. Goidel et al., supra note 20, at 170.

45. Anthony Gierzynski, Money Rules: Financing Elections in America 48–49 (2000).

46. Id.

47. 424 U.S. 1 (1976).

48. Id. at 142.

49. See Sullivan, supra note 14, at 668 (explaining the concept of bundling).

50. Id. at 668. The problem of soft money was created by congressional action in 1979, when Congress amended the 1974 Act to permit parties to raise funds without the restrictions of contribution limitations, provided that the funds were set aside for "party building." 11 CFR § 100.7(b). See Herbert E. Alexander & Anthony Corado, Financing the 1992 Election 148 (1995). According to one commentator, "[a]ny limit on party expenditures of soft money would likely be struck down by the current Court in light of its recent decision that political parties may make unlimited independent expenditures on behalf of a particular candidate." Sullivan, supra note 14, at 669.

51. Frank J. Sorauf, Politics, Experience, and the First Amendment: The Case of American Campaign Finance, 94 Colum. L. Rev. 1348, 1356 (1994).

52. See, e.g., Colorado Republican Campaign Committee v. Federal Election Comm'n, 116 S. Ct. 2309, 2317 (1996) (holding that political parties have the First Amendment right to make unlimited expenditures on behalf of a particular candidate). In Nixon v. Shrink Missouri PAC, 120 S. Ct. 897 (2000), the Court, in reaffirming *Buckley*'s validation of contribution limits, distinguished *Colorado Republican Campaign Committee* on the grounds that the earlier decision had concerned a challenge to limitations on expenditures.

53. Congress enacted a law in 2000 expanding campaign contribution disclosure requirements. See Pub. L. No. 106–230 (2000). However, no efforts to expand direct restrictions on campaign finance have succeeded.

54. William P. Marshall, The Last Best Chance for Campaign Finance Reform, 94 Nw. U. L. Rev. 335, 339–42 (2000).

55. See Daniel A. Farber & Phillip P. Frickey, The Jurisprudence of Public Choice, 65 Tex. L. Rev. 873 (1987) (general discussion of public choice theory).

56. Marshall, supra note 54, at 376–86.

57. Jamin Raskin & John Bonifaz, The Constitutional Imperative and Practical Superiority of Democratically Financed Elections, 94 Colum. L. Rev. 1160, 1160 (1994).

58. Sullivan, supra note 14, at 669.

59. These statistics are taken from Bradley A. Smith, Faulty Assumptions and

Undemocratic Consequences of Campaign Finance Reform, 105 Yale L.J. 1049, 1050–51 (1996).

60. 120 S. Ct. 897, 910 (2000) (Stevens, J., concurring).

61. U.S. Const. Amend. V; Amend. XIV, § 1. When property rights are involved, legislative regulation will be found unconstitutional solely when the Court finds the legislation to fail the rational basis test, a standard that is virtually never satisfied. See, e.g., West Coast Hotel Co. v. Parrish, 300 U.S. 379 (1937).

62. 424 U.S. at 16–21.

63. See Nixon, 120 S. Ct. at 903–5.

64. 198 U.S. 45 (1905).

65. See Sunstein, supra note 5 at 1397 ("In rejecting the claim that controls on financial expenditures could be justified as a means of promoting political equality, *Buckley* seems highly reminiscent of the pre–New Deal period. Indeed *Buckley* might well be seen as the modern-day analogue of the infamous and discredited case of *Lochner v. New York*.").

66. This is a view, however, that I reject. See discussion infra notes 80–165 and accompanying text.

67. I have discussed the concept of ancillary First Amendment rights in an earlier work. See Martin H. Redish, Freedom of Thought as Freedom of Expression: Hate Crime Sentencing Enhancement and First Amendment Theory, 11 Crim. Just. Ethics 29, 34–35 (1992).

68. See, e.g., J. Skelly Wright, Politics and the Constitution: Is Money Speech?, 85 Yale L.J. 1001, 1005–6 (1976) (political spending and giving are a form of conduct related to speech, rather than pure speech, and therefore laws regulating these activities should be subject to a lesser standard of judicial review).

69. United States v. O'Brien, 391 U.S. 367, 376 (1968) (rejecting First Amendment challenge to federal law making it a crime to destroy a draft card).

70. Alexander Meiklejohn, Political Freedom 25–26 (1960).

71. See Chapter 2, supra.

72. See Robert H. Bork, Neutral Principles and Some First Amendment Problems, 47 Ind. L.J. 1, 26 (1971).

73. See discussion infra notes 128–40 and accompanying text.

74. 424 U.S. at 20–21 (contribution limit "entails only a marginal restriction upon the contributor's ability to engage in free communication. A contribution serves as a general expression of support for the candidate and his views, but does not communicate the underlying basis for the support. The quantity of communication by the contributor does not increase perceptibly with the size of his contribution, since the expression rests solely on the undifferentiated symbolic act of contributing."). The Court acknowledged that "the size of the contribution provides a very rough index of the intensity of the contributor's support for the candidate." Id. at 21. However, this apparently did not convince the Court that restrictions on the size of the contribution could affect First Amendment rights in a meaningful way.

75. The Court reasoned that while expenditure limits "preclude most associations from effectively amplifying the voice of their adherents," contribution limits "leave to contributor free to become a member of any political association and to assist personally in the association's efforts on behalf of candidates." Id. at 22.

76. Id. at 21.

77. Frank J. Sorauf, Inside Campaign Finance 38 (1992).

78. Id.

79. Ultimately, however, I do conclude that such limitations are, in fact, unconstitutional. See discussion infra notes 122–65 and accompanying text.

80. See United States v. O'Brien, 391 U.S. at 376.

81. 120 S. Ct. at 911 (Breyer, J., concurring).

82. Id. at 912.

83. The Court has instead referred to "the exacting scrutiny required by the First Amendment." Buckley, 424 U.S. at 16. See also Nixon, 120 S. Ct. at 903.

84. See, e.g., Barenblatt v. United States, 360 U.S. 109, 126 (1958).

85. 120 S. Ct. at 913.

86. Id.

87. Id.

88. See, e.g., Laurence Tribe, American Constitutional Law § 13.27 at 1135 (2d ed. 1988) ("If the net effect of the legislation is to enhance freedom of speech, the exacting review reserved for abridgements of free speech is inapposite."); Lillian R. BeVier, Money and Politics: A Perspective on the First Amendment and Campaign Finance Reform, 73 Cal. L. Rev. 1045, 1048 (1985) (noting that commentators have on occasion urged deference on the basis of "Congress' superior institutional capacity with regard to the governmental interests that the limitations are alleged to serve.").

89. See discussion infra at 000–000.

90. See, e.g., Nebraska Press Ass'n v. Stuart, 427 U.S. 539 (1976).

91. See, e.g., Time, Inc. v. Hill, 385 U.S. 374 (1967); Cox Broadcasting Corp. v. Cohn, 420 U.S. 469 (1975).

92. 5 U.S. (1 Cranch) 137 (1803).

93. See Korematsu v. United States, 323 U.S. 214 (1944).

94. See, e.g., Dennis v. United States, 384 U.S. 855 (1966).

95. I have discussed the theory of the counter-majoritarian principle in more detail in Martin H. Redish, The Federal Courts in the Political Order 124–25 (1991).

96. 5 U.S. (1 Cranch) at 178.

97. Cass R. Sunstein, Interest Groups in American Public Law, 38 Stan. L. Rev. 29, 29 (1985).

98. Id. (footnote omitted).

99. Id.

100. Abner Mikva, Foreword, 74 Va. L. Rev. 167 (1988).

101. William Eskridge, Politics Without Romance: Implications of Public Choice Theory for Statutory Interpretation, 74 Va. L. Rev. 275, 277 (1988). On the subject of public choice theory, see generally Daniel Farber, Free Speech Without Romance: Public Choice and the First Amendment, 105 Harv. L. Rev. 554 (1991).

102. Redish, supra note 95, at 24–25. See the discussion in Chapter 2, supra at 000–000.

103. See Michael J. Klarman, Majoritarian Judicial Review: The Entrenchment Problem, 85 Geo. L.J. 491, 498 (1997) ("The desire of representatives to perpetuate their hold on office may induce them to act contrary to the preferences of their constituents on a variety of issues; we might call this the 'agency' problem of representative government or 'legislative entrenchment.'").

104. See Marshall, supra note 54, at 341: "Nowhere . . . do the insights of public choice hold more resonance than in the area of campaign regulation. Unlike other legislative actions—which may or may not benefit incumbents depending on whether they appeal to voters—campaign reform is a direct regulation of the reelection process. Obviously, no self-interested maximizer is going to support legislation that makes her reelection more difficult."

105. See Elizabeth Drew, Politics and Money 154–55 (1983).

106. Marshall, supra note 54, at 339. See also Marlene Arnold Nicholson, Campaign Financing and Equal Protection, 26 Stan. L. Rev. 815, 847 (1974).

107. Goidel et al., supra note 20, at 41–44.

108. 120 S. Ct. at 912–13 (Breyer, J., concurring).

109. I have discussed the possibility of such friction in prior work. See Martin H. Redish, Freedom of Expression: A Critical Analysis 106–9 (1984).

110. See discussion infra notes 141–65 and accompanying text.

111. Marshall, supra note 54, at 350. Professor Marshall, it should be noted, was not necessarily endorsing this position, but rather merely summarizing one established line of scholarly thought. For an expression of a similar view, see Jamin Raskin & John Bonifaz, Equal Protection and the Wealth Primary, 11 Yale L. & Pl'y Rev. 273, 323 (1993).

112. Sullivan, supra note 14, at 671.

113. Neuborne, supra note 4, at 1062.

114. Id. (footnote omitted).

115. Id.

116. Id. at 1068.

117. Id.

118. Id. at 1070.

119. Id. at 1070–71.

120. See C. Edwin Baker, Human Liberty and Freedom of Speech 47–69 (1989).

121. See Chapter 1, supra.

122. See Smith, 105 Yale L.J. at 1060 ("Increased campaign spending trans-

lates into a better informed electorate."). See also Gary C. Jacobson, Money in Congressional Elections 31 (1980) (empirical studies have demonstrated that "the extent and content of information [voters] . . . have has a decisive effect on how they vote.").

123. Meiklejohn, supra note 70, at 27. "The principle of the freedom of speech springs from the necessities of the program of self-government."

124. Id. at 26–27.

125. The First Amendment, Meiklejohn argued, is concerned not at all about an individual's private right to speak. Id. at 26.

126. This is not to suggest that Meiklejohn himself would necessarily have viewed campaign finance regulation as a violation of the First Amendment. But to the extent he would have found such laws constitutional, it would have resulted from his own fallacy—what I have in earlier discussions referred to as the fallacy of the New England town meeting. See Chapter 1, supra; Chapter 3, supra. In that earlier discussion, I argue that Meiklejohn improperly analogized society to a self-contained New England town meeting, where we can operate with the assurance that all those present have been exposed to speaker communications. This is not an assumption we can reasonably make in general society. The point emphasized in text is simply that the process-based values recognized by Meiklejohn are threatened by restrictions on candidates' abilities to communicate their message to the voters, whether or not he would have recognized them as such.

127. See generally BeVier, supra note 88.

128. In *Buckley*, the Court expressly rejected the equality rationale as a constitutionally acceptable justification for expenditure limitations: "The interests served by the Act include restricting the voices of people and interest groups who have money to spend and reducing the overall scope of federal election campaigns. Although the Act does not focus on the ideas expressed by persons or groups subject to its regulations, it is aimed in part at equalizing the relative ability of all voters to affect electoral outcomes by placing a ceiling on expenditures for political expression by citizens and groups. Unlike *O'Brien*, where the Selective Service System's administrative interest in the preservation of draft cards was wholly unrelated to their use as a means of communication, it is beyond dispute that the interest in regulating the alleged 'conduct' of giving or spending money 'arises in some measure because the communication allegedly integral to the conduct is itself thought to be harmful.'" 424 U.S. at 17 (internal citation omitted).

129. Marshall, supra note 54, at 349 (footnote omitted).

130. This theory is considered in detail in Chapter 5, infra.

131. See, e.g., Kenneth Karst, Equality as a Central Principle in the First Amendment, 43 U. Chi. L. Rev. 20 (1975). The equality rationale is examined in the context of limits on corporate political activity in Chapter 3, supra. See, e.g., Police Dep't v. Mosley, 408 U.S. 92 (1972).

132. Note that the political equality argument, if accepted, simultaneously justifies both expenditure and contribution limitations. To the extent one were to reject the equality argument and instead focus exclusively on the avoidance-of-corruption rationale (as the Supreme Court did in *Buckley*), it is likely that only restrictions on contributions would be justified, though there exists debate on the point. See discussion infra notes 147–65 and accompanying text.

133. Reynolds v. Sims, 377 U.S. 533 (1974). See Sullivan, supra note 14, at 671 ("[The equality] argument starts from the principle of formal equality of suffrage embodied in the one person, one vote rule that emerged from the reapportionment cases."); Marshall, supra note 54 at 349 ("[T]he equal protection principle of one-person, one-vote supports the regulation of campaign finance in service of equality interests."); Sunstein, supra note 65 at 1392 ("The 'one person–one vote' rule exemplifies the commitment to political equality. Limits on campaign expenditures are continuous with that rule.").

134. See David A. Strauss, Corruption, Equality, and Campaign Finance Reform, 94 Colum. L. Rev. 1369, 1382–85 (1994).

135. New York Times Co. v. Sullivan, 376 U.S. 254, 270 (1964).

136. To the extent the argument for equality is employed to justify governmentally dictated access to existing communication sources, rather than governmentally imposed restrictions on campaign contributions or expenditures, this concern over creation of an equality of ignorance would not apply. However, such access rules give rise to their own serious constitutional difficulties. See Chapter 5, infra.

137. See discussion supra notes 105–6 and accompanying text.

138. See Marshall, supra note 54 at 339 ("Challengers generally need greater funds in order to promote name recognition."); Anthony Gierzynski, Money Rules: Financing Elections in America 42 (2000) (challenger spending yields a larger percentage of the vote, dollar for dollar, than incumbent spending); id. at 60 (candidates challenging incumbents have heavy burden to overcome through spending).

139. For example, scholarly advocates of campaign finance limitations have complained that "[i]n American society, there is a persistent . . . assumption that political power must serve business interests." They have also noted "the class inequalities manifest in our current campaign finance system." The goal of campaign finance regulation, these scholars assert, is "to bring about a reign of true social and economic equality." Raskin & Bonifaz, supra note 57, at 1160, 1203 (1994).

140. It might be argued in response that absent governmentally imposed limits, inequality will nevertheless prevail in favor of those with conservative leanings. But to the extent this assertion is accurate, it ignores the fact that those differences were not brought about by direct governmental regulation of expression, the way the inequalities resulting from the imposition of limits do.

141. 424 U.S. at 17.

142. Id. at 25. See also Federal Election Comm'n v. Colorado Republican Federal Campaign Committee, 2000 WL 554688 (10th Cir. 2000).

143. 424 U.S. at 45.

144. Id. at 29. See also Federal Election Comm'n v. Nat'l Conservative Political Action Committee, 470 U.S. 480, 497 (1985) (discussing corruption concern).

145. Id. at 26–27 (quoting United States Civil Service Comm'n v. National Ass'n of Letter Carriers, 413 U.S. 548 (1973).

146. 120 S. Ct. at 905–6.

147. Sorauf, supra note 51, at 1351 n. 17.

148. Cf. Federal Election Comm'n v. Massachusetts Citizens for Life, Inc., 479 U.S. 238, 259–60 (1986) ("We have consistently held that restrictions on contributions require less compelling justification than restrictions on independent spending.").

149. See discussion supra notes 77–79 and accompanying text.

150. See Buckley, 424 U.S. at 27 n. 28 (noting "the deeply disturbing examples surfacing after the 1972 election"); Nixon, 120 S. Ct. at 906.

151. Sorauf, supra note 51, at 1351 n. 17.

152. Nixon, 120 S. Ct. at 27 n. 28.

153. The Court in *Nixon* pointed to a newspaper report questioning the state treasurer's decision to use a certain bank for most of Missouri's banking business after the bank had contributed $20,000 to the treasurer's campaign. 120 S. Ct. at 907. However, at no point did the Court cite any evidence of an improper quid pro quo in the case.

154. Id.

155. Id. at 904–8. See also Buckley, 424 U.S. at 26–29. For a classic example of the doctrine of res ipsa loquitur, see Byrne v. Boadle, 159 Eng. Rep. 299 (Exch. 1863).

156. 18 U.S.C. § 201 (b)(1) (2000).

157. Neuborne, supra note 4, at 1073.

158. See, e.g., Jack C. Doppelt and Ellen Shearer, Nonvoters: America's No-Shows (1999). See also Robert D. Putnam, Bowling Alone 187–284 (2000). Many years ago, scholars developed theories of democratic elitism, which recognized the general alienation of the public at large. See, e.g., Joseph Schumpeter, Capitalism, Socialism, and Democracy 269–83 (1942). In 1967, political scientist Peter Bachrach recognized the widespread existence of alienation from the political sphere, and sought to redefine the concept of "political" to include such new areas as the corporate workplace. See Peter Bachrach, The Theory of Democratic Elitism (1967).

159. 120 S. Ct. at 905.

160. Sorauf, supra note 51, at 1351.

161. Neuborne, supra note 4, at 1072.

162. Sorauf, supra note 51, at 1351.
163. Id. at 1356.
164. See Fred McChesney, Money For Nothing 63–66 (1997).
165. Similar strategic uses of the First Amendment have already been seen in prior chapters. See, e.g., Chapter 2, supra; Chapter 3, supra.

NOTES TO CHAPTER 5

1. See, e.g., John Stuart Mill, On Liberty (1859); Abrams v. United States, 250 U.S. 616, 630 (1919) (Holmes, J., dissenting) ("[T]he best test of truth is the power of the thought to get itself accepted in the competition of the market.").

2. See, e.g., C. Edwin Baker, Scope of the First Amendment Freedom of Speech, 25 U.C.L.A. L. Rev. 964, 967–68 (1978).

3. See Jerome A. Barron, Access to the Press—A New First Amendment Right, 80 Harv. L. Rev. 1941 (1969); Owen M. Fiss, Liberalism Divided 9–20 (1996); Cass R. Sunstein, Democracy and the Problem of Freedom of Speech 17–51 (1993).

4. See sources cited in note 3, supra.

5. See Charles E. Lindblom, Politics and Markets 201–22 (1977); Fiss, supra note 3, at 10.

6. See sources cited in note 3, supra.

7. Id.

8. Red Lion Broadcasting Co. v. FCC 395 U.S. 367 (1969).

9. Miami Herald Publ'g Co. v. Tornillo, 418 U.S. 241 (1974).

10. Turner Broadcasting System, Inc., v. FCC 520 U.S. 180 (1997); Hurley v. Irish-American Gay, Lesbian and Bisexual Group, 515 U.S. 557 (1995).

11. See discussion infra notes 204–11 and accompanying text.

12. See Alexander Meiklejohn, Political Freedom (1960).

13. This is true to a lesser extent, however, than it might have been prior to the recent dramatic advances in communication technology. See discussion infra notes 204–11 and accompanying text.

14. See discussion infra text at notes 105–62 and accompanying text.

15. See, e.g., Fiss, supra note 3; Barron supra note 3.

16. See discussion infra notes 53–65 and accompanying text.

17. See discussion infra notes 53–65 and accompanying text.

18. See Fiss, supra note 3; Sunstein, supra note 3.

19. See, e.g., Vincent Blasi, The Checking Value in First Amendment Theory, 1977 Am. B. Found. Research J. 521 (First Amendment designed to check governmental misconduct).

20. See, e.g., Dennis v. United States, 341 U.S. 494 (1951); Abrams v. United States, 250 U.S. 616 (1919); United States v. O'Brien, 391 U.S. 367 (1968).

21. Compare Sunstein, supra note 3 (advocating governmental intervention

in order to produce expressive equality), with Cass R. Sunstein, Beyond the Republican Revival, 97 Yale L.J. 1539, 1546 (1988) (attacking legislative process as subject to interest group pressures).

22. See Chapters 1 and 2, supra.

23. Id.

24. See Chapter 4, supra.

25. See discussion infra notes 105–62 and accompanying text.

26. See discussion infra notes 146–62 and accompanying text.

27. See discussion infra notes 146–62 and accompanying text.

28. See, e.g., Wooley v. Maynard, 430 U.S. 705 (1977); West Virginia Bd. of Educ. v. Barnette, 319 U.S. 624 (1943).

29. See discussion infra notes 146–62 and accompanying text.

30. See discussion infra notes 157–58 and accompanying text.

31. See discussion infra notes 36–71 and accompanying text.

32. Id.

33. See discussion infra notes 73–162 and accompanying text.

34. Id.

35. See discussion infra notes 203–5 and accompanying text.

36. See sources cited in note 3, supra.

37. See, e.g., John Maynard Keynes, General Theory of Employment, Interest, and Money (1936).

38. See, e.g., Adam Smith, A Wealth of Nations (1799).

39. See, e.g., David Ricardo, The Principles of Political Economy and Taxation (1821).

40. David Held, Democracy: From City-States to a Cosmopolitan Order?, in Prospects for Democracy 13, 21 (David Held, ed. 1993).

41. Christopher Pierson, Marxist Theory and Democratic Politics 9 (1986).

42. According to one commentator, under Marxism "[t]he post-capitalist state would not . . . bear any resemblance to a liberal, parliamentary regime." Held, supra note 40, at 22.

43. Benjamin I. Page, Who Gets What from Government? 2 (1983).

44. Id. at 2–3.

45. See, e.g., Baker, supra note 2; Martin H. Redish, Freedom of Expression: A Critical Analysis 9–86 (1984).

46. Page, supra note 43, at 3.

47. John Rawls, A Theory of Justice 78 (1971).

48. Id. at 101.

49. Chapter 2, supra.

50. See Meiklejohn, supra note 12, at 27 ("The principle of the freedom of speech springs from the necessities of program of self-government. . . . It is a deduction from the basic American agreement that public issues shall be decided by universal suffrage.").

51. It should be noted that the phrase "democratic redistribution" is unique to this analysis. However, the term accurately describes a theory articulated by a number of modern political theorists.

52. Keith Graham, The Battle of Democracy: Conflict, Consensus and the Individual 56 (1986).

53. Id. at 56–57.

54. Robert A. Dahl, A Preface to Economic Democracy (1985).

55. Id. at 60.

56. Id.

57. Id.

58. Id. at 61.

59. Id. at 91 (footnote omitted).

60. A number of years prior to Professor Dahl's suggestion, political scientist Peter Bachrach argued: "If the political scientist is to be realistic, he must recognize that large areas within existing so-called private centers of power are political and therefore potentially open to a wide and democratic sharing in decisionmaking." Peter Bachrach, The Theory of Democratic Elitism 102 (1967).

61. See id. at 73–75.

62. It is interesting to note that certain points in his analysis, Dahl appears to justify his suggested method of democratic redistribution by resort to traditional substantive arguments in support of economic redistribution. See Dahl, supra note 54, at 58 (justifying redistribution on "[a]n elementary principle of fairness: In general, scarce and valued things should be allocated.").

63. See the discussions of this concept in Chapter 2, supra.

64. See discussion supra notes 36–44 and accompanying text.

65. The rationale for and contours and dangers of such a right of access, from the perspective of the theory of free expression, are examined infra notes 36–44 and accompanying text.

66. See discussion supra notes 36–44 and accompanying text.

67. See, e.g., Charles E. Lindblom, Politics and Markets 201–2 (1977) (noting the danger of "circularity"—the theory that, because of the distorting effect of those possessing economic power, political choices are effectively made by the very economic interests that the system was intended to regulate); Fiss, supra note 3, at 10 (under the circularity principle, "[v]oters were not actually considering the viability of capitalism, the justness of market distributions, or the structure within which organized labor was allowed to act because . . . of the control exercised by corporate interests over the political agenda.").

68. See discussion supra notes 36–44 and accompanying text.

69. In this category can be placed Lindblom, Fiss, and Sunstein.

70. See Chapter 2, supra.

71. See Meiklejohn, supra note 12, at 27 ("The principle of the freedom of

speech springs from the necessities of self-government. . . . It is a deduction from the basic American agreement that public issues shall be decided by universal suffrage.").

72. See discussion supra notes 36–44 and accompanying text.

73. While scholarly advocates of a right of access have occasionally argued that such a right is actually dictated by the First Amendment (see, e.g., Barron, supra note 3), in the relatively rare instance in which the Supreme Court has validated use of a right of access it has held only that governmental creation of such a right does not violate the First Amendment. See FCC v. Red Lion Broadcasting Co., 395 U.S. 367 (1969).

74. See Meiklejohn, supra note 12.

75. See generally Chapter 4, supra.

76. See Barron, supra note 3.

77. See Fiss, supra note 3.

78. See Dahl, supra note 54.

79. Fiss, supra note 3.

80. Id. For a detailed attack on this view, see Chapter 3, supra.

81. See Chapter 2, supra.

82. See Meiklejohn, supra note 12 (First Amendment protects only speech relevant to the political process); Alexander Meiklejohn, The First Amendment Is an Absolute, 1961 Sup. Ct. Rev. 245 (concept of speech related to political process defined broadly).

83. See Chapter 2, supra.

84. Fiss, supra note 3.

85. Meiklejohn, supra note 12.

86. Id.

87. Stephen A. Gardbaum, Broadcasting, Democracy and the Market, 82 Geo. L.J. 373 (1993).

88. Id. at 381.

89. Today, it might be argued that the technological advances embodied in development of the Internet have dramatically altered the ability of the private individual to make such instant nationwide contributions to public debate. Indeed, it should be noted that the overwhelming majority of scholarly and judicial advocacy of a right of access was premised on the communications structure that existed before the Internet was developed. It is my position that development of the Internet significantly reduces the First Amendment pressures for creation of a right of access. In describing the arguments in support of a right of access at this point, however, I omit any consideration of the Internet's impact.

90. Fiss, supra note 3.

91. Barron, supra note 3.

92. But see discussion infra notes 94–104 and accompanying text.

93. See, e.g., Benjamin Bagdikian, Media Monopoly 19, 20, 27, 28 (1983).

94. Of course, to the extent that the right of expressive access was premised on the needs of the individual speaker to self-realize, rather than exclusively the interest of either the listeners in self-realizing (as Professor Gardbaum posits) or the collective society in engaging in the function of self-government (as Professor Fiss urges), then the effect of the creation of such a right on the diversity of available information and opinion would be irrelevant. Under an individual self-realization model, the key would be the fact that it is the speaker herself whose expressive opportunities have increased. However, scholarly advocates of the right of expressive access have uniformly focused on the interests of the listeners, either as individuals or as part of a broader self-governing society.

95. See Benjamin I. Page, Who Deliberates? Mass Media in Modern Democracy 24–26 (1996).

96. Professor Fiss, for example, has argued that "[i]n a referendum or election . . . there is every reason to be concerned with the advertising campaign mounted by the rich or powerful, because the resources at their disposal enable them to fill all the available space for public discourse with their message." Fiss, supra note 3, at 16. While Professor Fiss provides not the slightest bit of empirical support for such a sweeping and counterintuitive notion, he also argues that speech by the economically powerful may drown out the expression of others, since "in politics, scarcity is the rule rather than the exception," because "[t]he opportunities for speech tend to be limited, either by the time or space available for communicating or by our capacity to digest or process information." Id. at 15–16 (emphasis added). See also J. Skelly Wright, Money and the Pollution of Politics: Is the First Amendment an Obstacle to Political Equality?, 82 Colum. L. Rev. 609, 637 (1982) ("Unchecked political expenditures . . . may drown opposing beliefs."). See generally Chapter 3, supra.

97. Serious doubt can be raised about its validity. See Chapter 3, supra. My analysis assumes the argument's validity at this point, solely to highlight what appears to be a clear inconsistency in the arguments of many of the scholarly advocates of a right of access.

98. PL 102–385, October 5, 1992, 106 Stat. 1460.

99. In general, a cable operator with twelve or less cable channels shall carry at least three local commercial stations. The cable operator of a cable system with more than twelve cable channels shall carry up to one-third of the aggregate number of channels of such systems in local commercial stations. 106 Stat. 1460, 1471.

100. Turner Broadcasting System, Inc. FCC, 512 U.S. 622 (1994) (*Turner I*); Turner Broadcasting System, Inc. FCC, 520 US 180 (1997) (*Turner II*).

101. See Justice Breyer's concurrence in *Turner II*. See also Sunstein, supra note 3.

102. Even if one assumes no limit to the channels available to a cable opera-

tor, it is still arguable that the must-carry provisions give rise to significant First Amendment difficulties.

103. Miami Herald Publ'g Co. v. Tornillo, 418 U.S. 241 (1974).

104. Cf. New York Times Co. v. Sullivan, 376 U.S. 254, 270 (1964) (allowing public officials to sue for defamation chills public debate by deterring criticism of such officials).

105. See discussion supra notes 51–65 and accompanying text.

106. See discussion supra notes 84–94 and accompanying text.

107. See discussion supra notes 66–71 and accompanying text.

108. Professor Barron, for example, seems to focus exclusively on process-oriented concerns traditionally associated with First Amendment theory. See Barron, supra note 3. The same could be said of Professor Gardbaum. Gardbaum, supra note 87.

109. Sunstein, supra note 3.

110. Sunstein, Supra, note 21.

111. Cass R. Sunstein, Pornography and the First Amendment, 1986 Duke L.J. 589.

112. As previously noted, Professor Fiss also advocates expressive redistribution on the basis of the enrichment rationale.

113. See Fiss, supra note 3.

114. See Fiss, supra note 3, at 10. The principle is discussed in more detail in Chapter 3.

115. Fiss, supra note 3, at 10.

116. See discussion supra notes 66–71 and accompanying text.

117. For a more detailed analysis of the principle of epistemological humility, see Chapters 2 and 3, supra.

118. See Turner Broadcasting System, Inc. v. FCC, 512 U.S. 622, 641 (1994).

119. See, e.g., Police Dep't v. Mosley, 408 U.S. 92 (1972).

120. It should be noted that even in the purely expressive-based context, the arguments in support of expressive redistribution on balance are unpersuasive.

121. See, e.g., Barron, supra note 3.

122. See, e.g., Fiss, supra note 3.

123. To the extent that government has actually engaged in efforts designed to bring about redistributive justice, of course, the argument of the circularity principle—that control of the political agenda by powerful economic interests precludes adoption of measures designed to bring about distributive justice—is significantly undermined. See Chapter 3.

124. Fiss, supra note 3; Sunstein, supra note 3.

125. Sunstein, supra note 21.

126. Cass R. Sunstein, Interpreting Statutes in the Regulatory State, 103 Harv. L. Rev. 405, 476 (1989).

127. See Abner Mikva, Foreword: Symposium on the Theory of Public Choice, 74 Va. L. Rev. 167, 170 (1988).

128. Jonathan R. Macey, Promoting Public-Regarding Legislation Through Statutory Interpretation: An Interest Group Model, 86 Colum. L. Rev. 223 (1986).

129. See discussion supra notes 98–102 and accompanying text.

130. Cass R. Sunstein, The First Amendment in Cyberspace, 104 Yale L.J. 1757 (1995).

131. See Turner II, 520 U.S. 187 (1997) (Breyer, J., concurring); Sunstein, supra note 130.

132. See discussion supra notes 97–102 and accompanying text.

133. Alien and Sedition Act of 1798, 1 Stat. 596–97 (1798).

134. See, e.g., Abrams v. United States, 250 U.S. 616 (1919).

135. See, e.g., Dennis v. United States, 341 U.S. 494 (1951); Gitlow v. New York, 268 U.S. 652 (1925).

136. See O'Brien v. United States, 391 U.S. 367 (1968).

137. See Vincent Blasi, The Pathological Perspective and the First Amendment, 85 Colum. L. Rev.

138. Miami Herald Publ'g Co. v. Tornillo, 418 U.S. 241 (1974).

139. See Red Lion Broadcasting Co. v. FCC, 395 U.S. 367 (1969).

140. See Thomas W. Hazlett & David W. Sosa, Was the Fairness Doctrine a "Chilling Effect"? Evidence from the Postderegulation Radio Market, 26 J. Leg. Stud. 279 (1979).

141. See discussion supra notes 133–37 and accompanying text.

142. O'Brien v. United States, 391 U.S. 367 (1968).

143. Id.

144. See discussion supra notes 133–37 and accompanying text.

145. See discussion supra notes 94–104 and accompanying text.

146. See, e.g., Wooley v. Maynard 430 U.S. 705 (1978); West Virginia St. Bd. of Educ. v. Barnette, 319 U.S. 624 (1943).

147. See discussion infra notes 47–71 and accompanying text.

148. See discussion infra notes 157–62 and accompanying text.

149. See Jack W. Brehm & Arthur R. Cohen, Explorations in Cognitive Dissonance 271 (1962).

150. Hannah Arendt points out that the totalitarian regimes of the twentieth century were the first of their kind in their total claim on the individual:

> Yet, insofar as individualism characterized the bourgeoisie's as well as the mob's attitude to life, the totalitarian movements (of the twentieth century) can rightly claim that they were the first truly antibourgeois parties; none of their nineteenth century predecessors, neither the Society of the 10th of December which helped Louis Napoleon into power, the butcher brigades of the Dreyfus Affair, the Black Hundreds of the Russian

pogroms, nor the pan-movements, ever involved their members to the point of complete loss of individual claims and ambitions, or had ever realized that an organization could succeed in extinguishing individual identity permanently and not just for the moment of collective heroic action.

Hannah Arendt, Origins of Totalitarianism 313–14 (1958).

151. Id. at 323–24.

152. Commentators have explained this breakdown in the following manner:

A slow disintegration affecting all human relations causes mutual distrust so that ordinary people are alienated from one another; all the bonds of confidence in social relationships are corroded by the terror and propaganda, the spying, and the denouncing and betraying, until the social fabric threatens to fall apart. The confidence which ordinarily binds the manager of the plant to his subordinates, the members of a university faculty to one another and to their students, lawyer to client, doctor to patient, and even parents to children as well as brothers to sisters is disrupted. The core of this process of disintegration is, it seems, the breakdown of the possibility of communication—the spread, that is, of the vacuum. Isolation and anxiety are the universal result.

Carl J. Friedrich & Zbigniew Brzezinski, Totalitarian Dictatorship and Autocracy 136 (2d ed. 1965)

153. Id.

154. Id. at 143.

155. Id.

156. Id. at 157.

157. Fiss, supra note 3.

158. But see discussion supra notes 94–104 and accompanying text.

159. See discussion infra notes 205–11 and accompanying text.

160. See discussion supra notes 149–50 and accompanying text.

161. One might of course respond that this concern would be rendered irrelevant were it possible to fashion a right of access that could be invoked only when the substance of the expression of the party granted access was not abhorrent or offensive to the party in control of the expressive resource. Whether a workable structural or doctrinal standard could be developed to implement this limitation is open to serious question. Moreover, even if such a standard could be devised, it is important to note that it would dramatically reduce the scope of a constitutionally valid right of access.

162. For example, the negative impact of forced access could presumably be great if Hugh Heffner of *Playboy* were required to provide access to the Christian Coalition, or if archconservative Robert McCormack, founder of the *Chicago Tribune*, had been required to provide access to the views of the Socialist Party.

163. See C. Edwin Baker, Human Liberty and Freedom of Speech 219 (1989).

164. See Chapter 3, supra.

165. That the Supreme Court recognizes the First Amendment right of private corporations against compelled speech—indeed, even against a state-created private right of access—is demonstrated by its decision in Pacific Gas & Electric.

166. See, e.g., Baker, supra note 163.

167. See Chapter 6, infra.

168. See Fiss, supra note 3, at 19–20.

169. See discussion supra notes 146–62 and accompanying text.

170. See discussion supra notes 149–52 and accompanying text.

171. See discussion supra notes 163–67 and accompanying text.

172. See Stanley v. Georgia, 394 U.S. 557 (1969).

173. In this sense, Fiss is similar to communitarian political speech theorists who came before him.

174. See, e.g., Jean Baechler, "Individual, Group, and Democracy," in Democratic Community (NOMOS XXXV) 15, 23–24 (John W. Chapman & Ian Shapiro, eds. 1993) ("Democracy defined as consensual obedience and delegated power has as its privileged interlocutor the individual as person. . . . This statement is self-evident because only free individuals can agree to obey other free individuals who are chosen by them."). See generally Chapter 2, supra.

175. See Frank Michelman, Law's Republic, 97 Yale L.J. 1493, 1526–27 (1988).

176. See discussion supra notes 133–37 and accompanying text.

177. See discussion supra notes 160–62 and accompanying text.

178. See discussion infra notes 133–37 and accompanying text.

179. Blasi, supra note 19.

180. See discussion supra notes 133–37 and accompanying text.

181. See discussion supra notes 37–71 and accompanying text.

182. It should once again be emphasized, however, that there nevertheless exist serious doubts about the empirical and intuitive support for the view that expressive redistribution through creation of a right of access will, in fact, lead to enrichment of public debate.

183. 395 U.S. 367 (1969).

184. 418 U.S. 241 (1974).

185. See Chapter 6, infra.

186. Turner Broadcasting System, Inc. v. FCC, 512 U.S. 622, 637–38 (1994).

187. Id. at 638. Despite acknowledging the questionable empirical basis of the scarcity rationale, however, the Court has indicated no willingness to reconsider the doctrinal implications of that distinction. Perhaps the reason for such reluctance is the fact that the FCC has itself revoked the Fairness Doctrine, rendering the need to reconsider the scarcity rationale largely hypothetical.

188. See Lee C. Bollinger, Freedom of the Press and Public Access: Toward a Theory of Partial Regulation of Mass Media, 75 Mich. L. Rev. 1 (1976).

189. Id. at 2–3.

190. See, e.g., Barron, supra note 3; Fiss, supra note 3.

191. 447 U.S. 74 (1980).

192. 515 U.S. 557 (1995).

193. See discussion supra notes 94–104 and accompanying text.

194. See discussion supra notes 149–62 and accompanying text.

195. See discussion supra notes 135–37 and accompanying text.

196. See discussion supra notes 149–62 and accompanying text.

197. In upholding the must-carry provisions, however, the Court in *Turner* did not rely on this rationale. To the contrary, the Court expressly found that in selecting which cable channels are to be carried, the cable operator is exercising an editorial function protected by the First Amendment. See *Turner I*: "The provisions do not intrude on the editorial control of cable operators. They are content neutral in application, and they do not force cable operators to alter their own messages to respond to the broadcast programming they must carry. In addition, the physical connection between the television set and the cable network gives cable operators bottleneck, or gatekeeper, control over most programming delivered into subscribers' homes." 512 U.S. 622, 623.

198. See Chapter 2, supra.

199. See Arkansas Educational Television Comm'n v. Forbes, 533 U.S. 666 (1998).

200. See discussion supra notes 149–62 and accompanying text.

201. See Chapter 2, supra.

202. See also Pacific Gas & Electric Co. v. Public Utility Commission of California, 475 U.S. 1 (1986) (power company may not constitutionally be required to include in its mailings to consumers inserts prepared by environmental groups). Cf. Glickman v. Wileman, 521 U.S. 457 (1997) (requiring fruit growers to contribute to payment for governmentally orchestrated advertising campaign does not violate First Amendment because fruit growers were in general agreement with message being conveyed).

203. See discussion supra notes 94–104 and accompanying text.

204. See Barron, supra note 3, at 1644–47.

205. ACLU v. Reno, 929 F. Supp. 824, 830–31 (E.D. Pa. 1996), aff'd, 521 U.S. 844 (1997). See also Adam R. Kegley, Regulation of the Internet: The Application of Established Constitutional Law to Dangerous Electronic Communication, 85 Ky. L.J. 997, 1000 (1996–97): "Physically, the Internet is nothing more than a network of computer networks. . . . Individual computers are linked together through telephone lines and they communicate via modems. . . . Servers are maintained by individuals, companies, and institutions. Internet service

providers lease dedicated phone lines from companies that in turn lease lines from telecommunications carriers."

206. ACLU v. Reno, 929 F. Supp. at 871.

207. Edias Software Int'l, L.L.C. v. Basis Int'l, Ltd., 947 F. Supp. 413, 417 (D. Ariz. 1996).

208. Panavision, Int'l v. Toeppen, 947 F. Supp. 1227, 1231 (N.D. Ill. 1996).

209. Edias Software Int'l v. Basis Int'l, Ltd., 947 F. Supp. 413, 419 (D. Ariz. 1996).

210. Heroes, Inc. v. Heroes Foundation, 958 F. Supp. 1, 4 (D.D.C. 1996).

211. Maritz Inc. v. Cybergold, Inc., 947 F. Supp. 1328, 1329 (E.D.N.Y. 1996).

NOTES TO CHAPTER 6

1. See infra text accompanying note 85 (discussing the funding of the vice president's travels as an example of a permitted limited employee subsidy).

2. 500 U.S. 173 (1991).

3. See infra text accompanying notes 105–11 (explaining regulation that prohibited clinics receiving funding from the Department of Health and Human Services from providing information about abortion).

4. See infra text accompanying notes 112–21 (describing and critiquing the Court's reasoning in *Rust*).

5. See discussion infra notes 163–96 and accompanying text (outlining and critiquing alternative models for analyzing governmental subsidization of speech).

6. See infra text accompanying notes 46–51 (articulating prevailing theories on the value of free speech); discussion infra notes 59–60 and accompanying text (explaining the effects of positive subsidies on free speech).

7. It is not always be possible to draw a strict dichotomy between the two situations. When this is so, my analysis seeks to draw an ex ante categorical balance. See discussion infra text accompanying notes 100–103 (arguing that the benefits of allowing governmental subsidies as a judgmental necessity outweigh the risks).

8. See infra text accompanying notes 54–56 (describing the difference between positive and negative subsidies and their constitutional implications).

9. See infra notes 82–99 and accompanying text (explaining the distinction between "policy" and "auxiliary" subsidies).

10. Subsidies of judgmental necessity are at times inevitably viewpoint-based. See infra notes 10–103 and accompanying text (describing the characteristics and analysis of subsidies of judgmental necessity).

11. The model's exception to the ban on viewpoint-based subsidies will include some of those subsidies that fall within the terms of the "judgmental necessity" category. See infra text accompanying notes 100–101 (arguing that the ben-

efits of allowing governmental subsidies made as a judgmental necessity outweigh the risks).

12. See infra text accompanying notes 100–101 (explaining the requirement that a decision to subsidize be "substantially related" to the pre-described goals and purposes of the program to fit under the judgmental-necessity provision).

13. See infra note 102 and accompanying text (explaining the structure of the inquiry to be used by the Court in analyzing a challenged subsidy).

14. See infra text accompanying notes 97–103 (discussing the possible ambiguities arising form the government's efforts to award viewpoint-neutral subsidies).

15. See discussion infra notes 121–24 and accompanying text (exploring the comparative merits of alternative models previously suggested for measuring the constitutionality of government subsidization of expression).

16. See discussion infra notes 163–96 and accompanying text (exploring the comparative merits of alternative models previously suggested for measuring the constitutionality of government subsidization of expression).

17. 29 N.E. 517 (1892).

18. Id at 517.

19. Not all scholars find persuasive the logic of the unconstitutional conditions doctrine. See generally Cass R. Sunstein, Why the Unconstitutional Conditions Doctrine Is an Anachronism (with Particular Reference to Religion, Speech, and Abortion), 70 B.U. L. Rev. 593 (1990) (arguing that the unconstitutional conditions doctrine should be abandoned). Moreover, in certain areas the Supreme Court has, without explanation, completely ignored the doctrine's logic. See, e.g., Northern Pipeline Construction Co. v. Marathon Pipe Line Co., 458 U.S. 50 (1982) (holding that under the "public rights" doctrine, when the federal government creates a substantive statutory right, it may condition acceptance of that right on adjudication of the right in a non–Article III forum); Atlas Roofing Co. v. Occupational Safety and Health Administration, 430 U.S. 443 (1977) (applying the "public rights" doctrine to Seventh Amendment right to civil jury trial).

20. See generally William Van Alstyne, The Demise of the Right–Privilege Distinction in Constitutional Law, 82 Harv. L. Rev. 1439 (1968) (contending that the erosion of "privilege" in the public-sector context has required the creation of substantive due process provisions to protect against the state).

21. U.S. Const. Amend. XIV, § 1: "No State shall . . . deny to any person within its jurisdiction the Equal Protection of the laws."

22. DeShaney v. Winnebago County Dep't of Soc. Servs., 489 U.S. 189, 195 (1989)("The [Equal Protection] Clause is phrased as a limitation on the State's power to act, not as a guarantee of certain minimal levels of safety and security.").

23. Kathleen M. Sullivan, Unconstitutional Conditions, 102 Harv. L. Rev. 1413 (1989).

24. Id. at 1419.

25. Id. at 1420.

26. Id.

27. Id. at 1421. Professor Sullivan notes that this approach "has never been prominent in the cases at all, but is suggested by contemporary debate among commentators about limits of permissible exchange." Id.

28. See, e.g., National Equipment Rental, Ltd. v. Szukhent, 375 U.S. 311 (1964) (due process objection to personal jurisdiction subject to waiver through contract). Similarly, the Seventh Amendment right to jury trial may be waived with relative ease. See Fed. R. Civ. P. 38.

29. Sullivan, supra note 23, at 1421.

30. Id.

31. Id.

32. Id.

33. Id.

34. Seth F. Kreimer, Allocational Sanctions: The Problem of Negative Rights in a Positive State, 132 U. Pa. L. Rev. 1293 (1984) (suggesting that affirmative governmental intrusion in the form of benefits has exceeded negative government action as a form of coercion); Albert J. Rosenthal, Conditional Federal Spending and the Constitution, 39 Stan. L. Rev. 1103 (1987) (measuring the extent to which conditions attached to congressional spending may exceed, in effect, direct regulations Congress would be barred from enacting). See generally Richard A. Epstein, The Supreme Court, 1987 Term, Foreword: Unconstitutional Conditions, State Power and the Limits of Consent, 102 Harv. L. Rev. 4 (1987) (explaining the various opinions about the unconstitutional conditions doctrine in judicial and academic circles).

35. See generally Sunstein, supra note 19 (stating that the validity of the unconstitutional conditions doctrine is subject to question).

36. See supra note 19 (citing cases in which the Supreme Court, inexplicably, opted not to employ the unconstitutional conditions doctrine).

37. U.S. Const. Amend. I: "Congress shall make no law . . . abridging the freedom of speech . . ."

38. The mere fact that a prima facie abridgement is shown does not necessarily mean that the regulation is unconstitutional.

39. Such physical prevention, however, may constitute at least a prima facie abridgement.

40. See, e.g., Walker v. City of Birmingham, 388 U.S. 307 (1967) (holding that punishment for violating an otherwise unconstitutional injunction is not a violation of a person's free speech rights). However, unlike defendants accused of violations of criminal statutes, under the so-called "collateral bar" rule a defendant prosecuted for contempt is generally not permitted to raise the unconstitutionality of the injunction as a defense. Compare id. (defendant accused of violating injunction not allowed to challenge constitutionality of injunction) with Shuttlesworth v. City of Birmingham, 394 U.S. 147, 150–51 (1969) (criminal ordi-

nance imposing limitation identical to injunction upheld in Walker held violation of First Amendment).

41. See, e.g., Near v. Minnesota, 283 U.S. 697, 713 (1931) (holding that prior restraints on expression have a strong presumption of unconstitutionality).

42. See, e.g., Dennis v. United States, 341 U.S. 494, 516–17 (1951) (upholding prison sentences imposed on individuals because of expressive activity).

43. Whether the speaker has been placed in a worse position because of his expression or because of an unrelated reason, of course, presents a factual issue that will have to be resolved in the individual case.

44. Examples are food stamps or Medicaid.

45. Of course, one could adopt a so-called "absolutist" position on free speech. See, e.g., Thomas I. Emerson, The System of Freedom of Expression 17 (1970) (explaining the absolutist view of free speech). Under this approach, the mere finding of "abridgement" will automatically lead to a finding of unconstitutionality. Neither the Supreme Court nor the majority of commentators has accepted this view. For a detailed discussion of the issue, see Chapter 2, supra. See also Martin H. Redish, Freedom of Expression: A Critical Analysis 52–55, 191–206 (1984).

46. It must be conceded that issues of free speech theory do not always fall into the terms of so simplistic a dichotomy. For present purposes, however, recognition of these two broad categories is sufficient.

47. Alexander Meiklejohn, Political Freedom 8–9 (1960). See also Vincent Blasi, The Checking Value in First Amendment Theory, 1977 Am. B. Found. Res. J. 521, 527–28 (1977) (explaining the ability of free press to expose actions of the government); Cass R. Sunstein, Beyond the Republican Revival, 97 Yale L.J. 1539 (1988) (articulating a republican belief grounded in a guaranteed right to participate in public deliberation).

48. C. Edwin Baker, Scope of the First Amendment Freedom of Speech, 25 UCLA L. Rev. 964, 966 (1978). See also Thomas I. Emerson, Toward a General Theory of the First Amendment, 72 Yale L.J. 877, 879 (1963) (asserting that free expression is essential to realizing the individual's character and potentialities as a human being); see generally Martin H. Redish, The Value of Free Speech, 130 U. Pa. L. Rev. 591 (1982) (arguing that the true goal of free speech is to promote "individual self-realization").

49. By "democratic communitarian," I mean one who believes in the value of communitarian self-determination. See Martin H. Redish & Gary Lippman, Freedom of Expression and the Civic Republican Revival in Constitutional Theory: The Ominous Implications, 79 Cal. L. Rev. 267, 290–94 (1991) (defining the "communitarian-determinative" model of civic republican theory).

50. See generally Meiklejohn, supra note 47.

51. See Geoffrey R. Stone, Restrictions of Speech Because of Its Content: The Peculiar Case of Subject-Matter Restrictions, 46 U. Chi. L. Rev. 20, 101 (1975)

(explaining that content-based restrictions distort the marketplace of ideas, leaving the public with an incomplete and possibly inaccurate vision of society's opinions).

52. To the extent the expression in question does not fall within First Amendment protection and thus could be regulated directly, this analysis of course becomes irrelevant.

53. See DeShaney v. Winnebago County Dep't of Soc. Servs., 489 U.S. 189 (1989) (holding that the Constitution confers no right to affirmative aid).

54. An example is expression categorized as legally obscene. See, e.g., Miller v. California, 413 U.S. 15, 34–37 (1973) (holding, in part, that obscene material is not protected by the First Amendment).

55. An example would be advocacy of unlawful conduct that is found to present a clear and imminent danger of harm. See Brandenburg v. Ohio, 395 U.S. 444 (1969) (per curiam) (explaining the level of imminent harm necessary to justify an infringement of free speech protection).

56. See discussion infra at 000–000 (discussing positive government subsidies of speech).

57. See supra text accompanying notes 46–52 (discussing the effects of government subsidies on free speech).

58. See, e.g., Erznoznik v. City of Jacksonville, 422 U.S. 205 (1975) (holding invalid a statute prohibiting drive-in theaters from showing movie containing nudity if screen is visible from a public street); Police Dep't v. Mosley, 408 U.S. 92, 99–102 (1972) (declaring as overbroad a statute prohibiting all picketing, other than peaceful picketing during a labor dispute, within 150 feet of a school). In both of these cases, the Court closely scrutinized content-based regulations. For an overview of the treatment of content-based restrictions, see John Hart Ely, Flag Desecration: A Case Study in the Roles of Categorization and Balancing in First Amendment Analysis, 88 Harv. L. Rev. 1482 (1975); Daniel A. Farber, Content Regulation and the First Amendment: A Revisionist View, 68 Geo. L.J. 727 (1980); Stone, supra note 51. Indeed, even if restrictions on speech are content-neutral, First Amendment principles might be undermined. See, e.g., Martin H. Redish, The Content Distinction in First Amendment Analysis, 34 Stan. L. Rev. 113, 131 (1981) ("[S]uch restrictions may undermine the functioning of the marketplace by keeping the public equally ignorant of all positions on issues, rather than merely of one viewpoint.").

59. See Edward G. Reitler, The Title X Family Planning Subsidies: The Government's Role in Moral Issues, 27 Harv. J. Legis. 453, 459 (1990) (refuting the argument that negative subsidies are far less insidious than direct restrictions because an entity can simply reject a subsidy and therefore eschew the silencing effect of that subsidy).

60. Mark Yudof has noted that the benefits and costs of government subsidization of speech, addressed briefly above and more fully below, apply specifi-

cally to government subsidization of speech because "[g]overnments have an almost unique capacity to acquire and disseminate information in the modern state. This stems in part simply from superior resources . . . [b]ut . . . also stems from the broad reach of the modern welfare state." Mark G. Yudof, When Government Speaks: Politics, Law, and Government Expression in America 9–10 (1983). Yudof believes that the potential harmful effects of this capacity are exacerbated by technological advances that have improved the government's ability to communicate. Id.

61. See, e.g., Wooley v. Maynard, 430 U.S. 705, 717 (1977) ("The state is seeking to communicate to others an official view as to proper appreciation of history, state pride, and individualism. Of course, the State may legitimately pursue such interests in any number of ways."); Joseph Tussman, Government and the Mind 13–14 (1977) ("Even in democratic societies, the community may legitimately act, through government, on the mind."); Yudof, supra note 60, at 41 ("it is absurd, then, in the modern contexts, to adopt the position that government speech, in its may manifestation and irrespective of its advantages, is an illegitimate enterprise in a liberal and democratic state."); Donald L. Beschle, Conditional Spending and the First Amendment: Maintaining the Commitment to Rational Liberal Dialogue, 57 Mo. L. Rev. 1117 (1992) (affirming the importance of the government's voice while exploring the current approach to conditional-spending issues); Reitler, supra note 59, at 458 ("[T]he question is no longer whether the government has any role in the inculcation of values. Instead it is a matter of how much governmental influence in individual choice is desirable.").

62. See infra notes 63–72 and accompanying text.

63. See generally Buckley v. Valeo, 424 U.S. 1, 92–93 (1976) (per curiam) (recognizing that public expenditures may "facilitate and enlarge public discussion"); Mark G. Yudof, When Governments Speak: Toward a Theory of Government Expression and the First Amendment, 57 Tex. L. Rev. 863, 868 (1979) ("The government is sometimes uniquely situated to acquire and disseminate particular information, and in some cases government may be the only actor with the willingness and the resources to present a particular side of a public issue."); Buckley v. Valeo, 424 U.S. 1, 92–93 (1976) (per curiam) (recognizing that public expenditures may "facilitate and enlarge public discussion").

64. Emerson, supra note 45, at 698.

65. Tussman, supra note 61, at 3.

66. Id at 11.

67. Id at 54.

68. See id. at 13–14; see also David Cole, Beyond Unconstitutional Conditions: Charting Spheres of Neutrality in Government-Funded Speech, 67 N.Y.U. L. Rev. 675, 702 (1992) ("[A] government functions in large measure through communication and persuasion, and would be disabled by a mandate that it maintain only neutral positions."); Yudof, supra note 63, at 866 ("Although they

do not serve individual values of self-expression and dignity, the communications emanating from [the government (among other institutions)] do provide information necessary to the exercise of the citizenry's judgment about political issues and candidates.").

69. Zechariah Chafee, Government & Mass Communications 755 (1947).

70. Id. As an example of this principle in action, Chafee explained that "[i]f the government makes [a serious public danger] plain to the people, they may be able to ward it off by private action." Id.

71. Reitler, supra note 59, at 483.

72. Yudof, supra note 60, at 43; see also Yudof, supra note 63, at 866 (stating that government speech, which "can amplify the voices of individuals," is one consideration for the support of "First Amendment rights for the government").

73. See Yudof, supra note 60, at 42 ("The power to teach, inform, and lead is also the power to indoctrinate, distort judgment, and perpetuate the current regime."); see also Steven Shiffrin, Government Speech, 27 UCLA L. Rev. 565, 611 (1980) (recognizing the danger of the "tyranny" of prevailing opinion).

74. Yudof, supra note 60, at 6; see also Yudof, supra note 63, at 898 (noting that, by "indoctrination and the withholding of vital information," government speech can undermine "the power of the citizenry to judge intelligently and to communicate those judgments."); Shiffrin, supra note 73, 611 (arguing that government "departures from neutrality are indefensible when they undermine respect for the democratic process."); see also Robert D. Kamenshine, The First Amendment's Implied Establishment Clause, 67 Cal. L. Rev. 1104, 1107 (1979) ("Government promulgation of political views presents dangers to the interests which the Framers intended the First Amendment to protect."). But see generally Frederick Schauer, Is Government Speech a Problem?, 35 Stan. L. Rev. 373 (1983) (reviewing Mark G. Yudof, When Government Speaks: Politics, Law, and Government Expression in America 9–10 (1983)) (questioning the distorting effect of government speech).

75. Yudof, supra note 60, at 6. See also Kamenshine, supra note 74, at 1105 ("If a government can manipulate [the marketplace of ideas], it can ultimately subvert the process by which the people hold it accountable[.]").

76. Yudof, supra note 60, at 15. See also Edward H. Ziegler, Government Speech and the Constitution: The Limits of Official Partisanship, 21 B.C. L. Rev. 578, 580 (1980).

77. Yudof, supra note 60, at 6. More specifically, Yudof feared that the government might manipulate the private mass media "by leaking selected information, creating pseudo-events, and lying about matters not easily verified by those outside government." Id. at 8. He was also concerned about the "tendency of executive-branch agencies to seek to influence legislative processes." Id. Additionally, Yudof feared the government's ability to speak, without limitation, in "public in-

stitutions whose mission, in whole or in part, [was] to indoctrinate, educate, or care for a particular group." Id. at 9.

78. Thomas I. Emerson and David Haber, The "Scopes" Case in Modern Dress, 27 U. Chi. L. Rev. 522, 522 (1960).

79. Kamenshine, supra note 74, at 1104. See also Ziegler, supra note 76, at 618 (arguing that "official partisanship in connection with structured political questions violates the First Amendment since it infringes the political rights of citizens by diminishing the effect and probability of its opponents' protected expression."); Shiffrin, supra note 73, at 607 ("If a system of free expression is to be preserved, either custom, or statutes, or constitutionally based limitations must provide assurances that government speech will not unfairly dominate the intellectual marketplace."). The Supreme Court has heeded these warnings in a number of cases. See, e.g., Keyishian v. Board of Regents, 385 U.S. 589 (1967) (holding that statute and regulations preventing the appointment or retention of subversive persons in state employment was unconstitutional). Zechariah Chafee identified a particular concern with the government's ability to shape public attitudes. Chafee's apprehension was that those in power would communicate with the public simply as a means for staying in power. Chafee, supra note 69, at 763. He believed that "an energetic information service [was] an excellent way [for officeholders] to entrench themselves in office." Id. See also Anderson v. City of Boston, 380 N.E. 2d 628, 637 n. 14 (Mass. 1978), appeal dismissed, 439 U.S. 1060 (1979) ("Surely, the Constitution of the United Sates does not authorize the expenditure of public funds to promote the reelection of the President, Congressmen, and State and local officials (to the exclusion of their opponents), even though the open discussion of political candidates and elections is basic First Amendment material."); Reitler, supra note 59, at 456 ("elected officials should not perpetuate themselves or their party through the spending of public monies.").

80. Whether a particular employee falls within the category of "core" employees presents an issue of fact, for individualized resolution.

81. See infra notes 82–99 and accompanying text.

82. Tussman, supra note 61, at 115.

83. See generally Martin H. Redish, The Constitution as Political Structure 154–58 (1995); Blasi, supra note 47, 521.

84. See Beschle, supra note 61, at 1144 ("The government's disproportionate power to communicate its opinions is at least partially curbed by the natural skepticism, perhaps even cynicism, which greets government messages clearly labeled as such."); Reitler, supra note 59, at 460 ("Today's Watergate-wise public is notoriously skeptical of what its government says.").

85. See supra text accompanying notes 61–62 (arguing that certain governmental subsidies support First Amendment values.)

86. See supra text accompanying notes 61–62 (describing the benefits of government subsidization).

87. Owing to its substantial resources, the government is uniquely capable of funding the promulgation of information on many matters of public concern. See Yudof, supra note 60 (describing the government's unique position to provide subsidies).

88. It may not be presumptively constitutional, however, if the subsidy is a policy subsidy or a subsidy of judgmental necessity that is inevitably viewpoint-based.

89. See supra text accompanying notes 82–86 (discussing subsidization of government employees and appointees).

90. See generally Stone, supra note 51 (explaining that content-based restrictions distort the marketplace of ideas, leaving the public with an incomplete and possibly inaccurate vision of society).

91. See generally Redish, supra note 58 (explaining that content-neutral restrictions may negatively affect the marketplace of ideas).

92. See id. (explaining content-neutral regulations also may undermine First Amendment principles).

93. See generally Stone, supra note 51 (discussing the dangers of viewpoint-based discrimination).

94. See supra text accompanying notes 82–86 (describing the benefits of subsidizing speech of policy-making employees).

95. It is conceivable that under narrowly defined circumstances, government may find it necessary to "farm out" one of its traditional policy expressions to a private contractor, as when government retains a private public relations firm to fashion a campaign in support of a government program. Arguably, the hypothetical of the private printer of the Congressional Record, supra, text accompanying note 3, would fit within this category. Such activity may properly be deemed "policy" subsidies only in those instances in which a reviewing court concludes that the expressive activity in question is one that, absent use of the private contractor, the government would definitely have had to perform itself.

96. See supra text accompanying note 76 (discussing dangers of governmental falsification of consent).

97. 429 U.S. 274 (1977). In that case, a fired untenured teacher challenged dismissal on First Amendment grounds. The Supreme Court initially required the plaintiff to establish that his constitutionally protected conduct had been a "substantial factor" in the school board's decision. Id. at 287. The burden then shifted to the school board to demonstrate "by a preponderance of the evidence that it would have reached the same decision as to [the teacher's] reemployment even in the absence of the protected conduct." Id. Although the Court did not elaborate on exactly how this was to be accomplished, the only conceivable method available to the board appears to have been to demonstrate the inade-

quacy of the teacher's record and performance. The Court elaborated upon this procedure in Price Waterhouse v. Hopkins, 490 U.S. 228 (1989).

98. Mt. Healthy, 429 U.S. at 287.

99. Id.

100. See supra text accompanying notes 90–99 (discussing prohibitions on viewpoint-based subsidies).

101. See supra text accompanying note 61–72 (describing the public's need for information).

102. See supra text following note 96 (requiring that categories be fashioned in a viewpoint-neutral manner).

103. See supra notes 61–72 and accompanying text (discussing the benefits and need for government subsidies).

104. 500 U.S. 173 (1991).

105. 42 U.S.C. § 300 et. seq. Under Title X, the Secretary of Human Health Services was "authorized to make grants to and enter into contracts with public or nonprofit private entities to assist in the establishment of voluntary family planning projects which shall offer a broad range of acceptable and effective family planning methods and services." 42 U.S.C. § 300(a) (1988).

106. 42 U.S.C. § 300a–4(a).

107. Rust, 500 U.S. at 179.

108. 42 C.F.R. § 59.8(a)(1).

109. 42 C.F.R. § 59.10.

110. 42 C.F.R. § 59.9.

111. 53 Fed. Reg. 2922.

112. 500 U.S. at 196.

113. Id. Indeed, elsewhere in the opinion, the Court asserted that "when the government appropriates public funds to establish a program it is entitled to define the limits of that program." Id. at 194.

114. Id. at 196 (citing 42 C.F.R. § 59.9) (emphasis in original).

115. See supra text accompanying notes 20–36 (discussing the theoretical limitations of the unconstitutional conditions doctrine).

116. "Self-referentiality" in this context refers to the evaluation of a governmental subsidy with reference to the subsidy's express purpose rather than to the effects the subsidy has on the wider sphere of available public choices in regard to expression. See supra discussion at text between notes 96–97.

117. The Court illustrated its logical fallacies when it reasoned that "[t]he government can, without violating the Constitution, selectively fund a program to encourage certain activities it believes to be in the public interest, without at the same time funding an alternative program which seeks to deal with the problem in another way. In so doing, the Government has not discriminated on the basis of viewpoint; it has merely chosen to fund one activity to the exclusion of the other." Rust, 500 U.S. at 193 (emphasis added). The Court erroneously believed that "the

government may 'make a value judgment favoring childbirth over abortion, and
. . . implement that judgment by the allocation of funds.'" Id. at 192–93 (quoting
Maher v. Roe, 432 U.S. 464, 474 [1977]). When, as here, the government's "value
judgment" is a pretext for stifling expression of an ideological position, the government discriminates on the basis of viewpoint. As Justice Blackmun argued in dissent, "for the first time," the Court has upheld "viewpoint-based suppression of
speech simply because that suppression was a condition upon the acceptance of
public funds." 500 U.S. at 207 (Blackmun, J., dissenting).

118. See supra text accompanying notes 93–97(analyzing the dangers to the
constitutional legitimacy of "auxiliary" subsidies).

119. See supra discussion at text accompanying note 88 (discussing the constitutional legitimacy of viewpoint-based subsidies).

120. To underscore the viewpoint-based nature of the regulations, it is helpful to transform them hypothetically into a proper categorical subsidy. This
would have been the case had the Regulations directed the subsidized clinics to
counsel on the general issue of family planning.

121. See supra text accompanying notes 96–97 (arguing that government may
not establish viewpoint-based categories).

122. Robert M. O'Neil, Artistic Freedom and Academic Freedom, 53 Law &
Contemp. Probs. 177, 191 (1990).

123. But see generally Edward C. Banfield, The Democratic Muse: Visual Arts
and the Public Interest (1984) (arguing that the federal government should not
engage in the aesthetic judgments required for art subsidies); William D.
Grampp, Pricing the Priceless: Art, Artists, and Economics (1989) (arguing that
public support of the arts is not economically justifiable).

124. See generally Stanley Ingber, Judging Without Judgment: Constitutional
Irrelevancies and the Demise of Dialogue, 46 Rutgers L. Rev. 1473 (1994); Jesse
Helms, Is It Art or Tax-Paid Obscenity? The NEA Controversy, 2 J.L. & Pol'y 99
(1994) (explaining Senator Helms's position that the NEA has been a tool for advancing moral relativism more than a legitimate public subsidy); Elizabeth E. De-
Grazia, In Search of Artistic Excellence: Structural Reform of the National Endowment for the Arts, 12 Cardozo Arts & Ent. L.J. 133 (1994) (advocating a return to NEA decision-making free from government-imposed content
restrictions); Carl F. Stychin, Identities, Sexualities, and the Postmodern Subject:
An Analysis of Artistic Funding by the National Endowment for the Arts, 12 Cardozo Arts & Ent. L.J. 79 (1994) (arguing that restrictions on art funding are unconstitutional because such restrictions deny some individuals a right to express
a political identity); John E. Frohnmayer, Giving Offense, 29 Gonz. L. Rev. 1
(1993/1994); Amy Sabrin, Thinking About Content: Can It Play an Appropriate
Role in Government Funding of the Arts?, 102 Yale L.J. 1209 (1993) (arguing for
more precise definition of artistic "content" in First Amendment jurisprudence);
Donald W. Hawthorne, Subversive Subsidization: How NEA Art Funding

Abridges Private Speech, 40 U. Kan. L. Rev. 437 (1992) (arguing that NEA criteria are impermissible under the First Amendment); Owen Fiss, State Activism and State Censorship, 100 Yale L.J. 2087 (1991); O'Neil, supra note 122 (discussing concepts of academic and artistic freedom); Note, Standards for Federal Funding of the Arts: Free Expression and Political Control, 103 Harv. L. Rev. 1969 (1990) (arguing against attempting to regulate art through conditional grants).

125. DeGrazia, supra note 125, at 133 (describing the formation of the NEA).

126. Note, supra note 125, 103 Harv. L. Rev. at 1972.

127. 20 U.S.C. § 954 (c)(1).

128. 20 U.S.C. § 954(d) (disallowing funding for any art the NEA chairperson deems to be obscene).

129. Id.

130. See supra at 000–000.

131. See supra text accompanying notes 87–97 (defining and discussing the constitutionality of "auxiliary" subsidies).

132. See supra text accompanying notes 100–103 (discussing the application of the "judgmental necessity" principle).

133. See supra notes 101–3 and accompanying text (defining the "substantial relationship" concept in the context of the normative selection process).

134. See, e.g., O'Brien v. United States, 391 U.S. 367, 374–75 (1968) (accepting at face value Congress's highly suspect assertion that its prohibition on draft and desecration was motivated by viewpoint-neutral, non-speech-related considerations. See also Laurence Tribe, American Constitutional Law 819 (2d ed. 1988) (discussing the Court's avoidance of a congressional-motive inquiry in *O'Brien*).

135. Nor could Congress redefine its goal to be to fund "decent" art. See discussion supra accompanying notes 73–79 (discussing the dangers inherent in governmentally sanctioned positive-speech subsidies).

136. See supra discussion at text accompanying notes 88–96 (arguing that viewpoint-based subsidies are unconstitutional).

137. 118 S. Ct 2168 (1998).

138. Id. at 2167.

139. Id.

140. Id.

141. Id. at 2177, where the Court pointed to educational projects as an example.

142. See Id. at 2178 ("Respondents do not allege discrimination in any particular funding decision. . . . Thus, we have no occasion ere to address an as-applied challenge in a situation where the denial of a grant may be shown to be the product of invidious viewpoint discrimination.")

143. See Id. at 2175 ("Respondents raise a facial constitutional challenge . . . and consequently they confront a 'heavy burden' in advancing their claim. . . . Facial invalidation 'is manifestly, strong medicine' that 'has been employed by the Court

sparingly and only as a last resort.' Broadrick in Oklahoma, 413 U.S. 601, 613 . . . (1970) (noting that 'facial challenges to legislation are generally disfavored').")

144. Broadrick v. Oklahoma, 413 U.S. 601,613 (1970).

145. See 118 S. Ct. at 2177–78.

146. See id. ("Any content-based considerations that may be taken into account in the grant-making process are a consequence of the nature of arts finding. The NEA has limited resources and it must deny the majority of the grant applications it receives, including many that propose 'artistically excellent' projects. The agency may decide to fund particular projects for a wide variety of reasons.").

147. See, e.g., Plyer v. Doe, 457 U.S. 202, 222 n. 20 (1982) ("The public schools are an important socializing institution, imparting those shared values through which social order and stability are maintained."); Ambach v. Norwick, 441 U.S. 68, 77 (1979)(discussing findings that public schools instill "fundamental values necessary to the maintenance of a democratic political system); West Virginia State Board of Education v. Barnette, 319 U.S. 624, 631 (1943) (finding that the love of country and government can teach "the guaranties of civil liberty which tend to inspire patriotism and love of country"); William B. Senhauser, Note, Education and the Court: The Supreme Court's Educational Ideology, 40 Vand. L. Rev. 939, 943–44 (1987) (stating that under the "cultural transmission ideology . . . the purpose of education is not to encourage individual growth, but to assure the internalization of established norms, with the child's need to learn societal disciplines receiving particular emphasis."); Mark G. Yudof, Library Book Selection and the Public Schools: The Quest for the Archimedean Point, 59 Ind. L.J. 527, 527–28 (1984) ("Children, however, are rightfully perceived as . . . instruments of larger societal purposes. Those purposes include the assimilation of the child into the larger culture, for the intergenerational, exogenetic transmission of values, knowledge, language, and customs is essential to the preservation of community and to the definition of persons within the community."); Richard L. Roe, Valuing Student Speech: The Work of the Schools as Conceptual Development, 79 Cal. L. Rev. 1269, 1274 (1991) ("The Supreme Court currently views the work of the schools to be the inculcation of values."); Moskowitz, The Making of the Moral Child: Legal Implications of Values Education, 6 Pepperdine L. Rev. 105, 134–36 (1978) (asserting that the state has a compelling interest in inculcating values to students).

148. Keyishian v. Bd. of Educ., 385 U.S. 589, 603 (1967). See also Pierce v. Society of Sisters, 286 U.S. 510, 535 (1925) (noting that students are not "the mere creatures of the state"); Tinker v. Des Moines Indep. Community School Dist., 393 U.S. 503, 511 (1969) (noting that students are not "closed-circuit recipients of only that which the state chooses to communicate."); Barnette, 319 U.S. at 637 (stating that the fact that schools "are educating the young for citizenship is reason for scrupulous protection of Constitutional freedoms of the individual, if we

are not to strangle the free mind at its source and teach youth to discount important principles of our government as mere platitudes."); Stephen Arons, Compelling Belief: The Culture of American Schooling 206 (1983) ("If the government were able to use schooling to regulate the development of ideas and opinions by controlling the transmission of culture and the socialization of children, freedom of expression would become a meaningless right."); Stanley Ingber, Socialization, Indoctrination, or the "Pall of Orthodoxy": Value Training in the Public Schools, 1987 U. Ill. L. Rev. 15, 16 ("Any effort to indoctrinate `official values' . . . is inconsistent with . . . personal autonomy."); Stephen E. Gottleib, In the Name of Patriotism: The Constitutionality of "Bending" History in Public Secondary Schools, 62 N.Y.U. L. Rev. 497, 498 (1987) (Indoctrination "may deny students an appreciation of the role that liberty, democracy and dissent have played in our achievements as a people." [citations omitted]).

149. Betsy Levin, Educating Youth for Citizenship: The Conflict Between Authority and Individual Rights in the Public School, 95 Yale L.J. 1647, 1649 (1986) ("[T]he very nature of the process of inculcating values in those who are not yet adults apparently necessitates that the constitutional rights of . . . students be somewhat circumscribed."); Roe, supra note 148, at 1276 ("An inherent conflict between the authority of the state to instill knowledge and values it deems important and the speech interests of individual students characterizes Supreme Court jurisprudence in the area of student speech"); Ingber, supra note 148, at 19 ("Paradoxically, education must promote autonomy while simultaneously denying it by shaping and constraining present and future choices."); Yudof, supra note 147, at 528 ("Children need to be socialized to societal norms, but they also need to grow up to be relatively autonomous beings within the confines of culture.").

150. See Levin, supra note 149, at 1678 ("In most instances, the interest of the educational enterprise in socializing students to particular values or in order and control is given considerable weight while that of the individual schoolchild is given relatively little."); Tyll van Geel, The Search for Constitutional Limits on Government Authority to Inculcate Youth, 62 Tex. L. Rev. 197, 239–40 (1983) ("For many years, the Supreme Court has shown ambivalence toward whether pupils in the public schools enjoy a right of freedom of belief that serves as a check on governmental efforts to indoctrinate them."); Tinker, 393 U.S. at 506 (holding that although students do not "shed their constitutional rights . . . at the schoolhouse gate, . . . [the] special characteristics of the school environment" reduce students' First Amendment protection.).

151. Yudof, supra note 147 at 563. See also Shiffrin, supra note 73, at 647–53 (arguing for a similarly "process oriented" solution to the conflict that would divide the authority to make curriculum-related decisions among school boards, parents, and teachers).

152. Kamenshine, supra note 74, at 1134 ("Short of general concepts of social responsibility . . . no such [uniform] values exist").

153. See Roe, supra note 147, at 1292–93 (advocating the use of a "conceptual development model"); van Geel, supra note 150, at 297 ("Empirical social science evidence shows that the government has no compelling interest in value inculcation.").

154. See, e.g., Emerson & Haber, supra note 78, at 526–28 (discussing the need for a "balanced presentation" of views in public education); Gottlieb, supra note 148, at 577 (detailing advantages to a fairness doctrinal approach in public education); Kamenshine, supra note 74, at 1130, 1137 (discussing application of a fairness doctrine); Van Geel, supra note 150, at 297 (advocating the adoption of a "fairness principle").

155. Gottlieb, supra note 148, at 577.

156. F. Fitzgerald, America Revised: History Schoolbooks in the Twentieth Century 47 (1979).

157. Gottlieb, supra note 148, at 505. See also James C. O'Brien, Note, The Promise of Pico: A New Definition of Orthodoxy, 97 Yale L.J. 1805, 1820 (1988) (citing Jean Anyon, Workers, Labor and Economic History, and Textbook Content in Ideology and Practice in Schooling 37 [M. Apple & L. Weis eds. 1983]) ("Anyon found that radical unions, their leaders, and their policies were ignored, insulted, or dismissed as dishonest . . . that [textbooks] discussed only strikes that ended in violence and ultimately did not get workers what they wanted; and that reformist leaders and moderate reform legislation were lauded." [citations omitted]).

158. See supra note 148.

159. Recall that the "judgmental necessity" concept allows the government to have some basis on which to select between competing applicants for funding. As long as the criteria used for selection are "substantially related" to the terms of the viewpoint-neutral category, the government can make a normative judgment between competitive candidates, even though this most likely will produce "viewpoint" contamination. See supra notes 100–103 and accompanying text (discussing "judgmental necessity"). Compare this with Rust v. Sullivan, 500 U.S. 173 (1991). In *Rust*, the government did not define the initial category neutral as a generic matter. Thus, as in NEA grants, government decision-makers can proceed to the next step. The government may make some value judgments in selecting among the competing candidates. *Rust* never gets past the first step because the government defined the category in a viewpoint-laden manner. See supra notes 103–21 and accompanying text (examining *Rust*).

160. See supra text accompanying notes 148–56 (providing a discussion of the role of public schools in the inculcation of values).

161. See Board of Ed. v. Pico, 457 U.S. 853, 864 (1982) (finding that the "discretion of the states and local school [ ] boards in matters of education must be exercised in a manner that comports with the transcendent imperatives of the First Amendment").

162. The obvious danger here is the evidentiary problem of establishing the

fact of the government's improper motive. See supra discussion at text accompanying note 97 (stating that the burden of establishing the government motive as improper is on the plaintiff).

163. See supra discussion at text accompanying notes 115–21 (critiquing *Rust*).

164. See Cole, supra note 68, at 748 ("A better way of accommodating the opposing interest implicated when government funds speech is to identify and enforce spheres of neutrality and independence.").

165. Id. at 702–8 (discussing of the problems associated with government funding of speech).

166. Id. at 712.

167. Courts recognize limited exceptions for obscenity, libel, and fighting words.

168. Cole, supra note 68, at 712.

169. Id.

170. Id. at 713.

171. Id. at 714.

172. Id. at 715.

173. Id.

174. Id.

175. Id. at 716.

176. Id. at 737.

177. Id. at 716.

178. Id. at 717.

179. Id. at 723.

180. Id. at 731.

181. Id. at 717.

182. Id. at 736.

183. Id. at 739.

184. Id. at 743.

185. See supra text accompanying notes 73–79 (outlining the dangers of government subsidization of speech).

186. Cole, supra note 68, at 740.

187. Id. at 736.

188. See id. at 739–40 (discussing the arts as "sphere of neutrality").

189. Fiss, supra note 124, at 2098.

190. Id. at 2099.

191. Id. at 2100.

192. Id.

193. Id. at 2101. Professor Ingber argues, in a manner similar to Fiss, that "[p]ublic subsidies of the arts . . . should be allocated so that more is said and more are exposed to that which is said than would exist without public subsidies. Public monies will advance public discourse by supporting the kind of art that

would not have found a ready patron in the private market, not by simply allowing more people to say the same thing." Ingber, supra note 124, at 1621–22 (footnotes omitted).

194. Fiss, supra note 124, at 2101.

195. See supra notes 46–51 and accompanying text (enumerating communitarian and autonomy theories as two broad theories of freedom of expression).

196. See supra notes 46–51 and accompanying text (discussing the values that underlie the First Amendment).

197. Perhaps anticipating this particular criticism, Professor Fiss argues later in his article that "[t]he duty to attend to effect does not mean . . . an end to merit. What it does mean is either a reexamination of the notions of merit that underlie funding decisions or, alas, a sacrifice of some of the values that might be furthered by notions of merit that do not incorporate, or, in fact, are antagonistic to, the constitutional goal of producing a public debate that is worthy of our democratic aspirations." Fiss, supra note 124, at 2103. However, Fiss merely proposes a redefinition of merit that devalues consideration of the inherent quality of a piece of art and substitutes a consideration of the ability of the art to contribute a voice to a debate on an issue.

198. An additional problem with an approach that turns on a determination of whether or not a work of art "reinforces the prevailing orthodoxy" is the obvious difficulty in making such a determination.

199. See Ely, supra note 58, at 1496 (advocating use of a priori balancing in free speech cases).

NOTES TO CHAPTER 7

1. Lochner v. New York, 198 U.S. 45, 75 (1905) (Holmes, J., dissenting).

Index

About the Author

Martin H. Redish is the Louis and Harriet Ancel Professor of Law and Public Policy at Northwestern University School of Law. A nationally recognized authority on free expression, federal jurisdiction, and civil procedure, Redish received his A.B. with highest honors in political science from the University of Pennsylvania and his J.D. magna cum laude from Harvard Law School. Redish is the author or coauthor of thirteen books and more than seventy scholarly articles. In addition to his teaching and scholarship, Redish litigates cases involving jurisdictional and constitutional issues with the law firm of Piper, Marbury, Rudnick & Wolfe. He has testified as an expert witness before numerous congressional committees on free speech and federal jurisdiction issues and lectured extensively on those subjects before judicial groups.

Reidsh is the winner of three awards for teaching excellence and was recently named to a list of the one hundred most cited legal scholars of all time. He has served as a visiting professor at Stanford, Cornell, and the University of Michigan law schools. Redish lives with his wife, Caren, and two daughters, Jessica and Elisa, near Chicago, where he is an avid fan of Northwestern football and the Chicago White Sox.